Contemporary Issues Series

Homelessness: A Social Dilemma

A Critical Analysis of the Question of Homelessness in the United States

G. Thomas Goodnight

National Textbook Company
a division of NTC *Publishing Group* • Lincolnwood, Illinois USA

Published by National Textbook Company, a division of NTC Publishing Group.
©1991 by NTC Publishing Group, 4255 West Touhy Avenue,
Lincolnwood (Chicago), Illinois 60646-1975 U.S.A.
Manufactured in the United States of America.

1 2 3 4 5 6 7 8 9 VP 9 8 7 6 5 4 3 2 1

Contents

Introduction to the Homeless Controversy

The specter of the homeless in the midst of a society of plenty has given rise to a new generation of debate over the causes and consequences of poverty in America. The debate crosses many public and private institutions, involving the law, public health, medicine, psychiatry, social welfare, as well as public and private housing policies. The debate occurs at many different levels: the federal government, state governments, local communities and private charities. The spectrum of issues is broad, ranging from general social and economic policies to assure the adequacy of housing and systems of societal support for the poor to the special dilemmas of addressing the needs of those children, women, and men who have "fallen through the cracks" and are not being served by any institution, public or private. These readings are designed to serve as an introduction to a crucial public policy debate which promises to shape social justice in America.

To understand the nature of the problem of contemporary homelessness, as well as the difficulty of finding a solution, one must turn to the historical development of attitudes toward poverty and social responsibility. The United States has always been a country that prided itself on a work ethic, individualism and diversity of local communities. For much of its history, poverty has been viewed as the failure of individuals to work or develop the characteristics necessary to succeed. Responsibility for taking care of the poor was largely left to the activities of private donations to charity, organized through the churches and other community organizations. Where government did become involved, it was either to provide poorhouses with a minimal amount of care for the destitute or jail services for the nonself-supporting. The nature of these efforts varied widely, according to the policies of local counties or towns.

Early 20th century reform movements sought to expand the domain of recognized social problems by arguing that collective social problems could be mitigated, if not resolved, by government action. The rise of American cities and development of urban life made visible the needs to address the common issues of alcoholism, crime, education, employment conditions, sanitation, and income. Progressivism, the chief reform movement of the early 20th century, made clear that government had some duty to maintain and enhance the quality of urban life, and that social problems were amenable to changes in government policy, at least at state and local levels. The reformist spirit was set aside by the First World War and the privatized era of the 20s. Nevertheless, the basis for debating the responsibility of government and society for dealing with issues of poverty and human welfare had been created.

The Great Depression put the issues of poverty and welfare on a national level. Prior to this deep, national economic downturn, political leaders had followed a prevailing philosophy of government noninterference in times of economic trouble. Indeed, the chief duty of the federal government had been to restrain spending, thereby insuring that its own economic house was in order. So widespread was the Depression, however, that soon the federal government itself had to find new ways to offset what was rapidly becoming a general failure of the social system. This failure was etched in the faces of farmers who had lost their land and respectable members of middle class America whose communities collapsed. Whereas the homeless had always been associated with misfits—hoboes and bums—who had reputedly chosen a way of life because they could not fit in, the homeless of the Great Depression were people who took to the road because they had no other choice. When California closed her golden gates to the homeless, it became clear that even the West, the mythic place of opportunity, was filled up and there was no where to go.

Roosevelt's social policies began a great experiment. He worked to preserve a democratic capitalist system by making adjustments that acknowledged some levels of social responsibility. The New Deal was less a systematic approach to the problem of poverty than a variety of experiments in the areas of labor, job training, income supplements, social security, education, and so on. In the New Deal, the federal government acknowledged a national responsibility to deal with issues of poverty and welfare. Whether or not New Deal policies would have been sufficient to offset a system of chaotic mergers, bank failures, predatory business practices, and capital/labor relationships is a mute issue. The Second World War, with its great demands for labor and resources, ended the threat of Depression.

The Great Society was a program, similar to the New Deal in many major respects, save for the fact that it was not a response to a prolonged economic downturn. The Great Society of the early 1960s sought to use federal initiatives as a means to stimulate state and local governments' responses to social problems. The War on Poverty had as its aims the provision of the basic means of support for individuals to compete and a way of getting people out of the intergenerational cycle of poverty. Thus, programs were developed to increases levels of government resources allocated to food, education, housing, and health care while providing job retraining and community development. The War on Poverty was never funded fully and became a victim of expenditures needed for the Vietnam War.

President Reagan took office sounding the themes of Rooseveltian rhetoric, the need for a thoroughgoing restructuring of government and social policy. The Reagan revolution, however, was based on the notion that social policy ought to be returned to the state and local levels. Thus, Reagan proposed the idea of a "social safety net," a minimal level of services that government would provide for those who could not help themselves. The idea was to maintain assistance only for deserving people, thereby encouraging people who might be able to work, albeit at not terribly attractive jobs, to do so. By reducing government programs, government costs could be diminished, taxes lowered, and the resulting rising tide of economic prosperity would "lift all boats," as it were. This philosophy of government, which harkened back to earlier views of poverty, was never to be tested. Shortly after Reagan took office, the economy plunged into the deepest recession since the 1940s. It was then that the "new homeless" began to appear.

The "homeless" in modern times have been associated generally with Skid Row, a section of the city where unattached males gather, many because of problems with alcohol or because of not fitting in with the norms of family life. Skid Row is a general name attached to specific areas of a town. It was a part of every community that provided a place for people who were not sorted into its neighborhoods, factories, and other places of work and life. In the recession of the early 1980s, it became clear that the homeless were no longer occupants of a limited section of town; people with nowhere to go became visible in the public places of cities. Sleeping on sidewalks, ambling through parks, often carrying their belongings in a bag or pushing all their worldly goods in a shopping cart, the new homeless became the most visible sign that the problems of poverty were increasing. Indeed, the issue of homeless itself became a way to dramatize the failure of the "social safety net" and the direness of poverty. Homelessness became an issue of broad societal consequence precisely because at a time when it was politically unpopular to create a new anti-poverty crusade, it kept alive discussion of minimal social responsibilities.

At a minimum, homelessness focuses on the basic obligations that society owes to its most destitute members, the issues of what rights to education and health services, as well as limiations, are required as a matter of law. Ian Loveland ("Homelessness in the U.S.A.") examines the complex social dimensions of the issues. He finds that homelessness itself has been transformed from the stereotypical problem of males who are down on their luck or who cannot fit in, to a more complicated issue involving women, families, people who want to work but can't, people who do but cannot afford housing, veterans, runaways, and the mentally ill. He overviews how homelessness challenges the federal government, state initiatives, city responses, and the voluntary sector.

The readings for this book take their cue from Loveland. They are designed to identify the complex nature of the issue of homelessness as well as the variety of possible solutions to the problem.

SOCIAL DIMENSIONS OF HOMELESSNESS

All commentators on homelessness agree that the cause for homelessness are complex and that the new homeless are a more diverse group of people than are identified by the stereotypical images of the bums (1910s), hobo (1930s), or welfare cheaters (1980s). Although this group shares a single common characteristic, the absence of shelter and a dwelling to call their own, the homeless are as diverse as are the conditions which lead to their detachment from relatives or neighbors who might take them in, community programs which might give them resources to purchase housing, and social networks which offer services to the displaced and destitute.

This section isolates three social dimensions of homeless: the problem of women and children who have been put on the streets due to the "feminization of poverty"; the problem of the homeless and employment or work; and the issue of homelessness and mental illness. In many cases, these issues intersect, as often a person is without a home due to the failure of more than one social institutions. However, the divisions do reflect significant lines of development of the contemporary problem.

Women and children have always been vulnerable to poverty due to their traditional dependency upon an adult male provider for income. As the rate of divorce, abandonment, teen age pregnancies, and abuse increased during the 1980s, women and children became less protected by the traditional social equation. As the economy constricted and eliminated lower paying jobs, many of which are traditionally occupied by women, and as recovery left many without a job, the problem of the "feminization of poverty" appeared, together with an exacerbation of teen-age runaways and displaced youths. Ellen Bassuk ("Who Are the Homeless Families?") details the dimensions of women and poverty as well as the general failure of the social system to deal with the issue. Peter Rossi ("The Family, Welfare and Homelessness") identifies the stresses of homelessness on family life and its consequences.

One of the stereotypes surrounding homelessness is that poverty in general is caused by individuals who simply do not want to work. First and Toomey ("Homeless Men and the Work Ethic") demonstrate that the situation among homeless men is more complex. In their study they find that some are disabled and cannot work while others need a range of services before being able to rejoin the work force. James D. Wright ("The Worthy and

Unworthy Homeless") indicates that the numbers of homeless who could work but chose not to are actually very small.

In addition to the social and economic causes of homelessness in the 1980s, the deinstitutionalization of Americans from mental hospitals is thought to be a significant contributor to the appearance of the homeless. Deinstitutionalization was brought about as the result of a patients' rights movements which advocated community treatment as a better means for people suffering mental health problems than locking the mentally ill away in asylums. In the 1950s, there were over a half million Americans in mental institutions, while presently there are just over 100,000. Some experts argue that these ex-patients are not contributing significantly to the homeless population, since deinstitutionalization was accomplished largely before the 1980s; others argue that the numbers of mentally ill, who are left on the streets without family or professional care, are significant and growing. Moreover, homelessness itself is seen as a cause of substantial emotional and psychological problems. Susser, Goldfinger and White ("Some Clinical Approaches to the Homeless Mentally Ill") examine the range of intervention strategies that are needed to deal with the mentally ill homeless. Marsha Martin ("The Homeless Mentally Ill and Community-Based Care") explores methods to reorganize the current hodge-podge of solutions provided through temporary shelters. Finally, Richard Lamb ("Involuntary Treatment for the Homeless") examines the possibility of compulsory reinstitutionalization as a means of assuring care.

THE ISSUES OF SHELTER AND SERVICES FOR THE HOMELESS

For much of the 1980s, the homeless debate turned on the question of whether or not there were enough emergency shelters and services for those in dire straights. In part, this issue was a result of a deepening recession which stretched the limits of private charities and state/local systems of relief. As the recession worsened, social services became vulnerable and the urgency of emergency measures increased. Yet even after the recession, the issue continued when it became apparent that there were increasing numbers of homeless—despite general economic recovery. Kim Hopper ("The Ordeal of Shelter") compares the short-term emergency measures with longer term needs for a solution. Dennis D. Hirsch ("Making Shelter Work: Placing Conditions on an Employable Person's Right to Shelter") balances social concerns for a "right to shelter" with social plans to use the shelter as a place for reintegrating the homeless into the work place.

During the 1980s, the federal government undertook to decentralize the provision of social services. This move was defended as an attempt to respond to the diversity of community concerns and social problems, and to encourage flexible and creative local responses to local conditions. Critics of the "new federalism" saw the shift from a federal to a local commitment as a way of shifting the burden of social expenditures and reducing an overall commitment to fighting poverty. Indeed, the privatization of government services, it was pointed out, seemed to be a pretext for reducing government efforts. Michael Sosin ("Decentralizing the Social Service System") evaluates the decentralization of government and the problems created in providing services for the homeless. He concludes that decentralization causes service problems. Dorothy Stephens, Elaine Dennis, Monica Toomer and Joan Holloway ("The Diversity of Case Management Needs for the Care of Homeless Persons") propose a "case management" approach which allows for meeting the diverse needs of homeless populations in ways that integrate and coordinate services.

PUBLIC POLICY RESPONSES TO HOMELESSNESS

Federal efforts to help the homeless are many and complex. The National Governors' Association ("Status of Programs Under the Stewart B. McKinney Homeless Assistance Act and Related Legislation") lays out the variety of programs relevant to relieving the harms of homelessness and mitigating some of the causes. Homelessness is more than a discussion of displaced persons, however. It is also a way of discussing the potential ramifications of poverty in America. In a sense, all of the poor are potentially homeless. Another deep recession, which brought about decreased employment and increased reliance on limited government services, would put many more people into the streets. The degree and nature of homelessness depends upon macro economic conditions and government policies. A key factor in this equation is the availability and quality of housing and housing programs in the United States. As a result, the solutions to homelessness have been discussed in terms of expanding the supply and availability of housing within the overall context of community development.

Jerome Weinstein ("Homesteading") suggests that an expanded federal/local partnership could result in the rehabilitation of existing housing that has been abandoned and is now owned by the federal government. This policy would have the benefit of reducing the number of homeless while giving to individuals the incentives and tools to redevelop the community. Homesteading, of course, would require commitments to additional jobs and social services to make the projects viable. Frederick Brown ("Creating More Dynamic Public Housing") presents another alternative, namely creating incentives that make possible home ownership of what has been provided as public housing. A popular conservative proposal involves developing areas of the city through tax relief. Robert Guskind ("Enterprise Zones") analyzes how well such solutions have worked.

The federal government is currently recovering its credibility in the area of housing. During the latter part of the Reagan administration, the McKinney Act was passed to provide some emergency relief for the homeless. Subsequently, its funds were expanded to over $1 billion. However, the Reagan years saw a substantial reduction in the federal government's commitment to housing, as HUD's budget was cut by over $20 billion. To add insult to injury, the HUD scandal, following just as Reagan left office, revealed that what few funds were left were often spent at the behest of lobbyists and to enrich consultants. The Bush administration has sought to recover federal credibility by expanding efforts in the housing area. Michael Stegman ("A Bush/Kemp Report Card") evaluates the success. He finds that the rhetorical promises of HOPE our not equal to the budgetary commitment. John Gilderbloom and Richard Applebaum ("Rethinking Rental Housing") suggest an alternative measure to assuring that there will be enough affordable, decent housing for all. "New Directions in Welfare and Housing Assistance" presents a diverse array of possible productive reforms in welfare and housing that would help mitigate homelessness.

CONCLUSION

The debate over homelessness is likely to grow in the future. From one perspective, the debate is about the failure of welfare and the need to restore social incentives for retaining the traditional values of work and family as a way of life. Among conservatives who now talk of a permanent under class, there is deep skepticism about the hope for finding a single solution and a fear that increased government services will further disintegrate community ties. Solutions for homelessness, within this purview, are seen as a responsibility of individuals, families, and local communities. Just as communities have the right to formulate different priorities and preferences for common assessment of taxes and expenditure of funds, so they have a right to decide levels of welfare and appropriate responses to the least economically rewarded among them. This view emphasizes the intractable nature of poverty and the limited amount of funds that can be spent without overburdening the sectors that produce jobs and wealth. Solutions to the problems of homeless and poverty are likely to be found within a redesigned set of programs that require work as a condition of government assistance and that take emergency action only under the most extreme circumstances, when private charity cannot fulfill its front line duties.

From another perspective, homelessness is a symptom of the general failure of society to address the growing disparity between rich and poor, between those who have access to social rewards, who have the skills and contacts to be successful, and those who have been excluded by reasons of prejudice, economic factors, and sheer bad luck from the American dream. Within this purview, the quality of life for all is diminished by the indifference toward the least among us. The poor are seen to be impoverished through no fault of their own; the victims of powerful economic and social forces, the poor are basically no different from the rich and deserve better.

On this side of the debate, there is growing concern that more and better alternatives be developed to assure adequate social services for children so that the cycle of neglect, abuse, and failure does not result in a lost generation. There is also concern to find a means of assuring protection for those women who are battered and have no where else to go, for those suffering from ill-health, drugs and alcohol and cannot get on their feet without help, and for a burgeoning older population that will need more homes equipped for special services.

Whether the debate is framed in how little should be done or how much can, there has yet to be a consensus framed on issues of social welfare in the American democracy. The readings in this book present an introduction into one of the most important controversies of this generation.

Homelessness in the U.S.A.

Ian Loveland

I. INTRODUCTION

As the Thatcher government continues to restrict access to social security benefits, deregulate private rented housing, and dismantle public sector housing provision, homelessness is again attracting considerable media attention. Recent press reports identify many single men sleeping rough, families occupying grossly overcrowded accommodation, and growing numbers of runaway children.[1] Some local councils, particularly in London, are apparently unable to cope with their homeless populations. Arguments that such logistical overloading is now widespread have gained credibility from recent reports that Nicholas Ridley has censored a DoE survey of local authorities' implementation of their statutory duties.[2] But increasing homelessness is not a uniquely British problem.

This paper reviews the current situation in the United States, where homelessness emerged as a major issue in the 1984 Presidential election campaign.[3] The American press continues to devote attention to reports by journalists who have "gone native" among the homeless populations of large cities, producing accounts charting the daily misery of a homeless existence.[4] The controversial issue of quantifying the homeless population receives similar prominence.[5] Press reports often dwell on individual tragedies, such as the freezing to death of 61-year-old Rebecca Smith in her cardboard box home in Washington D.C.[6] Constant media coverage of the difficulties suffered, and posed, by homeless Americans has kept the issue firmly in the

British Academy Post-Doctoral Research Fellow, Centre for Socio-Legal Studies and Nuffield College, Oxford University, U.K.

0165-0068/88/$3.50 © 1988 Elsevier Science Publishers B.V. (North Holland)

public eye, to which it has been presented as a social problem of considerable magnitude and complexity.[7]

Homelessness has attracted a voluminous literature in recent years. This paper necessarily presents a very selective culling of the data available. It is designed primarily to provide an overview of the main themes of the problem, and to offer some closer insight into particular aspects of the current situation. The selection process reflects to some degree the author's current interests in homelessness in Britain, which approaches the issue as a question of administrative law and central/local relations in the political context of the Thatcher government's restructuring of welfare services. Vestiges of this model remain, but the legal frameworks surrounding homelessness in America and Britain are too diverse to permit straightforward comparison. Nevertheless there are great similarities between the political and social contexts in which those legal frameworks are based, and since the paper is aimed at British readers occasional references are made to comparable aspects of Britain's homelessness problems to provide familiar reference points along the way.

Section 2 discusses how homelessness is presently defined. Sections 3 and 4 then examine competing analyses of the size and composition of the homeless population, and simultaneously outline various analyses of its causes. Section 5 assesses the responses made to the situation: particularly the extent to which homelessness is construed as a phenomenon demanding governmental solutions (and if so, from which tier of government). Section 6 then addresses how the homeless themselves, whether indirectly through litigation or via more direct political activism, are challenging current allocations of housing resources. The concluding section attempts to predict how effectively the newly elected Bush administration will handle this major social problem. Our starting point, however, is perhaps the most basic of questions: in the world's wealthiest nation, just what does "homelessness" mean?

2. DEFINING THE PROBLEM

"Homelessness" is a culturally specific phenomenon. Just as poverty is a relative concept, with its absolute level rising as societies become wealthier, so homelessness is a social condition accorded various definitions; whether over time, between societies, or indeed within them. Shelter considered inadequate in London or New York could for economic, political or even climatic reasons be broadly acceptable in some third world countries.[8]

The *Puhlhofer*[9] saga cogently illustrates the range of interpretations within Britain. Pressure groups such as Shelter advocate a wide definition, embracing anyone "who live[s] in conditions so bad that a civilised family life is impossible."[10] This would include not just people literally without roofs over their heads, but also those occupying overcrowded or poor-quality accommodation. The statutory definition in the Housing (Homeless Persons) Act 1977 made no precise reference to accommodation standards, leaving interpretation to the local authorities responsible for implementing the Act. This discretion is confined only by the loose constraints of administrative law, thereby affording councils considerable (lawful) scope to reach differing conclusions. Local authority decisions are generally only challengeable through judicial review, which precludes adjudication of the merits of individual cases.[11] Empirical studies reveal considerable variation in council decision making, much of which breaches lawful parameters.[12]

Despite consolidation of the 1977 Act into Part III of the Housing Act 1985, the question of what standard of accommodation constituted a home remained unanswered. Relevant case law was somewhat ambiguous.[13] The House of Lords' decision in *Puhlhofer* provided a more definitive, restrictive answer. The Puhlhofers, two adults and two young children, lived in a boarding house, occupying one room, without self-contained washing facilities, in a building without a kitchen. The court considered that families in such accommodation were not legally homeless. Their Lordships agreed that Diogenes, an Ancient Greek who reputedly inhabited a barrel, *would* be homeless; but anyone occupying a structure which could conceivably be regarded as accommodation would not.

The outcry which greeted the judgement prompted the DoE to introduce amending legislation. An applicant having accommodation is now homeless if it is not reasonable for her and "any other person who normally resides with him as a member of his family..." to remain there.[14] The concept of reasonable occupancy is not defined. It is not intended to impose absolute substantive quality standards, since in assessing reasonableness councils may have regard to the general housing circumstances prevailing in their respective areas.[15] Essentially therefore persons in the poorest accommodation are not homeless if such housing is representative of the area's stock, even if the accommodation contravenes statutory sanitation and overcrowding requirements.[16]

In the United States, there is broad acceptance of an even narrower definition.[17] The homeless are those without accommodation *at all* other than night refuge in emergency shelters.[18] These are the people who generally sleep in the streets, in subway stations, in airport lounges, in parks, on beaches, or in cars. Diogenes, it appears, would also be considered homeless in George Bush's America.

As in Britain, certain pressure groups advocate a wider definition, emphasising the physical standard of accommodation and its suitability as a home from which its occupants can effectively enter the mainstream of American cultural life.[19] More legalistically, Rosenthal suggests the category should include anyone lacking enforceable rights to occupy accommodation for at least one week ahead.[20] These are, however, long-term objectives; for reasons discussed below, the immediate concern of homeless people and their active supporters is simply to put a safe roof over the head of any homeless person who wants one. British observers might consider this approach rather restrictive. Temporary shelter in a hostel is still consistent with being homeless as defined by the Housing Act 1985;[21] although as *Puhlhofer* demonstrated, long-term occupancy and appalling conditions are not mutually exclusive concepts for Britain's homeless population.[22]

Homelessness is also widely perceived as an *urban* phenomenon.[28] It is undoubtedly incorrect to assume that rural America has no homeless population.[24] Rather the equation of homelessness with urbanism derives from the growing visibility of homeless people to the many affluent commuters passing daily through the business and shopping districts of large American cities. As one commentator observes:

> in most neighbourhoods of New York City it is. . . not at all unusual to see people stretched out in a subway station; tourists in Greenwich Village seem surrounded by these aimless wanderers; and everyone who uses Pennsylvania Station or the Port Authority Bus Terminal must have seen those who have made these public places their homes.[25]

Homelessness is no longer a problem about which the general public can remain ignorant; although this does not mean that many Americans cannot continue to ignore it.

Section 4 below discusses efforts to quantify America's homelessness problem. Such quantification relates solely to the narrow concept of "rooflessness". Families doubling-up with friends, in housing which is insanitary, impossible to heat, or far removed from community facilities, are not yet classified as homeless. A broader definition of the concept might suggest that the United States is currently suffering a housing crisis of which rooflessness is merely a minor part.[26]

3. WHO ARE THE HOMELESS IN AMERICAN SOCIETY?

There is a powerful (although no longer dominant) strand within popular opinion which equates the homeless with the "hobo".[27] The hobo is regarded as a disaffected male, usually white, unemployed and work-shy, and often having alcohol- or drug-related problems.[28] However, popular opinion and historical reality have little in common here. The American hobo originally served as the primary labour force for the mining, railroad and construction industries as industrialised society marched west towards the Pacific in the nineteenth century.[29] Hobos did indeed develop a distinctive culture. This was founded on two elements: transience and employment. Hobos sought as much of both as they could. "Tramps" might travel widely and seek to avoid work. The "home guard" might pursue many menial jobs in the same town. Neither group were hobos; both were regarded contemptuously by hobos themselves.[30]

The popular misconception derives from the economic panics of 1873 and 1891/2, when nervousness in the financial markets triggered prolonged recessions in the railroad and construction industries. Hundreds of thousands of workers became temporarily unemployed. The panics provide clear examples of structurally caused dislocation of a formerly self-sufficient, highly mobile labour force. Hobos became "homeless" firstly because widespread unemployment made travel (by jumping trains) a pointless exercise, thereby confining many men to a single area; and secondly because such immobility was caused by considerable poverty, which precluded access to the existing housing market. The mass presence of hobos within urban areas was not a new phenomenon: in times of high employment hobos congregated in specific districts, creating a distinct "hobohemia" or "skid row" within the larger metropolis. Hobohemia then functioned essentially as a giant labour exchange, within which transient workers sought information about new jobs, bought clothing, food and tools in cheap stores, and frequently blew saved wages on alcohol, prostitution and gambling.[31] While the service industries attending hobos enjoyed some degree of permanence, individual hobos did not. Few remained in the same town beyond several months; many stayed only days.

In this form, skid row was widely accepted as a legitimate, necessary part of the frontier-based economy.[32] But during economic crises this perception changed. Rather than being a large high-spending pool of cheap, mobile labour, hobohemia became a repository of idle, discontented and potentially dangerous working-class men. As such they frequently became the target for repressive policing. Vagrancy itself remained a criminal offence in most states, although much hobo "criminality" resulted from aggressive enforcement of other trivial misdemeanours, such as public drunkenness, breach of the peace, or begging. Many cities vigorously used the criminal law to encourage hobos to leave town, and discourage travellers from staying.[33] As noted below, this "not in my backyard" response to homelessness remains attractive to some city authorities.

The hobos' "dangerousness" assumed a more pervasive hue when they began to organise collectively for political ends. The earliest example is perhaps the march of "Coxey's Army" on Washington D.C. in 1894. Foreshadowing the new deal policies of the 1930s, Coxey's Army drew together unemployed hobos from all over the United States in a call for federally financed public works programmes to alleviate unemployment. The march was broken up by police before reaching Congress, in a larger-scale manifestation of the official hostility to homeless people already displayed in many towns and cities.[34]

Homelessness, in the sense of indigence rather than perpetual transience, was given a further structurally caused boost by a decline in the geographical scale of the as yet undeveloped American Frontier, and a simultaneous reduction in the number of men needed to exploit it because of developments in technology and rationalisation of working practices.[35] By the mid-1920s, the hobo had largely disappeared from America's social landscape. The misperception of the homeless man as a work-shy, feckless deviant, however, remains firmly rooted in public opinion, exercising considerable influence over contemporary analyses of the homelessness problem.

Nevertheless, it is perhaps a testament to the problem's current seriousness that, despite eight years of the individualist market liberalism[36] espoused by the Reagan administrations, a consensus has emerged in most public, political and academic circles that not all of today's homeless Americans can be held personally accountable for their disadvantaged circumstances. The range and quantity of people affected is too widely disparate to permit of such simplistic analyses. This belief does not enjoy universal support: as noted below, the individual pathology explanation retains considerable support within the federal government, and among various state and local administrations. Moreover, rejecting individualist analyses of the *cause* of homelessness does not automatically entail support for collectively based *cures*. This mismatch between diagnosis and prescription is returned to below. The following section identifies some half dozen distinct subgroups among the homeless population. The divisions are not rigidly drawn; many homeless people may be mobile between categories, and/or have characteristics common to several groups.

3.1. Single Men of Working Age

While this group might seem the most obvious successor to the pre-1920s hobo, the analogy is not particularly apt. A sizeable, visible, contingent of men sleeping in shop doorways or parks, panhandling passers-by for change, queueing outside bloodbanks or soup kitchens, is now a feature of most large cities and many smaller towns. The group's membership may be quite stable. These people might more accurately be portrayed as the descendants of the early twentieth century "home guard". Most are unemployed, or drift spasmodically between unemployment and causal low-skilled, low-paid jobs. But many manage to maintain regular employment, again in low-paying, predominantly service sector jobs. This is in itself a somewhat remarkable achievement, given the mechanical and social difficulties of finding and holding employment when one has no permanent address, nowhere to store clothes, to wash or to get regular rest.[37]

Homelessness among this group, particularly those in work, derives primarily from changes in the structure of the housing market since the mid-1970s. Regentrification of inner-city areas has decimated the number of high-density, low-quality, but very cheap single room occupancy (SRO) hotels where low-income workers have traditionally lived.[38] Many SRO hotels have been converted to "yuppie" owner-occupied condominiums,[39] although federal and local tax reforms have also made refurbishment and rental of very expensive apartments attractive investment options for many property companies.[40] As SROs continue to disappear, it becomes tempting to over-romanticise the accommodation they offered. The sector contained great variations in quality and cost; many were dirty, insect infested, with few facilities, and poor security: enforcement of statutory standards has always been erratic.[41] That the loss of SROs is so deeply lamented is an indication of the overwhelming nature of the current problem.

The consequent quantitative decline in the bottom tier of the private rented sector has forced up its cost; rises in SRO rent levels have greatly outpaced wage increases in the 1980s.[42] Nor can low-wage-earning single men move unproblematically into the lower reaches of the rented appartment market. Entrants to this sector must generally produce three months' rent in advance ("first, last and deposit"), an amount beyond many people's resources. A further financial strain on entry is that most rented accommodation is let unfurnished, thus necessitating further immediate expenditure. Insofar as black and other ethnic minority groups continue to face pervasive discrimination in both labour and housing markets, their vulnerability to homelessness is proportionally even more acute than that of working-class whites.[43]

There is thus a working class "affordability crisis"[44] in operation, deriving from the interactive effect of structural changes in the housing and labour markets which have been triggered and encouraged by federal government economic policies. But it is not just the single man, nor solely the working class, who have been affected.

3.2. Homeless Families: Nuclear Models

It is for this group that structuralist explanations of homelessness enjoy the most widespread public support. The appearance on the social landscape of large numbers of nuclear families, none of whose members appear individually deviant, powerfully challenges traditional individualistic explanations of poverty.[45]

Homelessness in this category again stems from an "affordability crisis".[46] For working- and lower-middle-class Americans this has several distinct components. The first derives from increasing unemployment, particularly among skilled and unskilled workers in manufacturing industries. Many adults who subsequently re-enter the labour market do so into less well paid jobs in the service sector, with consequent reductions in a family budget still suffering the impact of the catastrophic income reduction accompanying redundancy. Reductions in social security expenditure have further undermined many American families' capacity to withstand even short-term periods of unemployment without severely reducing their standard of living.

Interacting with this is an increase in the cost of both private rented and owner-occupied family housing which, as in the case of SROs, has greatly outpaced wage increases.[47] Again this is attributable largely to contraction in the number of units available. The past decade has seen significant reductions in building starts in both the public and private sectors. Some 2 million new homes were built in 1978. This fell to 1.3 million in 1980, and then to 1.1 million in 1982, in a trend which shows no sign of reversal.[48] In consequence, entry into the owner-occupied sector has become increasingly expensive in terms of the percentage of income required to finance a mortgage.

In contrast to Britain, there is little subsidised public sector housing for such families to move into. Despite increased right to buy sales through the Housing Act 1980, council housing still accounts for over 25% of Britain's housing stock. In the United States, that figure is 2%.[49]

However, as in Britain, American tax policy provides substantial subsidies to established owner-occupiers through tax relief on mortgage interest payments. Reductions in financial support to the public sector, coupled with rapid growth in the size of mortgage interest tax concessions, has shifted the relative worth of government subsidy firmly in the owner-occupiers' favour. In the United States, the imbalance is even more pronounced:

> Benefits from federal housing programs are so skewed that *the total of all the assisted housing payments ever made under all HUD assisted housing programmes, from the inception of public housing in 1937 through 1980, was less than the cost in the federal government of housing related tax expenditures in 1980 alone* [original emphasis].[50]

Consequently, for many American families mortgage arrears and foreclosure do not precipitate a move down-market, but out of the market entirely.[51] Many such families have become visibly homeless; how many conceal their homelessness by doubling up with friends or family, or by splitting the household into fragments is unknown.

The employment/housing squeeze has also adversely affected middle-income groups, whose members are increasingly restricted in terms of the quality, location and mobility which the market offers.[52] This problem is not qualitatively comparable to being physically homeless, but it has heightened public awareness of the influence exercised on people's housing circumstances by structural economic factors.[53]

These twin themes of labour market contraction and property market inflation set the socio-economic context within which the growth of the homeless population must be placed; at the risk of repetition they will be adverted to further below. For some homeless people, however, these structural changes are not exclusive causes of homelessness, rather they exacerbate pre-existing vulnerability.

3.3. The Deinstitutionalised Mentally Ill

In Britain the Mental Health Act 1959 heralded the beginning of a trend towards caring for the mentally ill in the community rather than in large institutions. The policy continues to arouse great controversy, primarily because the necessary community-based facilities have not been provided by many health authorities.[54] An inevitable consequence of exposing mentally ill people to the respective rigours of Britain's employment and housing markets in which they are unable effectively to compete is that many of them have become homeless.

For governments, one attraction of deinstitutionalisation is its cheapness; especially when community resources are not actually provided. This consideration was accorded particular importance in the United States, where the process began in the 1950s following the invention of the antipsychotic drug thorazine, accelerated rapidly in the 1960s, and has continued apace until the present day.[55] Providing institutionalised care was, and remains, the responsibility of state governments. Discharging patients into the "community", where they would be dependent on federally subsidised social security benefits, and local government health services, produces a major reduction in the state's fiscal liabilities.[56] Civil liberties lawyers lent further impetus to the American programme of "releasing" patients into the community. Many radical lawyers, inspired by the "new property" thesis developed by Charles Reich[57] and frequently financed by funds from Lyndon Johnson's Great Society initiatives,[58] made increasingly imaginative use of federal and state constitutions to impose constraints on the autonomy with which government organisations administered all manner of social welfare programmes.

In the political climate of the 1960s hospitalisation was widely regarded as equivalent to imprisonment—relatedly deinstitutionalisation was construed as a release for the patient, and victory for the lawyer.[59] In 1955 some 550,000 patients were resident in state institutions; by 1983 there were only 130,000.[60] For the lawyer, however, discharge ended his/her involvement with the health care system; the cause of civil liberties had been advanced by another oft-repeated procedural success in the familiar environs of the local court. For patients, deinstitutionalisation heralded entirely new substantive experience, in an often alien environment. As one observer graphically asserts, deinstitutionalisation was to prove a procedural success for lawyers, but a substantive failure for the people it was supposed to free:

[It] has meant a nightmare existence in the blighted centres of our cities, amidst neighbourhoods crowded with prostitutes, ex-felons, addicts, alcoholics and other human rejects now repressively tolerated by our society. Here they eke out a precarious existence, supported by welfare cheques they may not even know how to cash. They spend their days locked in or out of dilapidated "community-based" boarding houses.[61]

The concept of "freedom" for the mentally ill arguably embraces much more than simply being discharged on to the streets where they are unable to fend for themselves. The civil right inherent in deinstitutionalisation is essentially *negative;* it compels the government to lift a restriction. For many mentally ill Americans what was needed was a *positive* civil right, imposing upon government the duty to provide a structured, protective environment in which patients could attempt to maximise their potential for independent living. Such programmes simply have not been provided in sufficient quantity.[62] A corollary of deinstitutionalisation policies is the non-institutionalisation of citizens who would formerly have received hospital-based care. In quantitative terms restrictive admission policies to psychiatric hospitals probably presents a greater contribution to homelessness than discharge of existing patients.[63] The end result is, however, the same.

3.4. Military Veterans

In contrast to many social welfare programmes, financial and social support for veterans of the United State's many overseas wars has traditionally been both substantively generous and easily accessible. Veterans occupy a particularly "deserving" niche within the American welfare state.[64]

Nevertheless, Vietnam veterans now form a distinct segment of the homeless population. These Americans are exclusively male, both black and white, and generally in the 30–50-year age range. A number suffer some psychological or psychiatric disorders, frequently compounded by drug or alcohol addiction.[65] This category overlaps significantly with the deinstitutionalised mentally ill; its members have the same pervasive incapacity to cope with the mundane requirements of everyday life such as finding regular employment and secure accommodation. However, significant numbers are homeless because of acute poverty; many veterans received no marketable employment skills while in the armed forces, and it appears that many have also slipped through the Veterans' Administration safety net. For both groups the incidence of homelessness has risen during the 1980s because of wider structural changes in the housing and labour markets.[66]

3.5. Homeless Families: One-Parent Households

Exponents of the new property thesis were also active in seeking to establish that single mothers possessed enforceable legal rights in the welfare provision they received from federal and state governments.[67] Many states subjected these claimants to onerous "morality" tests before granting benefit, and subsequently to intrusive policing of their sexual behaviour. The so-called "unfit mother" and "man in the house" rules which some southern states used to disqualify many (predominantly black) women from any form of income support payments were among the most glaring examples of the states' readiness and capacity to defy the redistributive social policies of the Kennedy and Johnson administrations.[68]

Such tests necessarily subjected claimants to intrusive investigations by welfare administrators. "Midnight raids" in search of undeclared cohabitees were a favoured tactic of many welfare bureaucracies.[69] Welfare rights lawyers challenged such practices by asserting that they breached the citizen's constitutional right to privacy. That such legal action was necessary demonstrates clearly that the one (female)-parent household had yet to achieve "deserving" status in American public opinion; particularly if the mother was black.[70]

In the mid-1980s some 11 million children were being raised in households headed by a single women; over 30% of such families had incomes below the poverty level.[71] The high visibility of one-parent households in today's homeless population reinforces popular stereotypes about the individual fecklessness and culpability of homeless people; "scroungerphobia" is a transatlantic phenomenon.[72] Conversely (as discussed below), various state governments have seen such homeless families as exemplifying the multifaceted, structural nature of much current homelessness. Inadequate schooling, adolescent pregnancy, few job-training initiatives, lack of day care facilities, limited public sector housing, dependency-generating welfare benefits and insufficient government-funded employment programmes are seen as closely linked contributors to the problem. In this analysis, homelessness is but one manifestation of the market's pervasive failure to provide acceptable living standards to large sections of the American people. Such holistic analyses clearly demand similarly comprehensive responses;[73] these have rarely been forthcoming.

More women and children are now pushed into homelessness following divorce. The availability of no-fault divorce in many states, generally entailing 50/50 division of assets which necessitates sale of the family home, is regarded as a major cause of this phenomenon. Moreover, women tend to suffer appreciable reductions in disposable income after divorce, whereas men's income usually increases, generally because the woman assumes child care responsibilities which severely limit her earning capacity.[74]

3.6. The Unemployables

There has always been a rump of citizens for whom economic self-sufficiency through employment is not a feasible option.[75] For some "unemployables" dependent status derives from "deserving" causes, such as old age or chronic physical disability. For others, chiefly drug and alcohol addicts, unemployability compounds the social unacceptability of an already deviant lifestyle. The state of the housing and labour markets are largely irrelevant to homelessness among these people, given that few business would want to employ them, and few landlords would wish to house them.[76] Homelessness within this category highlights the variations in social service support and social security benefits across the country. As discussed below, such inconsistencies result both from the constitutional division of welfare responsibility between federal, state and local government, and from the readiness of the various tiers of government to lift certain sections of the unemployable poor out of the housing and labour markets. In this respect the federal government has taken a lead, albeit an unhelpful one.

One of the first Reagan administration's earliest social welfare initiatives was an eligibility review of people receiving Social Security Disability Insurance, a benefit paid to those with a mental or physical handicap rendering them unable to perform "substantial gainful work". When the review ended in 1984 some 200,000 people had been struck from the rolls. There is considerable dispute as to the accuracy of this weeding out process. Various commentators have suggested that many genuine claimants were too confused or too frightened to respond to the examination procedure and have become homeless as a result.[77]

Despite the current media obsession with America's drug problems, alcohol and narcotic addiction among the homeless are long-standing phenomena; Andersen's classic study of homeless men in 1920s Chicago charted widespread substance abuse in the city's skid row.[78] Now, as then, increased employment opportunities and lower cost housing would not in themselves assist addicts to overcome a web of problems of which homelessness is only a part. Provision of detoxification facilities for alcohol and/or drug abusers is erratic, as is the availability of counselling or resettlement programmes to assist former addicts to reintegrate themselves in the employment and housing markets. Without such facilities, which require extensive government funding, homelessness among this group is unlikely to diminish. This group is of course perhaps the most "undeserving" of the undeserving poor.

Similar problems surround homelessness among the mentally ill and mentally handicapped. Federal funding for supportive, rehabilitative health care for the mentally ill which might maximise their economic self-sufficiency has been woefully inadequate during the 1980s.[79] This failure of community-based care is partly hidden by the no-cost (to the government) support provided by patients' families, and partly compensated for by the many state and local administrations which do provide innovative and extensive facilities for the mentally ill. Such initiatives frequently make specific provision for overcoming the housing and employment difficulties suffered by patients for whom some degree of self-sufficiency may be achieved with regular social work support. Again, however, the federal structure of America's welfare state, and the ideological pluralism to which federalism gives rein, have produced marked inconsistencies in public sector provision. Some commentators identify major discrepancies in provision for the physically and mentally disabled; primarily because local communities often mobilise to prevent facilities being located in their particular neigbourhood.[80]

3.7. Runaways and Throwaways: Homeless Children

Like Thatcher's Britain, Reagan's America eulogised the family as the basic unit of social organisation, and as a major provider of care and financial support to its members. In both countries such sentiments have been accompanied by widespread breakdowns in family stability, often exacerbated by financial problems stemming from government economic and social security policies.[81] The consequences of such breakdowns are many and various. Physical and sexual abuse by parents is one manifestation of the problem; increased truancy or petty criminality among children themselves is another. In both countries, public awareness that family breakdown also results in many children without roofs over their heads has also increased in recent years.[82] In the weeks preceeding the 1988 Presidential election the National Academy of Sciences created considerable controversy by censoring a report on juvenile homelessness produced by its own academicians. The report suggested some 100,000 American children currently lived on the streets. The Academy cut the report because its authors were unable to maintain a dispassionate objectivity in the face of their findings, but rather felt compelled to reinforce their analysis with a short attack on the Reagan administration's social welfare policies.[83]

As the Academy study revealed, homeless children present a particularly emotive strand of the homelessness problem, insofar as they are at great risk of financial and/or sexual exploitation. Yet press coverage, while sensationalistic, is unlikely to present the problem accurately: many homeless children remain largely invisible to public scrutiny, whether through deliberate efforts to avoid detection by police or social service agencies, or simply because their age prevents them seeking mainstream employment and accommodation. Survival is necessarily achieved on society's economic margins, through means such as prostitution, petty theft or drug dealing.[84] As with unemployables, homelessness among children is not directly caused by tightening of the employment and housing markets. Both its causes, and its cures, lie in factors outside the market.[85] To some extent, therefore, recurrent media coverage of homeless children undermines efforts to portray homelessness generally as a structural economic defect. The indirect linkage between economic liberalism's housing and employment policies and family breakdown is rarely made in the popular press.

But having considered the *nature* of homelessness in today's United States, the next question concerns its *scale*. How many Americans currently lack regular access to even the most limited forms of accommodation?

4. QUANTIFICATION OF THE PROBLEM

The scale of homelessness in the United States, when restrictively interpreted as people without regular access to shelter, is a highly contentious issue. In the mid 1980s estimates ranged from a low of 250,000 to a high of 2.5

million. The low figure is advanced by the Department of Housing and Urban Development (HUD), in a study intended to arrive at a more methodologically defensible quantification of the homeless population than those previously produced.[86] HUD's analysis was designed to refute the high estimate of some 2.5 million homeless (a figure gaining growing public acceptance through constant media repetition), presented by a Washington-based homeless persons pressure group, the Community for Creative Non-Violence (CCNV).[87]

The methodological basis of CCNV's figure was somewhat suspect. CCNV projected its national aggregate from a limited telephonic survey of individuals and organisations closely involved with providing services to the homeless in a non-random sample of urban areas. Respondents were asked to give personal estimates of the number of homeless persons in their particular area. Neither the choice of sample areas, the basis of respondents' calculations, nor the method of extrapolation from local figures were explained. HUD was severely critical of these omissions, and sought "more systematic" analysis by combining four different methods of measurements to calculate a "most reliable range estimate". The technique led, as noted above, to the claim that only some 250,000 American citizens were then reliant for accommodation on emergency shelters.

However, HUD's own methodology has also been roundly condemned, primarily because of its peculiar assumption that an accurate conclusion could be reached by collating the aggregates derived from techniques which it had itself labelled as unsatisfactory. One commentator described this claim as

> sheer nonsense: if none of these approaches is based on any scientific, reliable methods, no amount of piling approach on approach will ensure reliability[88]

In contrast to HUD, CCNV made no effort to defend its estimate's methodological integrity. Its spokesman reported to a Congressional hearing that numbers were in themselves "meaningless": the problem's enormity rendered continued attempts at precise quantification irrelevant.[89] But numbers were not irrelevant to the federal government. The larger the problem, the more plausible it seems to demand a federal solution; the smaller the number then the more credible are arguments that the problem is remediable through locally based initiatives.[90] Given the massive cutbacks in federal housing subsidies since 1980 (discussed further below), HUD's low estimate is not altogether surprising.

Similarly there is little consensus concerning the respective proportions within the total homeless populations of the various subgroups identified in Section 3. Studies have been made of the clienteles of individual night shelters to assess the numbers of mentally ill, alcoholic, drug-dependent or simply unemployed citizens resident at particular times,[91] but given the difficulties inherent in extrapolating national figures from such data they are of little help in clarifying the overall picture.[92] On a largely impressionistic basis there is apparent agreement that the deinstitutionalised mentally ill constitute the largest segment of the visibly homeless (with estimates ranging from 35 to 60%),[93] but again no reliable national figures exist. It is also suggested that many homeless persons make strenuous attempts to remain invisible to both public sector and voluntary agencies, a factor further complicating attempts to construct accurate profiles of the homeless population.[94] But while answers to the numbers question remain elusive, government efforts to uncover it continue apace. Clearly, however, the numbers involved are vast, even if one accepts HUD's disputed estimate of 250,000. Given the government defined scale of the problem, it perhaps becomes pertinent to ask just what government is doing to reduce it.

5. THE SOLUTION: A PROBLEM OF GOVERNMENT?

Several pressure groups representing homeless people have argued that homelessness is now so pervasive that no rapid, straightforward solution is possible. Rather they advocate a tripartite response. The first phase should simply be one of crisis management, entailing a massive increase in the availability of safe, warm shelter of the most basic kind. The second involves the provision of a supportive package of social services, ranging from child-minding and health care, to job training and assistance in finding employment. The third, long-term, part of the solution is a large expansion in federal subsidies for new building and renovation in both the public and private rented sectors.[95] Each phase is clearly more costly than the last. The tripartite model also entails acceptance that America's homeless problem can only be solved through coordinated, collective action, and is therefore properly the responsibility of all tiers of government.

This section examines the extent to which federal, state and city government has accepted and acted upon the prescription. Clearly the multiplicity of state and city jurisdictions precludes more than a cursory assessment of the measures introduced. The intention is merely to provide an indication of the range of initiatives undertaken, and to cast light on the respective influences exercised by structural and individualistic analyses of the causes of homelessness.

Nor can this paper enter into a detailed analysis of the complexities of the constitutional mechanisms regulating federal/state/local relations.[96] Some reference was made to this above, and the implications are considered further below, but one may note here that the legal autonomy of state governments is to some extent constitutionally protected from federal aggression. This is in marked contrast to the situation in Britain, where local government is entirely a creature of statute, with the result that its functions, its financial autonomy, and indeed its very existence are completely controlled by central government.[97]

5.1. The Federal Government

The preamble to the still extent National Housing Act 1949 asserts that the objective of federal housing policy is to secure "a decent home and a suitable living environment for every American family". The Reagan administrations appear to have ignored this historical commitment, adopting instead a "conscious policy of federal withdrawal"[98] from the provision of affordable housing; federal housing expenditures have fallen from $27 billion in 1980 to $9.9 billion in 1986.[99] Although some commentators attribute recent increases in homelessness directly to the Reagan/Bush administrations' reductions in federal expenditure on public housing and social security programmes,[100] the federal government itself does not recognise any causal link between the phenomena. Reagan adhered to a more individualistic explanation, arguing that "the homeless are homeless, as it were, by choice".[101] His then Vice-President George Bush suggested homelessness was limited exclusively to the mentally ill (although he did not simultaneously propose expansion of health care facilities as a means to a cure). Unsurprisingly therefore, the federal government has not accepted homelessness as a problem requiring comprehensive federally designed, funded and administered responses. Indeed some officials denied that there was a problem at all.[102]

Federal inactivity is justified on two grounds. The first is context specific: if homelessness is a problem, then it is a localised problem whose solution demands the application of expert local knowledge which only state or city government is able to provide.[103] The second relates to the more general issue of the "correct" form of federal/state relations. The constitutional sanctity of the states themselves, in contrast for example to the legal ephemerality of the GLC and ILEA, provides for an appreciable degree of entrenched pluralism within the American welfare state. State governments which oppose federal policies cannot simply be legislated away. Indirect pressure can be applied through fiscal policy, particularly by setting thresholds for service provisions below which federal subsidies will not be paid, but its impact is not qualitatively comparable to rate-capping, for example.[104]

The states have devoted considerable effort to maximising their decision-making autonomy when implementing (or not implementing) federal government welfare programmes. Federal government has generally not sought to impinge greatly on the autonomy, with the result that enormous discrepancies exist in the substance and administration of welfare state benefits.[105] Roosevelt's New Deal policies, and subsequently the civil and welfare rights reforms introduced by the Kennedy/Johnson administrations, produced a series of particularly acute conflicts between federal and state governments over the latter's constitutional entitlement to dilute federal programmes or ignore Supreme Court judgements. The refusal of Governor

George Wallace to end racial segregation at the University of Alabama is perhaps the best-known example of this.[106] Similar controversies also flared during the 1960s over such issues as publication of welfare rolls[107] and the "midnight raids" on single women claimants.[108]

Such instances of flagrant disregard of legislative or judicial norms have provided federal officials in Democrat administrations with opportunities to erode the states' autonomy, but subsequent elections of Republican Presidents have generally led to renewed loosening of federal controls. The Reagan administrations continued this trend, arguing that close federal involvement in welfare administration was administratively inefficient as well as politically unpalatable. As a HUD spokesperson recently argued in opposition to calls for a federal assault on homelessness:

> It is almost a truism that when a federal bureaucracy imposes new requirements and regulations on local problems, costs are multiplied and decision-making and processing time result in delayed solutions and delivery of services [*sic*].[109]

Consequently, federal initiatives have been largely exhortatory, directed towards the states, cities and counties and voluntary organisations. The sincerity with which such calls to arms were made is of course open to question. The major exception to the Reagan administrations' "hands-off" policy was the Stewart B. McKinney Comprehensive Homeless Assistance Act. The McKinney Act appropriated approximately $1.5 billion in funds for 1988–1990, to be distributed between a mishmash of shelter rehabilitation programmes, services for the mentally ill, emergency food and medical provision, and an assortment of literacy and job training initiatives.

McKinney's fragmentory approach to the problem is entirely consistent with the Reagan administrations' refusal to accept homelessness as the result of structural inadequacies in the housing and labour markets. As such it could at best provide a piecemeal, temporary solution for small parts of the homeless population. The Act's conceptual limitations are exacerbated by its administrative mechanics. State and local governments must compete amongst themselves for McKinney financing: since Congress has authorised expenditure of only 60% of the appropriated funds many proposed projects receive no federal support. Moreover federal grants are made on a year-by-year basis with no guarantee of renewal, which of course precludes any efforts to initiate long-term solutions. Additionally federal funds are frequently released only if state or local government commits itself to dollar for dollar matching funding. Consequently McKinney is unlikely to assist homeless persons in states or cities unsympathetic to structuralist analyses of the problem, a shortcoming reinforced by the Act's requirement that managing organisations must meet the bulk of any administrative costs incurred in introducing new programmes.[110]

Reagan approved the Bill somewhat reluctantly towards the end of his second term. White House Aides reported that it was signed with "a lack of enthusiasm".[111] HUD has been similarly lacking in enthusiasm in its distribution of the federal funding involved. Its failure to meet an August 1988 deadline for allocating a mere 15 million dollars for new local government administered shelters prompted the National Coalition for the Homeless to begin court action to ensure that shelters could be established before the onset of winter.[112] It remains to be seen how much of the appropriated funding is eventually made available.

The Department's practical inefficiencies are allied with a somewhat bizarre analysis of the causes of homelessness:

> the problem is not so much the scarcity of housing, as it is a problem of low income families not having sufficient income to afford the housing that is available.[113]

The notion that housing is *not available* if potential consumers cannot afford it does not appear to have informed HUD's critique. Nor has the major initiative taken to bridge the affordability gap had a significant impact. Rather than producing cheaper housing, the Reagan administration has chosen to offer private tenants income supplements through the so-called "Section 8" programme. This resembles the British housing benefit scheme, although it is far more limited in scope. Housing benefit is essentially demand-led expenditure, with its total cost to central and local government dependent upon the number of claimants, their incomes and their housing costs. In contrast, Section 8 payments are made from a fixed supply of federal funding. When the annual budget is exhausted no further payments are made, irrespective of any unsatisfied demand. The system provides a limited number of recipients with vouchers for a fixed amount which claimants can present to prospective landlords as proof of their ability to afford rent payments.

HUD considers the Section 8 initiative to have made a major contribution to alleviating homelessness.[114] Critics have, however, suggested that its impact has been minimal. The scheme's primary inadequacy is quantitative. Section 8's initial annual budget of $200 million was rapidly exhausted;[115] in the Greater Boston area in 1984 some 20,000 applications were made for a fixed total of 1000 certificates. Nor does issue of a voucher automatically lead to housing. The sums awarded are invariably fixed at the lowest point of an area's private rented market, severely restricting both the range and quantity of potential housing. Moreover, claimants have only two months in which to secure accommodation, at the end of which period their vouchers expire. In a tight market two months may prove insufficient, given that claimants' stigmatisation as welfare recipients, coupled with possible bureaucratic problems with payment, renders them relatively undesirable as potential tenants compared with self-supporting competitors. The vouchers' efficacy has been further reduced because up-rating of Section 8 limits has not matched private rented sector inflation; consequently recipients in more expensive areas are simply unable to find affordable accommodation.[116]

Neither the McKinney Act nor Section 8 vouchers provide more than localised, crisis-management responses to homelessness. In seeking longer-term solutions one must direct attention at initiatives introduced by the states. The following section examines the responses made by the two states which have been most active in grappling with their homelessness problems: New York and Massachusetts.

5.2. State Initiatives

Left largely to their own devices, whether through constitutional pro-priety or federal disinterest, the American states have adopted a wide range of programmes in response to the needs of their respective homeless popula-tions. In Massachusetts, the then growing problem of homelessness was ac-corded maximum priority by Governor Michael Dukakis when beginning his second term in 1982.[117] The initiatives proceeded from the assumption that large-scale homelessness in Massachusetts resulted from a combination of inadequacies in the housing and labour markets, and the catastrophic failure of the state's social service bureaucracies to make adequate community-based provision for the mentally ill, thousands of whom had ef-fectively been discharged on to the streets since the late 1960s. The new ad-ministration introduced a number of state-financed multi-agency initiatives, in partnership with local government, church and other voluntary organisa-tions and homeless persons' pressure groups.[118] Equally important was the Governor's categorical assertion that homelessness is the result not of per-sonal inadequacy but of wider economic and social forces, an analysis which received increasing national media attention in the run-up to the 1988 Presi-dential campaign, when Dukakis ran as the Democrat nominee.

Mario Cuomo, Governor of New York State, has taken a similar view of the problem:

> Homelessness today is not primarily the result of personal fault or failure, but of larger misfortunes over which people have very little control.[119]

State initiatives have been launched at various levels. With some legal prod-ding (discussed below), Cuomo's administration has greatly expanded emer-gency shelter provisions. Total spending in the current year has allegedly reached some $300 million.[120] In a more preventative vein, the state has en-couraged New York City to use development control powers to restrict pri-vate sector developments in the housing market, for example through temporary moritoriums on conversion of SROs in certain areas. Longer-term measures have involved joint projects with private developers to pro-mote low- and mid-cost housing developments designed to loosen the affordability squeeze affecting working- and lower-middle-class families. The largest initiative, "Housing New York", will provide 40,000 new units by 1996.

The perception that homelessness is a "housing problem with distinctive social service components"[121] has also triggered re-evaluation of health care policies for the mentally ill and expansion of detox facilities for drug and alcohol abusers. Similarly the state's Department of Social Services has increased social work support to families at risk of breaking up, and also extended counselling and shelter facilities to runaway children. Despite the variety of initiatives Cuomo himself sees them as little more than palliatives, arguing that any long-term solution requires massive federal involvement.

This paper cannot do more than offer some indication of the scope and variety of state initiatives. The point to emphasise here is that the federal government's seeming indifference to the nation's homeless is not shared by many state governments. Furthermore the constitutional structure of American government accords the states sufficient autonomy to introduce and finance wide-ranging attempts to alleviate their respective homelessness problems. The quality and quantity of state assistance to the homeless varies widely; the New York and Massachusetts programmes are atypical both in their recognition of the structural economic causes of much homelessness and their multifaceted efforts to deal with it. Moreover, just as previous federal administrations have experienced difficulty in transmitting social policy objectives through recalcitrant state governments, so notionally sympathetic state policy-makers have found their initiatives towards homelessness significantly diluted or obstructed at local levels of citizen/government relations. Particularly acute difficulties have arisen in New York and New Jersey; these will be discussed further in Section 6 below. In the concluding pages of Section 5, attention centres on the responses made by local government and voluntary organisations.

5.3 City Responses

The absence of federally imposed legal constraints on the state's obligations towards the homeless, and the corresponding variations in the measures adopted, are mirrored in the equally disparate responses made by the nation's city and county authorities.

At one extreme lies the attitude typified by Phoenix and Tucson in Arizona. In the early 1980s Tucson's Mayor was elected on a manifesto whose main plank was to get "the transients the hell out of town".[122] The presence of dishevelled-looking homeless people, particularly the bizarre behaviour of the mentally ill, is considered both detrimental to business interests and unnerving for local residents. The city consequently introduced intensive policing of downtown areas to move the homeless on to other locations.[123] The concern of Phoenix's city authorities to encourage gentrification and commercialisation of its inner city core has led to a determined assault on facilities for homeless people. As in Tucson, city councillors and leading businessmen fear that providing services for homeless people would provoke a massive influx of homeless Americans from neighbouring towns and states. Neither city has any publicly funded shelters. Phoenix has gone somewhat further. Local business launched a "Fight Back" campaign to clamp down on unacceptable behaviour by homeless people. The city also took legal action to close down voluntarily funded and managed shelters, with the result that there was nowhere at all for homeless people to seek overnight refuge. Lest the homeless should seek to sleep in the open air, the city closed a major public park and introduced local ordinances (bye-laws) making it a criminal offence to sleep or even lie down on public property. It might safely be presumed that enforcement of such ordinances is somewhat selective. The prevailing mood is perhaps best captured by an editorial in the *Arizona Republic* newspaper:

We didn't tolerate prostitutes—why tolerate bums?.[124]

Such cities subscribe to the so-called "magnet theory" of homelessness.[125] Magnet theory holds that the size of an area's homeless population is exclusively determined by the level of public response made to it. City funding of shelter places or subsidised housing will inevitably trigger immigration by homeless people from surrounding areas. In many parts of the United States, the combination of magnet theory and the perception of homelessness as a purely voluntaristic, deviant phenomenon has led many cities, as in the years following the Cleveland panic, to adopt purely repressive responses to homeless persons. Removal of any publicly financed shelter provision, coupled with resistance to initiatives by voluntary organisations, effectively condemns homeless people to live permanently on the streets. Administrations such as Phoenix and Tucson hope that a complete lack of facilities will discourage the transient homeless from coming to the city, while simultaneously encouraging those already there to move on. Local ordinances forbidding sleeping in public, allied to aggressive and selective police enforcement of minor offences such as panhandling or vagrancy combine in a form of reverse magnet theory.[126] The NIMBY (not-in-my-backyard) response is of course a "solution" only for those Americans who prefer not to look upon their homeless fellow citizens: for the homeless themselves enforced mobility and greater exposure to the criminal justice system exacerbates an already desperate situation.

A slightly less repressive dispersal method is "greyhound therapy", a technique frequently practised by small towns and cities, which provides bus fares for homeless persons to transport them to the nearest large city.[127] A variation on the theme is practised in Chicago, where the police have reputedly taken to rounding up homeless men late at night and subsequently depositing them on the streets of some of the city's more salubrious suburbs.

Some cities also make extensive use of zoning laws to prevent facilities for homeless persons being introduced in particular localities.[128] Local opposition to community-based mental health care facilities has been a major contributor to the failure of deinstitutionalisation policies; similar obstacles have confronted local initiatives to provide hostels, supported housing or detoxification centres for homeless people in more affluent neighbourhoods.[129] Most resistance stems from concerns about falls in property values, although empirical evidence suggests that such facilities do not have noticeable long-term effects on the resale value of nearby housing.[130] Nevertheless considerable energy is now expended on designing strategies to persuade potential host communities that local provision for homeless people will not adversely affect the neighbourhood.[131]

While some cities have actively exacerbated the difficulties suffered by their homeless citizens, it must also be noted that many local administrations have adopted extensive and innovative techniques to ameliorate the situation. The multi-faceted nature of America's homeless population poses different problems to different areas. Homeless citizens in Portland, Oregon, are distinctive for their particularly high incidence of mental illness. Although the city has bucked national trends by expanding institutionalisation of the mentally ill and community-based facilities, such provision has not matched the growth of its mentally ill population. The city has also seen its supply of SRO accommodation shrink from 4,100 in 1980 to barely 1,700 in 1986. The city did not begin to address its homelessness problems until 1982, when a task-force was established to identify the homeless population and propose measures to reduce it. The task-force concluded that the high percentage of mentally ill homeless citizens means that straightforward efforts to increase housing supply would be an inadequate response. Consequently the city produced a 12-point action plan advocating coordinated action by housing welfare and health care organisations in both the public and voluntary sectors.[132] Some six years later, the city was able to reveal an impressive success rate in its programmes to reduce its homelessness problem, particularly among former drug and alcohol abusers.[133]

Los Angeles, which vies with New York for the title of homeless capital of America, has established various quasi-autonomous corporations in partnership with voluntary organisations to produce specific housing developments for different categories of homeless people. One of the most important is the Single Room Housing Occupancy Corporation, a body which has built or converted over 700 SRO units in the city's skid row areas.[134]

Among the more "informal" measures adopted is the traditional policy of the New York City Transit Authority to permit homeless people to ride the subways or sleep in stations throughout the night. However, the Transit Authority is now finding the problem quantitatively unmanageable; a 2 a.m. sweep of the system in September 1988 uncovered some 971 people asleep in trains or stations.[135] Since many of these people are mentally ill or substance abusers, they present a severe problem for the Authority, posing a threat both to safety and the delicate sensibilities of more affluent commuters. Investigation is currently being undertaken to devise a "humane" way of easing the homeless out of the transport system, Similarly lax enforcement of local bye-laws has led to the growth of a sizeable contingent of homeless men taking up night-time residence at Chicago's O'Hara airport, presenting some new arrivals to the United States with an extraordinary juxtaposition of affluence and poverty.

That permitting overnight shelter in a subway or airport lounge is seen in some quarters as a positive step in dealing with homelessness further underscores the very limited impact that local government can make on the nation's homelessness crisis. Yet insofar as a social problem is defined by the responses made to deal with it, city authorities wield enormous (if localised) influence over public perceptions of homelessness. The issue of homeless single women provides an apposite example of this. Readers may have observed that the various groups of homeless people identified in Section 3 did not include single women. This may in part be attributable to homeless women's more ready access to informal support networks of family and friends.[136] But the omission also reflects the minimal provision which any tier of government has made for homeless women without dependent children. City-based public shelters have been provided almost exclusively for men. To an extent the absence of facilities may derive from the traditional perception of homelessness as a male problem; the female hobo was a rarely observed phenomenon.[137] Additionally, it has been argued that many localities will not provide shelters for women on the grounds that such facilities encourage the break-up of marriages and families.[138] There is no empirical evidence to support the contention, but the theory is a graphic reminder of the influence exercised on housing policy by deep-rooted ideological beliefs regarding the desirabilty of maintaining the nuclear family as the basic unit of social organisation.[139] It is pertinent to recall at this point the differential attachment of personal responsibility and deservingness to the homelessness suffered by nuclear and one-parent families; this ideological commitment retains a powerful influence in many parts of the country.

Single homeless women also exhibit great reluctance to use mixed-sex hosted accommodation. The more pervasive shortcomings of many institutions cut across sex boundaries, and are considered further below. It may be noted here, however, that entering a male-dominated hostel exposes women to very real risks of robbery, sexual assault, rape and other male violence.[140] In response to these fears, and in some cases with no little legal pressure, some cities have recently opened women-only hostel accommodation. That these shelters have been filled immediately reinforces the argument that America harbours a huge, thus far invisible contingent of homeless women. It is perhaps stating the obvious to note that women's position in the labour market has traditionally been markedly inferior to that occupied by men with equivalent racial and class characteristics. But as a result of this sexual inequality, it is likely that women's access to affordable accommodation has been restricted particularly severely as employment and housing markets have become more brutal in the 1980s.

5.4. The Voluntary Sector

Government provision for the homeless is at best patchy. In many parts of the United States there is no effective public provision *at all* for people without shelter. For those seeking to avoid another night on the streets, recourse must be had to the voluntary sector. In the mid-1980s a HUD survey estimated that some 63% of shelter accommodation was financed by nongovernmental sources: the Reagan administration viewed this as a salute to the altruism of the American public, rather than a condemnation of federal inactivity.[141]

The voluntary organisations come from a bewildering range of sources, and provide an equally varied range of services. Systematic voluntary sector activity to alleviate homelessness dates from the 1860s, when the Charity Organisation Society established a residential facility in New York. The Society perceived homelessness to be the result of personal moral deficiencies. Such individual shortcomings were to be remedied during the client's residence in the Society's shelter, where he or she would receive instruction in the virtues of thrift, sobriety and hard work to counter the "indolence and dependence" that was presumed to cause homelessness. The Society accompanied its "correctional facilities" with vigorous campaigns to outlaw tramping and to prohibit the customary practice of providing overnight lodging in local police stations.[142]

This preoccupation with individual inadequacy, if not culpability, remains a strong informant of contemporary church responses. Much shelter provision is accompanied by programmes of personal counseling, job training and assistance to locate affordable housing which are designed to break what is seen as a "cycle of homelessness".[143] These initiatives generally recognize that structural economic factors underlie recent upsurges in homelessness. However, since resolving those problems is quite beyond their scope, voluntary schemes tend to regard making clients self-sufficient in the private sector employment and housing markets as their ultimate objective.

In contrast, some religious institutions offer food and shelter with no strings attached, beyond requiring clients not to disturb their fellows while in residence. The Pine Street Inn in Boston is the best-known member of this genre. Its ideology

> is emphatically not to rehabilitate the men, only to provide the essentials of life in a homelike atmosphere...To help the men optimally adapt to the lifestyle they sustain by choice or fortune, neither encouraging that lifestyle nor censoring it.[144]

Shelter provision of this kind provokes considerable criticism from conservative commentators, who equate "moral neutrality" with encouragement of the deviant social values which have caused the client's homelessness. Enabling the homeless to "adapt" to such lifestyles will, it is argued, increase both the numbers of people seeking shelter and their dependency on the services offered.[145]

Voluntary groups which take advantage of various tax concessions offered to charitable bodies are not permitted to engage in explicit political campaigns. Nevertheless religious groups have adopted a more overtly politicised role in addition to delivering housing and/or counselling services to homeless people. The Covenant House group of shelters in New York provides accommodation for homeless children and young persons, but is also actively involved in lobbying the federal government for changes in the legal frameworks protecting the young from financial and physical abuse.[146]

But religious institutions which provide assistance to the homeless are not invariably influenced by such progressive motives. Perceptions of homelessness as a voluntaristic, deviant phenomenon which can be cured by thorough instillation of suitable religious values lead many shelters to adopt quite repressive regimes. Residents may be required to "purchase" their night's accommodation and evening meal by submitting to prolonged sessions of "earbanging":

> fifteen minute sermon for breakfast or lunch, an hour for supper...You end up having to be there right when they open the door to get a seat, then you gotta sit there for half an hour until they start the sermon, and the sermon's an hour, and then you gotta wait another half hour before its your turn to eat... Mostly it's fire and brimstone.[147]

However, the voluntary sector is not dominated by religious groups. Increased homelessness has prompted the growth of numerous charitable organisations offering small-scale accommodation, health and legal advice services. Additionally many cities now have "Coalition for the Homeless" pressure groups which are concerned both with running local services and lobbying city and state government to expand public sector provision.[148] One of the more bizarre voluntary sector initiatives is provided by the Cameo cinema in Los Angeles, which permits homeless people to sleep through its all-night programmes for a reduced entrance fee.[149]

Many voluntary sector responses stem from joint ventures with local government, often involving provision of public facilties at reduced or nil cost which are then financed and managed by voluntary organisations. One of the more comprehensive examples of such public/private cooperation is Los Angeles' Skid Row Development Corporation. The Corporation provides hostel accommodation, alcohol and drug counselling, welfare benefit advice and job training programmes at several "Transition Houses". Residents subsequently enter a development of "move-on" appartments where they can live largely independent lives, with support facilities available if needed, before seeking total self-sufficiency in the housing and labour markets.[150]

The voluntary sector has also received some funding from the federal government. The Emergency Jobs Appropriation Act 1983 earmarked some $100 million to be distributed among voluntary oganisations providing food and shelter to homeless persons. An additional $170 million was pumped into the scheme between 1984 and 1986. However, as with the McKinney Act, the programme's efficacy was severely compromised by the federal government's refusal to allocate more than 2% of the federal grant to meet the administration costs involved. These fell primarily on the charity United Way of America, which assumed responsibility for overseeing and coordinating local responses. The United Way spent some $300,000 on administration costs in the scheme's first phase, a commitment it was unable to maintain in the long term.[151]

One of the largest voluntary sector initiatives has been the National Health Care Programme for the Homeless, established with a grant of some $25 million from the Robert Wood Johnson Foundation and the Pew Memorial Trust. The programme is notable both for its national character and its insistence that the sites chosen exhibited consensus between state, city and voluntary organisations as to how the funds should be spent. Some 19 of the country's 50 largest cities were eventually selected, each of which produced its own programme of health services. The project did not actually provide housing, but it was not therefore just a means of making homelessness more tolerable. Rather the initiative proceeded from the assumption that for some of the homeless, particularly substance abusers and the mentally ill, homelessness may be largely attributable to their poor health. Tackling illness may thus take a homeless person some considerable way towards solving his or her housing problems.[152] The initiative also succeeded in attracting additional funding from its host cities, although it is unclear if local government will undertake the full financial commitment necessary to continue the programmes when the Foundation money runs out.

Even the most cursory review of voluntary sector initiatives underscores the extent to which the United States harbours a pluralist approach to the analysis and treatment of social policy problems; this is perhaps too easily obscured by the successive elections of the Reagan and Bush administrations. But in the absence of federal leadership, localised responses to homelessness, be they the product of state, city or voluntary organisations, are inevitably piecemeal and fragmented. For many of America's homeless, escape from their situation requires a struggle with recalcitrant or hostile government bureaucracies. In Section 6 attention focuses on some of the forms those struggles have taken.

6. SELF-HELP (?) REMEDIES: POLITICAL AND LEGAL INITIATIVES

To an extent more marked even than in Britain, consumers of public sector welfare services in the United States exert minimal prescriptive influences on federal government policies.[153] American welfare groups are characterised by either chronological or geographical specificity. In the late 1960s the National Welfare Rights Organisation succeeded briefly in coordinating the legal and political activities of numerous local bodies, but its national role was short-lived.[154] Its most effective initiative was the so-called "crisis theory", a technique designed by Frances Fox Piven and Richard Cloward. The strategy called for massive campaigns to maximise benefit take-up, and thereafter to take full advantage of due process appeal rights to challenge all decisions made. It was intended that state and city welfare services would rapidly become administratively and fiscally overloaded, forcing Governors and Mayors to pressurise federal government to introduce radical reform of welfare provision. The initiative aroused much controversy, and achieved some short-term, localised successes.[155] In the 1980s, a more modest revival of the strategy on behalf of homeless persons has provided considerable insight into the readiness of government organisations to accept "law" as an effective determinant of their decision-making behaviour when administering welfare services.

6.1. Welfare Rights Advocacy: The New Jersey Experience

At both state and municipal levels the paucity of effective provision for homeless persons reflects a dearth of formal statutory provision obliging government organisations to offer support services. In those areas efforts to produce such obligations necessarily entail an explicitly political campaign to introduce new legislation. However, it is also the case that several states and cities have formal constitutional or statutory duties to assist homeless persons; as noted above, the substance of such measures varies widely. Moreover there is often an appreciable gap between abstract legal provision and the concrete services actually delivered to homeless persons. Scope for conflict between the homeless and government authorities may arise over both the interpretation and implementation of legal duties. In such circumstances the lines between political and legal activism become somewhat blurred, with the result that efforts to insert legalistic criteria into government decision-making processes can effect a marked substantive improvement in homeless people's circumstances. As the following case study suggests, such "welfare rights advocacy"[156] techniques expose both the potential and limitations of attempts to require welfare bureaucracies to respect existing legal constraints on their behavioural autonomy.

In the state of New Jersey all municipalities are legally obliged to provide food and shelter to any indigent person within their boundaries. Despite the apparently unambiguous nature of the "law" many local administrations simply refused to honour such obligations. Others adopted more indirect methods, such as closing their offices or providing the bus fare to adjacent communities, to deny assistance to homeless persons. In the city of Elizabeth (whose Mayor was an enthusiastic supporter of the "magnet theory"[157]), a coalition of church groups, legal advice agencies and private citizens sought to pressurise city authorities into accepting their legal responsibilities. Negotiation produced an informal agreement, which the city subsequently dishonoured; consequently the coalition adopted an aggressive, adverserial and legalistic campaign to produce compliance.

Sufficient funds were raised to finance a short-term advocacy service staffed by lawyers and other middle-class professionals well versed in the intricacies of the statutory obligations, and familiar with the subtleties of the city's decision-making machinery. All homeless persons who approached the coalition were accompanied through the decision-making process by one or more coalition advocates. The city administration responded firstly with denials of responsibility, which advocates were able to refute, and thereafter by subjecting applicants to day-long waits before granting access to shelter. Nevertheless the eventual outcome was that every accompanied homeless person did receive temporary accommodation.

The limits of the Elizabeth initiative are discussed further below. However, its initial success indicates that there is considerable scope for application of legal expertise to affect the distribution of housing resources without the need for litigation. However, such victories are likely to be organisationally specific: more pervasive reform may demand that the homeless do pursue their grievances through the courts. The most successful example of such a strategy has occurred in New York.

6.2. In Search of a "Right" to Shelter: The New Property Thesis Revisited

The efforts of civil liberties lawyers to secure the "release" of the institutionalised mentally ill was part of a wider movement to use constitutionally and statutorily derived legal rights as a vehicle more firmly to entrench the substantive benefits of America's welfare state in the fabric of social and political life.[158] Following an explosion in the numbers of homeless people in New York in the late 1970s, a lawyer named Robert Hayes has drawn on similar techniques to "encourage" the state and city governments to accept responsibility for the provision of basic accommodation to all those in need. The springboard for the campaign was the case of *Callahan v. Carey.*

As noted above in the discussion of deinstitutionalisation, while the United States constitution offers scope for welfare rights lawyers to redefine certain aspects of citizen/government relations in their clients' favour, constitutionally based "new property" rights,[159] such as prohibiting "midnight raids", are predominantly negative in character: they prevent government intrusion into certain spheres of an individual's life rather than impose positive obligations to provide material benefits. It is now widely accepted that the federal constitution does not oblige the federal government to ensure its citizens occupy adequate housing. The Supreme Court has been invited to establish such a right on several occasions; its refusal to do so has been unequivocal:

> the Constitution does not provide judicial remedies for every social and economic ill. We are unable to perceive in that document any constitutional guarantee of access to dwellings of a particular quality...assurance of adequate housing [is a] legislative, not judicial function.[160]

As seen above, the federal government has not produced any legislation from which a statutory right to shelter can be derived. However, the federal political structure of the United States means that each state has both its own constitution, and not inconsiderable legislative sovereignty. Such pluralism affords localized new property initiatives some prospect of success.

Callahan v. Carey was a class action on behalf of New York city's homeless men. Its objective was to force the city to provide emergency accommodation to anyone who requested it. Hayes' research into the legal structure of welfare provision in New York led him to believe that existing laws technically afforded homeless persons just such a right. Article 17 of New York State's constitution provides that:

> The aid, care and support of the needy are public concerns and shall be provided by the state and by such of its subdivisions, and in such manner and by such means, as the legislature may from time to time determine.

Hayes buttressed this constitutional entitlement by pointing to s.62(1) of the state's Social Services Law which required the welfare services to offer "assistance and care" to those unable to provide for themselves, and more specifically to the city's administrative code, which obliged the city's commissioner of public welfare to provide applicants for shelter with "plain and wholesome food and lodging for a night, free of charge".[161]

Existing case law on these constitutional and statutory rights interpreted them as idealistic objectives to which the executive should aspire, rather than to subjecting state and city government to positive obligations.[162] Legal precedent seemed to provide little support for the plaintiffs' contention. At this point Hayes' argument took a turn unavailable to British lawyers (for whom access to *Hansard* to determine legislative intent is not permitted), insofar as he resorted to records of debates at the 1938 New York State constitutional convention where Article 17 was introduced. Speeches by its supporters made clear that its purpose was to

> set forth a definite policy of government; a concrete social obligation which no court may ever misread...to remove from the area of constitutional doubt

the responsibility of the state to those who must look to society for the bare necessities of life....[163]

The suit's efficacy was enhanced by the ready availability of class actions in the American legal system,[164] and by the state and city governments' eventual decision not to contest the case. Consequently the original litigation was settled by a consent decree; given that New York's judiciary had in previous cases "misread" the supposedly unambiguous provisions of Article 17, it is not implausible to suggest that determined resistance by government lawyers could have convinced the court to uphold a far more restrictive interpretation of the public responsibility.[165] One commentator goes so far as to describe the *Callahan* decision as a "fluke"; a fortunate juxtaposition of a determined lawyer, a highly publicised social policy crisis, a politically sympathetic opponent, and a progressive court which are unlikely to be found in other parts of the country.[166] The subsequent election of Mario Cuomo as Governor of New York has enhanced the state's receptivity to the demands of homeless persons; Cuomo has been at the forefront of efforts to promote national responses to the homelessness problem.[167] The attitude of Ed Koch, the somewhat ideosyncratic Mayor of New York City, while harder to discern precisely, is not overtly unsympathetic.[168] Nevertheless there are both abstract and practical limits to *Callahan's* efficacy, which are discussed further below.

But the initiative represents a twofold advance on the original conception of the new property thesis. Firstly the end sought is a substantive right than merely procedural realignment of citizen/government relations. It is no longer assumed that due process decision-making will necessarily produce an acceptable outcome. In the aftermath of *Callahan* Hayes has had to make repeated appearances in court to compel a foot-dragging city to make available sufficient bed spaces for a perpetually growing homeless population. Nor was quantitative sufficiency the only concern; the inadequacies of New York's shelter accommodation also relate to its quality, which was frequently very poor.[169] Hayes' initial motivation sprang from a visit to some of the city's existing emergency shelters where conditions for residents were particularly unpleasant. Accommodation was in dormitories or vast halls, neither of which offered any form of privacy. Beds and bedding were frequently filthy and/or inadequate, as were shower and washing facilities. Few shelters made any provision for laundering clothes. All the hostels were overcrowded, with the result that many residents simply slept on floors with no bedding and no access to washing facilities of any kind. "Check-out time" was invariably before 8 a.m. the following morning. Considerable variation has also been recorded in the management style or house rules adopted by particular shelters. Intimidation or abuse of residents by shelter staff, many of whom function more as security guards than social workers, appears to be a widespread phenomenon. Nevertheless the city's shelters were turning people away every night.[170]

To a degree, poor conditions represent deliberate policy derived from the principles of England's 1834 Poor Law. The less eligibility principle intended to discourage the able-bodied poor from seeking relief in the workhouse continues to inform shelter provision in many parts of the contemporary United States. Its rather more sophisticated contemporary restatement holds that shelters are often of sufficient quality to represent an attractive option to the able-bodied poor, relative to seeking accommodation with family, with friends, or in the private rented sector. Minimal facilities, and restrictive admission policies are seen as necessary incentives to promote economic self-sufficiency in the prevention, as well as the cure of homelessness.[171] Such unpleasantness or indignity has no doubt discouraged many homeless persons from entering hostels. But the most pervasive worry relates to exposure to robbery, sexual abuse and other physical violence. Many of New York's homeless people have concluded that life on the streets or in the subways, even in the depths of winter, presents a less serious threat to their health and welfare than sheltering in emergency hostels.[172]

Even in a nominally progressive state such as New York, Hayes found it necessary to make constant forays into court to pressurise state and city officials to uphold minimum accommodation standards. The plaintiffs' case was assisted by statutory regulations introduced by the state's Department of Social Services as part of its efforts to improve housing quality. Clear evidence that public shelters were not meeting statutory criteria was readily available. The city's failure to uphold quality standards is attributable in part to financial pressures. Single, lockable rooms are more expensive than rows of beds in dormitories. Washing and laundry facilities are also costly; as are management personnel who can safeguard clients' physical welfare without riding roughshod over their dignity. Even at the most basic level of responding to the homelessness problem financial pressures may persuade notionally sympathetic local administrations to sidestep or dilute legal obligations. After *Callahan* the city found that improving shelter standards increased demand for accommodation as more and more homeless people came to view them as acceptable places to spend the night.[173] In the absence of federal funding to underwrite the costs of enhanced shelter provision, state and city concerns with prioritising limited financial resources would suggest that responses to the homelessness problem are always likely to be compromised by budgetary constraints.

New York is also one of the few cities to run hostels solely for women. It was suggested above that the apparently small number of homeless single women might largely be attributable to women's reluctance to enter mixed shelters for fear of sexual and other physical attack. The obvious solution to this fear would be to require government to provide women-only shelters. Following the success of *Callahan v. Carey* litigation was initiated against the city on behalf of its homeless women inhabitants. In *Eldredge v. Koch*[174] a class action was filed against New York city on behalf of its homeless women. The suit alleged that the *Callahan* standards in men's shelters were not being provided for women, with the result that women were effectively denied the constitutional and statutory rights accorded to the state's men. The New York courts readily accepted the plaintiffs' contention, with the result that the *Callahan* decree was extended to regulate emergency shelter provisions for women.

Despite the formal success of such litigation, it by no means promises a national solution. New York's constitutional and statutory commitments to its citizens' welfare go considerably farther than those made by most other states. Imaginative interpretation of vaguely defined government commitments is of no use when such commitments cannot be found.[175] The limited scope for the "new property" approach, together with the capacity of state and/or local governments to defy or evade constitutionally or statutorily based rights to shelter, suggests that the strategy will prove of limited worth to efforts to pressurise government into providing housing for the homeless. Other legal routes are therefore being sought. One of the more imaginative proposals is outlined below.

6.3. A "Tortuous Solution"

In an ostensibly more pragmatic vein, insofar as it is not dependent on pre-existing constitutional or statutory "rights", Mort advocates an attempt to broaden the scope of tortious liability owed by doctors and mental health institutions to their patients. It is argued that the adverse effects suffered by deinstitutionalised patients for whom no adequate community-based provision has been made were clearly visible by the mid-1960s. These effects included not simply rapid deterioration in patients' mental health as a result of receiving no further treatment, but also exposure to physical hardships occasioned by their incapacity to deal alone with the basic mechanics of day to day survival, such as finding employment or housing, or applying for welfare benefits. Government institutions which continued to discharge patients, whether in defiance or ignorance of so much evidence as to the patients' likely fate, would therefore be in breach of the duty of care owed to patients to treat them with the reasonable level of care and skill to be expected of professional physicians.[176]

The theoretical potential of this strategy is much enhanced by the ready availability of the class action in the American legal system.[177] Nevertheless, efforts to alleviate homelessness through the extension of tort liability would seem to require even more creative use of pre-existing legal concepts than rekindling the new property approach. There is as yet no evidence to suggest that the courts have embraced the argument. Even should they do so the remedy would assist only a fraction of the mentally ill homeless, who are themselves but a segment of the total homeless population. The concept is irrelevant to those whose homelessness is rooted in the structural inequities of a liberal market economy.

Furthermore, Mort's proposals fail to address a further criticism which has been levelled both at the legalistic strategies adopted by Hayes in New York, and the more overtly politicised welfare advocacy tactics pursued by groups such as the Elizabeth coalition. Both techniques place homeless persons in an acutely dependent position *vis-à-vis* their lawyer/advocate. Neither remedy amounts to a self-help solution in the sense of equipping homeless persons to achieve similar ends without such aggressive expert assistance. Nor is the lacuna simply one of knowledge on the homeless persons' part. When the Elizabeth project in New Jersey came to an end, several homeless people approached the city authority and articulated their demands in precisely the terms previously used so successfully by the expert, middle-class activists. These citizens were quite simply refused assistance, even though they had accurately identified a legal entitlement which mere months age had effectively determined the outcome of the city's decision-making processes.[178]

The implication to be drawn from the chronological specificity of the Elizabeth coalition's success, and from Hayes' constant returns to court, is that definition of the "law" in relation to housing provision for the homeless should be concerned more with the tangible long-term product of government decision-making received by its consumers than with the legalistic credibility of specific, abstracted analyses of constitutional or statutory obligation. In consequence, some homeless people have adopted rather more direct tactics in challenging governmental responses to the problem.

6.4. The Politics of Protest: A California Case Study

Despite the limited success of legalistic protest against government inactivity, the process of litigation has served further to publicise the nature of the homelessness problem. Moreover, by limiting protest to the constitutional method of court hearings, homeless people reinforce the perception that they are not deviant from, or threatening to, mainstream American values. Compartmentalisation of homelessness into a series of discrete court cases considerably defuses the extent to which public opinion construes the homeless as a dangerous collective phenomenon. Indeed, it is suggested that the public sympathy and private charity offered to homeless Americans by their more affluent peers is attributable to the "docility" with which individual homeless people have accepted their fate, and to the "gratitude" they have expressed when receiving public or private assistance.[179] As we saw above in discussing city responses towards the homeless, such sympathy disappears when local power elites regard the presence of any homeless person as an affront to moral decency and/or a threat to commercial interests. One such power elite operates in the California city of Santa Barbara. Until its homelessness problems attracted national press attention the city was best known as Ronald Reagan's holiday retreat. The city's method of "managing" its homeless population was not unusual; the response of those being managed was.[180]

Because of their temperate climate, the Pacific states are generally spared the winter time phenomenon of homeless people freezing to death on city streets. Nevertheless the nation's homeless are apparently found in disproportionately large numbers on the west coast.[181] By the early 1980s Santa Barbara was playing host to an increasing, and increasingly visible, population of homeless men and women. Several semi-permanent outdoor settlements existed in local parks, where homeless citizens established shelters of various kinds. A number of the inhabitants suffered mental health, alcohol or drug addiction problems. The private rental market is both small and expensive, primarily because of rigid zoning laws designed to maintain the city's aesthetic low-rise charm and so enhance its appeal to tourists. Recent development trends have involved gradual replacement of SROs with more luxurious holiday accommodation. The local economy's reliance on tourism also creates a preponderance of service sector employment. This is not seasonal in the British sense, but it is low-paid all the year round. Competition for both housing and casual employment is heightened by students from the city's university campus. The city has provided some high-quality public housing, although it comprises only 2% of the city's total stock. These various factors have combined to create a particularly acute affordability squeeze in the city's labour and housing markets, with the result that a substantial proportion of the homeless are homeless for purely economic reasons.

Since Santa Barbara has no detox clinics for drug and alcohol abusers, many homeless people pass their day wandering around the city's main tourist shopping area—panhandling, "dumpster diving" for food, hanging out, or simply doing their shopping. Local merchants took exception to the sometimes bizarre behaviour of the alcoholics and mentally ill, and to the unkempt appearance of other homeless people, whose presence was felt adversely to affect the tourist trade. In 1982 the city authorities and local business established a "task force" to determine how best to respond to the homelessness problem. The task force report set itself the following objectives:

Get rid of street people
A cost effective humanitarian dispersement plan
Eliminate "undesirables" who deter economic and
   physical development of the area
Isolate bad people—create containment area.[182]

Among the "cost effective and humanitarian" measures proposed were the following:

Aggressive police presence in the area...
Relocate and disperse street people to a *controlled* environment for either processing to travel out of the area or for rehabilitation...
Use an existing facility or create a village (out of city limits area) and transport transients there...Provide travel through a traveler's aid service (out of the area); in cases of illegal or improper conduct offer "get out of town" approach as an alternative to jail.

The city's pre-existing adherence to magnet theory was amply demonstrated by its complete lack of publicity funded shelter facilities.[183] But in addition to doing nothing to encourage homelessness, the task force was advocating positive steps to discourage homeless people from remaining in Santa Barbara. A major weapon in the containment and dispersal plan was reactivation of a rarely used local anti-sleeping ordinance, which made it a criminal offence to be asleep in a public place between 10 p.m. and 6 a.m. Aggressive police enforcement of this measure led to the arrests of over 1200 homeless people in 1985/6: since many could not pay fines they ended up in jail.[184] The local police also subjected homeless citizens to vigorous enforcement of other local ordinances such as not having one's dog on a lead, lighting camp fires, and drinking in public. While being homeless was not *per se* a crime, homeless people's constant exposure to prosecution for trivial offences essentially produced a *de facto* criminalisation of their homeless status.

More formal efforts to marginalise the homeless population included a county decision to refuse to enter them on the electoral roll on the grounds that their home address, 100 Montecito Street, was a public park, and thus insufficient as the "residence" which state registration statutes required. The local (privately funded) Legal Defence Center launched a class action on the homeless persons behalf seeking *mandamus* to compel the county to enfranchise them. In *Collier v. Menzel*[185] the county registrar's contention was upheld at first instance, but subsequently overturned by the California Court of Appeal. The appeal court adopted a somewhat strained interpretation of the relevant statutory criteria in a judgment that was clearly determined by broader political concern with the homeless appellants' civil rights:

Unlike other minority groups or disadvantaged persons, the "homeless", by the very nature of their living circumstances, have been unable to exercise any political influence in order to make their particular problems and needs known.
It is patently unjust that society ignores the homeless and yet also denies them the proper avenues to remedy the situation. Even more compelling, the denial of the vote to the "homeless" denies them electoral power. Powerlessness breeds apathy, and apathy is the greatest danger to society.[186]

While the county lost in court, its various initiatives had succeeded in creating a climate of hostility within the town. In its more innocuous forms this involved such measures as shopkeepers pouring bleach on unsold food to prevent homeless people retrieving it from dumpsters. Constant police harassment also continued, prompting the Legal Defense Center to initiate several suits for brutality against the local police force. More disturbingly, two homeless people were murdered as they slept, one stabbed 17 times by a local military cadet.

Santa Barbara was by no means unique among Californian cities for having and enforcing anti-sleeping ordinances. Moreover local public housing programmes and social service facilities compared favorably with adjoining areas. But the co-existence of (in the American sense[187]) liberal welfare provision for the respectable poor with repressive measures against the seemingly "undeserving" homeless is not atypical. Santa Barbara hit the headlines because, rather than moving on, its homeless population sought to challenge prevailing orthodoxy.

In addition to homeless people themselves, Santa Barbara's Homeless coalition contained various middle-class lawyers, academics and students, and local clergymen. These members were acutely aware of the need to provide support for the homeless people's campaign, rather than taking it over and imposing their own perceptions of the homeless's needs and preferences. This proved somewhat difficult to avoid in the early stages of the Coalition's activities. The homeless themselves had little experience in organising political campaigns, negotiating with local government officials, or initiating legal actions. Homeless activists have the additional handicap of lacking an office and home to work from and return to. Moreover those members suffering mental health or drug/alcohol problems could not be relied upon as consistent contributors to group strategies. Nevertheless many homeless Santa Barbarans were not affected by mental illness or substance abuse. They rapidly gained the expertise and confidence to pursue their demands both within the complex structures of local welfare bureaucracies, and when that failed, by mounting voluble, and visible, public demonstrations against city policy.[188]

The first major event was a rally outside the local court during the murder trial of the military cadet, during which the homeless protested against the climate of violence and hostility enveloping the city. Press coverage of the demonstration and subsequent protests against the anti-sleeping ordinance led to CCNV involvement in the town's politics. The CCNV's director, Mitch Snyder, visited the city to launch vituperative attacks on the city council at several public meetings. Snyder also threatened to organise a mass march and public "sleep in" on the city's beaches and parks over a forthcoming holiday weekend, with the intention of focusing the national media spotlight squarely on Santa Barbara's city council. Although the local newspaper dismissed Snyder as "a rabble-rouser", the prospect of such unfavourable publicity led the city council to dilute the anti-sleeping ordinance. The ban was still to apply to beaches, but the homeless were now to be permitted to sleep in vacant lots, public parks and cars. As a result the CCNV cancelled its planned demonstration, whereupon the city immediately re-extended the ban to cover the parks.[189] In the immediate aftermath of the campaign, police enforcement of remaining ordinances declined significantly; this was, however, a temporary respite. As media attention waned, and the CCNV turned to other concerns, so police activity among the homeless populations increased in intensity. Arrest rates have again risen for "dog at large" and public drinking, to the extent that weekends in jail now feature regularly in many homeless people's life cycle. It is perhaps not coincidence that Santa Barbara has a thriving trade in weekend breaks.[190]

Although there has been some appreciable substantive improvement in public provision for its homeless, Santa Barbara's city council now appears to regard itself as the victim not of the homeless themselves but of a nation-wide problem with which the federal government has failed to come to terms. This does not encompass seeing homeless people as victims of economic change, but as the Reagan era begins to fade into memory, it is to George Bush that more and more eyes, albeit for different reasons, look for a solution.

7. CONCLUSION

During the first Presidential debate of the 1988 campaign, Governor Michael Dukakis and Vice-President Bush were asked how, if they should be elected, they would deal with the growing homelessness problem. Their answers cogently illustrate the sharp divide between structuralist and individualistic critiques of the current situation.

Dukakis analyzed the problem in purely structural terms. The rapid increase in homelessness during the Reagan era was directly attributable to massive cuts in public sector housing expenditure:

> The problem, Mr. Bush, is that you cut back 90% on our commitment to affordable housing for families of low and moderate income. And when you do that, you have homeless families.[191]

Dukakis' solution lay in a massive federally funded and federally led programme of both new building and renovation of existing poor-quality stock:

> This isn't a question of a little charity for the homeless; this is a question of organising the housing community.[192]

The Governor had begun his second term by assigning primary importance to "organising the housing community" in an attempt to loosen the "affordability squeeze" that accounts for much contemporary homelessness. As noted above, the state government has devoted significant resources to initiatives designed to reduce Massachusetts' homeless population.

But the forty-first President saw a different way forward. The role of government was to go no further than affirming the limited commitments made in the McKinney Act:

> I want to see—when I talked at our—at our convention about a thousand points of light, I was talking about the enormous numbers of shelters and organisations that help.
>
> The Governor's wife has been very active in the homeless. My—my campaign chairman, Secretary Jim Baker's wife—this isn't government; these are people that care, that are trying to give of themselves...
>
> I think that we're on the right track, I don't see this, incidentally, as a Democrat or Republican or a liberal or a conservative idea. I see an involvement by a thousand points of light.[193]

That the voluntary organisations upon whom he relies have uniformly described themselves as quite unable to cope with current needs appeared to have escaped George Bush's attention.[194] Given the problem's enormity and complexity, and given that its roots clearly lie in the substantive inequities produced by the market in relation to employment opportunities, access to affordable housing, and mental health care, the federal government's continuing refusal to ameliorate those conditions suggests that no significant reduction in homelessness will be forthcoming. The appointment of Jack Kemp, a radical right wing ideologue, to take charge of HUD implies that no extensive federal initiatives will be taken. Kemp has voiced a commitment to restoring a free market in the private rented sector, involving abolition of such limited rent control as currently exists. He is also an admirer of the Thatcher government's "right to buy" policy for public sector tenants. In recent months Conservative lobby groups, foremost among them the Heritage Foundation think tank, have urged Bush to provide Presidential leadership to solve the problem; their proposed solutions appear, however, to go no further than deregulation of private rented housing.[195] Following his election victory, Bush described the situation as "a national shame"; he intends to address it "with sensitivity and the needed compassion". He has as yet neither advanced clear policy initiatives nor earmarked additional funding for putting his sensitivity and compassion into practice. Should President Bush's actions prove as complacent and vacuous as his speeches, one might indeed expect to see *many* thousand points of light illuminating the United States in the 1990s. Most of them are likely to be the camp fires of a growing number of homeless Americans for whom adequate, affordable housing becomes an evermore distant dream. Unless of course if, as in Ronald Reagan's holiday home town of Santa Barbara, lighting a camp fire is an imprisonable offence.

NOTES

1. See, for example, *The Observer*, 30 October 1988; *The Guardian*, 10 and 12 November 1988.

2. *The Observer,* 6 November 1988.
3. M. Stern (1984) "The emergence of homelessness as a public problem", *Social Services Review.* Writing in 1975, Feagin suggests that America's mass media operates a "poverty rollercoaster", rising and falling over an approximately 15-year cycle. Poverty was a major issue in the 1930s, invisible in the late 1940s and early 1950s, rediscovered (as in Britain) in the 1960s, and then ignored in the 1970s. Its re-emergence in the late 1980s indicates that the trend is continuing. J. Feagin (1975) *Subordinating the poor: welfare and American beliefs* pp. 1–2.
4. See, for example, J. Coleman (1983) "The diary of a homeless man", *New York,* Vol. 16, in which the author recounts a ten-day foray into New York's public shelter system. The report is startling for its description of the constant abuse and threatened and actual violence to which shelter users are subjected, from their peers, assorted police forces and hostel staff themselves.
5. See, for example, J. Alter (1984) "Homeless in America", *Newsweek,* 2 January 1984. For a more geographically specific estimate see *The New York Times,* 17 June 1987. For an example of the "human interest" type coverage see K. Anderson (1984) "Left out in the cold", *Time,* 19 December.
6. *Washington Post,* 4 February 1982.
7. See, for example, the series of articles in *The New York Times,* 18–22 December 1988.
8. L. Burns (1987) "Third world solutions to the homelessness problem", in: R. Bingham, R. Green and S. White (eds.), *The Homeless in Contemporary Society* (Sage Publications, New York).
9. *R v. London Borough Hillingdon, ex parte Puhlhofer* (1986) 18 HLR 158.
10. Shelter (1974) *The Grief Report,* p. 9.
11. A. Arden (1988) *Homeless Persons,* 3rd edn., chapter 3. The *Puhlhofer* decision was also notable for its explicit disapproval of efforts to challenge local authority decision-making through the courts, on the grounds that the legal system was being overwhelmed by litiguous applicants presenting frivolous claims. There appears to be little empirical justification for such claims; see M. Sumkin (1987) "Myths of judicial review", *LAG Bulletin,* September.
12. P. Burkinshaw (1982) "Homelessness and the law—the effects and response to legislation", *Urban Law and Policy.* Doe (1988) *Responding to Homelessness: Local Authority Policy and Practice.* Institute of Housing (1988) *Who Will House the Homeless?* Association of London Authorities (1988) Camden's homelessness policies and procedures. NACAB (1988) *Homelessness: A National Survey.*
13. See, for example, *Parr v. Wyre Borough Council* (1982) HLR 71.
14. Housing Act 1985 s. 52(2B) as amended by the Housing and Planning Act 1986 s. 14(2).
15. *Ibid.*
16. On the subsequent case law see A. McAllister (1987) "Homelessness since *Puhlhofer*", *LAG Bulletin.*
17. Department of Housing and Urban Development (1984) *A Report to the Secretary on the Homeless and Emergency Shelters,* p. 7.
18. For a review of the current debate see K. Peroff (1987) "Who are the homeless and how many are there?", in: C. Hartman (ed.), *America's Housing Crisis.*
20. R. Rosenthal (1987) *Homeless in Paradise,* University of California at Santa Barbara, PhD thesis, p. 63.
21. For example, *R v. Ealing LBC, ex parte Siddhu* (1982) 80 LGR 534, in which the court rejected Ealing's contention that admission to a battered woman's hostel meant that an applicant was no longer homeless.

22. See, for example, *R v. South Herefordshire District Council ex parte Miles* (1983) 17 HLR 82 in which occupancy of a rat-infested hut was considered reasonable. For contrasting decisions, relating to overcrowding, see *R v. City of Westminster ex parte Ali* (1983) 11 HLR 83 and *Krishnan v. London Borough of Hillingdon* (1981) June *LAG Bulletin*.

23. J. Koch (1987) "The federal role in aiding the homeless" in: Bingham et al. *op. cit*. It is not proposed here to engage the debate as to how one might best define "the urban" in advanced western societies. An incisive summary is provided in P. Dunleavy (1980) *Urban Political Analysis*, pp. 50–56. One might note that Dunleavy's own rejection of an urban/rural dichotomy within Britian, on the grounds of the entire country's proximity to large towns or cities, may have less applicability to the much larger land mass of the United States.

24. M. Stefl (1987) "The new homeless: a national perspective" in Bingham et al. *op. cit*.

25. T. Main (1983) "The homeless of New York". *Public Interest*, Summer 1983, p. 3.

26. See generally the collection of essays in C. Hartman (ed.) (1985) *America's Housing Crisis*.

27. See C. Hoch (1986) "Homeless in the USA". *Housing Studies*.

28. M. Stefl. *op. cit*.

29. N. Anderson (1925) *The American Hobo*.

30. *Ibid*., chapter 6.

31. J. Schneider (1984) "Skid row as an urban neighbourhood 1880–1960". *Urbanism Past and Present*.

32. See N. Anderson (1975) *The American Hobo: An Autobiography*, pp. ix–xii. Schneider, *op. cit*.

33. C. Hoch (1987) "A brief history of the homeless problem in the United States", in: Bingham et al., *op. cit*.

34. *Ibid*.

35. On the early impact of the principles of scientific management on manual labour, popularly known as Taylorism or Fordism, after two of its earliest exponents, see H. Braverman (1975) *Labour and Monopoly Capital*.

36. It should be noted that in this paper "liberalism" is used in its British sense, to describe the extreme right wing position exposed by philosophers such as Hayek, and pursued in varying degrees by both the Reagan and Thatcher administrations. In its American incantation liberalism most closely resembles what British observers would characterise as moderate social democracy, i.e. the belief that government should undertake modest initiatives to ameliorate the most inequitable socio-economic consequences of market autonomy. For a summary of this position, in both the British and American context, see V. George and P. Wilding (1976) *Ideology and Social Welfare*, chapters 2 and 3.

37. For an account of the problems involved see Rosenthal *op. cit*., chapter 10. R. Jahiel (1987) "The situation of homelessness", in Bingham et al., *op. cit*.

38. New York lost 30,000 SRO (60%) places between 1975 and 1981; San Francisco 5,700 (17%) between 1975 and 1979; Cihcago 10,000 (45%) between 1973 and 1984; see C. Hoch and R. Slayton (1987) "The new homeless and the skid row SRO in the United States", paper presented at the American Collegiate Schools of Planning Conference, Los Angeles, 7 November 1987.

39. P. Kasinitz (1984) "Gentrification and homelessness". *Urban and Social Change Review*.

40. R. Sanjek (1986) "Federal housing programs and their impact on the homeless", in: J. Ericson and C. Wilhelm (eds.), *Housing the Homeless*.

41. H. Siegal (1986) "A descriptive portrait of the SRO world", in: Erikson and Wilhelm, *op. cit.*
42. See E. Achterberg and P. Marcuse (1985) "Towards the decommodification of housing: a political analysis and a progressive program", in: Hartman, *op. cit.*
43. See, for example, J. Wright (1987) "The national health care for the homeless program", in: Bingham et al., *op. cit.*
44. Stone, *op. cit.*
45. M. Stefl (1987) "The new homeless: a national perspective", in: Bingham et al., *op. cit.*
46. Stone, *op. cit.*
47. Between 1970 and 1980 median rents rose some 123%; the median income of private sector tenants by only 67%; see Achtenberg and Marcuse, *op. cit.*
48. C. Hartman (1985) "Introduction: a radical perspective", in: Hartman, *op. cit.*, pp. 20–21.
49. J. Atlas and P. Dreier (1985) "Mobilise or compromise? The tenants' movement and american politics", in: Hartman, *op. cit.*
50. C. Dolbeare (1983) "The low income housing crisis", in: Hartman, *op. cit.*, p. 69.
51. M. Hope and J. Young (1986) "The politics of displacement: sinking into homelessness", in: Erikson and Wilhelm, *op. cit.*
52. Dolbeare, *op. cit.*
53. Robbins, T. (1986) "New York's homeless families", in: Erikson and Wilhelm, *op. cit.*
54. See *The Guardian,* 29 November 1988.
55. R. Collin (1984) "Homelessness: the policy and the law", *The Urban Lawyer.*
56. H. Lamb (1984) "Deinstitutionalisation and the homeless mentally ill", in: H. Lamb (ed.), *The Homeless Mentally Ill.*
57. See C. Reich (1963) "Midnight searches and the Social Security Act", *Yale Law Journal;* (1964) "The new property", *Yale Law Journal;* (1965) "Individual rights and social welfare: the emerging legal issues", *Yale Law Journal.*
58. For an overview and critique of these programmes see E. Cahn and S. Cahn (1964) "The war on poverty: a civilian perspective", *Yale Law Journal.*
59. N. Rhoden (1982) "The limits of liberty: deinstitutionalisation, homelessness and libertarian theory", *Emory Law Journal.*
60. Lamb (1984) *op. cit.*
61. A. Scull (1979) *Decarceration: Community Treatment and the Deviant: A Radical View,* p. 2, cited in Collins, *op. cit.*
62. Lamb (1984) *op. cit.* E. Bassuk (1984) "The homelessness problem", *Scientific American.*
63. Rosenthal, *op. cit.*, pp. 231–235. B. Pepper and H. Ryglewicz (1982) "Testimony for the neglected: the mentally ill in the post-deinstitutionalised age", *American Journal of Orthopsychiatry.*
64. See G. Steiner (1971), *The State of Welfare,* chapter 7, for an analysis of the sacrosanct nature of veterans' benefits. That their importance has grown, rather than diminished in the 1980s, is indicated by the creation in the final months of the Reagan presidency of a cabinet post exclusively concerned with veterans' interests. Goerge Bush has retained the position in his first administration.
65. H. Goldin (1982) *Soldiers of Misfortune* (Office of the Comptroller, New York).
66. M. Robertson (1987) "Homeless veterans: an emerging problem", in: Bingham et al, *op. cit.*

67. Reich (1963) *op. cit.*
68. Reich (1963), (1964), (1965) *op. cit.*
69. Reich (1963) *op. cit.* A. Bendich (1966) "privacy, poverty and the constitution", in: J. Ten Broek (ed.), *The Law of the Poor.*
70. Cf. Steiner's assertion that "the popular image of the chief beneficiaries [of welfare benefits] has changed from that of old, respectable white people to that of young, immoral Negro men and women"; (1966) *op. cit.,* p. 7. For confirmation that such "old" prejudices remain highly important in determining allocation of contemporary housing resources see Stern, *op. cit.*
71. P. Sullivan and S. Damrosch (1987) "Homeless women and children" in: Bingham et al., *op. cit.*
72. For its relevance to post-war American welfare policy, and an analysis of its roots in the ideologies underpinning British models of poor relief, see Feagin, *op. cit.*
73. See C. Mowbray (1985) "Homelessness in America: Myths and Realities," *American Journal of Orthopsychiatry.*
74. L. Weitzman (1985) *The Divorce Revolution,* cited in Sullivan and Damrosch, *op. cit.*
75. See, for example, Anderson (1925) *op. cit.,* pp. 104–106.
76. Nor is this solely a private sector phenomenon. Heskin reports how a city-financed project on Los Angeles' skid row, designed to cater for all homeless people, was rapidly filled entirely by the elderly and disabled (deserving) poor; (1987) "Los Angeles: innovative local approaches", in: Bingham et al., *op. cit.*
77. Bassuk, *op. cit.;* J. Erikson and C. Wilhelm "Introduction", in: Erikson and Wilhelm, *op. cit.*
78. (1925) *op. cit.,* pp. 67–69; for a review of the literature since then see Stefl, *op. cit.*
79. R. Lamb (1986) "Deinstitutionalisation and the mentally ill", in: Erikson and Wilhelm, *op. cit.*
80. Lamb (1984) *op. cit.*
81. Sullivan and Damrosch, *op. cit.*
82. In the British context see *The Observer,* 30 October 1988. In the USA see N. Karlen et al. (1986) "Homeless kids: forgotten faces", *Newsweek,* 6 January.
83. National Academy of Sciences (1988) *Homelessness, Health and Human Needs.* The condemnation of the Reagan administration was eventually released in the form of a supplementary statement to the main report, published privately by ten of the thirteen members of the investigatory panel; see *The New York Times,* 20 September 1988.
84. For a harrowing account of the lifestyles forced upon homeless children in one of California's most prestigious resorts see Rosenthal, *op. cit.,* chapter 7.
85. J. Erikson and C. Wilhelm (1986) "Introduction", in: Erikson and Wilhelm, *op. cit.*
86. Department of Housing and Urban Development (1984) *A Report to the Secretary on the Homeless and Emergency Shelters* (Washington, DC).
87. CCNV (1980) *A Forced March to Nowhere* (Washington, DC).
88. C. Hartman (1984) Testimony before a Joint Hearing of the Subcommittee on Housing and Community Development of the Committee on Banking, Finance and Urban Affairs, and the Subcommittee on Manpower and Housing of the Committee on Government Operations. *United States Congress* (Washington, DC, 24 May).
89. *United States Congress, op. cit.,* p. 32.

90. S. Kondratas "A strategy for helping America's homeless", *The Heritage Foundation Backgrounder*, No. 431.
91. For a snapshot of New York's (male) shelter population, see S. Crystal et al. (1982) *Chronic and Situational Dependency: Long Term Residents in a Shelter for Men;* (1982A) *New Arrivals: First Time Shelter Clients* (Human Resources Administration of the City of New York).
92. Crystal's studies suggested that while the majority of occupants in New York's male shelters suffered from readily discernible psychiatric or physical disability, some 20% could not be so categorised, and were in terms both of their current health and previous employment history ostensibly capable of being self-supporting. This has led one conservative commentator to argue that there is a clear, empirically sustainable basis for dividing the homeless into deserving and undeserving categories; see Main, *op. cit.*
93. E. Bassuk (1984) "The homelessness problem", *Scientific American*.
94. P. Applebaum (1984) "Testimony", in: *United States Congress, op. cit.*
95. N. Kaufman (1984) "Homelessness: a comprehensive policy approach", *Urban and Social Change Review.* C. Mowbray (1985) "Homelessness in America: myths and realities," *American Journal of Orthopsychiatry.* Erikson and Wilhelm, *op. cit.*
96. An introductory overview is provided by J. Wedemeyer and P. Moore (1966) "The American welfare system", in: J. Ten Broek (ed.) *The Law of the Poor.* The social welfare field has proven a major battleground between the federal and state governments, particularly under Democrat Presidents who have sought to expand the scope of welfare programmes. For a survey of such battles from a social policy perspective see Steiner (1966) *Social Insecurity,* pp. 85–89; Feagin (1975) *op. cit.,* pp. 68–75. A more legalistic critique is provided by D. Herzer (1970) "Federal jurisdiction over statutorily-based welfare claims", *Harvard Civil Rights—Civil Liberties Review.*
97. On the constitutional basis of Britain's central/local relations, and the shifts therein in recent years, see generally M. Loughlin (1986) *Local government in the modern state.* Readers no doubt need not be reminded in detail of the changes effected during the past ten years. Suffice it to say that techniques such as ratecapping or total abolition of states whose governments diverged from federal orthodoxy are not available to American presidents.
98. M. Cuomo (1987) "The state role: New York's approach to homelessness", in: Bingham et al., *op. cit.,* p. 205.
99. *Ibid.*
100. See, for example, E. Bassuk and A. Lauriat (1984) "The politics of homelessness", in: R. Lamb (ed.), *The Homeless Mentally Ill.* M. Carliner (1987) "Homelessness: a housing problem", in: Bingham et al., *op. cit.*
101. Quoted in M. Hope and J. Young (1986) "The politics of displacement", in Erikson and Wilhelm, *op. cit.*
102. In 1982 HUD's Deputy Assistant Director was sufficiently removed from the realities of the situation to be able to assert that "no-one is living on the streets"; cited in R. Sanjek, *op. cit.,* p. 315.
103. Kondratas, *op. cit.*
104. For an analysis of the development of the distribution of social welfare responsibilities between state and federal government in the post new deal period see Steiner (1966) *op. cit.,* pp. 46–60. Steiner suggests that America's welfare state was built upon "a states' rights philosophy, a policy of providing federal support for categorial programs drawn by and tailored to the interests of the indi-

vidual states with an absolute minimum of insistence upon uniformity"; *ibid.* p. 46.

105. See G. Steiner (1971) *The State of Welfare,* p. 78.
106. See generally the collection of essays in part 3 of T. Becker and M. Feeley (eds.) (1973) *The Impact of Supreme Court Decisions.*
107. Steiner (1966) *op. cit.,* pp. 92–97.
108. Reich (1963) *op. cit.*
109. J. Koch (1987) "The federal role in aiding the homeless", in: Bingham et al., *op. cit.*
110. Alter et al., *op. cit.* For a summary of the McKinney Act's programmes, and an indication of its general inefficacy, see Illinois State Support Centre (1989) *A Report on the Implementation of the McKinney Act in Chicago 1987–1988* (available through the American Bar Association Special Committee on Housing and Urban Development Law).
111. *The New York Times,* 27 September 1987.
112. *Ibid.*
113. Koch, *op. cit.,* pp. 225–226.
114. Koch, *op. cit.*
115. Alter et al., *op. cit.*
116. Rosethal, *op. cit.,* pp. 205–209.
117. Kaufman, *op. cit.* Alter et al., *op. cit.*
118. For a slightly less sanguine view of Dukakis' initiatives, premised on the view that he was as much concerned with consolidating political support from welfare and social service groups, see R. Gaines and M. Segal (1988) *Dukakis,* pp. 283–287.
119. Cuomo, *op. cit.,* p. 200.
120. *The Guardian,* 15 December 1988.
121. Cuomo, *op. cit.,* p. 210.
122. Cited in Alter et al., *op. cit.,* p. 12.
123. Alter et al., *op. cit.*
124. Cited in P. Secton (1983) "The life of the homeless", *Dissent.* For a deeper examination of Phoenix's homelessness policies see P. Stark (1982) "Phoenix: war on the homeless", *Village Voice,* 28 December 1982.
125. Rosenthal, *op. cit.,* pp. 539–541.
126. The Miami Police Department has recently proposed introduction of local byelaws carrying a ten-day jail sentence for sleeping, cooking, bathing or urinating on public streets or in parks. The police do not, however, intend to jail the homeless, merely to arrest them and thereafter deposit them in different, less visible, parts of the city. The police force is the only public body in Miami currently "catering" to the city's homeless population; see *The New York Times,* 3 November 1988.
127. K. Peroff (1987) "Who are the homeless and how many are there?" in: Bingham et al., *op. cit..*
128. See P. Tuoni (1981) "Deinstitutionalisation and community resistance by zoning restrictions", *Massachusetts Law Review.*
129. M. Ritzdorf and S. Sharpe (1987) "Portland Oregon: a comprehensive approach", in: Bingham et al., *op. cit.*
130. See M. Ritzdorf (1984) "Strategies for reducing community fears of group homes in American municipalities", *Housing and Society.*
131. For example, the city of Boston and the Massachusetts state government have successfully established a number of hostels for single women with children in Boston's most affluent suburbs by presenting the facilities as essentially educa-

tional initiatives; *The International Herald Tribune,* 7 February 1988. See further Ritzdorf, *op. cit.*

132. For a detailed account of the Portland initiatives see Ritzdorf and Sharpe, *op. cit.*
133. See *The New York Times,* 22 December 1988.
134. A. Heskin (1987) "Los Angeles: innovative local approaches", in: Bingham et al., *op. cit.*
135. *The New York Times,* 5 September 1988.
136. P. Sullivan and S. Damrosch (1987) "Homeless women and children", in: Bingham et al. (eds.), *op. cit.*
137. Anerson (1925) *op. cit.,* chapter 10.
138. L. Stone (1984) "Shelters for battered women: a temporary escape from danger or the first step towards divorce?", *Victomology.*
139. *Ibid.* For a broader analysis of the impact of the pre-occupation with the nuclear family on American welfare policies see L. Kosimar (1976) *Down and Out in the USA.*
140. Sullivan and Damrosch, *op. cit.*
141. Koch, *op. cit.*
142. See C. Hoch (1987) "A brief history of the homelessness problem in the United States", in: Bingham et al., *op. cit.*
143. The job training programme adopted by the Council of Churches in Washington DC is a typical example of such initiatives. The programme rejected the idea that "to simply house and feed the homeless was the end of what we had to do. We had to...help the homeless become self-sustaining and independent human beings"; *The Washington Post,* 1 February 1984.
144. Quoted in Main, *op. cit.,* p. 24.
145. *Ibid.*
146. Sullivan and Damrosch, *op. cit.*
147. Quoted in Rosenthal, *op. cit.,* p. 329.
148. M. Cooper (1987) "The role of religious and non-profit organisations in combatting homelessness", in: Bingham et al., *op. cit.*
149. Heskin, *op. cit.*
150. Heskin, *op. cit.*
151. Cooper, *op. cit.*
152. See J. Wright (1987) "The national health care for the homeless program", in: Bingham et al., *op. cit.*
153. Steiner (1966) *op. cit.,* pp. 153–157.
154. F. Piven and R. Cloward (1972) *Regulating the Poor,* pp. 300–320.
155. *Ibid.*
156. For an analysis of the strategy and a detailed study of the New Jersey episode, see M. Fabricant and I. Epstein (1984) "Legal and welfare rights advocacy: complementary approaches in organising on behalf of the homeless. *Urban and Social Change Review.*
157. Rosenthal, *op. cit.,* p. 540.
158. Jones, *op. cit.;* Reich (1964) *op. cit.*
159. Reich (1964) *op. cit.*
160. *Lindsey v. Normet* 405 US (1972) at 56.
161. New York City Administrative Code s.604–1.0 (b).
162. G. Mort (1984) "Establishing a right to shelter for the homeless", *Brooklyn Law Review.*
163. Cited in Mort, *op. cit.,* pp. 944–945.

164. For a comparison of the British and American situations see R. Cranston (1984) *Consumers and the Law* (2nd edition), pp. 95–99.

165. The city initially filed a voluminous defence to the suit, but was subsequently persuaded by the trial judge to seek a mutually acceptable compromise; K. Hopper and L. Cox (1986) "Litigation in advocacy for the homeless", in: Erikson and Wilhelm, *op. cit.*

166. Mort, *op. cit.*, p. 947.

167. R. Bingham, R. Green and S. White (1987) "Preface", in: Bingham et al., *op. cit.*

168. Although in recent months the city has adopted somewhat repressive tactics. In early November 1988 the Parks Authority carried out an "eviction" of a homeless persons encampment, nicknamed Kochville, in City Hall Park. The city did not actually throw the campers out of the park, rather it seized their tents, blankets and food; a course of action tantamount to a *de facto*, if not *de jure* eviction; see *The New York Times*, 1 November 1988.

169. The problem is not unique to New York, as the following testimony to a Congressional committee from a Los Angeles shelter resident suggests: "I pay $220 a month for rent for a room 10' by 10'. I have to share the toilet and shower with 70 other rooms. The toilet rooms...have feces on the walls and stuff like that. There is roaches and fleas in my room. And I am so afraid of the rats and mice in my room that I keep my cluth handy. The window...has never closed and I have lived here for a year and a half. And we hardly ever have hot water ...And when I complain to the manager, she tells me, if I don't like it get out. So I have a place to stay, but I am still homeless" (cited in Jahiel, *op. cit.*, p. 106).

170. Coleman, *op. cit.*

171. Main, *op. cit.*

172. For a review of the problem posed to, and caused by, the homeless see J. Fischer (1987) "Criminal activity and victimization among the homeless", in: R. Jahiel (ed.). *Homelessness and its Prevention.*

173. Cuomo, *op. cit.*

174. 116 Misc. 2d (1983).

175. R. Collin (1984) "Homelessness: the policy and the law", *The Urban Lawyer.*

176. Mort, *op. cit.*, pp. 991–994.

177. Cranston, *loc. cit.*

178. Fabricant and Epstein, *op. cit.*, p. 19.

179. Stern, *op. cit.*

180. The most comprehensive account of Santa Barbara's homeless population is provided by Rosenthal, *op. cit.*, from which this brief summary is drawn.

181. Department of Housing and Urban Development, *op. cit.*

182. Excerpts are drawn from the *Summary Report of Task Force on Lower State Street Problems,* Santa Barbara, 13 June 1986. My thanks to Willared Hastings of the Santa Barbara Legal Defence Center for furnishing me with a copy of the document.

183. *The Los Angeles Times,* 31 March 1986.

184. *Ibid.*

185. 221 Cal. Rptr. 110.

186. *Ibid.,* p. 116.

187. *Supra,* note [36].

188. See Rosenthal, *op. cit.*, pp. 94–104.

189. *The Los Angeles Times,* 20 August 1988.

190. My thanks to Willard Hastings of the Santa Barbara Legal Defense Center, Jane Hagstrom of the Santa Barbara Homeless Coalition, and many inhabitants of "the jungle" for providing further insight into recent developments in the city.
191. For a transcript of the debate see *The New York Times,* 26 September 1988.
192. *Ibid.*
193. *Ibid.* This is an accurate and entire record of President Bush's analysis. Nothing has been edited out. The sentence structure is his own creation.
194. See Collin, *op. cit.*
195. See *The New York Times,* 14 December 1988.

Who Are the Homeless Families? Characteristics of Sheltered Mothers and Children

Ellen L. Bassuk, M.D.

INTRODUCTION

Since the early 1980s, alarming numbers of families have lost their homes and have turned to emergency shelters for refuge. Because of the overflow, many families have also been housed in dilapidated welfare hotels and motels. Based on a 29 city survey, the U.S. Conference of Mayors (1987) reported in 1987 that families comprise 34% of the overall homeless population, are the fastest growing subgroup, and are predominantly headed by women.

We may well be witnessing the "feminization of homelessness" (Bassuk, 1987a). Reflecting the remarkable increase of female-headed families in the general population—now estimated at one out of seven American families (Wilson, 1987)—70% to 90% of homeless families are headed by women (Bassuk, 1988b). The figures vary regionally, with the lower percentage in the mid-west and west and the higher in the east. The remaining families are headed by couples who generally become homeless after the man has lost his blue-collar job (Bassuk, 1988b).

The numbers of homeless families do not at first glance reflect the enormity of the tragedy since the figures do not account for individual family members as well as the life-long impact of homelessness. Homeless mothers are defined as those women who are pregnant or are on the streets with their children. Usually they have 2 to 3 children, the majority of whom are 5 years or less. The preschoolers are growing up in shelters or on the streets during their formative years without the emotional, social, or economic re-

Dr. Bassuk is Associate Professor of Psychiatry, Harvard Medical School and President, The Better Homes Foundation.

For reprints, contact Dr. Bassuk at The Better Homes Foundation, 189 Wells Avenue, Newton, MA 02159.

sources they need for basic development. Based on data from a descriptive study that we completed of 80 families and 156 children residing in 14 Massachusetts family shelters (Bassuk, 1986; Bassuk, 1987b) as well as relevant literature, this paper reviews what is known about homeless mothers and children.

CHARACTERISTICS OF THE MOTHERS

Demographics

The average age of most homeless mothers, regardless of the locale, is approximately 27 years (Bassuk, 1986; Dumpson, 1987; McChesnesy, 1986). Despite a widespread belief that homeless persons are overwhelmingly from minority groups, the distribution of families mirrors the percentage of poor persons in a given location; no group is spared the degradation of becoming homeless. In the overall Massachusetts sample, for example, most mothers are white. However, when the distribution of minorities was looked at regionally, the majority of those in Boston are black, while most suburban families are white (Bassuk, 1986). Information about rural homeless families is lacking.

Marital status also varies according to location, but this too most likely reflects the general ethnic composition of the region. The marital status of homeless mothers reflects the tendency for black women to never marry and for whites to marry, but to have high divorce rates (Bassuk, 1986; Garfinkel, 1986; Wilson, 1987).

Contrary to the common assumption that homeless persons are poorly educated, the Massachusetts data show that almost two-thirds of the mothers have at least a GED or high school education with more than one-fifth completing several years of technical school or college (Bassuk, 1986). Unfortunately, for these women, educational achievement did not translate into occupational skills, suggesting that other factors such as economic or emotional problems may be interfering with their capacity to work. Most homeless women had not worked for more than a month at a time or had never worked.

Given this profile, it has been assumed that homelessness is primarily a problem of teen mothers and that many are unable to work because of the real burdens of childcare. Although there are teen mothers with special needs in our study, the mothers' ages spanned three decades from adolescence to midlife. Overall, the average age is 27 years; only six mothers were less than 20 years at the time of the study, and the average age at the birth of the first child was 19 years. Because of the combined burdens of child-care and poverty, teen mothers, when compared to their older counterparts in the Massachusetts study, had completed fewer years of high school, had rarely worked, and had more children. Otherwise their experiences were similar (Bassuk, 1986).

Another small group of mothers with special needs are those who are homeless and pregnant. Most of the women in the Massachusetts study who were pregnant were becoming mothers for the first time. Although they were terrified about bringing a newborn into a world without shelter, support, and security, only one mother planned to place her child for adoption.

Housing History

Generally, homeless mothers had moved many times prior to coming to the shelter or welfare hotel. In our study they had moved more than 3 times in the year before becoming homeless and an average of 6 times in the previous 5 years.

Where had these families been living? Eighty-five percent of the mothers had been doubled or tripled up with relatives or friends in overcrowded apartments. Unable to find affordable housing quickly, families often exhausted all potential supports and then had no place to turn except the shelters. With several families and many young children living together, little personal space or privacy, and infrequent respite from child care responsibilities, it was not unusual for family members to feel stressed and to fight. Sometimes, they parted amicably, but occasionally relationships were permanently disrupted.

In addition to doubling up in overcrowded apartments, more than half the mothers had previously lived in emergency shelters or welfare hotels, indicating that homelessness has become an episodic or chronic problem for some. A smaller group of mothers and their children had also lived in abandoned buildings, in cars, or on the streets before coming to the shelter. Representing a fifth of the sample, most of these families had also previously lived in emergency shelters as well as with friends or family (Bassuk, 1986).

Some mothers had moved from other cities and states to Massachusetts, but the vast majority had not. Most mothers tended to reside and move within the area where they grew up—often within a 5 mile radius—and to be sheltered in emergency facilities in that community.

Income Maintenance

How do these mothers survive? Ninety percent of the Massachusetts homeless families were receiving Aid to Families with Dependent Children (AFDC). Many were receiving other entitlements as well, such as food stamps and WIC. However, these combined benefits had not helped to prevent homelessness. In general, AFDC benefits, which vary considerably from state to state, have failed to keep pace with the inflation rate. When the poverty level for a family of three in 1985 was defined as $8,850 in Massachusetts, the AFDC cash benefits combined with the value of food stamps fell well below this level, amounting to only $7,000 (Bassuk, 1987a). If it is estimated that the median monthly rent for a one bedroom apartment in a city such as Boston is $500, then this family has only approximately $83 a month left for all other expenses. Even if this family could find decent housing, they would be spending 86% of their income for rent—far above the estimated 30% to 40% that is considered reasonable (Bassuk, 1984).

In general, most poor families use AFDC intermittently and briefly to survive acute personal or situational crises or to supplement inadequate income, but usually for not longer than 2 to 3 years (Bane, 1983). In contrast, a majority of the homeless mothers were chronically dependent on AFDC. Although 30% of Massachusetts AFDC recipients have been receiving AFDC for more than two years, 56% of shelter mothers had been AFDC recipients for at least this long (Bassuk, 1986). According to Bane: "Almost 50 percent of all spells end within two years. Of those who remain for at least two years, 60 percent will have spells lasting at least six years, and one third will have spells of over eight years" (Bane, 1983, p. 13). The data suggest that homeless mothers are likely to become part of the small percentage of welfare mothers in this country who will remain persistently poor.

Inadequate Supports

In its strictest sense, homelessness can be equated with lack of shelter. But lacking shelter is only one dimension of homelessness; a home implies connectedness with supportive persons and institutions as well as with community networks. Only a small percentage of AFDC mothers turn to the emergency shelter system or are on the streets despite the invidious effects of poverty and the depth of the housing crisis. Many turn to other persons to help them through crises. For example, many families who are precariously housed depend on extended kin and non-kin domestic networks to provide the safety net that prevents homelessness (Stack, 1974; Susser, 1982). Stack (1974) wrote in her book, "All Our Kin": "I learned that poverty creates a necessity for this exchange of goods and services. The needs of families living at bare subsistence are so large compared to their average daily income that it is impossible for families to provide independently for fixed expenses and daily needs . . . The poor adapt a variety of tactics in order to survive. They immerse themselves in a domestic circle of kinfolk who will help them." (p. 29) Stack (1974) broadened her definition of family to include both "kin and non-kin who interact daily, providing domestic needs of children and assuring their survival" (p. 31).

Although many families may remain doubled up for years, and by definition are homeless, they are spared the further degradation of having to turn to the emergency shelters. Unfortunately, the recent alarming increase in homeless families nationwide indicate that a growing number of people lack adequate supports and have difficulty getting the help they need.

Homeless mothers generally are isolated and alone. When asked to name three persons they can turn to during times of personal crises, only a third were able to name at least three people who they could depend on. Twenty-two percent were unable to name any supports. The remainder named one or two persons and many in this group mentioned a recent shelter friend or professional contact. In addition, over one-fourth named their minor child as a primary support during times of personal stress (Bassuk, 1986). In contrast to the homeless mothers who have few supports, adults in the general population report that they have 8 to 15 persons in their network (Shulz, 1985).

However, even for mothers who were able to describe 3 or more persons, these individuals were unable to rescue them from the streets. Most often, they offered emotional support, but could not provide instrumental help, such as financial aid, child-care, transportation or most importantly, shelter.

Why did so many mothers lack adequate supports? For some, homelessness stressed or weakened existing, but already fragmented supports. Many mothers who are now homeless had been severely deprived as children and come from disrupted families. As adults they are less able to depend on parents, siblings, or extended family. The reasons for the family disruption and later estrangement ranged from severe conflict to divorce, illness and death of a parent (Bassuk, 1986).

The existence of an intact family, however, in no way ensures that the now homeless mothers had received adequate parenting when they were children. Almost a third of the homeless mothers stated that they had been physically abused, generally by their own mothers. Not surprisingly, some homeless mothers now have difficulty parenting their own children. A small minority of homeless mothers suffered from a drug or alcohol problem or a psychiatric disability, but the numbers in this group were small (Bassuk, 1988a).

McChesney (1986), in a study of 80 homeless families in Los Angeles County family shelters, described the families' lack of support in similar ways: "In the process of trying to stave off their slide into homelessness, families tried many varied and creative means to shelter themselves and their children. Where possible, families routinely turned to their own parents and brothers and sisters first. However, what was most striking about the families in the sample was the fact that in the main, they could not call on their own parents and brothers and sisters as resources. There were three major reasons...: either their parents were dead, their parents and siblings didn't live in the Los Angeles area, or their parents and siblings were estranged (p. 6)." McChesney (1986) commented on the "surprisingly high number of deceased parents" and the percentage of homeless mothers who had been orphaned (16%).

Another possible source of support for homeless mothers was in their relationships with men (Bassuk, 1986). When asked how many meaningful relationships they had with men, most described one long-standing boyfriend. They reported, however, that the men they had been involved with had many problems including joblessness and drug and alcohol problems. Forty percent of the sheltered homeless women had also been involved in at least one relationship in which they had been battered. Most of the violence was drug-related. As the man's alcoholism spiraled out-of-control, he tended to become abusive, precipitating the break-up of the relationship and the mother's slide into homelessness.

Mental Health Status

Overall about a fourth of the homeless mothers suffered from a major psychiatric clinical syndrome (e.g., schizophrenia, major affective disorder, alcoholism), but these did not cluster into a single diagnostic category (Bassuk, 1986, 1988a). In contrast to many adult individual homeless persons who have been reinstitutionalized and suffer from psychoses, such as schizophrenia, these illnesses were not overrepresented among homeless mothers. Unlike the many homeless adult individual women with major mental disorders, these women do not have problems reality testing, do not require medication, and in general are not chronically mentally ill.

However, more than two-thirds of the mothers suffer from DSM-III Axis II diagnoses of personality disorders. In contrast, based on large scale random sampling, estimates of the prevalence of serious personality disorders in the adult population range from 5 to 15 percent (Bassuk, 1986). What does this label mean? A personality disorder diagnosis indicates the presence of a chronic pervasive pattern of emotional difficulties, usually evident by adolescence. It reflects an impaired capacity to respond adaptively to stress, as well as difficulty functioning in multiple areas of one's life— such as working, forming and maintaining relationships, parenting, and living independently. It is certainly not surprising that parents who lack the essential early nurturance of a mothering figure, have been abused, have lived in chaos during their formative years, have suffered major family disruptions, or who lack positive role models, often manifest this profound deprivation by developing behavioral disorders later in life.

Although these disorders, in general, have not been caused by shelter or hotel living, the mothers' problems are invariably exacerbated by their homeless experience. The diagnosis of personality disorder in our study was made on the basis of a careful developmental history—not on the degree of depression and anxiety manifested by the mothers while they were living in the shelter or hotel. The mothers' difficulties had to predate the current homelessness episode, to be evident during early adolescence, and to indicate a long-term enduring pattern of emotional distress and difficulty functioning (Widiger, 1985). Problems forming and maintaining supportive relationships were often a major feature of this disorder. Generally, attachments to others tended to be tenuous, often troubled, and were more easily disrupted during times of stress.

Pregnancy-Related Problems

In the only systematic study of homeless pregnant women to date, Chavkin et al. (1987) concluded that, in comparison to women living in housing projects, homeless mothers residing in New York City welfare hotels were more likely to have higher infant mortality rates, to have babies of low birth weight, and to receive less prenatal care.

Physical Health

Using data from the 16-city Health Care for the Homeless Project, Wright (1987) described the health problems of homeless adult family members (15% of overall sample) who presented at their clinics for treatment. He found that, compared to a group of ambulatory patients from the general population (National Ambulatory Medical Survey—MAMCS), they tended to have more acute and chronic physical illnesses. However, compared to homeless adult individuals, they had fewer visible health care problems.

CHARACTERISTICS OF THE CHILDREN

In the Massachusetts study of sheltered homeless families, 156 children were interviewed (Bassuk, 1987b). Approximately two-thirds of the children were preschoolers, five years or less. Almost half of the homeless preschoolers manifested severe developmental lags (using the Denver Developmental Screening Test), often in multiple areas tested. In addition to language development, this included gross motor skills, fine motor coordination and personal/social development. Lenore Rubin, a child psychologist who interviewed many of these children, explained that these severe impairments were related to their mother's difficulties: "The greatest issue for them is their mother's depression. They don't get played with, or talked to, and as a result, they get left behind" (Hirsch, 1986, p. 10). Although these children require greater stimulation and more opportunity for interaction, very few were in infant stimulation, daycare, or headstart programs.

Using various standardized instruments, the school-age children manifested high levels of anxiety and depression. Overall, approximately half of these children required psychiatric referral and evaluation. Not surprisingly, their school performance reflected these difficulties. Forty-three percent were currently failing or doing below average work. Twenty-five percent were in special classes and 43% had already repeated a grade (Bassuk, 1987b).

"School is a living purgatory for homeless kids. Deeply ashamed of their circumstances, they invent addresses. If their homelessness becomes known, they are bullied, taunted and often beaten up by other children. Teachers treat them harshly, according to officials of the Department of Public Welfare, either because no one has warned them that these children may express their insecurities by being too aggressive or withdrawn, or because the homeless child, having become the target of playmates' abuse, turns into the teacher's scapegoat as well. Until very recently, children forced to move from shelter to shelter had difficulty transferring into the school districts where their shelters were located" (Hirsch, 1986, p. 10). Not surprisingly, many of these children attend school erratically, if at all. To date, few communities have successfully reduced the barriers to education faced by homeless children.

In addition to their emotional and learning problems, homeless children also suffer from various health problems. Using data from the Health Care for the Homeless Project, Wright (1987) observed that "the rate of chronic physical disorders among the homeless children is nearly twice that observed among ambulatory (NAMCS) children in general" (p. 4). Other researchers have reported immunization delays (Acker, 1987), lead poisoning (Gallagher, 1986), and poor nutritional status (Acker, 1987; Gallagher, 1986) among homeless children.

DISCUSSION

As the Massachusetts study indicates, homeless mothers are generally young, currently single, have had a high school education, have poor job histories, and have been on welfare for a long time. Although each family has a unique history, a mother's extreme isolation and disconnectedness from supportive relationships and caretaking institutions has contributed to her need to seek refuge in emergency shelters. Regardless of the reasons, most sheltered homeless mothers have been unable to depend on their supports to help prevent the slide into homelessness. There is no doubt that being doubled-up stresses or weakens a person's supports, but the data suggest that for many homeless mothers their supportive relationships with friends and family were already fragmented by interpersonal conflict, substance abuse, illness, or divorce. Although economic factors, including the severity of the low income housing crisis and inadequate welfare benefits, are enough to explain homelessness, we must also be attuned to the social and psychological needs of the families. Otherwise, once housed, the quality of life of these families will remain severely compromised.

REFERENCES

Acker P.J., Freeman A.H., Dreyer B.P: 1987. An assessment of parameters of health care and nutrition in homeless children. Amer J Dis Children 141:388.

Bane M.J., Ellwood D: June 1983. The Dynamics of Dependence. The Routes to Self-Sufficiency. Washington DC: US Dept. of Health and Human Services.

Bassuk E.L., Rosenberg L: 1988a. Why does family homelessness occur?: A case-control study. Amer J Public Health 78:783–788.

Bassuk E.L., Reisman D. 1988b. Health care needs of homeless families: An overview. Unpublished.

Bassuk E.L., 1987a. Feminization of homelessness: Families in Boston Shelters. AM J Soc Psych 7:19–23.

Bassuk E.L., Rubin L: 1987b. Homeless children: A neglected population. Amer J Orthopsych 56:279–286.

Bassuk E.L., Rubin L, Lauriat A: 1986. Characteristics of sheltered homeless families. Am J Public Health, 76:1097.

Bassuk E.L: 1984. The homelessness problem. Scientific American. 251:40–45.

Chavkin W., Kristal A., Seabron C, Guigli P: 1987. The reproductive experience of women living in hotels for the homeless in New York City. New York State J of Med 87:10–13.

Dumpson J.R: March 1987. A Shelter Is Not A Home. Report of the Manhattan Borough Presidents' Task Force on Housing for Homeless Families.

Gallagher E: 1986. No Place Like Home. A Report on the Tragedy of Homeless Children and Their Families in Massachusetts. Mass. Committee for Children and Youth, Boston.

Garfinkel I., McLanahan S: 1986. Single Mothers and Their Children. A New American Dilemma. Washington DC: The Urban Institute Press.

Hirsch K: Jan. 21, 1986. Childhood without a home. A new report on the youngest victims. The Boston Phoenix.

McChesney, K.Y: 1986. New findings on homeless families. Family Professional. 1(2).

Shulz R., Ran J.T: 1985. Social Support Through the Life Course. In Cohen S., Syme S.L. Edu Social Support and Health. Florida: Academic Press, pp 129–149.

Stack C.B: 1974. All Our Kin. Strategies for Survival in a Black Community. New York: Harper and Row.

Susser I: Norman Street: 1982. Poverty and politics in an urban neighborhood. New York: Oxford Univ. Press.

U.S. Conference of Mayors: 1987. A Status Report on Homeless Families in American Cities. A 29-City Survey, Washington, DC.

Widger T., Frances A: 1985. Axis II Personality Disorders: Diagnostic and treatment issues. Howard Comm Psych 36: 619–627.

Wilson, William J: 1987. The Truly Disadvantaged. The Inner City, The Underclass, and Public Policy. Chicago: The Univ. of Chicago Press.

Wright J.D: 1987. Effects of homelessness on the physical well-being of children, families and youth. Unpublished.

The Family, Welfare and Homelessness

Peter H. Rossi

Although the problem of homelessness manifests itself by definition as a housing and poverty problem, that by itself leads to only a superficial diagnosis. The thesis of this paper is that homelessness is much more than a problem of housing the poor, and that a full understanding of it must extend deeply into issues involving the nature of our social welfare system as it interacts with our kinship system. Of course, this does not deny the housing shortages but rather identifies equally important processes in housing policy. Three analyses constitute the evidentiary foundations of this argument: First, we consider the social characteristics of the homeless and of comparable extremely poor people who are housed. Second, we examine the nature of our current social welfare system and illustrate how it is poorly suited to serve the kinds of people who are homeless. Third, we consider the nature of kinship obligations and show how those basic defenses against adversity offered by the family are inadequate for coping with members who then become homeless persons. A final section of this paper suggests how our current social welfare system may be altered better to provide reasonable and sensible help to the homeless and other extremely poor people.

I. CRITICAL FEATURES OF CURRENT HOMELESSNESS

Homelessness has always existed to a greater or lesser degree throughout our history, waxing and waning mainly according to the health of the economy.[1] In recent times the last heavy resurgence of homelessness occurred during the 1930s' depression when as many as several hundred thousand homeless persons filled the emergency shelters set up in the early days

S.A. Rice Professor of Sociology and Acting Director, Social and Demographic Research Institute, University of Massachusetts, Amherst, MA.

of the New Deal.[2] Nevertheless, America's collective memories of the homeless of the Great Depression homeless have faded. Today, America's consciousness is informed by more recent portraits and understanding of the homeless population. Our views of "normal" homelessness are influenced more strongly by fresher recollections of the Skid Rows of the 1950s and 1960s.

On first glance one can note how the "old" homeless and the "new" homeless differ.[3] A primary difference is the character of "shelter". Perhaps the most critical difference is that the old homeless were not literally without shelter; rather, they were concentrated in Skid Rows, neighborhoods dominated by "flophouse" hotels, cheap restaurants and mission shelters. Few of the old homeless slept in the streets or in public places such as railroad and bus terminals. They slept in the mission shelters and in the inexpensive "flophouse" hotels whereas the new homeless of the 1980s are housed in shelters and can be found on the streets and in public access places. Neither the mission shelters nor the flophouse hotels were housing adequate by even minimal standards, but they provided shelter. The concentration of the old homeless on Skid Row was enforced by police practices that swept up the homeless who wandered off their allotted turf. In contrast, today's homeless can be found more widely dispersed throughout downtown urban areas. But, more strikingly, the new homeless of the 1980s are considerably more deprived in their housing. As many as half of the homeless resort to "emergency" shelters and the remainder live on the streets or in public places. The emergency shelters are arguably on a par in quality to the old flophouse hotels; certainly living in bus stations or on the streets can only be viewed as a more severely deprived housing condition.

Another significant difference is the socio-economic and demographic make-up of the homeless populations.[4] For instance, consider the demographic changes in age. In the 1950s and 1960s, the average age of the homeless as reported by social researchers was in the fifties. The current homeless average in the middle thirties. Close to a majority of the old homeless were old men, many of them living on old age pensions. All of the 1980s studies of the homeless find only small percentages who are over 60. Senior citizens are rare among today's homeless whereas in the earlier period they predominated. The older homeless were part of the labor force. The old homeless who were not on old age pensions were employed, earning their rent and food money at casual labor and enjoyed an income (in constant dollars) that on the average was three times the income of the current homeless, few of whom have any employment at all. The old homeless were poor but the new are virtually destitute. The average monthly income from all sources of the new homeless was less than $100 and more than one in five report zero income.

There were virtually no women or families on Skid Row; today at least one in five are women and half of them are accompanied by young children.

Although families that consist of both parents and children are still rare, many single mother families are found among the new homeless, and the number seems to be growing.

Moreover, few of the old homeless were recruited from among minority groups; the current homeless have proportions of Blacks and Hispanic that are four to five times their representations in the general communities in question. Virtually all of the homeless female-headed households are drawn from minority groups. The "typical" old homeless was a white male on the verge of old age who lived on earnings from intermittent employment or minimum Social Security old age payments. The "typical" homeless person of the 1980s is a Black or Hispanic male in the middle thirties and has lacked steady work for up to a decade[5].

There are also continuities over time. Disabling conditions, including physical disabilities, chronic mental illness, alcoholism, and criminal records involving serious felony offenses plague both the "new" and "old" homeless. Chronic mental illness appears to occur slightly more among the new homeless (one in three as compared to one in five) and, not surprisingly, drug abuse is higher among the current homeless population. Among the current homeless, these disabilities are cumulative and four out of five have one or more of the conditions listed above.

the most conspicuous and significant feature common to both the old and the new homeless is family status. The homeless in America, whether the old or new, are unmarried, either never having married or having been divorced, widowed or separated, a condition that applies as well to the single parent[6] homeless with their children. Homelessness is equivalent to "spouse-lessness".[7]

Understanding these similarities and comparing these differences of the new and old homeless provide clues to the reasons why homelessness has increased since the early 1980s. First of all, homelessness has increased precisely among that portion of the American population who have experienced catastrophically high levels of unemployment since the mid-1970s, namely young minority men. These unemployment rates, with the diminishing pool of males who are potential spouses and economic providers partly account for the increase in unmarried mothers and their children among the homeless. Second, the decline of elderly homeless attests to the more generous Social Security benefits available to the aged since the early 1970s. Third, the rise in chronically mentally ill reflects the deinstitutionalization movement of the 1960s and the decline in the use of mental hospitals for the chronically mentally ill. Finally is the growth in extreme poverty brought about by both unemployment and a major decline in the real value of welfare benefits.

II. THE HOUSED AND HOMELESS EXTREMELY POOR

The unattached (i.e. unmarried) homeless persons described above represent merely a small portion of the unattached extremely poor. A consideration to the "extremely poor", those with annual incomes of $2,000 or less, illustrates this thesis. For example, in 1986 over four million unattached persons between the ages of 22 and 59 earning less than $2,000 existed, compared to less than two million in 1969 (income adjusted for inflation and presented in constant 1985 dollars).[8] This age range is significant because it represents the ages at which most adults are expected to be self-supporting. These adults constitute the housed extremely poor, living in conventional dwellings.[9] Although we lack precise estimates of the number of homeless, our best estimates range around 500,000, with a range of 100,000 plus or minus.[10] In short the homeless represent about 10% of the extremely poor.[11]

It is very instructive to consider the living arrangements of those extremely poor who are housed. Aside from female-headed households (unmarried women living with their minor children), the majority of the extremely poor live in households with other people, mainly their parents and less frequently with other relatives. In contrast, female-headed households live separately in their own dwellings, supported largely by AFDC grants.

These data indicate great numbers of adults old enough to be expected to be economically self-supporting who are dependent on welfare benefits for income or on their kindred for at least shelter and most likely food and clothing. The fact that unmarried mothers live by themselves often reflects the eligibility requirements of the AFDC program, that unmarried mothers establish independent households to receive full benefits. For those who have not taken on responsibility for the care of children, the welfare benefits available are either non-existent (in some states) or are not enough to support a single person living alone.[12]

For many non-parents, relying on their kin may have been a temporary expedient. For example, in April of 1987, about one in three of the people who earned $2,000 or less in 1986 were employed, possibly steadily enough so as to deliver them from the extremely poor and to enable them to pursue independent life plans. For relatively well-off parents and other heads of families, the burden of caring for a dependent adult relative may not be so onerous. Indeed, typically such is the case: The average 1986 incomes of the households who take in a dependent adult are close to the overall United States median household income, so most may be able to take in an unemployed son or brother at least "temporarily". But, many of the host households, particularly those of nonrelatives, are poor themselves and such hospitality may impose a severe burden.[13]

Unfortunately, we learn very little from the Current Population Survey about the prevalence of disabilities among the dependent adults identified above insofar as such information is not collected. For this information we must consult local surveys. Surveys conducted among General Assistance (GA) and AFDC clients in Chicago[14] provide strong evidence that disability levels are much lower among the housed extremely poor than the homeless extremely poor. Virtually all GA and AFDC clients are unmarried. The unmarried mothers on AFDC mainly lived independently; the unmarried men on GA mostly lived dependently, that is, with their parents or other relatives. Less than one in twenty of GA men and AFDC women had ever been hospitalized for mental illness or had trouble with alcohol or been imprisoned for felony offenses. The men, mostly on General Assistance, had been unemployed for much shorter periods of time than the homeless population.

Piecing these bits of information together, one can offer an intriguing set of interpretations. First, the striking differences between the housed and homeless extremely poor are that the latter come from the poorest levels of society, have been unemployed for long periods, and have high disability levels. The poverty of their kindred, in addition to high levels of disabilities, provide an explanation of why they are homeless. Their presence in the households of their relatives constitutes a serious drain on the income and housing resources of very poor families and their disabilities render any accommodations difficult to their presence in the household. Second, the lack of welfare programs providing support to unattached males and the presence of welfare programs providing support to unmarried mothers explain why the latter are housed: AFDC payments, although not very generous, are enough to allow most unmarried mothers to rent housing while GA payments are simply inadequate to support a single person living independently.

The rising numbers of "families" among the homeless require some additional considerations. First, the families in question are almost entirely women and their minor children; husband-wife couples, with or without children, are very rare among the homeless. Second, such families typically remain homeless for short periods before finding conventional housing. Homelessness, then, is apparently a transitional step between one housing arrangement and another. Third, this group among the homeless demonstrates the least prevalence of disability. Their major problem is poverty, a situation exacerbated by the low levels of benefits available under AFDC. The problems presented by homeless "families" are therefore quite different from those of the single homeless.

III. SUPPORT OBLIGATIONS AMONG ADULT KIN[15]

The first line of defense for people against the many turns of fortune that lead to adversity is their kindred, those to whom they are related closely by marital or blood ties. In this respect the most important kinship tie is the marital bond, a strength of obligation reflected both in the traditional marriage vows and in the law. Husbands and wives are so strongly obligated to provide support, spiritual, moral and financial, to each other that we tend to take it for granted. The support obligations may not correspond symmetrically but they are strong in both directions; husbands may have a stronger obligation to provide steady income, but wives who refuse to seek employment when their husbands are incapacitated are also looked upon as not fulfilling their marital obligations. It is to break the marital bond to refuse to share shelter and sustenance with a spouse. It is also a reflection of the strength of that bond that virtually all of the homeless are either single, separated, widowed or divorced.

The next kinship line of defense against adversity is the parent-child bond. Both the law and the custom of parental obligations to provide shelter and sustenance to their minor children are well-settled. Parents neglecting to provide shelter, food and a reasonably safe environment to children under 12 would surely meet widespread disapproval among their friends and neighbors and likely face legal action for neglect. It is, however, ambiguous when minority status and the corresponding parental obligation to provide support end. Most Americans would certainly state that parents possessing adequate means should provide support to teenagers and young adults who are going to school, but there is no legal obligation to pay the tuition and maintenance costs of a 20-year-old undergraduate. One would certainly regard reasonably well-off parents who refuse to send their children to college as not fulfilling their parental duties. At the same time, one would esteem 20-year-old undergraduates who earned a major portion of their schooling costs. One also expects some degree of subsidy to children entering the labor force; an unmarried 19-year-old seeking employment is typically living at home and even provided with spending money. At the same time, if that child were not seeking employment, some degree of disapproval would occur. After completing high school, children are more or less expected to help partially to support themselves or to continue further schooling.

It is not clearly defined in our cultural expectations at which age children should become self-supporting and should live separate form parental households. Nor is it clear how the circumstances of the parents modify their obligations to provide shelter and sustenance to their adult or near-adult children. Surely, few would expect nearly destitute or chronically ill parents to provide the same degree of support as those parents who are well-off. To make sacrifices for children is expected from all, but the sacrifices are scaled roughly to parents' circumstances.

Nevertheless, one can assert certain general principles. First, the cultural prescription that a child should be self-supporting and living separately increases in strength as the child grows older. Dependency on parents becomes less acceptable when involving an older child. This dependency likely reaches its low point in the middle twenties and remains low with additional years. Second, one regards the marriage of a child as a move into adulthood with the preferred living arrangements of married couples being separate from both parental families. Third, "emergency" conditions providing for exceptions abound. Reverses in children's fortunes brought about by events such as serious illness, marital disruptions, or unemployment sanction return to parental folds at least "for a while". Indeed, we suspect that many of the unattached adults living with their parents identified earlier returned to their parental homes under such "emergency" conditions. Fourth, adult children who are not competent to function fully as adults by reason of mental retardation, chronic mental illness or chronic physical disability may be exempted from the cultural prescriptions for self-support and separate living arrangements. The exemption is most clearly defined when the condition in question results not from the child's own actions and results not in unacceptable behavior. Parental households incorporate a passive, borderline mentally defective child more easily than a chronic alcoholic or a child whose mental illness involves floridly aggressive episodes. The status of long-term chronic unemployment as an acceptable reason for returning to a parental home is likely ambiguous, depending on such conditions as societal or community levels of unemployment.

The preceding discussion's main point illuminates that parental obligation to offer and provide shelter and sustenance to children does not end abruptly at some point in the life courses of the children but extends throughout adulthood. Perhaps for some parents that obligation is never invoked, and for others the obligation is activated for temporary emergencies. For a small minority of parents, the burden of providing for a dependent adult child for some extended period of time may weigh heavily.

The support obligations of more distant kin are even more ambiguous. One may regard grandparents as remiss if they showed no concern for their grandchildren. Still, to extend more than love and caring beyond the grandchild's childhood is neither legally nor culturally prescribed. Of course, the circumstances of someone who is the grandparent of an adult in his or her twenties or thirties (and hence at least in his or her late fifties and most likely in his or her sixties and seventies) may be such that no obligation in practice exists.

Next to the parental relationship, the kin tie involving the strongest obligations is that between siblings. The same conditions concerning grandparents most likely apply with respect to siblings, with perhaps more emphasis placed on the resources of the obligated sibling. Compared to a single person, someone with strong obligations to a spouse and to children may have less obligation to a sibling.

Beyond the kin ties discussed above, the obligations of kin drop off rapidly in strength.[16] Uncles and aunts have minimal obligations to their nieces and nephews. Nor do we owe much to cousins.

The living arrangements of extremely poor persons reflect the struction of kinship obligations. First of all, whether homeless or not, the majority of extremely poor persons are not married or living with their spouses. Virtually all the homeless are either not married or not living with their spouses. More than three quarters of the housed extremely poor are unmarried. We cannot tell from the cross-sectional surveys used to make those statements whether the extremely poor are not married because of their poverty or because poverty was a factor in the breakup of their marriages. Secondly, aside from unmarried mothers, the living arrangements of the extremely poor reflect the strength of kin obligations, as described. Most extremely poor single persons live with relatives. More precisely, the majority living with relatives are living with parents most of the remainder with siblings, and a very small proportion with more distant kin.

Up to this point, we have looked upon the obligations that people may have towards their kin in adversity. Shifting now to the viewpoint of people who for one reason or another are suffering from destitution or are threatened with that condition, surely the worst off are those who have no living primary kin. Without parents or siblings to call upon for help in adversity, the safety net of kindred is simply missing. Mortality can bring about this condition, especially the absence of living parents, but also parents can abrogate their responsibilities. Mortality can also affect the presence of siblings and, in addition, single children never had siblings.

The prevalence of being without living primary kin is very high among the homeless. Slightly under half (42%) of the Chicago homeless interviewed in 1986 had no living parents and one in four had no living siblings.[17] Both prevalences are extremely high considering the average age of the homeless, in the middle thirties. Some evidence also signals that many have lacked parents for much of their lives. Foster parents raised one fifth of the Minneapolis homeless interviewed in 1986.[18] This indicates either orphanhood or abandonment. Clearly, many of the homeless simply lack any primary kin who could help them by providing shelter and sustenance.

Nevertheless, most of the homeless have living parents and/or siblings, thus raising the question of why they are not living with their primary kin. Several characteristics of the homeless provide clues to the answer to this question. First, the primary kin of most of the homeless are themselves poor and thus have limited resources. The act of providing shelter and sustenance to another adult would surely constitute a strain. Second, many of the homeless face poor prospects of becoming self-supporting. The average time elapsed since last full-time employment for the homeless is about four and a half years with approximately one in five being unemployed for more than a decade.[19]

Some evidence suggests that these people have a persistent dependency that has severely taxed the capacity for generosity among their primary kin. Being homeless for less than two years suggests that their primary kin did provide support for a long period but were no longer able to do so. Third, the disability prevalences among the homeless make them unattractive as household members; it may be difficult to extend hospitality to someone who is chronically mentally ill, a chronic alcoholic or who has a felony conviction record. The fact that most of the Chicago homeless state that their Chicago relatives would not welcome them as household members even if there were room available in their homes illustrates this unattractiveness.[20]

This discussion demonstrates that primary kin represent the first line of defense against adversity, especially if short-term, for most adults, but that line weakens, often to the point of failure, when the resources of the kin are meager, when adversity turns into long-term condition, and when the supplicant adults are potentially disruptive household members.

IV. THE PUBLIC SAFETY NET

If primary kin constitutes the first line of defense against adversity, public agencies and their programs constitute the second line. This second tier safety net consists of a number of government programs, including income maintenance, rehabilitation, and full-care institutions.

The decline of poverty among the aged brought about by changes in the early 1970s in the Social Security system dramatically marks the potential effectiveness of the public-supported safety net. In the 1950s and 1960s one in three to one in four of the homeless on Skid Row were old men eking out their existence on the minimum old age pension of about $150 monthly (in 1985 dollars).[21] The changes made increased the average benefit available and subsequently tied the benefit level to inflation. The net effect was a rise in the average old age monthly benefit in constant 1985 dollars from $295 in 1968 to $479 in 1985.[22] The general consequence was a dramatic reduction of the persons 65 and over who were below the poverty line dropping 13% between 1970 and 1980. As far as homelessness goes, the effect was even more dramatic with less than 5% of the homeless of today being over 65 compared to 20% to 30% in the early 1960s.

Trends in the opposite direction reduced the value of AFDC payments, declining from a national average of $520 (1985 dollars) in 1968 to $325 in 1985, a 30% decline offset to some degree by such in-kind benefits as food stamps and Medicaid.[23] One can attribute partially the appearance of female-headed households among the homeless to this serious decline in benefits that made the most inexpensive housing difficult to find.[24] It is the difficulty of finding housing that can be afforded under such AFDC grants that makes for female-headed households being placed "temporarily" in the welfare hotels and motels in urban centers, such as New York, that have tight low-rent housing markets.

Unattached adults under 60 have never had a substantial safety net. Someone who lacks sole responsibility for minor children is not eligible for AFDC in most states.[25] One may obtain old age benefits if one is over 60 and has been employed in covered industries. One may obtain disability benefits under Social Security, provided one had an eligible disability and can prove it to examiners. One may seek unemployment benefit payments for a limited number of weeks, with eligibility contingent on previous work. But for other persons, many of whom remain unemployed for a long time, financial aid must be sought from other programs. This is the situation of most homeless persons. They are long-term unemployed, they are rarely single parents, and are more rarely living with a spouse. Given the level of disabilities among the homeless, one might surmise that many would be eligible for support as disabled persons, but only chronic mental illness, an ambiguous diagnostic category, qualifies as a covered disability.

In many states, General Assistance, a program financed by state or county funds, stands as the only income maintenance program available to such people. Some states, such as Texas, lack a General Assistance program.[26] Other states restrict eligibility to one or two months every year. The amount of payments also varies. In Los Angeles County, General Assistance payments amount to $212 per month (1988) whereas in Chicago monthly payments are $154. General Assistance benefit levels generally have not kept pace with inflation. In Illinois, the constant value (1985 dollars) of General Assistance payments declined over 50% from $322 in 1968 to $154 in 1985.[27] Few General Assistance clients in Chicago were able to afford separate living arrangements; most were part of their parental households.

For unattached persons who for one reason or another cannot count on the generosity of their primary kin, the income maintenance programs available in even the most generous localities have benefit levels insufficient for many to afford housing and sustenance. These persons constitute the bulk of the our current homeless population. Surprisingly, only a fraction of the eligible, about one in five, participate in General Assistance programs. Although $154 per month certainly will not pay the rent for even the most inexpensive housing,[28] the payments are still higher than the average homeless income and certainly better than the zero income reported by about one in five. We suspect that the public welfare system may be too difficult and arcane for the homeless to navigate easily.[29] In any event, the current American income maintenance system works well for the aged, poorly for single-headed households with young children, and abominably for the destitute unattached. Furthermore, in the same period when homelessness was growing, the system's levels of support deteriorated drastically for the latter two groups.

Chronic mental illness also affects the old homeless: Bogue estimated that from 15% to 20% of the 1958 Chicago homeless were mentally ill. Putting aside the tricky issue of diagnosis,[30] there appears to be increase in the proportion of the homeless showing signs of current psychosis or affective disorders to our present day 33%. Undoubtedly, the decanting of the state mental hospitals in the 1970s produced at least some of this increase, and the current practice of avoiding institutionalization maintains the high prevalence rates among the homeless.

A total care institution such as a mental hospital, represents part of the societal safety net, providing shelter and sustenance to clients who are presumably unable to function appropriately outside the institution.[31] The deinstitutionalization movement derived its impetus and rationale from the fact that hospitalization typically did not rehabilitate the chronically mentally ill while maintaining them in squalid and often cruel conditions. The expansion of the Social Security Disability program promised to provide income support to discharged patients who would be treated in the community under conditions that would maximize freedom and decent living conditions. Furthermore, the new psychopharmacology would enable the chronically mentally ill to function well enough to live in the new community treatment organizations.

Unfortunately, it proved far easier to discharge patients into local communities than it was to provide the community facilities to receive them.[32] In addition, it proved difficult to insure that those discharged connected effectively with local psychiatric care facilities. Consequently, the presence of the chronically mentally ill among the homeless grew apace. Of course, not all of the initially released patients and the subsequent non-hospitalized mentally ill ended up among the homeless. Many may have been incorporated into the households of primary kin, contributing to the increase in adult dependency noted earlier.

Nor did the anticipated income maintenance materialize for many of the mentally ill through Social Security Disability or Supplemental Security payments. Although the state recognizes chronic mental illness as a qualifying disability, an adjudication of eligibility does not come easily. The process of establishing eligibility is a complicated one, difficult for many mentally ill to negotiate successfully. Periodic administrative eligibility reviews are almost as complicated. Thus, few of the homeless mentally ill receive disability income maintenance.[33] In any event, those homeless released and those homeless never institutionalized represent another category of persons who have slipped through both the first and second tier of our social safety net.

Alcoholism and drug addiction constitute disability conditions that affect another third of the homeless.[34] No income maintenance safety nets exists at all for these disabilities, except for those whose abuse has led to serious physical deterioration. Of course, whether or not chronic alcoholism or drug addiction ought to be considered for purposes of income maintenance eligibility disabilities of the same order as paraplegia or schizophrenia is a complicated issue that is not likely to be answered affirmatively in the public arena in the near future.[35] However, there are signs of change: Over the past few decades, the view of alcoholism as a character defect has changed to that of a disease entity. Perhaps future changes may shift views of addiction to that of a disability. In that event, we will come to regard chronic alcoholism or serious drug addiction as a condition rendering victims eligible for societal support and possibly intervention.

V. ACCOUNTING FOR THE RECENT INCREASE IN HOMELESSNESS

Describing the characteristics of homeless people leads to an understanding of who is vulnerable to that condition. These characteristics, however, do not reveal why homelessness has increased in the past decade. No evidence shows a recent decline in the strength of obligations to help primary kin or a sudden increase in either mental illness or alcoholism. The last section of this paper provides a partial explanation in the decline since the 1970s of the capacity of our public safety net to provide adequate support to vulnerable groups. In addition, trends over that period have increased the prevalence of adult dependency and have also undermined the capacities of people to provide support to their dependent adult primary kin.

Perhaps the extraordinarily high unemployment rates affecting young minority males over the period 1975 to the present time, reaching highs of 30% to 40% unemployed among males 18 to 22, two to four magnitudes higher than for whites, signals the major factor in the homeless equation. Among older minority males unemployment rates were also high. Consequently, this increased the prevalence of adult dependency and diminished the capacities of families to aid their primary adult kin.

When inner city unemployment rates for young males reached highs of 30% to 40%, the vulnerable became steadily unemployed. The high male unemployment rates also explain how family formation through marriage has declined since impoverished males are unattractive as mates and since the latter are both less able and less willing to undertake the responsibilities for providing a household income. The burden of providing for the unemployed young men fell upon their parental families. In 1970, 39% of young Black men, aged 18 to 29, lived with their parents; by 1984 that proportion had risen to 54%.[36] At the same time, the further impoverishment of poor families reduced their capacities to provide help.

The conjunction of these trends changed both the age and racial composition of the homeless, dropping the average age into the middle thirties and producing large increases in the proportions of those homeless from minority groups as well as producing an overall increase in their numbers.

The failure of our urban housing markets to provide inexpensive housing have compounded the difficulties of the poor. The largest cities, such as New York and Los Angeles, have seen the most precipitous decline in low-cost housing stock but in degrees that have characterized all cities of all sizes. The Annual Housing Surveys, conducted annually by the Census for the Department of Housing and Urban Development, have recorded declines in city after city in the supply of housing that rents for 40% or less of poverty level incomes. These declines ranged from 12% in Baltimore between 1978 and 1983, to 40% in Washington, D.C. between 1977 and 1981, and to 58% in Anaheim, California in the same period. In 12 large cities surveyed between 1978 and 1983, the amount of inexpensive rental housing available to poor families dropped by about 30%. At the same time, the number of households living at or below the poverty level in the same cities increased by 36%. The consequence of these two trends is that in the early 1980s there developed a severe shortage of that housing affordable by poor households without imposing excessive rent burdens. These calculations assume, incidentally, that poor households can "afford" to spend 40% of their income on housing, a higher figure than the customary and more prudent 25% suggested by mortgage lenders.[37]

In addition, federal programs that support the construction of public housing or provide housing subsidies for poor households have seen either severe cut-backs or stringent funding levels in the 1980s, further exacerbating the shortage of low cost housing for families.[38]

Most of the rental housing discussed above consists of multi-room units appropriate to families. If we restrict our attention to that portion of the rental housing stock ordinarily occupied by poor unattached single persons, then the declines are even more precipitous. Chicago's Planning Department estimated that between 1973 and 1984, 18,000 single person dwelling units (largely, rooms in SRO hotels and small apartments), amounting to 19% of the stock existing in 1973, were demolished or transformed for other uses.[39] The Chicago experience is not unique. Similar losses in the SRO stock have occurred in Seattle, Boston, New York, Nashville, Los Angeles, Philadelphia, and probably most other cities. Indeed, a recent report indicated that between 1970 and 1985, more than half of the SRO units in downtown Los Angeles had been demolished.[40]

Some cities experienced the almost complete demolition of the flophouse hotels in the 1960s and 1970s. In 1958, such units in Chicago accommodated about 8,000 homeless men; by 1980, none of these units remained in Chicago. Although no one can mourn their passing, their demolition was not accompanied by housing that was inexpensive enough to be afforded by the extremely poor.[41]

The decline of "affordable" housing affected the vulnerable among the extremely poor in two ways: First, their primary kin who are also poor faced increased rent burdens thereby lessening their capacity for generosity. Second, the supply of extremely inexpensive housing for persons living alone has shrunk drastically. Ironically, the emergency shelters, clearly the cheapest housing currently available, have replaced the flophouse.

VI. WHAT CAN BE DONE?

The new homeless should remind us that the social welfare safety nets that we started to build during the Great Depression and significantly augmented in the 1960s are failing to prevent extreme destitution among increasingly large numbers of the American population. The failure of the welfare system to cover those who are vulnerable to homelessness is a long-standing fault of a system that essentially ignores the income support problems faced by unmarried and unattached adults. The Reagan Administration has not succeeded in dismantling any significant portion of the net, but it has certainly made the mesh so coarse and weak that many fall through and hit the bottom. Those who are disabled by the handicaps of minority status, chronic mental illness, physical illness, or substance abuse easily fall through this net.

The social welfare system has never paid much attention to unmarried and unattached men, but now the system appears to be as unresponsive to women in the same position. The slow erosion of the safety net has left gaps in the system through which have fallen the men and women of the streets, the shelters, and the welfare hotels. Likewise, the social welfare system does little to help families support their dependent adult members. Many of the old homeless, those of the 1950s and early 1960s, were pushed out or thrown away by their families when they passed the peak of adulthood; many of the new homeless are products of a similar process, but one which commences at age 25 or 30 rather than at 50 or 60.

As a consequence, homelessness now looms large on our political agenda, and there is much anxious concern about what can be done. Without going into detail, there are a number of measures that might be taken to reduce homelessness to a more acceptable level. These include: (1) compensating for the failures of our housing market by fostering the retention and enlargement of our urban low-income housing stock, especially that appropriate for unattached persons;[42] (2) reversing the policy of the last two decades that has put personal choice above institutionalization for those so severely disabled that they are unable to make choices that will preserve their lives and physical well being;[43] (3) enlarging our conception of disability to include conditions not purely physical in character, and in particular, recognizing chronic mental illness and chronic alcoholism for the often profound disabilities that they are; (4) restoring the real value of welfare payments to levels above that of bare subsistence, to the purchasing power that they had in the late 1960s; and, (5) extending the benefits of the income maintenance provisions of our welfare system to unmarried and unattached adults who are not senior citizens and to the households that provide them with shelter and support.

There is considerable public support in the United States for a social welfare system that guarantees a minimally decent standard of living to all. Homelessness on the scale currently being experienced clearly evinces that we do not yet have that system in place. That homelessness exists amidst national prosperity literally without parallel in the history of the world is likewise clear evidence that we can do something about the problem if we choose to. The analysis presented in this paper stressed the point that public policy decisions have in large measure created the problem of homelessness; they can solve the problem as well.

The measures suggested above address the short term problems presented by the current high levels of homelessness. The long run solutions must address the problem of providing employment and thereby income to young people entering the labor market and of providing reasonable employment and income levels throughout the life course. Insuring that minority youths integrate into the labor force presents a critical point. When every able-bodied and able-minded person in our society in his or her life course can make a smooth transition to self-supporting adulthood and when everyone who fails to do so because of disabilities is supported generously by a strong social welfare safety net then the problem of homelessness will be diminished to acceptable levels.

NOTES

1. *See* Hopper, *The Public Response to Homelessness in New York City: The Last Hundred Years* in ON BEING HOMELESS: HISTORICAL PERSPECTIVES (R. Beard ed. 1987); Hopper, Susser & Conover, *Economies of Makeshift: Deindustrialization and Homelessness in New York City*, 14 URB ANTHROPOLOGY 183 (1986).

2. N. ANDERSON, MEN ON THE MOVE (1940); J.P.H. SCHUBERT, TWENTY THOUSAND TRANSIENTS: A YEAR'S SAMPLE OF THOSE WHO APPLY FOR AID IN A NORTHERN CITY (1935); Wickendon, *Reminiscences of the Program for Transients and Homeless in the Thirties* in ON BEING HOMELESS: HISTORICAL PERSPECTIVES (R. Beard ed. 1987).

3. The descriptions of the homeless of the 1950s and 1960s is based on empirical social research undertaken in those years. In particular, I have relied most heavily on monographs by Bogue, Blumberg, and Bahr and Caplow who conducted surveys of homeless persons respectively in Chicago, Philadelphia and New York. *See* H.M. BAHR & T. CAPLOW, OLD MEN: DRUNK AND SOBER (1974); L. BLUMBERG, T.E. SHIPLEY, JR. & I.W. SHANDLER, SKID ROW AND ITS ALTERNATIVES (1973); D.B. BOGUE, SKID ROW IN AMERICAN CITIES (1963).

4. The data lying behind the statements in this section concerning the current homeless come from more than 40 studies of homeless people conducted in the 1980s and are summarized in detail in P.H. ROSSI, DOWN AND OUT IN AMERICA: THE ORIGINS OF HOMELESSNESS (1989). Particular reliance is based on data derived from a survey of the Chicago homeless conducted by the author in 1985 and 1986 and reported in P.H. ROSSI, G.A. FISHER & G. WILLIS, THE CONDITION OF THE HOMELESS OF CHICAGO (1986).

5. Interestingly enough, the current homeless resemble more closely the transient homeless of the thirties, except for the heavy representation of minority groups. The transient homeless of the Great Depression were young males, many of whom had never been employed since entering the labor market.

6. Almost all of the homeless "families" are unmarried women whose families consist of their minor children.

7. Indeed, that is the meaning of homelessness as applied to the Skid Row populations of the 1950s and 1960s. Almost all had shelter but none was living with a spouse.

8. These are also people who are not students or living on farms. Computed from the Current Population Surveys, an annual survey of 55,000 households conducted annually by the Bureau of the Census. Details of these calculations can be found in P.H. ROSSI, *supra* note 4, at 75–78.

9. The Current Population Survey is based on households living in apartments, single family homes, and mobile homes. Persons living in hotels or motels, boarding houses, or in group quarters such as shelters are not sampled.

10. Existing social statistics are based on surveys and censuses of persons living in conventional dwellings. Hence our major sources of information on the demographic composition of Americans miss those who live in shelters or out on the streets. The best current national estimate of the homeless is based on surveys conducted within shelters and with users of food kitchens set up to serve homeless persons. M. BURT & B.E. COHEN, FEEDING THE HOMELESS: DOES THE PREPARED MEAL PROVISION HELP? (1988).

11. If we take $4,000 annually as the upper boundary of the extremely poor, their numbers almost double and the proportion homeless drops to around 5%.

12. *See generally* P.H. ROSSI, *supra* note 4, at 190–94. In Illinois, maximum General Assistance payments are $154 a month certainly insufficient for living alone. For a discussion of the Chicago General Assistance Study (GAS), see *id*. at 85.

13. *Id*. at 80–81.

14 M. STAGNER & H. RICHMAN, GENERAL ASSISTANCE PROFILES; FINDINGS FROM A LONGITUDINAL STUDY OF NEWLY APPROVED RECIPIENTS (1985). M. STAGNER & H. RICHMAN, HELP-SEEKING AND THE USE OF SOCIAL SERVICE PROVIDERS BY WELFARE FAMILIES IN CHICAGO (1986).

15. Much of the evidence bolstering the arguments presented in this section are given in great detail in A.S. ROSSI & P.H. ROSSI, OF HUMAN BONDING: PARENT CHILD RELATIONS ACROSS THE LIFE COURSE (1989).

16. A.S. ROSSI & P.H. ROSSI, *supra* note 15, report that the strength of intra-kin obligations is directly proportional to the number of descent linkages intervening between the kin in question. Hence the strength of the parental bond.

17. P.H. ROSSI, *supra* note 4, at 169.

18. Piliavin & Sosin, *Tracking the Homeless*, FOCUS, Winter 1987–88, at 20.

19. P.H. ROSSI, *supra* note 4, at 114–15.

20. *Id*. at 170–71, 188–90.

21. *Id*. at 31. *See also* D.B. BOGUE, *supra* note 3.

22. P.H. ROSSI, *supra* note 4, at 191.

23. *Id*. at 191 & n. 13.

24. *Id*. at 191–92.

25. In states that have enacted Aid for Families with Dependent Children— Unemployed Parent (AFDC-UP), husband and wife families with dependent children are eligible.

26. P.H. ROSSI, *supra* note 4, at 85 n.4. Indeed, in most states, welfare departments try to get destitute people on federally subsidized programs, defining General Assistance as that program for which people are eligible if they are extremely poor and not eligible for any other programs.

27. *Id*. at 191.

28. Average monthly rental in Chicago's SRO (single room only) hotels was $195 in 1984. *Id*. at 183.

29. Applying for General Assistance in Illinois involves a sequence of several interviews which may not be formidable for most but may be difficult for persons who have neither appointment books or watches. *See id.* at 192–93.
30. Bogue used interns and residents to review the protocols of interviews undertaken with homeless persons to provide diagnoses of disabling conditions. Current studies used a variety of methods from psychiatrists' examinations to standardized interviews. As noted earlier, the prevalence rates for current studies converge on 33%. For a discussion on mental illness among the homeless, see *id.* at 145–56.
31. *See generally* Lamb. *Involuntary Treatment fort the Homeless Mentally Ill*, 4 NOTRE DAME J.L. ETHICS & PUB. POL'Y 269 (1989). For a discussion of alcoholism and drug abuse among the homeless, see P.H. ROSSI, *supra* note 4, at 156–67.
32. *See generally* Lamb, *supra* note 31.
33. Of course, this finding may merely reflect that those who managed to qualify for disability payments are by that fact lifted out of the homeless category. Payments in 1985 under SSDI averaged almost $484 and under SSI $261 per month. P.H. ROSSI, *supra* note 4, at 191.
34. For a discussion of alcoholism and drug abuse among the homeless, see *id.* at 156–57.
35. *See* Bowen v. City of New York, 476 U.S. 467 (1986) (concerning procedure utilized by the Social Security Administration in determination of eligibility for disability benefits).
36. Glick & Lin, *More Young Adults Are Living with Their Parents: Who Are They?*, 48 J. MARRIAGE & FAM. 107 (1986). The comparable proportions for white males were 39% in 1970 and 41% in 1984.
37. All these figures are taken from Wright & Lam, *Homelessness and the Low Income Housing Supply*, SOC. POL'Y, Spring 1987, at 48.
38. Salsich, *Nonprofit Housing Organizations*, 4 NOTRE DAME J.L. ETHICS & PUB. POL'Y 228 (1989).
39. During the same period, incidentally, 11,000 subsidized senior citizen units were added to the stock and 8,500 Section 8 senior citizen housing vouchers were issued. Thus, provision was made for the replacement of lost housing stock, but overwhelmingly, the replacements consisted of subsidized housing for persons 65 and over. For more information, see CHICAGO DEPT. OF PLANNING, *Housing Needs of Chicago's Single, Low Income Renters* (June 1985) (manuscript report) and C. HOCH & D. SPICER, SROS, AN ENDANGERED SPECIES: SINGLE-ROOM OCCUPANCY HOTELS IN CHICAGO (1985). The latter reports that 22,603 SRO rooms in Chicago were lost (condemned, demolished, or converted to other uses) between 1973 and 1985.
40. HAMILTON, RABINOWITZ & ALSCHULER, INC., A SOCIAL SERVICES AND SHELTER RESOURCE INVENTORY OF THE LOS ANGELES SKID ROW AREA (1986).
41. *See* Salsich, *supra* note 38.
42. *See* Salsich, *supra* note 38.
43. *See* Lamb, *supra* note 31.

Homeless Men and the Work Ethic

Richard J. First
Ohio State University

Beverly G. Toomey
Ohio State University

This article discusses policy development and service delivery issues for homeless men. Data from a statewide study of 793 homeless men are analyzed to identify disability and dependency levels. Three groups are defined: about a quarter are severely disabled; a third need a moderate range of services; and the remainder are displaced from the work force but capable of independence. Clearly, homeless men are not a single population, different levels of intervention are suggested.

INTRODUCTION

The presence of working-age homeless men presents a serious problem in a society organized around the work ethic and individualism. To provide benefits to these men, it is argued, is to encourage their non-participation in the labor market, reduce their motivation, and possibly increase their dependency on the working members of society. Yet these individuals still have needs related to their survival and sustenance. Thus, a basic value conflict exists that limits our ability to understand and to act effectively in response to the problem of men who cannot or do not work to support themselves.[1]

The provision of services to homeless men in the United States has traditionally been left to religious and charitable endeavors. Programs involving cash and in-kind benefits in the public sector have served the needs of women and children, the elderly, and the handicapped. Able-bodied males, who neither fit these categories nor meet the demands of the job market, are left with very few sources of support. The stigma of public dependency persists for males. Such dependency is clearly at odds with the work ethic that is at the foundation of policy making in relation to the problem of homelessness. Because homelessness carries with it the label of adult male dependency, solutions, or the lack thereof, are linked to a value structure that continues to focus on the personal deficits of homeless men and the perceived threat that these nonproductive single males pose for the larger society.

This article is concerned with the task of policy development and service delivery for homeless men. Findings are based on a statewide study in Ohio of 979 homeless persons (793 men) completed in 1985.[2] The intent is to focus on homelessness among males,the largest and most visible subgroup within the homeless population.[3]

STATEMENT OF THE PROBLEM

Since the beginning the 1980s, the public has been exposed to increasing numbers of single individuals, largely male, living on the streets and in public places.[4] High visibility has resulted in growing public recognition of their social condition and desperate plight as the poorest of the poor. Although visibly present on the streets, individual homeless men are, ironically, unrecognizable. This phenomenon is described by Michael Harrington in *The New American Poverty* "In conservative periods we become honestly, sincerely myopic: we literally cannot see the poor."[5] These individuals are a reminder that there are holes in the social safety net with respect to housing, health care, and economic well-being.

As with most emerging or rapidly changing social problems, there is not an accepted definition of the problem, and solutions are elusive. Systematic intervention strategies designed to address long-term dependency continue to founder. Policymakers at all levels of government seem unable to make choices that move beyond short-term emergency relief. A major issue remains unresolved. Where is the locus of responsibility, in the victim or in the social system?

Barriers to action rest on fundamental value assumptions about individualism and on the belief that the provision of welfare benefits leads to the perpetuation of dependency. Alexis de Tocqueville in his 1835 "Memoir on Pauperism," defined the problem: "Any measure that establishes legal charity on a permanent basis and gives it an administrative form thereby creates an idle and lazy class, living at the expense of the industrial and working class."[6]

This 150-year-old definition of the problem is still alive in the current debate on policy development for homeless persons. Traditional values of individualism and the work ethic are deeply rooted and serve to block efforts to answer such basic questions as, Who should be helped? What kind of aid/benefit should be provided? What outcomes can be achieved?

This article will examine policy questions with respect to homeless males. Utilizing a sample large enough to represent the various types of homeless conditions, levels of disability are identified, and differential implications for policy making are presented.

METHODOLOGY

Using a combination of random and purposive sampling methods, 979 interviews were conducted in 19 Ohio counties, including 5 major urban counties and 14 predominantly rural counties with small cities. Sampling methods varied by urban and rural location. After a random selection of rural counties, all persons identified as homeless by key informants in the county during the project data collection period were interviewed. Following the purposive selection of five urban counties, all possible sites where homeless people could be found were identified, with the assistance of key informants, and subjects were randomly selected within sites. A maximum of five homeless persons were interviewed in any one location.

The definition of homelessness guiding the study included people living on the streets with no shelter, those living in cars and in abandoned buildings, those staying in shelters, missions, or drop-ins, those staying for short periods in single room occupancy (SRO) hotels, and those moving between family and friends. An individual was deemed to be homeless if he had been living in a particular location less than 45 days. This cap was used to make the distinction between people who move in and out of hotels or family and friends' homes and those who intend to stay in a particular location on a more permanent basis.

A total of 979 individuals (793 men and 86 women) were interviewed face-to-face from March to August 1984. Interviewers were selected who could engage and develop rapport with subjects. The instrument included items on the conditions of homelessness, needs, demographic characteristics, health problems, and mental status as measured by 10 scales from the Psychiatric Status Schedule (PSS).[7] The length of interviews averaged about 1 hour. Contact logs maintained by interviewers revealed about a 10 percent refusal rate. Analysis of demographic characteristics indicates refusers did not differ substantially from individuals included in the study.

Categorizing Needs Groups

Findings were analyzed to identify factors associated with dependency and to examine the levels of disability which limit self-support. A psychiatric severity index was created using standardized cutoffs from four of the PSS scales; a behavioral disturbance index was created in the same fashion using five of the PSS scales. Using scores on these scales, history of prior hospitalizations, and evidence of alcohol abuse, categories of disability were formed. This categorization is suggested as a description not only of the level of functional impairment but also the potential to benefit from various programs and services. Three subgroups, as shown in table 1, were formed: (1) long-term needs group; (2) moderate needs group; and (3) short-term needs group.

Diversity in the homeless population has been well established in prior work.[8] The causes of differences in service needs and the ability of the homeless to respond to services are less clear. Therefore,education/ employment history, health/disability status, and social/family supports were analyzed to establish each group's relative psychosocial resources and needs. This description cannot be interpreted to provide causal linkages between disability conditions and demographic or resource variables. The relationships between demographic characteristics, social supports, and mental health status of homeless persons are not yet clearly understood. Nevertheless, categorizing by need group may enable the design of specialized and more effective interventions for homeless men.

Characteristics of Homeless Men

The homeless men interviewed in this study have a median age of 35 and have been homeless for an average of 90 days. Sixty-five percent are white, 31 percent are black, and 5 percent are of Hispanic or other racial origin. More than one-half (53%) did not finish high school, and 65 percent state that they have been in jail or prison. Only 8 percent were married or living with someone at the time they were interviewed. Thirty-nine percent are veterans and approximately 10 percent served in the Vietnam War (see table 2).

While the vast majority of homeless people are living in urban areas, this study included rural homeless: 16 percent of the men in the sample were living in rural areas. Contrary to the popular image, the majority of homeless men do not tend to be either mobile (moving within the city) or transient (moving between cities and states). Almost two-thirds of the homeless men were either born in the counties in which they were interviewed or had lived there longer than a year (see table 3).

Men were homeless for a variety of reasons, but economic and family problems emerge as central themes. Half of the respondents cited economic factors such as unemployment, problems paying rent, eviction, or termination of benefits as the primary reasons for their loss of a permanent home. Family conflict or dissolution was the cause of homelessness for 18 percent.

GROUP 1: LONG-TERM NEEDS GROUP

Group 1 homeless men are defined as those who are the most severely disabled. This group includes men who had scores indicating serious mental illness on three or four of the four scales used in the psychiatric severity index or scored high on four or five of the five scales used in the behavioral disturbances index. Also included are those who had been hospitalized for mental illness five or more times and those who reported they had been treated for alcohol abuse and were currently drinking "a lot." This group included 188 men, 23.7 percent of the total number of men interviewed. These men have serious personal limitations and also lack the resources to establish an independent life-style to meet their basic needs for food, clothing, and shelter.

Comparison with other groups reveals that group 1 comprises more older men, more veterans, more whites, and men more likely to have been in jail or prison (see table 2). They are more frequently found living "on the street" and more often in contact with religious missions or other services offered on a drop-in basis. These men have many serious problems: 14 percent have serious psychiatric disabilities and another third have mild impairments; serious or mild behavioral disturbances afflict 56 percent; and 61 percent are using alcohol excessively. Forty-eight percent of the men in this group have been hospitalized for mental illness with a mean number of hospitalizations of 6.5 (see table 4).

Table 5 displays limitations in employment and education, which indicate a negative prognosis for return to total independence. A series of questions revealed that about a fifth of this group reports they are too disabled to work, 17 percent left their last job for poor health or alcohol abuse, and 27 percent are currently receiving disability or other pensions. Limited support from family and friends (see table 6) combined with the high incidence of mental or behavioral disorders and substance abuse have resulted in a very isolated life-style. The prospects for individuals in this group returning to total independence are very limited. Many will need consistent, long-term support at a level that assures that basic needs for food, shelter, and related social supports are provided.

GROUP 2: MODERATE NEEDS GROUP

Group 2 homeless men are moderately disabled but can be viewed as having the potential for maintaining a semi-independent life-style. They have a higher level of personal and social resources than group 1. The criteria for inclusion in this group were men who had scores indicating serious impairment on one or two of the PSS psychiatric severity scales or two or three of the behavioral disturbance scales or were hospitalized for mental illness two to four times. These criteria defined a group of 263 men, 33 percent of the sample. These men are not seen as seriously disabled, but rather in need of income plus intensive training and rehabilitation services to help them return to a more independent and comfortable existence. Members of this group have more moderate disabilities and a stronger personal potential for independent maintenance. The men of group 2 are younger than those of group 1, there are a greater percentage of blacks, more Vietnam veterans, and more men who have never married. Men in this group frequently find shelter in SROs and with friends and relatives.

Fifty-four percent of the men in group 2 were found to have mild psychiatric impairment as measured by the psychiatric severity index, but, by definition, none with severe and protracted mental illness are in this group.

Many (61%) have mild behavioral disturbances. About a third of the men in this category have been hospitalized for mental illness but only 14 percent indicate they have been drinking "a lot." Only 13 percent of this group report they are not working because they are disabled, 7 percent left their last job due to health or alcohol abuse reasons, and only 11 percent are on disability payments or pensions. In comparison with the other categories, more of these men were fired from their last job or have never held a job. Better mental health status, less substance abuse, and better employment history in this group indicate the potential benefit of rehabilitative efforts. The immediate needs of this group of homeless men are a combination of economic and social supports. Serious barriers exist for their long-term success in a secondary job market that involves episodic and part-time employment.

GROUP 3: SHORT-TERM NEEDS GROUP

Group 3 consists of men who are the least at risk of long term homelessness. Men were specifically placed in this group if their scores did not fall in the impaired range on the PSS and if they did not meet the criteria for inclusion in group 1 or group 2. The indicators of dependency are lower and fall more in the area of economic factors. These individuals had an immediate crisis in their housing, family composition, or employment. The term "episodic homeless" has been used to describe this portion of the population. Group 3 members have the fewest serious disabilities and the most positive work histories (see tables 2-5). Service needs for single males in this category are minimal except for shelter under the auspices of voluntary and religious organizations. The number of homeless men who fall in this category is high, 342 (43%) of the study sample.

IMPLICATIONS

The traditional idea that the public benefits for able-bodied men weaken the work ethic presents a serious barrier to policy-making and change in the provision of services to the homeless. Common myths and stereotypes defining homeless men as "skid row buns," transients, alcoholics, or loiterers reduce the prospects for recognition of the underlying disabilities and economic barriers confronting homeless persons.

Economic Barriers

The data reported in this study clearly document that a substantial portion of homeless men have been and probably can be in the labor force. The men in group 3 are mainly employable; however, current public policy does not adequately address employment issues for this group of men, preferring instead to label as unworthy those who cannot secure or maintain their place in a changing labor market. These men are the reserve that makes cheap labor possible. In a secondary labor market, which is marked by unemployment and low wages, many homeless people have reached the bottom. With changes in employment policy that increase wages for low skill jobs, they can be employed and can be helped to return to independent living with minimal investment from human service programs—retraining, job finding, and emergency shelter. These men are caught in the squeeze because their skills are marginal and their family relationships are marked by conflict. Confronted by unemployment and high cost housing, they are pushed into the streets where many may simply stop trying.

Diversity and Disability Levels

This data indicated that homeless men are not a single population with one common, problem condition. While short-term assistance is appropriate for some (group 3), the moderately and seriously disabled (groups 2 and 1) require intense and perhaps long-term services to interrupt the cycle of homelessness.

The men in group 2 are in need of substantial services. Many need physical and mental health care, and some need alcohol rehabilitation. A great percentage could benefit from vocational training to improve employability and counseling to reduce family alienation. For this third of the homeless males there is reason to be optimistic but only with extensive rehabilitation efforts. Policy efforts should be aimed toward flexible employment, which recognizes their limitations and promotes their strengths. One possible future strategy is to develop more sheltered employment and public service jobs in conjunction with supportive services.

There is an unwillingness to accept the idea that some homeless men, such as those in group 1, will need continuous community care and the constant investment of community resources. Recognition of the problem of long-term dependency of working-age males is still absent from the literature on homelessness. Often, the work ethic is applied to this group with little recognition of these individuals' limited capacity to become self-sufficient.

Policymakers are becoming aware of the diversity of the homeless population: persons unable to find work because of lack of job skills, persons whose families have disintegrated and are no longer able to live in low-income housing or SRO hotels, seriously mentally and physically ill men without family or friends, and young people who are unable to enter the labor market but cannot continue to reside with their family of origin. This knowledge is beginning to affect the design of services in major cities of America. Nevertheless the work ethic—deeply ingrained in the morals of this country—is a barrier to this recognition.

It is probable that almost half of these homeless men could return to independence following short-term interventions and policy initiatives leading to job creation. It is also evident that another third of the homeless men would benefit from intensive rehabilitative services so that they could return to some form of independent or at least semi-independent living arrangements. However, the data in this study reveal that a quarter of our homeless male population is seriously disabled. These men have extremely limited personal and social resources to support attainment of independent living status. The solution for this group cannot be found in the traditional belief that we must "fix" the needy so that they are restored to independence; rather, this society must accept the evidence that some relatively few of our members cannot take care of themselves and do not have family support systems to take responsibility for them.[9] The burden of their care falls to society. The social policy of a humane society ought to reflect this reality if its neediest members are to be removed from the shame of living in the streets.

NOTES

This research was carried out by the Ohio Department of Mental Health and funded by the National Institute of Mental Health grant 1R18MH38877-01. We gratefully acknowledge the assistance of Jerry Bean, Terry Buss, Harvey Hilbert, Thomas P. Holland, Steven R. Howe, James A. King, Nancy Lust, William Muraco, Dee Roth, and Mary E. Strefl.
1. Frances Fox Piven and Richard A. Cloward, "The Contemporary Relief Debate," in *The Mean Season*, ed. Fred Block et al. (New York: Pantheon, 1987), pp. 45–108.
2. Dee Roth, Jerry Bean, Nancy Lust, and Traian Saveanu, *Homelessness in Ohio: A Study of People in Need* (Columbus: Ohio Department of Mental Health, Office of Program Evaluation and Research, 1985).
3. Additional analysis of this data base has addressed the equally important characteristics and service needs of homeless women. See Dee Roth,Beverly Toomey, and Richard First, "Homeless Women: Characteristics and Needs," *Affilia* 2 (Winter 1987): 6–19.
4. See Kim Hopper and Ellen Baxter, *Private Lives/Public Spaces: Homeless Adults on the Streets of New York City* (New York: Community Services Society, 1981); M. J. Stern, "The Emergence of Homelessness as a Public Problem," *Social Service Review* 58 (June 1984): 291–301; Dee Roth, Beverly Toomey, and Richard First, "Gender, Age and Racial Variations," in *Homelessness: The National Perspective*, ed. Marjorie Robertson and M. Greenblatt (New York: Plenum, 1989), in press.
5. Michael Harrington, *The New American Poverty* (New York: Holt, Rinehart & Winston, 1984), p. 94.
6. Alexis de Tocqueville, "Memoir on Pauperism," in *Tocqueville and Beaumont on Social Reform*, ed. and trans. Seymour Drescher (New York: Harper Torchbooks, 1968), pp. 1–27.
7. R. L. Spitzer, J. Endicott, and J. Cohen, "The Psychiatric Status Schedule: A Technique for Evaluating Psychopathology and Impairment in Role Functioning,"*Archives of General Psychiatry* 23 (1970): 41–55; R. L. Spitzer, J. Endicott, J. Cohen, and J. Nee, "The Psychiatric Status Schedule for Epidemiological Research," *Archives of General Psychiatry* 37 (1980): 1193–97.

8. See Dee Roth, Beverly Toomey, and Richard First, "Gender, Age and Racial Variations"; Richard First,Dee Roth, and Bobbie Darden Arewa, "Homelessness: Understanding the Dimensions of the Problem for Minorities," *Social Work* 33 (March–April 1988): 120–24.
9. See Robert N. Bellah, Richard Madsen, William M. Sullivan, Anne Swidler, and Steven M. Tipton, *Habits of the Heart* (New York: Harper & Row, 1985), pp. 167–274; Diana M. DiNitto and Thomas R. Dye, *Social Welfare Politics and Public Policy* (Englewood Cliffs, N.J.: Prentice-Hall, 1987), pp. 1–21.

Table 1

CLASSIFICATION OF NEEDS GROUPS

Group	Need Category	Level of Psychological Impairment	Level of Natural Social Supports	Potential Independence Status	Intervention Strategy
1	Long-term needs	Severe	Poor	Dependent	Stabilization and long-term care
2	Moderate needs	Mild	Poor	Semi-independent	Extended economic support and intensive rehabilitation
3	Short-term needs	Low	Fair	Independent	Immediate economic assistance and vocational support

Table 2

DEMOGRAPHIC CHARACTERISTICS OF HOMELESS MEN BY NEEDS GROUP

VARIABLES	TOTAL SAMPLE (N = 793 [100%])	GROUPS		
		(1) Long-Term (n = 188 [23.7%])	(2) Moderate (n = 263 [33.2%])	(3) Short-Term (n = 342 [43.1%])
Median age (in years)	35	39.0	34.0	36.0
Race:				
White	64.9	69.6	55.1	69.7
Black	30.5	26.6	37.6	26.3
Other	4.5	4.3	5.3	4.1
Education:				
Less than high school	53.0	50.5	54.9	52.6
High school graduate	31.5	27.7	33.5	31.6
Some college	15.5	19.2	12.3	15.8
Marital status:				
Married, living together	8.3	3.7	8.4	10.8
Separated/widow/divorced	44.6	50.0	40.3	45.1
Never married	46.7	45.7	49.8	44.2
Jail or prison	65.1	75.5	61.2	62.3
Veteran status	38.5	42.6	33.1	40.1
Vietnam service	10.3	9.6	12.2	9.4

NOTE.—All numbers except age indicate percentages.

Table 3

CHARACTERISTICS OF HOMELESS CONDITIONS BY NEEDS GROUP

VARIABLES	TOTAL SAMPLE (N = 793 [100%])	GROUPS		
		(1) Long-Term (n = 188 [23.7%])	(2) Moderate (n = 263 [33.2%])	(3) Short-Term (n = 342 [43.1%])
Mobility:				
Permanent resident	41.2	43.1	47.2	33.3
Longer than 1 year	22.3	24.5	21.3	21.9
Less than 1 year	36.4	31.9	29.3	44.5
Median no. of places stayed last month	2	2	2	2
Reason for homelessness:				
Economic	49.7	44.7	49.8	52.3
Alcohol/drug abuse	8.7	21.3	6.5	3.5
Family conflicts	17.6	16.0	17.1	18.7
Homeless type:				
Street	15.6	18.6	17.5	12.6
Shelter	58.8	60.6	53.2	62.0
Resource	21.8	15.9	25.5	22.2
Type of county:				
Urban	83.9	92.0	83.7	79.5
Rural	16.1	8.0	16.4	20.0

NOTE.—All numbers except places stayed last month indicate percentages.

Table 4

SEVERITY OF HEALTH-RELATED PROBLEMS

PROBLEMS	TOTAL SAMPLE (N = 793 [100%])	(1) Long-Term (n = 188 [23.7%])	(2) Moderate (n = 263 [33.2%])	(3) Short-Term (n = 342 [43.1%])
			GROUPS	
Medical problems	28.6	31.1	32.3	24.3
Serious psychiatric impairment	3.4	14.4	0	0
Mild psychiatric impairment	26.3	36.2	53.6	0
Serious behavioral disturbance	7.4	31.4	0	0
Mild behavioral disturbance	26.6	25.0	61.4	0
Alcohol	12.0	61.2	13.7	7.3
Hospitalized/mental health	29.9	47.9	31.9	18.4

NOTE.—All numbers indicate percentages.

Table 5

INDICATIONS OF ECONOMIC DEPENDENCY

VARIABLES	TOTAL SAMPLE (N = 793 [100%])	GROUPS		
		(1) Long-Term (n = 188 [23.7%])	(2) Moderate (n = 263 [33.2%])	(3) Short-Term (n = 342 [43.1%])
Reason for not working:				
Disabled	14.3	20.2	13.3	11.7
Why last job ended:				
Fired	10.5	10.6	13.3	8.2
Poor health (physical/mental/alcohol abuse)	11.1	17.0	7.2	10.8
Quit	9.0	9.5	9.1	8.5
Never had a job	11.9	11.6	12.2	3.8
Receiving pension (Veterans' Administration/disability/age)	14.6	26.6	10.7	11.1

NOTE.—All numbers indicate percentages.

Table 6

LIMITATIONS IN SOCIAL SUPPORT INHIBITING INDEPENDENCE

SOURCES	TOTAL SAMPLE (N = 793 [100%])	GROUPS		
		(1) Long-Term (n = 188 [23.7%])	(2) Moderate (n = 263 [33.2%])	(3) Short-Term (n = 342 [42.1%])
No relatives to count on	62.8	67.0	69.2	55.6
No friends to count on	59.6	64.3	65.0	52.9

NOTE.—All numbers indicate percentages.

The Worthy and Unworthy Homeless

James D. Wright

Americans have always found it necessary to distinguish between the "deserving" and "undeserving" poor—the former, victims of circumstances beyond their control who merit compassion; the latter, lazy, shiftless bums who could do better for themselves "if they wanted to" and who therefore merit contempt. The ensuing tension in our collective attitude toward the poor is reflected both in public policy and in public opinion surveys. A 1984 survey asked people to agree or disagree, that "most people who do not get ahead in life probably work just as hard as people who do." Forty-seven percent agreed with this sentiment, 44 percent disagreed, and the remainder were neutral or had no opinion. In the same survey, 84 percent agreed that "any person who is willing to work hard has a good chance of succeeding" but 80 percent also agreed that "even if people try hard they often cannot reach their goals."

Poverty in America has become visible again, both as a phenomenon and as a public policy issue. I refer specifically to the apparently dramatic increase in homelessness that has occurred in the past several years and to the media and political attention that the problem of homelessness has received. These days, homeless and destitute people can be found wandering the streets of any large urban area; no one can possibly remain oblivious to their existence. What to do about or for the homeless has likewise become an important political issue, with some thirty-two separate bills introduced

James D. Wright is the Charles and Leo Favrot Professor of Human Relations in the Department of Sociology at Tulane University. He has written thirteen books, including: *The State of the Masses*, with Richard Hamilton; *Under the Gun*, with Peter Rossi and Kathleen Daly; and, most recently, *Homelessness and Health*, with Dee Weber.

in the Hundredth Congress that deal with one or another aspect of the homelessness problem.

So far, the homeless seem to be included among the "deserving poor," at least by the general public. A recent national survey by the Roper Organization reported by *Newsweek* on September 21, 1987, asked what problems we should be spending more money on. "Caring for the homeless" was the top priority item, favored by 68 percent. (In contrast, foreign aid was mentioned by only 5 percent, and "military, armaments, and defense" by only 17 percent.) Thus, most people seem to feel that the homeless deserve our help, if not our compassion. But an opposite, more mean-spirited view has also begun to surface. On December 1, 1986, Stuart Bykofsky wrote a "My Turn" column for *Newsweek* magazine entitled "No Heart for the Homeless." The analysis turned on the division of the homeless into three groups: "(1) the economically distressed, who would work if they could find work; (2) the mentally ill, who can't work; (3) the alcoholic, the drug-addicted, and others who won't work." His solution to the problem was workfare for the first group, mental institutions for the second, and indifference to (or outright hostility toward) the third.

Bykofsky's simplistic categorization was unburdened by numbers or percentages, and so we are not told how many of the homeless fit his various types. Concurrent with the increased media and political attention being given to the problem, there has also been an outpouring of research studies that provide reliable guides to the relative proportions of "worthy" and "unworthy" homeless. My aim here is to review the findings of some of these studies, to see if we cannot be more precise about how many homeless deserve our sympathies and how many do not.

The many recent studies available for our use are uneven in coverage and quality. The largest and most geographically dispersed sample of homeless people available is that contained in *Homelessness and Health*, my study of clients seen in the National Health Care for the Homeless Program (HCH). Data for the first year of the HCH program describe nearly 30,000 homeless people seen in health clinics in sixteen large cities all over the country. Because of its size, geographical dispersion, and my familiarity with the results, I use the findings from this study extensively in the following discussion.

A second study upon which I have drawn is the Peter H. Rossi et al. survey of homeless people in Chicago, *The Condition of the Homeless in Chicago*. One problem faced by many studies is that they are based exclusively on shelter users; it has long been recognized that the shelter users are only one of two important components of the homeless population, the other being "street homeless" who, for whatever reason, rarely or never use the shelter system. One among many virtues of the Rossi et al. survey is its extremely thorough and systematic sampling of the street homeless. This fact, coupled with the breadth of topics covered and the general degree of sophistication in the conduct of the research, make the Chicago survey especially useful.

Neither of the above sources provides answers to all the important questions, and so in some cases I have relied on other research. In all cases, I have sacrificed technical niceties for completeness of coverage, knowing full well that new and better research will no doubt change the picture, at least in small details.

For convenience, it is useful to begin by imagining a sample of 1,000 homeless people, drawn at random, let us say, from the half million or so homeless people to be found in America on any given evening. Based on the research I have sketched, we can then begin to cut up this sample in various ways, so as to portray as graphically as possible the mosaic of homelessness in this country. Our strategy is to work from "more deserving" to "less deserving" subgroups, ending with the absolutely least deserving—the lazy, shiftless bums. Along the way, I call attention to various characteristics of and problems encountered by each of the subgroups we consider.

HOMELESS FAMILIES

Among the many tragedies of homelessness, there is none sadder than the homeless family—often an intact family unit consisting of a wife, her husband, and one or more dependent children, victims of unemployment and other economic misfortune, struggling in the face of long odds to maintain themselves as a unit and get back on their feet again. How many members of homeless families can we expect to find among our sample of 1,000 homeless people?

Although the rising number of homeless families has become a matter of considerable policy concern, evidence on their proportion in the larger homeless population is hard to come by. Most of the pertinent research has been done in homeless family shelters, or in facilities for homeless women and children; and while this material is useful for descriptive purposes, it does not tell us anything about relative proportions.

Some useful information appears in my HCH study. Across the sixteen cities covered in the study, 16 percent of all clients seen were described as members of homeless family groups. In six of the sixteen cities, family status was not systematically reported; among the 18,842 clients seen in the remaining ten cities, 28 percent were members of homeless family groups. Thus, somewhere between 160 and 280 of our 1,000 homeless people will be members of homeless families—whether male or female, adult or child. Let us take the midpoint of the range, 220 members of homeless families, as our best and final estimate, consistent with most other studies of the topic. The remainder are lone individuals.

The HCH study further suggests that among the 220 members of homeless families, 99 will be children (under age sixteen) and 121 will be adults; among the adults will be 83 adult women and 38 adult men. One important conclusion, then, is that nearly a tenth of the homeless on the streets of American cities today are homeless children in the care of their adult parent or parents.

A second important conclusion, one that follows form the relative preponderance of women to men among the adult family members, is that most homeless families consist of single mothers with their children rather than intact nuclear families. (There would also be a few single fathers with children, but their numbers are minuscule in all studies.) If each of the 38 adult men is coupled with one of the 83 adult women, then we get 38 male-female pairs and 45 single females among the total of 121 adult family members in our hypothetical sample of 1,000. Somewhat more than half of the homeless families are single-parent (typically, single mother) units, somewhat less than half are intact nuclear families.

Most of the intact nuclear families have children of dependent age, but only about half of them actually have their children with them. The most common arrangement among the remainder is that the children are living with other relatives; in some cases, the children are in foster care. Thus, only 17 or 18 of the intact male-female pairs would also include children as part of the family unit. The 99 children would thus be distributed among, say, 18 mother-father pairs and 45 single parents (mostly mothers). Thus, most homeless children live in broken families, one among the many problems homeless children face.

Studies of the effects of homelessness on children paint a uniformly shocking and depressing picture. According to Ellen Bassuk, in the *American Journal of Public Health* in 1986, developmental delays of varying severity are observed in more than half. My research has confirmed that homeless children suffer various physical disorders at rates two to ten times those seen among children in general. Some of the problems encountered by homeless children are depression, anger, anxiety, low self-esteem, and uncertainty about life (at a psychological level); and inadequate nutrition, dangerous living conditions, violence and abuse, a lack of parental authority, no quiet place to do homework, and so on (at a more concrete, palpable level). One homeless child that I have met—she lives with her mother and siblings in a welfare hotel in New York City—described her "dream" as "a clean apartment and a safe place to play out of doors." This does not seem like too much to ask. We might wonder what kind of world it is where this can only be a dream to some children.

As for the adult members of homeless family units, the picture is somewhat brighter; among both men and women, rates of alcohol and drug abuse, and mental illness, are lower than they are among lone homeless individuals. The adult family members also suffer fewer chronic physical disorders, are more likely to be short-term (or situationally) homeless, and are rated as having better housing and employment prospects than the lone homeless are. In general, their prospects for the future are much brighter; compared to the lone homeless, the adult family members are simply more intact. Many of these families need little more than a "helping hand" to get them through a rough stretch. Many of the single mothers with dependent children need little more than an expedited Aid to Families with Dependent Children (AFDC) process. Helping hands and more efficient AFDC processing would certainly not solve all the problems these families face, but it would make a considerable dent.

Members of homeless families constitute a significantly large fraction of the homeless population; my guess is that we would find 220 of them in a sample of a thousand homeless people, nearly half of them homeless children. Not only would most people look on homeless families as most deserving of help, there is also reason to believe that they need the least help (in that they appear to have the fewest disabling problems and tend generally to be the most intact), and that even relatively modest assistance would make a substantial difference in their life chances and circumstances. If the available resources are such as to require triage, then homeless families should be the top priority.

LONE WOMEN AND CHILDREN

By these calculations, there remain in our hypothetical sample of 1,000 some 780 lone homeless persons—single individuals on the streets by themselves. Based on the HCH study, some 6 percent of these 780 are children or adolescents age nineteen or less (which amounts to 47 additional children in the sample of 1,000), 20 percent are adult women (156 additional women), and 74 percent are adult men (which leaves, from the original sample of 1,000, only 580 adult males not members of homeless family groups). Adding these to the earlier results, we get two significant conclusions: First, among the total of a thousand homeless persons, 99 + 47 = 146 will be children or youth aged nineteen or less, approximately one in every seven. Second, among the remaining 854 adults, 156 + 83 = 229 will be women, which amounts to 229/854 or 27 percent of all adults. Combining all figures, homeless children and homeless adult women themselves comprise 146 + 229 = 375 of the original 1,000—three of every eight. Adult men comprise the majority of the homeless, but not the overwhelmingly majority; a very sizable minority—nearly 40 percent of the total—are women and children.

Most of the lone children found in these calculations are teenagers, which is also to say that nearly all homeless preteen children are still living with one or both of their parents. Still, children as young as twelve or thirteen will be found in sizable numbers in these data. Although men predominate among homeless adults, boys and girls are found in equal numbers among homeless children and teenagers; in the HCH data that form the basis for the preceding calculations, 51 percent of the lone homeless aged nineteen or less are boys, and 49 percent are girls; among all children (under age sixteen) in these data (whether lone individuals or members of homeless family groups), the split is also nearly 50:50. The heavy preponderance of males to females is observed only among the adults.

Although precise numbers are hard to come by, there is little doubt that many of these homeless teenagers are runaway or throwaway children fleeing abusive family situations. Among the girls, the rate of pregnancy is astonishing: 9 percent of the girls ages thirteen to fifteen, and 24 percent of the girls ages sixteen to nineteen, were pregnant at or since their first contact with the HCH clinic system; the rate for sixteen-to-nineteen-year-olds is the highest observed in any age-group. There is impressionistic evidence, but no hard evidence, to suggest that many of these young girls are reduced to prostitution in order to survive; many will thus come to possess lengthy jail records as well. Drug and alcohol abuse are also common problems. Indeed, the rate of known drug abuse among the sixteen-to-nineteen-year-old boys—some 16 percent—is the highest rate recorded for any age-group in our data.

I am discussing a time in life when the average adolescent's biggest worries are acne, or whom to invite to the high school prom, or where to go to college—a time of uncertainty, but also a time of hope and anticipation for the future. In contrast, homeless adolescents must worry about where to sleep tonight, or where the next meal is coming from, or who is going to assault them next. What hope for the future can be nourished under these conditions? Many of these kids—tough kids on mean streets, but kids nonetheless—face an unending downward spiral of booze, dugs, crime, and troubles with the law. They too must surely be counted among the deserving" homeless; indeed, anything that can be done should be done to break the spiral and set them back on a path to an independent and productive adult existence.

Among the 854 adults remaining in our initial sample of 1,000 homeless will be 229 adult women, or 27 percent of all adults. Again, this is very close to the figure reported in most studies. In the Chicago survey, 24 percent were women, and no recent study has reported a figure of less than 20 percent. Homeless women are not a new phenomenon; studies by D.L. Jones in Massachusetts, published in the 1974 *Journal of Social History*, and by P.F. Clements in Philadelphia confirm sizable fractions of women among the homeless, at least since colonial times. (Clements's work is published in E.H. Monkkonen's *Walking to Work: Tramps in America*.) Compared to homeless adult men, homeless women are younger by about two years on the average; 42 percent of the adult HCH women, but only 30 percent of the adult men, are under thirty. Compared to the men, the women are much more likely to have psychiatric impairments, but much less likely to abuse alcohol and drugs.

There are many different kinds of homeless women, and it is a mistake to think of "the" problems of homeless women as though all homeless women faced the same problems. One large and important subgroup is comprised of the lone mentally impaired women from whom the "bag lady" stereotype has been derived. This is the subset of homeless women that in some sense has been created by deinstitutionalization and related changes in our mental health treatment system. A reasonable guess is that they constitute about a third of all homeless women. Compared to other homeless women, they are much older (the median age of the group is forty) and predominantly white (58 percent); their principal need is for vastly improved community mental health services.

A second group, accounting for more than a quarter of the total, are mothers with dependent children in their care. These women tend to be young (the median age is twenty-seven), and their rates of mental disorder and substance abuse are relatively low. Only about half receive AFDC; many would presumably be employable if day care were available. Yet a third group are the homeless teenage girls, some of whose problems I have already discussed. the remainder of the women fall into a residual "other" category' the distinctive feature of this group is that alcohol and drug abuse is much more widespread than among the other women, rivaling the rates found generally among homeless men.

Most people would feel comfortable counting the adult women among the "deserving" homeless as well. Just as women and children are the first to be evacuated from a sinking ship, so too should women and children be the first to be rescued from the degradations of street life or a shelter existence. If we add to the group of "deserving" homeless the relatively small number of adult men in homeless family groups, then our initial cut leaves but 580 persons from the original 1,000 yet to account for.

LONE ADULT MEN

What is to be said about those who remain—the 580 lone adult males, not members of homeless families? A small percentage of them, much smaller than most people would anticipate, are elderly men, over age sixty-five; in the HCH data, the over-sixty-fives comprise about 3 percent of the group in question, which gives us 17 elderly men among the remaining 580. In fact, among all HCH adults, just about 3 percent are over age sixty-five; the lone adult men are not exceptional in this respect.

Since, in the national population as a whole, about twelve percent are over sixty-five, our 3 percent figure means that there are many fewer elderly homeless than would otherwise be expected—a "shortage" or "deficit" of elderly homeless that has been remarked upon in several studies. What explains the apparent shortage of homeless persons over sixty-five? First, a number of entitlements become available to persons once they turn sixty-five, chief among them Medicare and Social Security payments. It is possible that these benefits are adequate to get most older homeless persons off the streets or out of the shelters and into some sort of reasonably stable housing situation. A second possibility is premature mortality; homeless persons, that is, may only rarely survive to age sixty-five in the first place.

Little research has been done on mortality among the homeless, but the few studies that are available suggest that the mortality hypothesis is not to be taken lightly. Alstrom and his colleagues, in a study reported in the *British Journal of Addictions* in 1975, followed 6,032 homeless Swedish men for a three-year period. Observed mortality during the study period (n = 327 deaths) exceeded the age-adjusted expected mortality (n = 87 expected deaths) by a factor of approximately four; the average age at death among the 327 men was about fifty-three years. My own study of the topic has produced a similar result; among 88 deaths occurring among clients seen in the HCH program, the average age at death was fifty-one. Based on these findings, we can conclude that homeless men die some twenty or so years earlier than they "should." Thus, premature death must certainly account for at least some portion of the elderly "deficit."

The shortage of over-sixty-fives is not the only striking aspect of the age distribution of the homeless; the fact is, homeless people are surprisingly young. The median age of HCH adults is thirty-four years; all recent demographic studies of homeless populations have remarked on the low average age, perhaps because the stereotype is that the homeless tend to be old. Today, the average homeless adult male is somewhere in his early to middle thirties.

The low average age of the homeless sustains an important and often overlooked conclusion, namely, that the rise of the "new homeless" is in some sense a result of the so-called baby boom, the immensely large generations born in the United States between 1947 and 1964. As a cohort, the average age of the baby boom is now in the early thirties, almost identical to the average age of homeless people.

The baby boom has posed serious problems for virtually every institution it has touched in the course of its life span, beginning with the crisis in elementary education that commenced in the early 1950s, continuing through to a serious national housing shortage today, and ending ultimately with what will be a serious shortage of burial space around the year 2020 and thereafter. The more affluent members of the baby boom generation have come to be known as "Yuppies" (young urban professionals), whose housing preferences and purchasing power are in many respects responsible for the current housing crisis. What is often overlooked in discussions of the Yuppies is that they sit at the upper end of an income distribution, the other end of which reaches down into the poverty population. In the lowest reaches of this income distribution one finds the "new homeless," whose numbers have clearly begun to strain the capacity of the existing social welfare system.

As for the elderly, those over sixty-five, surely they are to be included within the "deserving" group. As it happens, only about half of them receive Social Security benefits. Many of those who do receive Social Security payments find that no housing can be purchased or rented within their means. Well over half have chronic physical health problems that further contribute to their hardships. Certainly, no one will object if we include the elderly homeless among those deserving our sympathies.

LONE VETERANS

We are now left with, let us say, 563 nonelderly lone adult men. If we inquire further among this group, we will discover another surprising fact: at least a third of them are veterans of the United States Armed Forces. Indeed, over a number of recent studies, reviewed by M. Robertson in Bingham, Green, and White's *The Homeless in Contemporary Society*, the percentage of veterans among the men varies from a low of 32 percent to a high of 47 percent. The one-third figure is clearly conservative; the true figure might be as high as one-half. As a point of comparison, 41 percent of all adult men in the United States are also veterans; in this respect, the homeless are not much different.

The studies reviewed by Robertson show the homeless veterans to be slightly older and proportionally more white than homeless nonveteran men; compared to the national veteran population, Vietnam-era veterans are over represented. About one in five have service-related disabilities sufficiently serious to prevent them from working; service-related psychiatric difficulties, while not always disabling, are also widespread. Among the Vietnam-era veterans, posttraumatic stress syndrome may be the most common psychiatric problem. Most of the veterans, especially the younger ones, report chronic unemployment problems as well. No more than about a third receive any form of assistance from the Veteran's Administration.

Most homeless veterans are drawn from the lower socioeconomic strata, having enlisted to obtain, as Robertson has put it, "long term economic advantages through job training as well as post military college benefits and preferential treatment in civil service employment,"; only to find that their economic and employment opportunities remain limited after they have mustered out. The lure of military service proves to have been a false promise for many of these men: "Despite recruitment campaigns that promote military service as an opportunity for maturation and occupational mobility, veterans continue to struggle with postmilitary unemployment and mental and physical disability without adequate assistance from the federal government." One of the Vietnam veterans in Robertson's study summed up the stakes involved: "If they expect the youth of America to fight another war, they have to take care of the vets."

Many of the homeless veterans are alcoholic or drug abusive, and many are also mentally ill; the same could be said for other subgroups that we have considered. Whatever their current problems and disabilities, these men were there when the nation needed them. Do they not also deserve a return of the favor?

LONE DISABLED MEN

Sticking with the admittedly conservative one-third estimate, among the 563 adult men with whom we are left, 188 will be veterans; 375 nonelderly, nonveteran adult men are all that remain of the initial 1,000. Sorting out this subgroup in the HCH data, we find that a third are assessed by their care providers as having moderate to severe psychiatric impairments—not including alcohol or drug abuse. Many among this group have fallen through the cracks of the community mental health system. In the vast majority of cases, they pose no immediate danger to themselves or to others, and thus they are generally immune to involuntary commitment for psychiatric treatment; at the same time, their ability to care for themselves, especially in a street or shelter environment, is at best marginal. Compassion dictates that they too be included among the "deserving" group.

Just what they "deserve" is hotly contested; I cannot do justice here to the many complex issues involved. Some, for example New York's Mayor Ed Koch, think that they deserve involuntary commitment if their lives or wellbeing are imperiled by the material conditions of their existence; civil libertarians think they deserve the right to die on the streets if they want to. Many mental health professionals seem to feel that reopening the large state mental institutions is the only viable solution; others think that coming through on the promise of community-based mental health care—the explicit promise upon which deinstitutionalization was justified—is the only morally defensible approach. All agree that for many of the mentally ill homeless, the least restrictive treatment has meant a life of scavenging food from street sources and sleeping in alleys and gutters—and this, no one intended.

Subtracting the 125 or so mentally disabled men from the remaining group of 375 leaves 250 of the original 1,000. Among these 250 will be some 28 or so men who are physically disabled and incapable of working. This includes the blind and the deaf, those confined to wheelchairs, the paraplegic, those with amputated limbs, and those with disabling chronic physical illnesses such as heart disease, AIDS, obstructive pulmonary disease, and others. Like the mentally disabled, these too can only be counted among the "deserving" group. Subtracting them leaves a mere 222 remaining—nonelderly, nonveteran adult males with no mental or physical disability.

Of these 222, a bit more than half—112 men—will be found to have some sort of job: my data suggest that 7 will have full-time jobs, 27 will have part-time jobs, and 78 will be employed on a sporadic basis (seasonal work, day labor, odd jobs, and the like). Rossi's Chicago data show largely the same pattern. The remainder—110 men—are unemployed, and among these some 61 will be looking for work. All told, then, among the 222 will be 173 who are at least making the effort: looking for work, but so far with no success, or having a job but not one paying well enough to allow them to afford stable housing. This then leaves us with 49 people from the initial 1,000 who are not members of homeless families, not women, not children, not elderly, not veterans, not mentally disabled, not physically disabled, not currently working, and not looking for work. Call these the "undeserving homeless," or, if you wish, lazy shiftless bums. They account for about 5 percent of the total—a mere one in every twenty.

NO EASY SOLUTION

There are many different kinds of homeless people, and it is pointless even to think of "the" homeless as though they were a homogeneous, undifferentiated group. Many of them—some 40 percent by my estimates—are alcohol abusive; a tenth abuse other drugs; a third are mentally ill; many have long-term chronic employment problems; most are estranged from their families and disaffiliated from the larger society. But very few of them are "homeless by choice" (to adopt a most unfortunate, although characteristic, phrase of Ronald Reagan), and all but a residual fraction merit our compassion on one or more counts.

There are no cheap or easy solutions to the problems of homelessness. At varying levels of analysis, homelessness is a housing problem, an employment problem, a demographic problem, a problem of social disaffiliation, a mental health problem, a substance abuse problem, a family violence problem, a problem created by cutbacks in social welfare spending, a problem resulting from the decay of the traditional nuclear family, and a problem intimately connected to the recent increase in persons living below the poverty level, as well as others.

In puzzling through the complex array of factors that cause homelessness, in the hopes of finding some solutions, coldheartedness is not the proper sentiment. Should we, as Bykofsky suggests, have "no heart" for a disabled thirty-three-year-old Vietnam veteran suffering from posttraumatic stress syndrome, or for a pregnant fifteen-year-old runaway girl whose father has raped and beaten her once too often, or for a feverish infant in the arms of her homeless mother, or for an entire family that has been turned out because the factory where the father worked was shut down, or for an arthritic old gentleman who has lost his room in the "welfare hotel" because he was beaten savagely and relieved of his Social Security check? These are very much a part—a large part—of today's homeless population, no less than the occasional "shiftless bum." Indifference to the plight of "shiftless bums" comes all too easily in an illiberal era; but indifference to the plight of homeless families, women, children, old people, veterans, and the disabled comes easily only to the cruel.

Some Clinical Approaches to the Homeless Mentally Ill

Ezra Susser, M.D., M.P.H.
Stephen M. Goldfinger, M.D.
Andrea White, M.S.W.

ABSTRACT: Clinicians who work with homeless people are likely to encounter a very broad spectrum of mental disorders and residential patterns. As with any other patient population, the particulars of clinical interventions must be guided by the specific constellations of biological, psychological, and social needs. However, for individuals who not only suffer from serious psychiatric disorders, but are also homeless, effective approaches may require significant modifications of traditional techniques and changes in the prioritization, timing, and framing of specific interventions. In this article we will focus on people who are severely and persistently mentally ill and who have been sleeping for months or years in shelters or in public spaces such as parks, streets, and bus terminals.

Rather than attempting to construct a comprehensive theoretical framework, we will focus on a number of significant therapeutic paradigms and clinical strategies which we have found particularly relevant and effective. The areas emphasized are those that differentiate work with this population from general clinical practice with the chronically mentally ill in clinics, hospitals, and other more traditional settings. Naturally, for those among the homeless mentally ill who are actively seeking treatment and willing and able to receive services in conventional outpatient settings, these unusual methods may not be necessary nor appropriate.

The discussion traces the steps that a team of clinicians would take in working with individuals. Thus, we begin by noting the unusual nature of the settings where the clinical work occurs, and then proceed to differentiate

Dr. Susser is at the Statistical Sciences and Epidemiology Division, Nathan Kline Institute for Psychiatric Research and is a Research Assistant Professor, Department of Psychiatry, New York University School of Medicine.

Dr. Goldfinger is Associate Clinical Director, Mass. Mental Health Center, and Assistant Professor, Department of Psychiatry, Harvard Medical School.

Ms. White is Associate Director, Columbia University Community Services.

the target population, the nature of the initial contact, the introduction of treatment, the services provided to enrolled patients, and the transition to housing, from what is typical in psychiatric care. The general principles suggested are illustrated with applications in a variety of settings.

ETHNOGRAPHIC ADAPTATIONS

Learning about the ethnographic context and the institutional system within which one will be working should generally precede direct clinical intervention with the homeless (Gounis and Susser, 1990). Although perhaps familiar with the literature on soup kitchens, shelters, and other institutions serving this population, few clinicians have direct knowledge and personal experience in these settings. Reliance on experiences with domiciled patients may lead to false assumptions regarding expectations, acceptable activities, and appropriate behavior. Often, after only a brief investigation of the setting or limited contact with members of the population, it becomes clear that a radical deviation from past clinical approaches is required.

The first step in establishing effective therapeutic interventions in a setting is an examination of the feelings, attitudes, and assumptions about mental health care in the prevailing culture of that particular setting. Thus, for example, in one transitional hotel for homeless women an appraisal of the subculture made it clear that conventional approaches to initiating contact with mentally ill women were likely to meet with little success. Mental illness and treatment for it were highly stigmatized; the entry of a psychiatrist as a consultant to the mental health team was seen as intrusive as well as threatening. Therefore, the women would be unlikely to present for treatment voluntarily, and referrals by staff might be seen as a humiliation and be resented. As an alternative, the psychiatrist initiated contact with the community by running the weekly Bingo game. Bingo provided a friendly and non-threatening atmosphere; was the best attended activity in the hotel; and allowed for an alteration of roles such that the psychiatrist became a guest, to be treated with hospitality rather than feared (Susser, in press). The approach was successful. Once the psychiatrist became a familiar and accepted figure in the hotel, women who had avoided him at first began to seek treatment, and staff could assume that referrals would not cause shame.

In a shelter, it is not only the attitudes of shelter clients, but of the shelter staff as well, that shapes the appropriate form of intervention. Mental health workers may be seen by shelter staff as agents of social control or as a source of justification for evicting or terminating uncooperative or disliked clients. Collusion by clinicians in accepting such a role quickly undermines their ability to gain the trust and cooperation of shelter residents. However, ignoring or refusing such demands endangers their ability to work collaboratively with permanent shelter staff who might otherwise serve as an important, and sometimes critical, resource.

In one large municipal shelter for men in the South Bronx, field experience and research prior to initiation of a mental health program had suggested that the program was likely to be viewed by mentally ill shelter dwellers as a resource for long term shelter living, and by staff as a resource for managing disruptive behavior. The usual intake approach for a mental health program would combine self-referral with referrals by shelter staff. It seemed likely, however, that with this approach the program would have to fight an uphill battle to establish a role as a bridge to community living, rather than as another component of shelter living.

At the moment of entry to the shelter feelings of demoralization and vulnerability are at a peak and the men may be most receptive to outreach (Susser, Struening and Conover, 1989). In time, social networks and institutional adaptation within the shelter emerge, and community ties recede, as men "settle" there. The new program therefore concentrated on aggressive outreach to men at the moment of entry to the shelter, when they tend to perceive that they are in acute crisis and still have some access to community resources (Gounis, et. al., 1987).

OUTREACH

Many homeless individuals will have had prior inpatient psychiatric hospitalizations, often involuntary in nature. A large number will have, at some point, undergone periods of outpatient care of various durations. These may be viewed by the patient as not having been helpful, however, or even as having been coercive and destructive. Although often attributed to an inability of the patients to cooperate with treatment, the attitudes of such patients can also be seen as due to a failure of the system to appropriately address the patients' needs (Goldfinger and Chafetz, 1984).

We believe that the emphasis in outreach programs for the homeless must be on accommodating our techniques to the needs of people who refuse to be treated elsewhere, rather than on selecting those who are easier to work with and who, therefore, may be able to make use of other mental health agencies. The outreach clinician then becomes the "clinician of last resort" rather than a substitute for other accessible services. A vigorous approach to engaging these "hard to reach" patients will frequently mean departing from the norms of clinical practice. Since the structure of traditional mental health programs rarely attracts these "hard to reach" patients—in fact, it may scare them away—other grounds for establishing a therapeutic alliance have to be developed. A clinical program may provide a sanctuary, a place to sit quietly or to talk and be heard out respectfully; food; showers; clothes; coffee; a telephone; a social network; and many other services that are perceived as useful by homeless persons and so provide a meaningful context for the initial contact between clinician and patient (Segal and Baumohl, 1985.) What is critical is that, in these early encounters, the client views what is offered as supportive and helpful. This may, on many occasions, mean relegating such interventions the clinician may view as most useful to a position of low priority. Instead, what must be paramount is the initiation of a sense of mutual trust, respect, and alliance (Frances and Goldfinger, 1986). This may mean postponing treatment of flagrant symptoms which, in a more traditional approach would be a subject of immediate concern and intervention. However, the clinician working with this population must learn to sacrifice immediate for long term goals, and like the client, to "live" temporarily with such symptoms. Premature or overly aggressive attempts to address pathology may recreate earlier negative therapeutic experiences and further convince the client that you will be no more helpful nor understanding than your predecessors.

Clinical outreach teams use widely differing approaches to introduce the role of the program as a treatment provider, once initial contact has been made. We suggest that the clinician introduce himself or herself as a mental health professional at the start. It is often preferable, however, to allow patients to set a gradual pace in terms of accepting treatment for mental problems per se. The priority at first is to befriend an individual, to develop trust, and familiarity. Thus, one might spend a good deal of time with people who are not actually enrolled in a program, to allow trust to develop; and even some who are enrolled may be receiving assistance in only a few concrete areas (e.g. getting clothes and food).

If a person is seriously disabled with mental illness, at some point one must proceed to treatment even if the person is not eager to be treated. The process of reaching some agreement with the patient as to the level of clinical intervention can be quite delicate and requires therapeutic skill. Some patients are more comfortable when the treatment is framed in medical terms, and are willing to accept medication and other inventions so long as they are being treated for a medical problem. Others reject medication and treatment for medical problems, but seek therapy and accept the psychiatric patient status with ease; they may agree to monitor symptoms and even to episodic hospitalizations. More "resistant" patients might be willing to talk to a mental health professional, even a psychiatrist, as long as they are free to define the nature of the conversation. They will then be able to avoid areas that they fear to discuss (e.g. psychotic symptoms), and may also avoid formal assessment and treatment, until they are more comfortable. Although such "chatting" is time-consuming and may be frustrating to some professionals, it can be an essential first step. Chatting regularly with a psychiatrist involves an implicit recognition of need for treatment; trust can develop over time and other interventions become possible.

From these various starting points, one can proceed to more comprehensive treatment in a gradual way. One seeks opportunities to discuss the patient's illness and the need for treatment without pushing too fast—titrating the dose, as it were. For instance, one psychiatrist used a letter to SSI as the basis for discussing mental illness with a woman who was willing to take medications but not to accept that she had a psychiatric problem. She insisted that she received SSI because of a knee injury, and wanted an increase in payments as she could hardly survive on the meager amount. Together with the psychiatrist, she composed a letter to SSI requesting an increase. In the process, she acknowledged that the letter would have to state that she had a mental disability, whether or not this was true, and composed her own description of her disability. This proved the opening for frank discussion of mental illness, and the nature of schizophrenia, after which psychiatrist and patient "agreed to disagree' as to whether the patient had schizophrenia. After that point, treatment proceeded with more explicit goals, such as improved hygiene, but still without insisting that the patient accept that she had a psychiatric diagnosis.

The purpose of outreach is to recruit patients into treatment and other services without resorting to strong-arm tactics. Ongoing negotiation over treatment is not only a means to an end, but also an end in itself. Patients are respected as active participants in defining the nature, and the level, of intervention. Thus, it is hoped that in the future they will be more likely to perceive treatment of their illness as a right, and play an ever more active role in planning and shaping the treatment they receive.

Since the introduction of treatment for mental illness may be a gradual process, and since clients often refuse to undergo the lengthy interviews used for assessment in most outpatient clinics, programs need to develop approaches to assess clients during the course of outreach. Information may have to be gathered gradually, in the course of many short conversations that are not primarily directed to taking a history. Task oriented groups, such as bingo or theater groups, sometimes provide an opportunity to observe a person interacting with others. As much time as possible should be spent outside of shelters and other "homeless" environments, to observe a person in a range of community settings; for instance, a worker might accompany a client to a coffee shop, to a grocery store, or to the movies.

There are of course individuals who are so severely ill that they cannot care for themselves, but who cannot be brought into treatment by these means. Involuntary hospitalization might be the only feasible option. When resorting to hospitalization, however, outreach work should remain an integral part of the process. The process of hospitalization offers many opportunities to establish a relationship with a patient. A case manager who accompanies a patient through an arduous and frightening process of involuntary admission sometimes finds that his or her presence is appreciated as never before. In the hospital, frequent visits and well chosen gifts might be remembered years later. The case manager might be needed to serve as liaison to the patient's social network in the mental health program or elsewhere in the community, or at least to assist a friend or relative to do so. By bringing news and gifts to and from the patient, the liaison helps to maintain the social network.

ACCOMMODATING TO DIFFICULT PATIENTS

A policy of accommodation implies, in addition to a focus on the "hard to reach," an open door to patients who are rejected elsewhere. A program should not routinely reject patients with a diagnosis of substance use disorder as well as mental illness; patients who have a history of violence; patients with HIV infection; patients who are mentally retarded; patients who continually "sabotage" treatment plans and frustrate staff; and others who are unwelcome in some agencies.

This stance will again fashion clinical work toward the unorthodox. Generally, the patients' problems will be remarkably severe and complex, program resources will be scarce, and conventional approaches will turn out to be inapplicable because they were designed and tested on quite different patient populations and in clinical settings where more resources were available. Above all, treatment plans must be of interest to the patient and feasible, requirements that often lead to unusual strategies when one is working with a "difficult" patient population in a marginal setting.

One of us, as a consultant to a team in a hotel for formerly homeless women, interviewed a 56 year old woman with a combination of chronic alcoholism (with consequent severe liver damage), atypical psychosis, post-traumatic stress disorder, and diabetes (with blood sugars that were often dangerously high). Her only intimate relationship wa with a pimp who sold and injected drugs and was likely to infect her with the HIV virus if the relationship continued. Previous attempts at education and treatment of each of these illnesses had failed, partly because she did not keep appointments or follow medical advice. The team then decided to pursue the one area in which she expressed genuine interest—resolving feelings about her family of origin, especially the grandmother who had raised her. This could at least improve the quality of her remaining years, and might serve as a prelude to further work. She was deeply touched by these efforts, and later was willing to confront her drinking and her sexual behavior.

Another example concerns a homeless young man in the large South Bronx men's shelter mentioned above. He was episodically violent, used drugs, had an uncontrolled seizure disorder, and was at very high risk for the HIV infection. Much of his childhood, and almost all of his adult life, had been spent in institutions, mainly jails, hospitals, and shelters. In spite of some appealing qualities to counterbalance these factors, it seemed highly unlikely that, in the near future, any supportive residence in New York City would accommodate him. Even in the shelter,he was unwelcome and was periodically evicted. Therefore, contrary to the program philosophy of serving as a bridge to housing rather than an agent of "social control" in the shelter, an approach was developed to foster longterm social adjustment in the shelter. Efforts could then be made to address his illnesses and behavioral problems over a period of time.

TRANSITION TO COMMUNITY LIVING

A key issue dividing the community involved in providing services for the homeless is the question of the permanence of homelessness. It is plausible to argue that the growing homeless population represents an inevitable, albeit unfortunate, result of current trends in political economy that are likely to persist in the foreseeable future. The alternate view is that, even in the short-term, homelessness may be dramatically reduced by changes in our social and political priorities. From questions about the advisability of constructing large scale humane and comfortable shelters to issues of clinical decision making for individual clients, one's underlying stance on this fundamental question inevitably colors one's planning and practice.

A discussion of the broader implications of this question falls outside the scope of this paper. However, we must state *a priori* that our approach is based on the presumption that life on the streets or in aggregate shelters must be viewed as an unacceptable condition. Efforts to obtain and stabilize clients in permanent, safe, and acceptable housing must be seen as one of the fundamental goals of interventions with this population. As a corollary to this, clinical work with homeless people must be seen as differing from other sorts of outpatient treatment in that it is essentially transitional. The goal of mental health programs, in addition to addressing dysfunction, disability, and symptomatology, is to serve as a bridge to community resources. Long term treatment within a program for the homeless is not a desired outcome.

Unfortunately, it is often difficult to maintain such a stance within the real world of clinical practice. The availability of safe and affordable housing options for homeless populations in most communities is simply insufficient to meet current needs. Thus, many shelter residents, even those in "emergency shelters" (sic), may have been there for many years. Nevertheless, in our view, clinicians must continue to struggle to find more reasonable housing options for all clients under their care, and programs for the homeless mentally ill must establish and maintain a self-definition of themselves as transitional. In the absence of such a stance, programs may unwittingly contribute to the continued institutionalization of homelessness and a reluctance to continue the search for more appropriate options.

Many programs find it difficult to adopt a transitional approach even when some form of community housing and psychiatric treatment is available. As in most types of programs, staff find it difficult to break strong attachments to clients who are well-known and relatively easy to work with, to turn to clients who are unknown and unstable. In programs for the homeless, these anxieties are intensified by the evident contrasts between clinical practice in such programs and practice in other agencies.

Program staff may be hesitant to turn clients over to fragmented systems of care, especially if the clients have experienced rejection in the past. Clients may be reluctant to leave the program, fearing change or fearing that a similarly tolerant staff cannot be found in other agencies.

These concerns are not unfounded, and there is no easy way to address them. Appropriate referrals frequently do not, in fact, exist in the community. Supportive residences often reject clients on the basis of past history or current noncompliance with treatment. Mental health programs may refuse to treat patients who abuse drugs or alcohol. Programs that do admit patients tend to offer limited case management and outreach and insist on a level of motivation and initiative that many clients cannot maintain. In general, patients and staff are correct in assuming that clients will be, at best, tolerated at another agency, often "lost to follow-up," and at worst rejected.

At the level of mental health systems, the alternative to maintaining patients in long-term treatment in programs for the homeless is to build comprehensive and continuous services (Lamb, 1984). These should encompass housing and other social needs and must be "universal" in the sense that all severely and persistently ill psychiatric patients can be accommodated. At the level of individual clinical work within most existing systems, however, the only alternative may be to extrude patients into an environment that has proved unfriendly in the past, risking a repetition of homelessness and other traumata.

We have found this to be one of the most fundamental problems for clinicians and programs for the homeless. Some continue to case manage clients for years after they find housing, because other agencies cannot do so with the same intensity. Others provide long-term psychiatric and other medical treatment, because patients will not attend other clinics, even when they are available. When clinicians do refer out and withdraw services, clients frequently cannot adjust and become homeless again.

STRATEGIES FOR "ESCAPE"

In order for both clinicians and patients to cope with such difficult external realities, new strategies must be designed to help ensure that the state of homelessness for the mentally ill remain as brief as possible. We have found that the most promising approach is one which we label as "Advocacy and Empowerment." We highlight four components.

1. *Advocacy* Advocacy is certainly the most "traditional" of the strategies that we recommend, and one that has long been recognized as an essential component of general case management services (Lamb, 1980, Harris and Bachrach 1988, Kanter 1985). However,in work with the homeless mentally

ill, the range of appropriate targets and means of advocacy is significantly expanded from that which is generally accepted. Thus, for example, appropriate targets for one's advocacy efforts will frequently extend beyond what is usually defined as a practitioner's clinical caseload. One often advocates on a limited basis for people who are not even officially enrolled in a mental health program. Many clients may refuse all psychiatric intervention, but require and will accept access to other services for clothing, housing, or medical care.

Programs that offer limited advocacy to all potential clients can proceed to more comprehensive case management for some. In a 200-bed women's shelter in Manhattan, many clients enrolled in a mental health program ostensibly as a means to get a more regular supply of soap, toilet paper and other basic necessities. After they began to attend the program, some asked for help in other areas such as obtaining welfare or negotiating with the shelter bureaucracy. When the program had gained credibility as an advocate in these areas, the team offered to help clients to extract needed services from more threatening systems such as hospitals and clinics. Treatment for mental illness was then presented as another entitlement, countering the prevailing view among the women that it was a form of punishment. In fact, posters in the shelter advertised the mental health program as an entitlement analogous to veteran's benefits, available only to "veterans" of the mental health system. Yet, some women still declined to enter treatment, preferring a more limited type of assistance.

2. *Demystification*   Educating patients regarding the cause and nature of their symptoms and helping them to understand when and how to use medication and other treatment interventions is becoming a more established part of clinical practice (Goldman and Quinn, 1988.) The clinician-educator may also function in the role of a consultant who is not part of the treatment team. The assumption of such an approach is that knowing about one's illness will assist the patient in making prompt and appropriate use of available treatment interventions and in developing appropriate coping strategies. To underscore the broader implications of the educational process, we describe our expanded version of psychoeducation as "demystification."

Given the reluctance of many agencies to open their services to homeless populations, we feel it is important for clients to approach these services with as much knowledge, expertise, and "clout" as possible. Thus, the focus of our approach is to have the patient acquire as much knowledge about his or her illness as is required to successfully negotiate with mental health centers, welfare offices, housing agencies, hospitals, and other services providers. This involves educating the client not only about illness, but also about systems.

Two basic components are involved. First the patient is encouraged to describe his or her own view of his disabilities and symptoms and to compare it with labels that have previously been used to describe him. Such activities as reading the DSMIII-R together can be a helpful adjunct to having the patient understand, if not agree with, the diagnoses that he has received. It is preferable, but not essential, that the patient agree with the professionals' characterization of his illness and appropriate treatment (Susser, 1988). What is critical, however, is that he learn to describe what others think is wrong with him in words that are most effective in helping him to receive the entitlement, program, or service which he desires. Secondly, clients and clinicians engage in active dialogue about how service agencies are structured and the overt, and covert, barriers to providing what is needed or wanted. With some clients this may involve reading entitlement regulations or other entry criteria together. Having clients share their previous experiences with having services denied can help provide realistic examples of how such rejection can be prevented in the future.

One homeless man had been consistently denied social security disability payments despite clear clinical evidence that he did, in fact, suffer from a major mental illness of sufficient duration and disability to qualify. By discussing his previous application attempts, he and his clinician were able to clarify the ways that he had participated in providing the system with grounds for rejecting his application. Together, they rehearsed how he would approach his next application process and how he would answer various questions that might occur. It is remarkably effective (and rather startling for the entitlement worker) to have a patient appear who simply states "I am schizophrenic, and have been diagnosed as such three different times at the following hospitals. Although I was able to work prior to my diagnosis, I have not been employed for the last four years. I have only $1,100 in total savings, and therefore, believe that I qualify for SSI benefits." Agencies are, in our experience, rather reluctant to deny benefits to such "educated consumers."

3. *Constructive sociopathy* Some patients are rather ineffective in negotiating with mental health professionals and others on whom they depend for resources. Good techniques have been developed to teach patients social skills that enhance survival in a relatively responsive system (Anthony and Liberman, 1986). In the public system, for patients who are socially marginal and may be unwelcome at the treatment site, these techniques need adaptation. We try to acquaint patients with as many paths as possible to pressure unresponsive and bureaucratic systems to meet their needs even when they do not ordinarily fall within the purview of a given agency.

In order to get what they need and deserve, homeless mentally ill individuals must learn how to use the system. However, given the frequently arbitrary and discriminatory nature of services, these clients often must be taught ways to "outwit" the system at its own game. Given the difficulty of survival as a homeless person, many of those that we encounter are already masters at some of these techniques. Others can, and must, learn them.

A group in a women's shelter categorized the skills needed to be a good panhandler. These included understanding the neighborhood, "sizing up" potential givers, and having a convincing story. Clients then applied these skills in negotiating for carfare in the shelter. They learned the criteria for getting carfare, "sized up" the worker who provided it, and showed the worker the necessary appointment slips. (The approach proved more effective than the screaming technique that was popular previously). Later, the same skills were used in applying for welfare, a task that became less foreboding when broken down to a set of familiar practices, now used to obtain money from a different channel.

Widely practiced examples of "constructive sociopathy" abound. One of the most common is helping chronically mentally ill individuals figure out how to write job applications and creatively answer job interview questions relating to those missing periods of time when they were hospitalized or otherwise involved in treatment activities. It is no secret that employers often actively discriminate against those with psychiatric histories and that a forthright offering of one's treatment history will often preclude the applicant's being hired. A more minor example might include helping a client to obtain a jacket and tie, even though such attire has never previously been a part of his wardrobe.

PEER SUPPORT

Peers can provide social networks that might persist while case managers and treatment sites change. Peer support sometimes develops in the course of a group activity in a program. The group described above, which began by studying panhandling skills, later evolved into a peer support group. Group members who had been through a welfare application started to take others through the process. Some developed into leaders and recruited new members into the group.

Peer groups can also create new treatment approaches. In New York a formerly homeless woman originated groups in hotels and shelters where women with drinking or drug problems could discuss their experience of homelessness as well as their addictions (White, 1988). With the exception of the leader, group members were not abstinent. These groups became a "pretreatment" option for those who were not yet ready for treatment. Over time, many women who attended the groups built the motivation needed to give up alcohol and/or drugs.

When a support group extends itself to participate in outreach to others, to shaping the nature of treatment within a program, or to other collective goals, its value is further enhanced, and one might use the term "empowerment" to describe the process. In a men's shelter in the South Bronx, a group of mentally ill men proved more effective in outreach to other mentally ill men than did the program staff. In the same shelter, a group called HEAT (Homeless Empowerment Assistance Team) contacts new arrivals to the shelter to orient them to the social milieu as well as to available services, runs a Narcotics Anonymous group, and helps men apply to educational programs and to find jobs. HEAT has also acquired an important influence in the mental health program. It is unusual, however, to reach that point for groups of persons who are chronically mentally ill and homeless. HEAT, for instance, is dominated by men whose disabilities derive from substance abuse rather than an illness such as schizophrenia.

"Advocacy and empowerment" represents an adaptation of clinical practice to a setting that is marginal and a program that is transitional. The focus is on patients acquiring resources, social skills, and social supports that are needed for a mentally ill person to survive in an unaccommodating community environment. Patients are encouraged to perceive the program as a temporary resource that might be of help in the endeavor. Whenever possible, the approaches should be supplemented by temporary work with the family and other social networks that are likely to be present over the long term; usually one searches for ways in which these networks can continue to be available without becoming overwhelmed.

Unfortunately, it generally requires a long period of time (months) to have an appreciable impact. When stabilization of symptoms must precede participation in the process,it takes even longer. By that time, many of the clients who remain in the program have become quite dependent on it, while those who have found some housing arrangement without learning these skills remain vulnerable to future displacement.

A further problem is that the approach was developed for patients with Axis I diagnoses. Patients with severe personality disorders may already be skilled in negotiating systems. In some cases, these patients become group leaders, teaching skills and motivating others to join, a role that is beneficial to everyone. A promotion ladder with clear conditions and gradations can be used to structure their movement to leadership positions. In general, however, programs for the homeless, like other programs for the chronically mentally ill, lack effective strategies for patients with personality disorders.

The approach also was not designed for mentally ill persons whose social disabilities are mainly the consequence of episodic violence of substance use dependence. These patients sometimes need special approaches, because their behavior can be so disabling even when they trust their case manager, understand their illness and can access resources. Again, like other programs, programs for the homeless need to focus on improving their work with this subgroup.

TEACHING ABOUT HOUSING

Housing should be a central focus of virtually any program for the homeless mentally ill. Whenever possible, the clinician should actively create new community housing options for his clients. At a minimum, he needs a strategy for teaching clients about what housing already exists and how to make use of it.

There are three areas of special importance to patients in the transition from homelessness to housing: 1) learning about available housing options, including the full spectrum of supportive living arrangements in a given community 2) improving community living skills such as shopping, cooking, setting aside money for rent, avoiding dangerous conflicts with neighbors 3) transforming skills used to survive while sleeping in shelters and public spaces to becoming assets rather than liabilities when the patient is no longer homeless.

When a client is enrolled in a program, the treatment plan should be designed to prepare that person for housing. For those that can attend, a housing group can serve to set the treatment plan. Information on housing is presented, the kills required to live in each type of housing are specified, and prior experiences are discussed. Thus, group members develop a keener sense of their preferences, their capabilities, and their options, before making a choice. For instance, in choosing a supportive residence, a member will want to consider cost, access to stores and to transportation, proximity to relatives, need for peace and quiet, tolerance for a curfew, the level of on-site services, and many other factors.

In a housing group, each person might initially see himself or herself in a two-bedroom apartment and see others in the group as only capable of living in a special facility for the disabled. One strategy to open discussion is to announce that all housing offered by the program has strings attached. Each option is an entitlement; the criteria to qualify for it include specific skills. Clients are asked to choose one type of housing and then begin to develop the skills needed by participating in the program, where they can practice these skills. After assessing the time needed to pay for and maintain a two-bedroom apartment, some clients readily accept other options in the interim. More typically, the process of adjusting hopes and expectations occurs over weeks or months.

Teaching and transforming living skills are most important when people have been homeless and/or in institutions for long periods, or perhaps for all their adult life. Those who are accustomed to institutions often do not know much about shopping, cooking, doing the laundry, making friends, and using leisure time outside of an institution. On the other hand, they may have highly developed skills for living in institutions that become a handicap in housing. In the Bronx men's shelter, for instance, it is normative to protect one's reputation by fighting, to steal when opportunity presents, and to develop a social life centered on drug use. Several men referred to community residences got into trouble when they continued to observe these norms after leaving the shelter. One threatened a landlord with a knife in response to an insulting comment, a second stole the common television set from a community residence, and a third invited his friends to his YMCA room for an extended drug party.

In any teaching about housing, it is helpful to keep at the fore a broad perspective on the causes of homelessness (Susser, Lovell, Conover, 1989), and to avoid the assumption that there is some form of housing available to everyone. Many people will be legitimately resentful if they feel that their difficulty in finding a place to live is being attributed only to a lack of knowledge or of social skills. Others will perceive correctly that for the time being their only real option is to adapt to living in shelters or public spaces. Some young homeless men, in particular, are not going to be accepted into any supportive residence, because of a persistent tendency to violence and/ or to drug use.

SUPPORT IN HOUSING

Most programs for the homeless are poorly designed, because they are expected to follow clients only until "placement" in housing, or for a short period thereafter. Longterm homelessness, however, is not usually a discrete event with a clearly defined onset and ending. More commonly, it is a dynamic process in which a person moves between shelters, public spaces, and marginal living accommodations over an extended period of time (Hopper, et al., 1985), Chafetz and Goldfinger, 1984). Thus it makes little sense to routinely terminate clients from a program when they move to a fragile community living arrangement (and receive them again when it collapses).

It would be preferable to provide support over an extended period of time, in which use of shelters or other homeless arrangements declined and use of housing increased. Clients could then practice strategies for finding out which places they prefer and how to stay in them. Episodic returns to homelessness would not need to be seen as a failure for either the client or the program, but rather could be considered as part of the process of adjustment.

In the minority of cases in which a permanent and suitable supportive residence is an option, it may be better to transfer care to an on-site team at the time of placement. However, clients will still make use of familiar and well-known resources. A client who moved from the Bronx men's shelter to one such residence returns to the shelter for a stay when he is acutely psychotic; a wider range of behavior is tolerated in the shelter than in the residence, and he prefers to stay in the shelter than the hospital while awaiting recovery.

Even with continuity of care over an extended period, many clients will be episodically homeless in the future. Homelessness has its roots in broad social processes, for the mentally ill as well as for others (Gounis and Susser, 1990, Hopper et al., 1985). For people who are poor and have a chronic mental illness, treatment and rehabilitation may reduce but will not eliminate vulnerability. Nevertheless, continuity would permit the work of individual programs with individual clients to be more meaningful and to have a more lasting impact, and represents a better model of care. Continuity also would ease the conflicts over transition to community living noted in an earlier section.

CONCLUSION

We have presented a viewpoint on good clinical work with people who have been chronically homeless and chronically mentally ill. Clinicians who work with homeless people do not always agree as to the best approach, and research findings are limited (an up-to-date bibliography of reports and publications on clinical work with the homeless mentally ill is maintained by Policy Research Associates, under contract with the NIMH). Therefore, while the chapter represents a synthesis of a good deal of clinical experience, it expresses opinions rather than known facts.

The clinician needs to adapt his or her practice in a number of important ways. He must learn about the milieu in which he will practice; he must define as the target population those who are usually turned away; he must serve as a bridge to community living rather than as an option for long-term treatment; he must have specialized knowledge about housing and the skills needed to stay in it. Some of these adaptations would improve clinical work with chronically mentally ill persons in other settings too; all are essential to good clinical work with those who are homeless.

REFERENCES

Anthony WA, Liberman RP. The Practice of Psychiatric Rehabilitation: Historical, Conceptual, and Research Base. Schizophrenia Bulletin, 12:542, 1986.

Chafetz L, Goldfinger SM. Residential instability in a psychiatric emergency setting. Psychiatric Quarterly, 56: 20–34, 1984.

Frances A, Goldfinger SM. "Treating" a homeless mentally ill patient who cannot be managed in a shelter system, Hospital and Community Psychiatry, 37: 577–579, 1986.

Goldfinger SM, Chafetz L. Designing a better service system for the homeless mentally ill, in Lamb HR (Ed.). The Homeless Mentally Ill: A Task Force Report of the American Psychiatric Association, Washington, DC, 1984.

Goldman CR, Quinn FL. Effects of a patient education program in the treatment of Schizophrenia. Hospital and Community Psychiatry, 39: 282–286, 1988.

Gounis K, Conover S, Susser E, Drucker E. First timers at the Franklin Men's Shelter: A program to prevent shelterization of newly homeless men. Report to New York City Department of Health, 1987.

Gounis K, Susser E. Shelterization and its implications for mental health services. In Cohen N (ed.). Psychiatry takes to the streets. New York: Guilford Press (1990).

Harris M and Bachrach LL. Clinical Case Management. New Directions for Mental Health Services, No. 40, San Francisco: Jossey-Bass, 1988.

Hopper K, Susser E, Conover S. Economies of makeshift: deindustrialization and homelessness in New York City. Urban Anthropology, 14: 183–236, 1985.

Kanter JS. Clinical Issues in Treating the Chronically Mentally Ill. New directions for Mental Health Services, No. 27, San Francisco: Jossey-Bass, 1985.

Lamb HR. Therapist-Case Managers: More than brokers of services. Hospital and Community Psychiatry, 1980, 762–764.

Lamb HR (Ed.) The Homeless Mentally Ill: A Task Force Report of the American Psychiatric Association. American Psychiatric Association, Washington, D.C., 1984.

Segal S and Baumohl J. The Community Living Room. Social Casework, 111–116, Feb. 1985.

Susser E. The med-psych consumers group. Unpublished report to Columbia University Community Services, New York, 1988.

Susser E. Working with people who are homeless and mentally ill: the role of a psychiatrist. In Jahiel R (Ed.) Homelessness: A Preventative Approach. John Hopkins Press, (in press).

Susser E, Lovell A, Conover S. Unraveling the causes of homelessness, and of its association with mental illness. In Copper B and Helgasson T (Eds.) Epidemiology and the Prevention of Mental Disorders. London: Routledge, (1989).

Suser E, Struening E, Conover S. Psychiatric Problems in Homeless Men. Archives of General Psychiatry, 46:845–850, 1989.

White A. Triple-trouble—Homelessness, Substance Abuse and Mental Illness. Community Psychiatrist, 3: 7–8, 1988.

The Homeless Mentally Ill and Community-Based Care: Changing a Mindset

Marsha A. Martin, D.S.W.

ABSTRACT: The care of persons with severe, persistent and disabling mental illness has received increasing attention during the past ten years. This focus is due, to some extent, to the increased visibility of a subset of this population, the large number of individuals with psychiatric problems who have become homeless. These men and women, who are without homes or in temporary residences, present a sophisticated array of needs and a multiplicity of problems which have rendered most communities impotent to provide appropriate and adequate rehabilitative services. To date, there is no "perfect" community-based system of care for these men and women. What exists is a hodge-podge of shelter, outreach and drop-in center services. Most of these provide little more than a bed (or a chair) to sleep on, a hot meal and refuge from inclement weather. This article discusses some of the issues and assumptions that inhibit and foster the development and provision of a comprehensive system of community-based care for persons with serious and persistent mental disorders who have become homeless. A framework, useful in reconceptualizing the clients, the services and the interaction between them is presented.

It is a commonly held assumption that communities can, theoretically, respond to the needs of the homeless mentally ill. However, the current operational framework is one that is designed around institutional settings, not free-standing community-based systems of care. In many communities the hospital is both the foundation of the health and mental health system and, at the same time, the institution of last resort, providing not only essential inpatient care, but also functioning as the locus of general health mainte-

Ms. Martin is at Hunter College School of Social Work 129 East 79th Street New York, New York 10021

Dr. Martin is an Associate professor at Hunter College School of Social Work in New York City. She is on the Board of the Coalition of Voluntary Mental Health, Mental Retardation and Alcoholism Agencies.

nance services. Although some communities offer a broad array of services and supports, even these are rarely conceptualized as coordinated and collaborative systems of care in which the hospital, rather than functioning as the center of activity, serves merely as another treatment modality. If community-based mental health care is to be successful in reaching the homeless mentally ill and providing appropriate services, a change in the mindset of those planning, delivering and receiving services will be necessary.

ASYLUM: A NEW DEFINITION

Since the establishment of asylums (as institutions of the mentally ill or aged), the care of persons with disabling and long-term mental illness has fallen within the public mental health arena. More often than not, this has been interpreted to mean outside of community attention, community domain and community care. Not only did these institutions offer asylum (a place offering safety, the protection afforded by a sanctuary), they also attempted to offer everything necessary for meeting the bio-psycho-social needs of individuals requiring mental health care. Among the services provided were: sleeping accommodations, food and clothing services, showers and personal hygiene services, medical and mental health services, daily living skills development, socialization and daytime activities training, on-site rehabilitation and vocational training services, off-site aftercare services, advocacy and entitlement support, family intervention and supportive services. These services were usually available on three levels: short-term, intermediate and long-term, each level corresponding to an assessment of the individual's current level of functioning and his/her corresponding level of need. If levels of functioning and levels of need fluctuated within the individual, it was possible to "travel" back and forth among all three levels (without leaving the grounds of the facility) until satisfactory rehabilitation was completed or the patient stabilized at some level of need. The provision of this system of care and these services was no small accomplishment, in and of itself. Additionally, by providing a physical plant and (at best) a nurturing environmental landscape, these institutions assisted in the establishment of alternative social and psychological supports. For individuals with fragmented and insufficient ego boundaries, this helped them cope with the demands and challenges resulting from the manifestation of their illness and the tasks involved in daily living. "Control" of the individual's behavior was assumed to result from both the treatment and the setting itself. If the internal boundaries were non-existent or insufficient to meet the needs of the individual and society, then external boundaries would be imposed and/or re-defined.

With the introduction of effective antipsychotic and thymoleptic medications an alternative to the asylum was available to those whose behavior could now be controlled by an active pharmacological treatment regime. Men and women who had been hospitalized for varying periods of time could return to the community, to their family and to their own home. To support this process of deinstitutionalization, federally funded community mental health centers were established to provide mental health care in the community. No longer was it absolutely necessary to send persons with severe, persistent and disabling mental illness to institutions; asylum was to be provided within the community. However, this time, new alternatives frequently lacked the structural and rehabilitative support of the variety of professional and nonprofessional staff and services, walls or beds of the old state hospitals. If the residents of the institutions were "ready" for this new form of asylum, the receiving community, the mental health and human services sectors were not. What was to have been the "least restrictive alternative" (a noble idea, indeed) became no alternative at all: out of their beds and into the streets, mentally ill and homeless.

COMMUNITY-BASED CARE: A DREAM DEFERRED

In 1974, the National Institute of Mental Health (NIMH) began to explore and develop a model for the delivery of community-based care for persons with long-term and disabling mental illness (Stroul, 1986). By the late seventies and early eighties it had further developed its conceptual framework, which resulted in the establishment of the Community Support System (CSS) program, integrating medical, social and rehabilitative treatment strategies and models. As a clinical structure around which to design community-based care, the CSS model of services suggested that every community "have arrangements to perform the following ten functions" (Stroul, 1986, NIMH, 1980):

- location of clients/outreach—reach-out, assure access to services, provide information;

- assistance in meeting basic human needs—food,clothing, shelter, safety, entitlements, etc.;

- mental health care—diagnostic assessment, prescription of medication, counseling, etc.;

- 24-hour crisis assistance—quick, round-the-clock intervention, in and out-patient services;

- psychosocial and vocational services—a continuum services aimed at community living;

- rehabilitative and supportive housing—a range of rehabilitative and supportive housing;

- assistance/consultation and education—support to families, friends and others;

- natural support systems—involvement of consumer, family and self-help in all aspects of service and care;

- grievance procedures/protection of clients rights—establish grievance procedures to protect rights of clients;

- case management—facilitate effective use by clients of the informal and formal helping networks and systems.

Although these ten functions were not designed with the homeless in mind, taken together, they provide the necessary support for the mentally ill who have become homeless to live, as independently as possible, within the community. As is evidenced by the large numbers of persons with mental illness on the streets across the United States, the transition from asylum to a CSS community-based mental health care system has not been fully realized. This is due to a variety of factors, not the least of which were the assumptions that the clients were essentially the same as they had always been (same needs, same problems); that necessary services existed; that capital and workforce resources count be tapped for new initiatives; and that suitable, supportive and rehabilitative housing opportunities were available, affordable and accessible to persons with serious, disabling mental illness. As with most assumptions, these did not hold true. The clients had different needs, the necessary services were non-existent, capital and workforce resources were inaccessible and housing opportunities were not available.

A NEW LOOK AT AN OLD PROBLEM

Since the early eighties, homelessness and mental illness have received a great deal of attention. (See, for example, Arce, 1983: Bassuk, 1984; Baxter and Hopper, 1981; Roth, et at el, 1985.) From the well-publicized debate about the incidence of mental illness among the homeless, to the renewal of the discussion of the need for asylum, the needs of this population have been the topic of many professional conferences and journals, symposia at annual meetings of professional organizations and task force discussions.

In 1982, the National Institute of Mental Health in an effort to increase the understanding of the phenomenon of homelessness among persons with serious and disabling mental illness began to fund a number of research projects (see Morrisey, 1986; Spaniol and Zipple, 1985; Bachrach, 1984). In 1984, a Task Force of the American Psychiatric Association issued a report on the homeless mentally ill (Lamb, 1984). In 1986 the Robert Wood Johnson Foundation supported the development of model mental health programs for the homeless in 18 cities across the United States. In 1988, NIMH awarded grants to municipalities for the development of services for the homeless mentally ill through the Stewart B. McKinney Act (NMHA Summary Report, 1987). Much has been learned about the homeless since the early eighties, and a tremendous amount of effort has been expended in the hope of curbing the tide of homelessness among the mentally ill. What follows is a discussion of some of what has been learned and the implications for service delivery and on-going care.

THE CLIENT: MENTALLY ILL AND HOMELESS

The homeless mentally ill are many different people with many different problems and needs. The NIMH supported research projects report that they are individuals with: histories of residential instability, limited familial support,limited histories of involvement in the criminal justice system, limited work histories, and limited access to the social welfare and human service system (See Morrisey, 1986; Morse, 19855; Mowbray, 1985; Mulkern, 1985; Roth, 1985).

Treatment approaches and services programs designed to reach the homeless mentally ill must understand that living on the street, more appropriately "in the out of doors" is a survival strategy, not a temporary solution to a situational problem (Martin, 1982). Mentally ill men and women do not make an eccentric or idiosyncratic choice to be homeless, rather they do it to survive. This "survival drive" sparks a process of adaptation which continues as long as the mentally ill person remains homeless and is outside of the mental health and social welfare systems (Martin, 1987). Strategies emerge that are utilized by the homeless to meet basic needs and that serve to lessen the immediate impact of stress. Many enable homeless mentally ill persons to maintain some sense of self-worth (for more discussion, see Martin, 1982). They include such defense mechanisms as denial ("I don't live on the street"), rationalization ("I'm waiting for a bus"), displacement (yelling at the mental health team for being forced to eat the food at the shelter), compensation (acquiring money and large quantities of "belongings", wishful thinking ("I'm waiting for a room at the hotel across the street. The manager is looking out for me.") and the ability to maintain and experience a sense of humor, fantasy and self-entertainment (talking, laughing, singing, dancing with self and others), which enable the homeless mentally ill to remove themselves from the every day stress of living in the outdoors. Behavioral strategies are developed that assist homeless mentally ill men and women in the acquisition of resources to meet basic needs. These include the ability to eat anything (be it from a soup kitchen, food pantry, breadline or garbage receptacle), the ability to sleep sitting up (for example, in chairs in hospital emergency rooms, drop-in centers and transportation centers), the ability to repeatedly articulate needs and request assistance (panhandling, begging for food and financial support).

The homeless mentally ill have what appears to be a remarkable capacity for adaptation and coping under extremely difficult conditions. They live without a "fixed," "permanent," or even "temporary," residence and with the uncertainty of being able to satisfy their routine basic human needs. Their "success" in satisfying basic needs suggests a certain degree of mastery and competence in relation to the tasks and demands of their street and "sheltered" environments. Derived from cumulative experiences of effectiveness,this competence and mastery results in an efficacy heretofore unknown by many mentally ill individuals. While life outside of the institution was not meant to be synonymous with "life on the street," life on the street, for some mentally ill men and women has become synonymous with "true" independent living (Martin, 1988).

For some homeless, the random care and giving, offered on the street by the passersby, local shopkeepers and merchants, seems to surpass that which they may have experienced in previous environments, familial or institutional. This results in a kind of intermittent positive reinforcement, which is very difficult to interrupt when attempting to offer an alternative to life on the street (Martin and Nayowith, 1986).

Treatment approaches and service programs must understand this condition of living. These men and women no longer think of themselves as "homeless" but see themselves as surviving. This shift in the psychological mindset accounts for the tenacity of homeless people in their efforts to continue to live in the outdoors, in shelters and drop-in centers when "more appropriate" alternatives are offered or suggested (Martin, 1988). It is not enough to offer the homeless mentally ill a shelter and a hot meal. Homeless mentally ill men and women learn to live on the street. They no longer experience their existence as "out of the ordinary." An alternative ego reality begins to structure the day- to-day experiences of life. Rehabilitative efforts must acknowledge this adaptive process, the strengths and abilities of homeless mentally ill men and women, and provide services that affirm and build on the ingenuity and creativity of their survival strategies (see Margin and Nayowith, 1986). Only by participating in re- structuring their internal processes and ego reality, rather than by offering services and resources that become external alternatives to the lifestyle, can mental health professional and shelter workers begin to help the homeless mentally ill make a new adaptation. More simply put: by "teaching the rules of indoor living" (Martin and Nayowith, 1986) homeless mentally ill men and women can learn to reorganize their lives.

THE SERVICES

Individuals with severe, persistent and disabling mental illness who have become homeless almost always want help. All of the research efforts supported by NIMH found this to be true (Morrisey, 1986). However, the current service delivery system is often not well-organized to provide the help they seek or would accept. The challenge to the service delivery system is to make the services responsive to the expressed needs of the homeless mentally ill. The services must be delivered in a flexible manner, with accessibility and acceptability as priorities. The service delivery system must include not only traditional health and mental health services but all of the same components that were available within the institution, incorporating the same degree of integration, coordination, collaboration and continuity (Goldfinger and Chafetz, 1984).

THE NEW YORK CITY EXPERIENCE

The Coalition of Voluntary Mental Health, Mental Retardation and Alcoholism Agencies is a non-profit umbrella organization representing more than 100 licensed mental health and alcoholism agencies in New York City (Coalition, 1987). In 1987, it established a task force to examine the needs of the homeless mentally ill, and the needs of the public and private voluntary mental health system, in an effort to create a more responsive network of services and system of care.

The task force found the existing system of care for the homeless mentally ill in New York City to be limited in its understanding of the nature of homelessness among the mentally ill men and women, fragmented and limited in scope. Although a variety of services exist within the public and private sectors, these suffered from a lack of coordination, integration and basic knowledge about homelessness and mental illness (Coalition, 1987b). Existing program models and strategies resulted in a poorly organized and under-utilized network of services. Based on discussions with voluntary mental health agencies, the Coalition developed a framework for reconceptualizing a comprehensive system of care for the homeless mentally ill that includes full participation from government, the non-profit community and the private sector. The elements of the framework include planning and organizing services, housing development, education and training (Coalition, 1987-88).

Planning Services

Prior to 1980, planning, organizing and development of services for the homeless mentally ill was largely a consequence of a few individuals and groups who, acting out of their own varied and intense interests, were able to obtain the necessary public and private support to create basic and essential services for the population. Although categorical and targeted funding streams became available for the development of services, these two fiscal incentives were not a substitute for a much needed planning process. In New York City, as in most municipalities around the country, these fiscal incentives resulted in little more than an expansion of existing services and a scattering of outreach and day programs. Since that time, the increases in the homeless population in general, and the homeless mentally ill in particular, have necessitated the development of both a more carefully designed landscape and a more thoughtfully crafted planning and funding process.

Planning and distribution of funds for programs serving the homeless mentally ill must take place within the context of a continuum of services. Implementation of such programs must follow an assessment of the distribution and integration of funds and services within a particular community. Funding of programs and services would be contingent upon a community's identified need, the existing network of services and the extent to which services are linked to one another. For example, outreach programs could be linked to drop-in centers, as well as to shelter and residential programs. Residential programs and drop-in centers could be linked to day programs and vocational and work-readiness programs. The implementation plan is key to the success of the continuity of services and should reflect a collaboration between government, the non-profit community and the private sector.

ORGANIZING SERVICES

Recognizing the importance of flexibility in successfully responding to the needs of the homeless mentally ill, service systems must also provide the necessary structure to enhance the rehabilitative process. Entry points, rehabilitative shelter, day and drop-in center programs, non-temporary housing opportunities and employment options are necessary components of community-based care. The organization of these components into a comprehensive system of community-based care, one which also provides continuity of services, requires focused attention on rehabilitation and community living.

Entry points must be well-publicized and provide access to a variety of services. They must recognize the importance of the engagement process and allow for the time to establish and solidify the involvement of those they intend to serve.

Rehabilitative shelter, day and drop-in center programs that go beyond meeting basic needs are critical elements in the rehabilitative process. They must be organized to support movement between each component of the system, while at the same time creating an incentive to move beyond this level of services.

Homeless mentally ill men and women require a range of housing alternatives and opportunities that support re-learning to manage a "household," be it a room in a single room occupancy (SRO) hotel, a shared room in an adult home, a room at a board and care home or an apartment. Learning to live indoors again will require support and supervision. While some homeless mentally ill men and women may benefit from most housing that provides a structured living environment, others may live quite comfortably in the general community with only limited support.

From work readiness to competitive employment, vocational rehabilitation must reflect the needs of the homeless mentally ill for practicing and re-learning the various aspects and expectations of the world of work. Structured work readiness programs re-introduce homeless men and women into the arena of formal employment. Transitional work programs provide a necessary "next step" toward competitive employment. Frequently, rehabilitation is not a linear process. It is often a slow progression of a cyclical, interactive nature, in which homeless men and women move between, around and through several service and/or program components before adaptation to indoor living and regular activities is secure. The organization of services must reflect this dynamic process rather than relying on a preconceived notion of how each individual "should" progress. Many homeless mentally ill men and women are quite capable of utilizing services toward the goal of indoor living, but only if the services are organized to meet their needs and affirm and reflect their ability and desire to care for themselves.

HOUSING DEVELOPMENT

The absence and/or inadequacy of housing in communities across the United States has resulted in many mental health agencies "getting into the housing business." Building, leasing, financing and/or rehabilitating housing has become a central activity for many agencies serving the homeless mentally ill. However, most of these organizations are ill-equipped to deliver services and simultaneously secure or build housing. Additionally, the "role of landlord" is an unfamiliar one to most mental health providers and may cause a great deal of added stress to already over-taxed workers. Collaborative non-profit housing development corporations must be formed, which can provide technical assistance to agencies willing to assume the housing function. Government, the non-profit community and the private sector have an opportunity to create a model for problem solving through the development of such a housing/technical assistance entity.

In the spring of 1988, The Coalition began to explore the creation of a housing development corporation to address the problems resulting from the lack of capacity of mental health agencies to acquire and develop property and the inability of local government to accomplish its housing goals (see Coalition, 1987a). it was hoped that a non-profit housing development corporation could and would assume the development of housing on behalf on community-based mental health agencies. Specifically, the corporation would acquire property, develop appropriate housing program models, finance housing projects, and manage these projects should agencies request management assistance.

EDUCATION AND TRAINING

There are many issues and problems facing community agencies as they try to provide services to the homeless mentally ill. One critical problem is the lack of knowledge and data about effective treatment strategies for the population. A second concern is the integration of service components for the homeless mentally ill into more traditional services. A third problem is the lack of a regular address for the client, resulting in a concern about difficulty maintaining agency contact. A fourth issue is the lack of coordination and cooperation among agencies.

Large scale community education and agency-based staff development and training programs are essential in moving toward a comprehensive system of care. Conferences, meetings with community and civic leaders and organizations, and the formation of community-wide coalitions and task forces all provide an educational function. Although the content may vary from setting to setting, education and training play a key role in the successful development of community-based services for the homeless mentally ill.

TOWARD THE FUTURE

If the responses to the needs of the homeless mentally ill are to be effective, they must take into consideration the multiple needs of the homeless mentally ill, the community, and both the public and private sector. In defining, creating and re-organizing services, a holistic approach will require a commitment to the provision of a variety of health, mental health and social welfare programs. Thus far, services for the homeless mentally ill have clustered around three program models: outreach services, drop-in center services and transitional shelters. Taken together, these programs comprise the essential components of a good "emergency relief" system of care. However, emergency relief is only one of the necessary elements in a comprehensive community-based system. To be successful, all of the essential elements must be present and fully operations.

Public mental health services cannot accomplish the task alone, nor can they be expected to provide the sole source of funding. Still, the current crisis in the care of persons with severe and persistent mental disorders both those who have become homeless and those at risk of homelessness, demands a bold and challenging response from within the field of mental health itself. The questions are no longer: Who are the homeless? Are they all mentally ill? What are their service needs? Whose responsibility is it to do something about the problem? The questions are: How can the field of mental health organize its services to create asylum within the community? Can mental health's response to the articulated needs of the homeless mentally ill be as creative as the responses of the individuals and families it wishes to serve? Answering these questions will provide the much-needed catalyst for change.

CONCLUSION

The development of a comprehensive system of community-based care for persons with serious, persistent and disabling mental illness who have become homeless requires a shift in the mindset of those currently planning, funding and providing services. Efforts have to move in the direction of creating asylum within the community. No longer can states afford the luxury of housing men and women on large state campuses, staffed by thousands of employees. However, this time,the community (including the individuals it seeks to serve) must participate in shaping the plans and creating the system. Interventive and rehabilitative services and strategies must recognize this dynamic process, if we are to successfully face the ethical and clinical challenges raised by this population.

REFERENCES

Arce, AA, Vergare, MJ, et al.: (1983), A Psychiatric profile of street people admitted to an emergency shelter. Hospital and Community Psychiatry 34:812- 817.

Bachrach, L: (1984) Report and Analytical Summary of a Meeting of DHHS-Supported Researchers Studying the Homeless Mentally Ill. Office of State and Community Liaison, NIMH.

Bassuk, EL: (1984) The Homelessness Problem. Scientific American 241: 40-45.

Baxter, E. Hooper, K: (1981) Private Lives/Public Spaces: Homeless Adults on the Streets of New York City, New York, Community Services Society.

Coalition of Voluntary Mental Health, Mental Retardation and Alcoholism Agencies,Inc. (1987a) Brochure New York, NY.

Coalition of Voluntary Mental Health, Mental Retardation and Alcoholism Agencies,Inc. (1988), Housing Corporation Concept Paper New York, New York, Spring.

Coalition of Voluntary Mental Health, Mental Retardation and Alcoholism Agencies, Inc.)1987b), Task Force Report. New York, New York.

Coalition of Voluntary Mental Health, Mental Retardation and Alcoholism Agencies,Inc. (1987-88), Year-end Summary Report of the Homeless Mentally Ill Project.New York, New York.

Frances, A. Goldfinger, S: (1986) "Treating" a Homeless Mentally Ill Patient Who Cannot be Managed in the Shelter System. Hospital and Community Psychiatry 37:577-579.

Goldfinger, SM, Chafetz, L:(1984) "Designing a Better Service Delivery System for the Homeless Mentally Ill" in Lamb, HR, (ed) The Homeless Mentally Ill: A Task Force Report of the American Psychiatric Association. Washington, D.C.

Lamb, HR: (ed.) (1984) The Homeless Mentally Ill: A Task Force Report of the American Psychiatric Association. Washington, D.C.

Lamb, HR: (1988) Deinstitutionalization at the Crossroads. Hospital and Community Psychiatry 39:941- 945.

Levine, IS et al.: (1986) Community Support Systems for the Homeless Mentally Ill in the Mental Health Needs of Homeless Persons edited by Bassuk, EL.San Francisco, California: New Directions for mental Health, 30:27-42.

Martin, MA: (1988) From Homelessness to Self-Sufficiency, Unpublished paper.

Martin, MA: (1987) Homelessness Among Chronically Mentally Ill Women in Issues Treating Chronically Mentally Ill Women edited by Nadelson, C., Bachrach, L. American Psychiatric Association.

Martin, MA: (1989) No Room at the End: The Homeless Elderly in Understanding and Serving Vulnerable Populations edited by Harel, Z, Erhlich, P. and Hubbard, R. Forthcoming, Fall.

Martin,MA: (1982) Strategies of Adaptation: Coping Patterns of Urban Transient Females. Unpublished Dissertation, New York: Columbia University.

Martin, MA: (1986) The Implications of NIMH-Supported Research for Homeless Mentally Ill Racial and Ethnic Minority Persons,NIMH.

Martin, MA, Nayowith, SA: (1989) Creating Community: Groupwork to Develop Social Support Networks with the Homeless Mental Ill in Group Work with the Poor and Oppressed edited by Judith Lee. Forthcoming, Summer.

Martin, MA, Nayowith, SA: (1986) Groupwork with the Homeless Mentally Ill: In Drop-in Centers, Shelters, and SRO Hotels. Unpublished paper.

Morrisey, J: (1986) NIMH-funded Research on the Homeless Mentally Ill: Implications for Policy and Practice. Albany, New York: Bureau of Evaluation Research, NYS Office of Mental Health.

Morse, G. et al.: (1985) Homeless people in St. Louis, St. Louis, MO: Four County Mental Health.

Mowbray, C: (1985) Identifying the Needs of the Chronically Mentally Ill Homeless in Detroit. Research and Evaluation Division, Michigan Department of Mental Health.

Mulkern, V: (1985) Homelessness Needs Assessment Study. Boston, MA: Human Services Research Institute.

National Institute of Mental Health. (1980). Essential CSS Functions. In Announcement-Community Support Systems Strategy and Development and Implementation Grants. Rockville, MD: National Institute of Mental Health.

National Institute of Mental Health (1987). The Homeless Mentally Ill: Reports Available from the National Institute of Mental Health. NIMH.

National Mental Health Association (1987). Urgent Relief For Homeless:A Summary of the Steward B. McKinney Homeless Assistance Act of 1987 (PL 100-77). Alexandria, Virginia: NMHA.

Rosnow, M.: (1985) Listening to the Homeless. Milwaukee, WI: Human Services Triangle, Inc.

Roth, D. et al.: (1983-1985) Homelessness in Ohio. Columbus, OH: Ohio Department of Mental Health.

Spaniol, L, Zipple, A: (1985) NIMH-Supported Research on the Mentally Ill Who are Homeless. Boston, MA: Center for Psychiatric Rehabilitation, Boston University.

Stroul, BA (1986): Models of Community Support Services: Approaches to Helping Persons with Long-Term Mental Illness. Community Support Program. NIMH.

U.S. Department of Housing and Urban Development: (1984) Report to the Secretary on the Homeless and Emergency Shelters. Washington, D.C.

Involuntary Treatment for the Homeless Mentally Ill

H. Richard Lamb, M.D.

A 26-year-old man was first hospitalized at age 18 and many times since.

He had been asked to leave his parents' home at age 20 because they were afraid of him. They had taken him back twice, but at age 22 had decided not to take him back again, after he had broken his mother's arm. He has been homeless for the past four years. sometimes in shelters, but mostly on the streets and in parks.

He is extremely paranoid, guarded and irritable to the point where any contact with people quickly escalates to physical violence. Voices constantly tell him that various people want to hurt him.

He wanders from city to city and place to place, only occasionally receiving his Supplemental Security Income (SSI) check because of his constantly changing whereabouts.

He is totally resistant to antipsychotic medications when not in hospitals and is medicated only with great difficulty during his brief hospitalizations. He refuses all housing placements.

He has had several arrests for assaults on strangers whom he had instantly incorporated into his delusional system. His longest stay in jail has been a week, and each time he has been sent to a psychiatric hospital. he is, at this time, living on the streets.

A 32-year-old man was first hospitalized at age 20. He has had multiple hospitalizations since, because of delusions, hallucinations and severe depression. He lived at home until age 26 when his mother died.

He has been in a variety of placements since the death of his mother, including halfway houses and board and care homes, but has been asked to leave by all of them because of his constantly putting his hands on women and his masturbating in public. He refuses to take medications.

Professor of Psychiatry, University of Southern California School of Medicine.

For the past year he has been living on the streets. He has been beaten and robbed twice. He has even been thrown out of soup kitchen lines for open masturbation—the ultimate rejection.

He has been hospitalized with increasing frequency in the past year because of delusions, hallucinations and suicidal ideation. In the hospital his symptoms quickly disappear, and he no longer meets the criteria for ongoing involuntary treatment.

He refuses long-term hospitalization or another locked facility, and discharge is usually to the streets.

Unfortunately, these are not unusual cases, but are simply two of the many thousands of homeless mentally ill persons in this country. To what extent has deinstitutionalization, and especially problems in its implementation, contributed to this homelessness? The purpose of this article is to examine the problems of deinstitutionalization not just with regard to the homeless mentally ill but for the long-term mentally ill generally, to draw upon our experience, especially our clinical experience, and to discuss one aspect of the problem in particular, involuntary treatment for the homeless mentally ill.

I. THE SEDUCTIVENESS OF "FREEDOM"

There is sometimes a tendency on the part of those who advocate institutionalizing the mentally ill to underestimate the humanizing effects of long-term mental patients' simply having free movement in the community.[1] Even patients who live in "mini-institutions" in the community—i.e., in community-based settings such as board and care homes that share some characteristics of state hospital social structure—often enjoy the benefits of residence in unlocked facilities, as well as free access to a range of community resources. Although some of these patients may require structured residential settings, and although most of them may be unable to withstand independent employment, they may still experience living in the community as a positive event.

At the same time, however, not all long-term mental patients benefit equally from even limited amounts of freedom. For a portion of the population, that which requires a highly structured and controlled environment, freedom may result in intense anxiety, depression and deprivation, and, increasingly often, in a chaotic life on the streets. These patients often require ongoing involuntary treatment, sometimes in 24-hour settings like California's locked skilled-nursing facilities with special programs for psychiatric patients[2] or, when more structure is indicated, in hospitals where security is greater.

A recent task force report of the American Psychiatric Association[3] traces the evolution of this concern:

The purported effectiveness of deinstitutionalization was predicated both on the availability of effective treatment in the community, and on the willingness of patients to accept treatment voluntarily. Unfortunately, a majority of the proposed community treatment facilities were never created, and many of the discharged patients continued to be unwilling to accept treatment voluntarily, and discontinued treatment immediately after discharge. Further, a growing number of young adult chronic patients did not accept the need for treatment and could not be treated involuntarily because they failed to meet the criteria of reformed commitment laws designed to limit the use of involuntary hospitalization. Many of these patients responded well to treatment when hospitalized, but rapidly relapsed after discharge, leading to the "revolving door" syndrome of repeated brief hospitalizations followed by relapse after discharge.

It can be seen then that freedom for the chronically and severely mentally ill is a much more complex issue than it might appear at first glance. Each patient must be evaluated individually and society and the mental health system must provide a range of options allowing varying degrees of autonomy for these persons.

II. DEINSTITUTIONALIZATION

Probably nothing more graphically illustrates the problems of deinstitutionalization than the shameful and incredible phenomenon of the homeless mentally ill. The conditions under which they live are symptomatic of the lack of a comprehensive system of care for the long-term mentally ill generally. Though the homeless mentally ill have become an everyday part of today's society, they are nameless; the great majority are not on the caseload of any mental health professional or mental health agency.[4] Hardly anyone is out looking for them, for they are not officially missing. By and large the system does not know who they are or where they came from. We can see first hand society's reluctance to do anything definitive for them; for instance, stop-gap measures such as shelters may be provided, but the underlying problem of a lack of a comprehensive system of care is not addressed.[5] We can see our own ambivalence about taking the difficult stands that need to be taken—for instance, advocating changes in the laws for involuntary treatment and the ways these laws are administered. When we get to know homeless mentally ill persons as individuals, we often find that they are not able to meet the criteria for the programs that most appeal to us as professionals: those that require a higher degree of patient functioning. For the citizenry generally, the homeless mentally ill represent everything that has gone wrong with deinstitutionalization and have persuaded many that deinstitutionalization was a mistake.

Yet, many things have gone right with deinstitutionalization. For instance: the chronically mentally ill have much more liberty, in the majority of cases appropriately so; we have learned what is necessary to meet their needs in the community; and we have begun to understand the plight of families and how to enlist their help in the treatment process. In this article, however, the focus is on what has gone wrong with deinstitutionalization, and in particular the ways that various forms of involuntary treatment could help resolve the problems of the homeless mentally ill.

III. HOSPITAL AND COMMUNITY

Has deinstitutionalization gone too far in terms of attempting to treat long-term mentally ill persons in the community? We now have over three decades of experience to guide us. *Some* long-term mentally ill persons require a highly structured, locked, 24-hour setting for adequate intermediate or long-term management.[6] For those who need such care, do we not have a professional obligation to provide it,[7] either in a hospital or a hospital-like alternative such as California's Locked Skilled Nursing Facilities with Special Programs for Psychiatric Patients?[8] Where to treat should not be an ideological issue; it is a decision best based on the clinical needs of each person. Unfortunately, deinstitutionalization efforts have, in practice, too often confused locus of care and quality of care. Where mentally ill persons are treated has been seen as more important than how they are treated. Care in the community has often been assumed almost by definition to be better than hospital care.[9] In actuality, poor care can be found in both hospital and community settings. But the other issue that requires attention is appropriateness. The long-term mentally ill are not a homogeneous population; what is appropriate for some is not appropriate for others.

For instance, what of those persons who are characterized by such problems as assaultive behavior; severe, overt major psychopathology; lack of internal controls; reluctance to take psychotropic medications; inability to adjust to open settings; problems with drugs and alcohol; and self-destructive behavior. When attempts have been made to treat some of these persons in open community settings, they have required an inordinate amount of time and effort from mental health professionals, various social agencies, and the criminal justice system. Many have been lost to the mental health system and are on the streets and in the jails.

Moreover, the result has often been seen as a series of failures on the part of both mentally ill persons and mental health professionals; as a consequence, a number of long-term mentally ill persons have become alienated from the system that has not met their needs, and some mental health professionals have become disenchanted with their treatment. Unfortunately, the heat of the debate over this issue of whether or not to provide intermediate and long-term hospitalization for such patients has tended to obscure the benefits of community treatment for the great majority of the long-term mentally ill who do not require such highly structured, 24-hour care.

IV. FUNCTIONS OF THE STATE HOSPITALS

In the midst of very valid concerns about the shortcomings and anti-therapeutic aspects of state hospitals, it was not appreciated that the state hospitals fulfilled some very crucial functions for the chronically and severely mentally ill. The term "asylum" was in many ways an appropriate one, for these imperfect institutions did provide asylum and sanctuary from the pressures of the world with which, in varying degrees, most of these patients were unable to cope.[10] Further, these institutions provided such services as medical care, patient monitoring, respite for the patient's family, a social network for the patient as well as food and shelter and needed support and structure.[11]

In the state hospitals what treatment and services that did exist were in one place and under one administration. In the community the situation is very different. Services and treatment are under various administrative jurisdictions and in various locations. Even the mentally healthy have difficulty dealing with a number of bureaucracies, both governmental and private, and getting their needs met.

Further, patients can easily get lost in the community as compared to a hospital where they may have been neglected, but at least their whereabouts were known. It is these problems that have led to the recognition of the importance of case management. It is probable that many of the homeless mentally ill would not be on the streets if they were on the caseload of a professional or paraprofessional trained to deal with the problems of the chronically mentally ill, monitor them, with considerable persistence when necessary, and facilitate their receiving services.

V. SOME BASIC QUESTIONS

It should be emphasized that the majority of long-term mentally ill persons are able to live in the community. With regard to this majority, we need to ask ourselves if we have truly established this population as the highest priority population in public mental health. If so, does this priority include our concern, our resources and our funding? We have learned a great deal about the needs of the long-term mentally ill in the community. Thus, we know that this population needs a comprehensive and integrated system of care;[12] such a system would include an adequate number and range of supervised, supportive housing settings, adequate, comprehensive, and accessible crisis intervention, both in the community and in hospitals, easier access to involuntary treatment, and ongoing treatment and rehabilitative services, all provided assertively through outreach when necessary. We know the importance of a system of case management such that every long-term mentally ill person is on the case-load of some mental health agency which will take full responsibility for individualized treatment planning, linking these persons to the needed resources and monitoring these persons so that they not only receive the services they need, but are not lost to the system. Have we done enough to put our knowledge into practice? For most parts of this nation, the answer is clearly no.[13] If this comprehensive system of care were in place, fewer patients would deteriorate to the point where they need involuntary treatment.

VI.   CIVIL COMMITMENT

In 1969, California's then-novel civil commitment law, the Lanterman-Petris Short Act, went into effect.[14] Within a decade every state (and Puerto Rico) modified its commitment code to make similar changes.[15] Such a rapid and complete consensus among legislatures is virtually unprecedented; more important, it reflected a nearly universal view, which I share, that past inattention to the rights of the mentally ill needed to be corrected.

In effect, the new civil commitment laws accomplished three things. First, the laws changed the substantive criteria for commitment from more general criteria simply embodying concepts of mental illness and need for treatment to more specific criteria that embodied either dangerousness or the incapacity to care for self with the presence of mental illness as a requisite for commitment. Second, the laws changed the duration of commitment from indeterminate and extensive to determinate and brief. Third, the new laws explicitly provided that persons civilly committed have rapid access to the courts, to public defenders, and, in some cases, to jury trials; this access secured for civilly committed persons the kinds of due process guarantees that criminals had obtained over the prior decade.

Numerous motivations may have accounted for these changes. The most straightforward should not be dismissed: legal reformers were concerned that mentally ill individuals, persons who often had difficulty defending their liberty interests, should not be civilly committed without a deliberate process, and then only when specific criteria were met. Still, such an explanation would not be considered complete. Throughout the works of Szasz,[16] Goffman,[17] and Laing,[18] many attorneys had almost come to believe that mental illness indeed was a myth and that the so-called mentally ill were otherwise ordinary people who were "choosing an alternative life-style."

This last perspective, and it is difficult to ascertain how wide-spread it was, clearly helped to shape the new laws. Moreover, libertarian perspectives appear to have taken precedence over clinical ones; commitment periods in most states are not geared to the clinical needs of acutely psychotic and depressed patients. Thus the new laws frequently, though unwittingly, contributed to the toll of chronic mental illness by providing unrealistically short treatment durations for both psychotic and depressed patients.

Consideration of the duration of commitment, then, suggests that legislators were more preoccupied with the rights than the needs of involuntary patients.

If one accepts the findings of various studies that suggest that, irrespective of commitment criteria, about 85 percent of persons committed are not dangerous,[19] then commitment laws that base civil commitment only on dangerousness reduce the potential number of patients who could be helped by commitment by that same amount, 85 percent. In fact, however, many, though not all, of the new laws allow involuntary hospitalization of mentally ill persons who are incapable of providing for their basic necessities, such as food, clothing, and shelter.[20]

Yet because of the way in which the new laws were drafted, the courts have often applied the new criteria literally. That is, a patient who obviously is seriously mentally ill, though less floridly psychotic than when first admitted, may not be retained in the hospital because he has avoided starvation (thus he must be providing himself with sufficient food), has obtained the rags he is wearing (has clothing), and claims to prefer living in a cardboard box (has shelter). Such interpretations should not be dismissed as the capricious acts of the judiciary, but should be viewed as the nearly inevitable result of narrowed commitment criteria.

Only the seriously mentally ill should be committed. However, the new commitment laws affected the chronically mentally ill by limiting commitment to those who are dangerous or are so deteriorated that they can generate only the most minimal efforts to sustain their own life. This restrictive scope, coupled with other changes that shorten commitments and provide more opportunities to challenge their legality, has made commitment a less effective vehicle for detecting, evaluating, and treating the seriously mentally ill.

What has been the result? Consider the homeless mentally ill as an example. Given that the estimates of the seriously mentally ill in the urban homeless population range from 25 to 50 percent, [21] and that the true percentage is most likely in the upper end of that range, the changes in commitment laws have, in my opinion, contributed substantially to this grave nationwide problem. For instance, it has been shown that involuntary hospitalization has an important role to play in the treatment of the homeless mentally ill.[22]

Often overshadowed by the concerns about the laws governing emergency involuntary commitment are the importance and the therapeutic potential of ongoing involuntary treatment. Such treatment, includes conservatorship or guardianship, outpatient commitment,[23] and treatment as a condition of probation. They will be discussed later.

VII.   RECOMMENDATIONS

To begin with, the civil commitment laws need to be redrafted and the criteria for commitment should be altered in a substantive way. Proposed revisions should include many of those found in the American Psychiatric Association's Model State Law on Civil Commitment of the Mentally Ill.[24] The criteria for commitment should include the following. First, the person suffers from a severe mental illness. Second, the person is likely to cause harm to others (including substantial damage to property) or harm to self, or is gravely disabled (that is, he is unable to satisfy his basic needs for nourishment, medical care, shelter, or safety without prompt and adequate treatment, or, from repeated history, is likely to suffer substantial mental or physical deterioration). Third, hospitalization is necessary to prevent harm to the person or to others.

It is important to note that expansion of the criteria of grave disability to allow commitment of a person who is likely to suffer deterioration represents a reintroduction of a need-for-treatment standard, in addition to the now-usual dangerousness criteria. Legislation expanding the criteria of grave disability to include deterioration has already been enacted in such states as Alaska, Texas, and Washington.

Under the ideal law, in nonemergency situations or after three days of emergency commitment, a judicial hearing would be required as a prelude to commitment for 30 days, a length of time that makes sense clinically. Although the patient would have the right to be present, to be represented by counsel, and to have a record of the hearing kept, informal rules of evidence would be employed. For example, testimony could be heard from all parties with relevant information without rigorous adherence to such doctrines as the hearsay rule and without observance of conventional courtroom procedure, with its strict adherence to rules of direct examination and cross-examination. The use of informal rules of evidence would make the judicial hearing much less countertherapeutic than it has been, and that informal rules are more appropriate for a commitment hearing than the model based on courtroom procedures for criminals. Subsequent recommitment, following another court hearing, would be for up to 60 days; thereafter patients could be recommitted for 180-day periods.

Guardianship (conventionally granted by probate courts) and conservatorship are potentially important resources for that relatively small proportion of the long-term mentally ill who need ongoing legal controls in the community as an alternative to total control in a hospital. Unfortunately in many states these legal mechanisms have only theoretical value, since the authority available through guardianship laws is often inadequate, and the procedures are discouraging.[25]

In California, conservatorship provides continuous control and monitoring of patients who need social controls while also providing adequate legal safeguards. Conservatorship is granted by the court for one-year renewable periods for patients found gravely disabled (that is, as a result of mental disorder, they are unable to provide for their basic needs for food, clothing, and shelter). Patients under conservatorship may be hospitalized when necessary, and for an indefinite period; their money may be managed when they cannot manage it themselves; and they may be compelled to live in a suitable community residential facility that meets their needs for care and structure. Such a facility may be a board and care home or, if needed, a locked skilled nursing facility with special programs for psychiatric patients, as exists in California.[26]

Why is greater use not made of conservatorship? Among the problems are bureaucratic obstacles, the opposition of some lawyers, and the lack of recognition by mental health professionals of the need for ongoing controls of patients who are in the community. A major problem here, as well as in emergency commitment, has been the narrowness of the definition of grave disability. This definition should be expanded to include those who are currently able to provide for their basic needs but have a history of repeatedly suffering substantial mental and physical deterioration whenever involuntary treatment is discontinued.

The system also needs a new treatment philosophy. Ideally, this new philosophy should recognize that external controls, such as conservatorship, are a positive, even crucial, therapeutic approach for those who lack the internal controls to deal with their impulses and to organize themselves to cope with life's demands.[27] Such external controls may interrupt a self-destructive, chaotic life on the streets and in and out of jails and hospitals.

In California, conservatorship has become an important therapeutic modality. This is particularly true when conservators are psychiatric social workers or persons with similar backgrounds and skills who may become a crucial source of stability and support for chronically mentally ill persons. Conservatorship thus enables patients who would otherwise be long-term residents of hospitals to live in the community and achieve a considerable measure of autonomy and satisfaction in their lives.

Other promising modalities are commitment to outpatient treatment[28] as an alternative to involuntary hospitalization (so long as the patient complies with treatment, he can remain in the community) and, when the criminal justice system is involved, treatment as a condition of probation.

CONCLUSION

Suppose I were acutely or chronically psychotic to the point of incompetency to make a decision about treatment and were living on the streets, vulnerable to every predator, eating out of garbage cans, and in and out of jail. I would fervently hope that the agent of society who saw my plight would not simply tell me that I have a right to live my life that way but instead would do something to rescue me—"against my will" if necessary. Society owes us that much.

Thus, the mentally ill have another crucial right. When, because of severe mental illness, they present a serious threat to their own welfare or that of others and at the same time are not able to ask for or even to accept treatment, they have a right to involuntary treatment. Not to grant them that right is inhumane.

NOTES

1. H.R. Lamb, Treating the Long-Term Mentally Ill 29 (1982).
2. Lamb. *Structure: The Neglected Ingredient of Community Treatment*, 37 AR-CHIVES GEN. PSYCHIATRY 1224-28 (1980).
3. American Psychiatric Ass'n, Task Force Report No. 26, Involuntary Commitment to Outpatient Treatment 1 (1987).
4. Lamb, *Deinstitutionalization at the Crossroads*, 39 HOSP. & COMMUNITY PSYCHIATRY 951-445 (1988).
5. *See* American Psychiatric Ass'n, The Homeless Mentally Ill (H.R. Lamb ed. 1984).
6. Belcher, *Defining the Service Needs of Homeless Mentally Ill Persons*, 39 Hosp. & Community Psychiatry 1203-05 (1988); Dorwart, *A Ten-Year Follow-up Study of the Effects of Deinstitutionalization*, 39 Hosp. & Community Psychiatry 287-91 (1988).
7. Group for the Advancement of Psychiatry, The Positive Aspects of Long Term Hospitalization in the Public Sector for Chronic Psychiatric Patients (1982).
   See supra note 2.
9. Bachrach, *A Conceptual Approach to Deinstitutionalization*, 29, Hosp. & Community Psychiatry 573-78 (1978).
10. Lamb & Peele, *The Need for Continuing Asylum and Sanctuary*, 35 Hosp. & Community Psychiatry 798-802 (1984).
11. Bachrach, *Asylum and Chronically Ill Psychiatric Patients*, 141 Am. J. Psychiatry 975-78 (1984).
12. Bachrach, *The Challenge of Service Planning for Chronic Mental Patients*, 22 Community Mental Health J. 170-74 (1986).
13. Talbott, *The Fate of the Public Psychiatric System*, 36 Hosp. & Community Psychiatry 46-50 (185).
14. Cal. Welf. & Inst. Code §§ 56000-5599 (West 1984 & Supp. 1989).
15. Lamb & Mills, *Needed changes in Law and Procedure for the Chronically Mentally Ill*, 37 Hosp. & Community Psychiatry 475-80 (1986).
16. T.S. Szasz, The Myth of Mental Illness (1961).
17. E. Goffman, Asylums: Essays on the Social Situation of Mental Patients and Other Inmates (1961).
18. R.D. Laing, The Divided Self (1960).
19. Monahan, Ruggiero & Friedlander, *The Stone-Roth Model of Civil Commitment and the California Dangerousness Standard: An Operational Comparison*, 39 Archives Gen. Psychiatry 1267-71 (1982).
20. American Bar Foundation, *Involuntary Hospitalization*, in The Mentally Disabled and the Law 34-63 (S.J. Brakel & R.S. Rock eds. rev. ed. 1971).
21. Arce & Vergare, *Identifying and Characterizing the Mentally Ill Among the Homeless*, in American Psychiatric Ass'n, *supra* note 5, at 75, 88.
22. Bennett, Gudeman, Jenkins, Brown & Bennett, *The Value of Hospital-Based Treatment for the Homeless mentally Ill*, 145 Am. J. Psychiatry 1273-76 (1988).
23. Miller, *Commitment to Outpatient Treatment: A National Survey*, 36 Hosp. & Community Psychiatry 265-67 (1985); Miller & Fiddleman, *Outpatient Commitment: Treatment in the Least Restrictive Environment?*, 35 Hosp. & Community Psychiatry 147-51 (1984).

24. Stromberg & Stone, *A Model State Law on Civil Commitment of the Mentally Ill*, 20 Harv. J. on Legis. 275 (1983).
25. Peele, Gross, Arons, & Jafri, *The Legal System and the Homeless*, in American Psychiatric Ass'n, *supra* note 5, at 261.
26. *See supra* note 2.
27. Lamb & Grant, *The Mentally Ill in an Urban County Jail*, 39 Archives Gen. Psychiatry 17–22 (1982).
28. *See supra* note 23.

The Ordeal of Shelter: Continuities and Discontinuities in the Public Response to Homelessness

Kim Hopper

Late in the ill-fated 1988 Democratic bid for the presidency, but still early enough for the outcome to be in doubt, the writer Joan Didion was traveling with the Dukakis campaign. She discovered that some of the young team of advisers, policy analysts and media consultants that the candidate had assembled around him had taken to referring to themselves as "the best and the brightest." They did this, Didion reports, "with no sense of irony and none, therefore, of history."[1]

Santayana, of course, had said it earlier. And before him, Marx (echoing Hegel) had remarked how all great events and personages on the world stage occurred twice—the first time as history, the second as farce. No one even remotely conversant with the shambles of the emergency shelter effort in our country today can fail to be impressed with the wisdom of these observations; or to be dismayed, as if additional reason for dismay were needed, at the lack of familiarity with even rudimentary Poor Law history on the part of our policy makers.

But it is not merely ignorance of precedent that cripples the effort. It is, I would suggest, a set of fundamental tensions at the core of the provision of public shelter, tensions that have their roots in the elemental ambiguities that permeate the problem of how—under what terms and conditions, and protected by what safeguards—are public resources to be used for meeting private needs in market-based economies.

Visiting Assistant Professor of Anthropology, New School for Social Research, New York.

I. THE HOMELESS IN HISTORY

Old Homer had it right: there is nothing so charged with sentiment as the unexpected homecoming of a loved one—especially when that arrival means setting right a gross injustice. Even the most jaded undergraduate can barely suppress a cheer when, in that final scene of *The Odyssey*, a disguised Odysseus reveals his identity and routs the parasites who have been pestering his wife, humiliating his son and squandering his wealth. Odysseus had returned home clad in the rags of a beggar, a figure that was held in low regard by the ancient Greeks.[2] To press the point, Homer had earlier on, in a textbook instance of dramatic irony, set us up nicely for that rousing conclusion. It is an offhand remark about beggars by (of all people) a swineherd, but it does the job:

> Wandering men tell lies for a night's lodging, for fresh clothing; truth doesn't interest them.[3]

Mythology may alert us to the abiding resonances of "home," but it was government's responsibility for the room and board of itinerant strangers and the local "friendless poor" that would provoke the debates over the terms, conditions and the telltale signs of "deservingness" that are with us even today.

The situation of the dependent poor, and the basis and stipulations of public provision for their support, have been troublesome issues for Western governments since they were first broached in a systematic way in the sixteenth century.[4] The earliest attempt to design a comprehensive public relief apparatus, *De Subventione Pauperum* (1526), was the work of Thomas More's friend, the Spanish scholar Juan de Vives, at the behest of the good citizens of Bruges. They were especially struck by the importunings of beggars lining the way to the cathedral—thrusting oozing stumps in the faces of churchgoers, displaying sickly infants, and otherwise making a menace of their appeal for alms. Vives' treatise draws an explicit connection between poverty and crime and makes it clear that the chief impetus behind a decent provision for the poor is civic self-interest. For when the indigent, "driven by need," turn to "open brigandage" or "thieve in secret" it will be too late; the welfare of the entire community will have been jeopardized. (Elsewhere, Vives compares the threat of mendicancy to that of the plague.)

Vives' solution, one that will be replayed in many variations by governments down to our own, is first to classify the needy by circumstance and ability and then to devise corrective measures accordingly. Above all, recipients of relief were to be set to work. Those without a trade would be taught one; those competent in one would be given an opportunity to practice it, either by local merchants or in state-subsidized workshops. Few are exempt: the elderly and simple-minded could be taught "to dig, to draw water, to sweep, to push a barrow, to be an usher in court, to be a messenger;" even the blind could be taught to sing, play an instrument, turn a lathe or spin. The basic premise had a brutal simplicity about it: "no one is so enfeebled as to have no power at all for doing something."[5]

Canon Law had charted the course for learned discourse much earlier. Ecclesiastical attention to the problem of almsgiving dates at least from the time of the late patristic writings of Augustine, who counseled against giving alms to those who "neglected righteousness." By the twelfth century, Church commentaries on the *Decretum* of Gratian had identified the core issues that would henceforth command the attention of relief specialists:

> [W]hether eligibility for relief should be determined by need alone or by other considerations, whether there should be any fixed order of preference among eligible applicants, whether the principle of selection should be conditioned by a desire to reform or, alternatively, to punish, the pauper seeking relief.[6]

This growing rationalization of charity went along with a changed attitude toward poverty. By the thirteenth century, the high medieval attitude that had prized poverty as a purification state—one that was personified in the figure of Francis of Assisi—was in abeyance and would soon be supplanted altogether.[7] There were a number of reasons for this change. First, what had been founded as mendicant orders of friars (Franciscan and Dominican especially) had grown rich and complacent over time. Disillusionment and indignation followed.[8]

Second, the composition of the poor had changed as a consequence of the dislocations of war, plague, economic displacement, and civil uprising. No longer were the roads home largely to the aged, infirm and pilgrims; now they were joined by brigands, demobilized soldiers, and peasants released from the manor (especially in the period following the Black Death). Word had it that the arduous journeys of many "pilgrims" were rather chiefly pleasure trips, and the rowdy example of janglers, tale-tellers and liars was thought to be "an encouragement to laziness and idle living."[9]

Third, not only had the Church desanctified poverty, it had elevated industry to a virtue. The obligation to work was now seen as an essential part of human nature. Though by no means a wholesale transformation, the new emphasis is quite striking in some popular confessional guides. *Labor*, which, in Gregory the Great's exegesis of the Book of Job, had meant "suffering," came to mean "work;" *quies*, which for Augustine had signified "tranquillity," became synonymous with laziness. The old anchorite vice of *acedia* (the temptation to neglect one's spiritual exercises or seek release from the rigors of a desert monk's life) was "laicized." By the late Middle Ages, the sin of sloth included not only spiritual slackness, but the neglect of one's worldly responsibilities as well.[10]

Lastly, of course, the sheer numbers of the wandering poor had reached numbers never seen before.[11]

The Church's recasting of "holy poverty" in the late Middle Ages set the stage for a decidedly less benevolent, more discerning and demanding attitude on the part of people at large toward the dependent poor. Formerly, writes Braudel, "the beggar who knocked at the rich man's door was regarded as a messenger from God, and might even be Christ in disguise." With the roads swollen by the addition of large numbers of displaced laborers, ex-soldiers, robbers, and occasional bands of vagrants, only the foolhardy still believed such notions. No longer was the legitimacy of need, in this the lowest station of a pauper's life, to be taken as self-evident. The figure of the beggar became suspect and the poor at large were tainted by association: "Idle, good for nothing and dangerous, was the verdict passed on the destitute by a society terrified by the rising tide of mendicancy."[12]

Nor, experience would soon teach, was there much hope that this rising tide was a transient thing. As the years passed, the numbers of the poor continued to grow, and it was this "conjuncture of older problems with poverty, with population growth and economic expansion" that spurred the "international movement for welfare reform" on the European continent in the sixteenth century.[13] The forces behind this conjuncture, in the main, are not difficult to identify. As capitalism began its slow ascendancy to a global economic system,[14] the settled verities of the feudal world gradually came undone. Custom would give way to competition, the security of a manor-bound peasantry would yield to the uncertainty of the landless proletariat, and the medieval institution of charity would soon prove unequal to the task of assistance. One cardinal feature of this need was its routine character: "destitution [emerged] as a normal and not, as heretofore, an abnormal element in social life."[15]

The sheer volume of need with which cities and parishes were expected to cope, more than anything else, probably explains the uniform move toward rationalized poor relief at this time. In order that the growing ranks of the innocent poor (those whose "infirmities were merely providential," as Defoe would later put it) might be justly served, it was necessary to devise means of distinguishing them from those whose need was counterfeit. The attempt to divide the villainy of "sturdie beggars and vagabonds" from the true need of the "impotent poor" was the first of many to draw workable distinctions between the deserving and undeserving poor.[16]

And so, with a force wholly out of proportion to his actual contribution to the social burden of dependency, the figure of the vagrant would assume a pivotal role in the development of public policy toward the indigent. The Webbs, for example,[17] argued that the roots of state poor relief schemes are to be found in these early efforts to control the wandering poor. In the ensuing centuries, forced imprisonment, compulsory work, banishment, branding, pillory, and torture would all be resorted to as means of curbing the movements of the rootless poor.[18]

In retrospect, the fear animating such repressive measures appears to have been threefold. In an era when footpads and highwaymen made road travel hazardous, vagrants were widely assumed to be robbers in disguise. Even when a beggar's harmlessness could be vouched for, the integrity of his need was open to question; many believed that he could find work or secure assistance elsewhere if only he would try. Lastly, and perhaps most importantly, the example of the vagrant (especially in a society soon to be introduced to the discipline of the factory on a massive scale) was thought to pose a threat: if idleness could be turned to profit, or at least assured subsistence, how then could the ranks of "free labor" be harnessed to arduous and ill-paid jobs? So long as it could be pursued with impunity, vagrancy was a standing mockery of the decent poor's submission to the new regime of work.

Animus toward the vagrant, of course, sufficed in the long run neither to discipline the working poor nor to deter the needy. But the intent was there, an insistent reminder of the necessity to discriminate among classes of the potentially dependent poor.[19] Need must be reasoned if the public fisc is to be protected, the insidious example of the idle be quelled, and the outlandish notion that a livelihood might be had without being earned kept in check. If envy is a revolutionary sin,[20] refusal to work is its secular accessory. Vagrancy fed the suspicion among the poor at large that the terms and conditions of work as they were presently constituted need not be immutable. In a laboring populace whose loyalty to the wage and shop-floor was tenuous at best, such suspicions bordered on the seditious.

II. THE SOCIAL RECOGNITION OF HOMELESSNESS

Homelessness in the most encompassing sense of the term has to do with various kinds and degrees of residential instability. In the absence of secure and stable dwelling, people have devised makeshift shelters that span everything from shared (and overcrowded) living quarters to a nomadic life on the streets. Officially, only those improvisations that are on display in public spaces, and the need that declares itself to public or charitable authorities, are classified as "homeless." Until that threshold of visibility is crossed, hardship may exist and suffering may occur—but they happen off stage, to people who although "at risk" are, for the time being, "coping." "Unmet need," to put it bluntly, is publicly irrelevant need.

My remarks here will shuttle between the narrow, official definition of homelessness and the broader, increasingly common set of survival strategies that (following Olwen Hufton) I will refer to as "economies of makeshift."[21] Clearly, the precise dimensions of the problem, and the type of coping arrangements to be considered as legitimate instances of "homelessness," are contested matters, not likely to be solved by the wand of classification or the wizardry of statistics. Tradition too has its political aspects and advocacy—not logic—plays the larger role in reasoning the need.

A. Varieties of Homelessness

Even in the strict sense adopted here, caution should obviously be exercised in applying the notion of homelessness to other times, places or cultures. While homelessness probably occurs in most societies, great variation is found not only in the forces of displacement but also in the configuration and meaning of the ensuing transient state. Nor is the reference point against which homelessness is to be measured always clear: the rudimentary Western notion of home as a place of domesticity is of comparatively recent origin. Rural housing for the majority of the population of the *ancien regime* amounted to little more than hovels, shared with animals, and "fulfilled no social function," not even the minimal one of "serv[ing] as homes for families."[22]

Resort to irregular forms of accommodation—what, with some reservations, might be called "homeless ways of life"—may describe the usual situation of whole communities (such as gypsies, Irish "travellers," or nomadic hunters and gatherers), or the chosen practice of certain groups (religious mendicants, warring or hunting parties), or, it can be the lot of specific occupations (migrant workers, prospectors, itinerant preachers). A kind of professional homelessness may even make its appearance from time to time, as in the figure of the American tramp. Official attitudes toward these atypical persons and practices vary greatly, depending in part (I suggest) on the threat that such symbols of unearned livelihood are thought to pose.

For centuries, to take an unusually colorful example, companies of unemployed scholars roved the medieval countryside. Having taken minor orders in the church, they readily found refuge at monasteries located a day's walk apart. The custom was that these guests repaid the hospitality of their hosts with ribald parodies of liturgical texts and deft lampoons of the established church. Their antics sufficiently provoked the church fathers of the day that denunciations of this *ordo vagorum* were regular items on the calendar of Council proceedings from the thirteenth century on. The Church's patience eventually wore thin and repressive measures were enacted. Vagrant clerics were shorn of their tonsure (and thus deprived of their protection against secular justice) and ecclesiastics who sheltered them were subject to fine or imprisonment.[23]

(If I may digress for the moment: I take it that one lesson of this medieval episode is that the privileges of even honorable mendicants were conditioned upon political tolerance of both their numbers and whatever cultural "commentary"[24] they dared to offer. A similar rule may well apply today to some of the more energetic efforts to rid city streets of mendicants and side-walk dwellers.)

Occasionally, the distinctive niche recognized as homeless was occupied by a miscellany of players, with little in common other than their mobility. In fourteenth century England, for example, "wayfaring" was an established way of life. The minstrels, laborers, musicians, pardoners, "pedlars" and pilgrims who made up its ranks provided valuable communication links between distant regions.[25] (And, just as the legacy of the wandering scholar is preserved in the *Carmina Burana*, so that of the wayfarer comes down to us as *The Canterbury Tales*.) But even recognizing their useful function, the wayfarers could not escape the traditional suspicion of strangers, a suspicion aggravated by the predations of robbers and the lawless example of runaway serfs.[26]

In eighteenth century France, an enumeration of the population on the road reads like an inventory of misfortune and artifice:

> [W]idows, orphans, cripples...journeymen who had broken their contracts, out-of-work laborers, homeless priests with no living, old men, fire victims... war victims, deserters, discharged soldiers and even officers...would-be vendors of useless articles, vagrant preachers with or without licenses, 'pregnant servant-girls and unmarried mothers driven from home,' children sent out 'to find bread or to maraud'...strolling players whose music was an alibi....[27]

Many others, Braudel remarks, were "virtually homeless, living in makeshift shelters (what we would call shanty-towns)."[28] And if random adversity was responsible for the displacement of some, the closer one gets to the modern period the more chronic is uncertainty about sources of subsistence and the more routine is irregularity in ways of life.[29]

B. A Confusion of Tongues

Diversity in form and content is the rule not only of the appearance but also of the names by which homelessness has been known. Victorian England would have recognized as "homeless" those whom its Elizabethan forebears would have hunted down as "masterless men;" each era would have readily identified the other's "vagrants." Late nineteenth century America would excoriate as "tramps" what New England colonists had occasion to refer to as "the strolling poor."[30] In the early decades of the twentieth century, America's "hobo" was equivalent to Canada's "bunkhouse man."[31] Closer to the present, when the *Saturday Evening Post* asked "Will Ours be the Century of Homeless People?"[32] it had in mind not the displaced poor but the vast numbers of political refugees that were making their ways to new lives across the globe.

Even today, certain anachronisms seem bound to sow confusion in the minds of urban visitors. Along Manhattan's thoroughfares, for example, there regularly appear small yellow signs, discolored by age, with the words

"Public Shelter" and an arrow directing one to a nearby building. Official capacity is also given. These signs refer not (as a perusal of the local press might lead one to suppose) to refuges for the homeless poor, but to civil defense precautions taken thirty years ago in surreal expectation of surviving an atomic war.

Nor is terminological ambiguity the exclusive preserve of the observer. In the course of my own fieldwork (and the observation has been reported by others as well), I regularly met people living on the street or in public places who denied being homeless. In the minds of some, such a term should be restricted to those of their compatriots who were clearly disordered in mind.

III. CORE THEMES IN THE HISTORY OF HOMELESSNESS

That public provision of shelter has suffered from a kind of institutional amnesia is not a novel observation. Writing in 1934, by which time the lodging house rolls were at an all time high and the city had logged over a century's experience in dealing with the problems of street beggars and the shelterless poor, one seasoned observer wondered if anything had been learned:

> Dependent homeless persons have always been a problem in New York City and, whether by discipline or charity, or both, the attention of the public has been challenged on numerous occasions. Each time the public seems to have met the challenge in the easiest and most expedient manner, with very little reference to previous experience and only intermittent, casual interest in the future.[33]

Specific measures to relieve the hardship of the homeless poor came into existence in the mid-nineteenth century in New York. In part, this was owing to a larger movement to differentiate subclasses of deviancy.[34] The upshot was that for the first time being homeless was recognized as a distinctive circumstance of need, one that would no longer be exhaustively defined by the traditional term vagrancy. Reformers were quick to perceive subcategories among the homeless poor and to propose appropriate measures to deal with each accordingly. Specialized and, for once, nonpunitive public shelters (rooms in police station houses) were designated for the use of the homeless. In a marked departure from the all-encompassing regimen of the old institutions of "indoor relief," use of these makeshift shelters was haphazard, part-time, on a first-come first-served basis, and entailed no submission to rules beyond the modest requirement of not interfering with the right of others in similar straits to get a night's rest. These were, in a word, marginal institutions, rigged up to meet a need that would otherwise have gone unheeded. They functioned by default not design. And they mark the initiation of a policy of improvisation that has endured to the present.

The history of the public response to homelessness can be described by identifying the core themes that have dominated the enterprise from the beginning.

A. Damaged, Disagreeable People

Despite stubborn indications to the contrary, homelessness has traditionally been viewed as a problem of troubled—and troublesome—individuals. The terms of opprobrium have changed, from the allegations of "barbarism" favored by nineteenth century reformers to the diagnosis of impaired capacity for social connectedness favored by latter-day sociologists, but the logic has not. Whether by predisposition, slow decline, or sudden trauma, this argument runs, such people are damaged and their homelessness serves merely to confirm and compound that fact.

Nineteenth-century reformers were convinced that the tramp was a kind of genetic throwback, an only partially civilized "savage," whose primitive nature was but tenuously held in check. Turn-of-the-century observers held up alcoholism, a congenital antipathy to work, and "feeble-mindedness" as the chief causes. Postwar analysts of "skid row" society saw "disaffiliation"—an inability to form, or refusal to abide by, the ties that bind us together as members of a common society—at the heart of the problem. Commentators on homelessness today refer to the deranged biochemistry of the urban street-dweller; to deficits in their ability to engage and sustain informal networks of support; and to a too-ready willingness on the part of shelter users to take municipal authorities on "a good housing deal."[35] In each instance, the assumption is that the distinctive shape of a social niche is best explained by examining the traits of its occupants.

In a word, the appeal of such an approach could be summed up as convenience. For if it is the character faults or pathology of the poor that best accounts for their poverty, then the deeper structural questions that their disturbing presence might otherwise provoke may be safely ignored.

B. Relief for a Price

Not only poor relief (institutional or office-based) was governed by the principle of "less eligibility,"[36] but emergency shelter as well. Proof of neediness was assessed in several ways. Submission to interrogation to determine whether one had responsible relatives in the area, and willingness to perform work (usually splitting wood or doing chores around the facility) or to endure a sermon in exchange for bed and board, were the most common. Artful lodgers could sometimes find their way around these requirements. But the essential "means test" was simplicity itself; the mere fact that one was willing to put up with the wretched conditions in the almshouse or municipal lodging house or police station house was de facto proof of the desperation of one's straights.

Given the condition of housing in the late nineteenth century city, strict enforcement of the principle of less eligibility would have amounted to an invitation to cruelty. In fact, reformers of that day repeatedly expressed their frustration at seasonal almshouse residents who found the facility—spartan and unforgiving as it was—of superior quality to their usual digs. Even so, the notion continued to hold sway and proved remarkably resistant to fluctuating circumstances. As shelter directors were quick to realize and powerless to change, the institutional routine was a rigid one, unvarying even when thousands of normally working men showed up at the shelter door. To have altered the routine, to have made allowances for a "different class of homeless man" (as some private shelters did during times of economic depression), would have been to confront the founding principle and operating premise of such institutions: these were temporary makeshift shelters, not subsidized alternatives, and anyone contemplating a longer stay had better think twice.[37] Writing in the pages of *The New Republic* in 1933, Matthew Josephson was astonished to discover that shelter policy, in the midst of the worst depression the country had ever seen, was still "premised on the theory of the bum."[38]

C. An Institutional Hybrid

Repeatedly, shelter administrators have been vexed to learn that this one facility was saddled with two quite contrary tasks. For the most part, it was to serve as a refuge of last resort for institutional castoffs, "inappropriate referrals," and people for whom the idea of the structured life of "indoor relief" was anathema—it had inherited, in short, the catch-all function of the colonial almshouse. In addition, as conditions in the labor market would demand, it was to be pressed into service as the temporary bivouac for the "reserve army" of the new industrial capitalist order. It as expected to be both a place of rehabilitation—"a great human repair shop" in Commissioner Kingsbury's phrase (1914)—and a public lodging house—a flop, where penniless men could find a bed and a meal. The two functions demanded wholly different programs and in the end neither took precedence. Instead, as Stuart Rice put it, an "institutional hybrid" evolved, "incoherent in policy and extravagant in operation."[39]

The same contradiction plagued the emergency programs for the homeless in the 1930s[40] and has returned to haunt contemporary shelters. At heart, the fundamental issue is not the quality of the shelters themselves, but an enduring ambivalence toward this category of relief whatever its guise.

D. Institutional Deterrence vs. Popular Makeshifts

Much as had been the case with reformist campaigns against street-begging, popular practice was out of joint with public policy with respect to the principle of "less eligibility" and the institution of the "means test."

Professional charity railed against "indiscriminate alms-giving;" common folks found it awkward and demeaning to try to divide "deserving" from "undeserving" and organized drives to distribute food, fuel and clothing during times of acute need. More pervasive still were the varieties of unobtrusive aid, the everyday practices of sharing and support to which ordinary people resorted as routine matters. These things were done quietly, out of sight, without any public declaration of need, and thus for the most part have eluded the social scientist's prying gaze.

The ingenuity and improvisations of the unemployed and their families that would so impress social scientists in the Great Depression were already well-established traditions among the urban poor in the late nineteenth century.[41] Hardship, bad luck and spells of real scarcity were familiar to working-class households and formal institutional aid, especially if it meant enduring humiliating rites of admittance and a bed in the anonymous democracy of a public flophouse, was an act of uncommon desperation. Recourse to kinship and custom—not the state—was the usual means for dealing with misfortune.

The larger story of emergency shelter is thus the informal one, and a cardinal feature of that assistance is that the need it meets never becomes a statistic of official relief. Acknowledged or not, the support extended by kin and neighbors was an indispensable prop—and continues to be an indispensable prop—to the formal relief apparatus charged with sheltering the homeless.

IV. CONTINUITIES AND DISCONTINUITIES

The homeless crisis besetting our cities today is of a markedly different sort than that traditionally dealt with in American urban settings. Still, while the singularities of the contemporary scene are striking, they should not be allowed to mask enduring staples of the public response to homelessness.

A. Discontinuities

1. Geography: Public homelessness and the institutions set up to relieve it are far more spatially dispersed phenomena in most cities today than at any time since the Great Depression. Skid row, that repository of official homelessness in the postwar era, has long since outgrown its former boundaries as a zone of disgraced social identity. The sheer visibility of much urban homelessness is markedly at odds with its picture in the past, again excepting periods of severe depression.

2. Demography: The homeless poor today are a more diverse population, one more obviously drawn from a cross-section of the urban poor, than at any time in the past. To take just two indicators: families make up the fastest growing subgroup within the class, and impoverished ethnic minorities are found in much higher proportions than in the population at large.[42] (Much variation is found regionally, of course.) At the same time, there are great differences in the mobility of local homeless populations, with western and southern areas tending to see more transient populations. Finally, although often overemphasized in popular accounts, the presence of unusually high frequencies of seven psychiatric disabilities among the homeless poor cannot be denied. The most recent authoritative review finds that in well-designed studies the prevalence of current mental illness ranges from 28 to 37 percent. Compared to their nondisabled counterparts, the psychiatrically disabled homeless differ chiefly in being homeless for longer periods and in having less contact with friends and family, more with the criminal justice system, and fewer employment prospects.[43]

3. Structural causes: Marked changes in the segmented composition of the labor force—and not, as was typically the case in the past, massive unemployment—figures centrally among the structural factors behind contemporary homelessness. The emerging polarized labor market of high tech, highly skilled, professional service jobs at one end, and low-paid, menial service work (maintenance, clerical, delivery) and some residual manufacturing at the other, coupled with the deteriorating situation of poor households at large, is what makes for the pronounced marginality of young black men in particular (in places like New York, the largest group of shelter users).[44] Abetting both these factors is a new dynamic of scarcity in urban housing markets. Briefly, this is a function of changed urban land values, the loss of much older low-cost housing (especially residential hotels), growing demand for higher priced dwellings, and a diminished capacity on the part of many poor households to keep up with rising rents. The net effects are an intensified demand for an increasingly scarce good—affordable housing—and, in many quarters, the mounting suspicion that to trust in the self-corrective tendencies of the market to rectify the situation is sheer folly.

4. Advocacy: An older, long dormant tradition of self-mobilization among the homeless poor has recently resurfaced and promises to be a shaping force in future advocacy efforts. Similarly, guerilla theatre—public marches and demonstrations, prolonged fasts and encampments, disruptions of official ceremonies—has played an important role in training popular attention on the issue. Organized lobbying and legislative action have begun to bear substantial fruit as well.[45] But the most distinctive feature of contemporary advocacy efforts to data has been the role of the courts, and the original right to shelter case will be examined in some detail below.

B. Continuities

1. Marginal people/Liminal relief: For the most part, public shelters continue to be physically and socially segregated, their institutional space mimicking the social status of their residents. The isolating and often forbidding character are elements in the traditional policy of deterrence. In New York, abandoned schools and psychiatric facilities, armories, refurbished troopships and ferries, and—the ideal site since the middle of the nineteenth century—islands, have emerged as the preferred sites for new shelters.

2. Almshouses in all but name: Recycled but unrecognized as such, the "undifferentiated" almshouse function has survived in the guise of contemporary shelters. With the exception of a recent (and only partially implemented more to restrict certain shelters or sections of shelters to specific clientele—men participating in work programs, ex-patients, men with outside jobs—the vast, cavernous facilities have been home indifferently to people of all manner of need and handicap. As early as the mid-1970s, moreover, it was clear to shelter staff that this erstwhile skid row haven had become the newest "dumping ground" for the misfits and discards of other public facilities. That recurring failure of the nineteenth century almshouse—proper "classification"—has been recycled along with the institution itself.

3. The poor bear the burden: Finally, as researchers in Los Angeles, Minneapolis, Chicago and New York have all found,[46] official shelter rolls tell only part of the story. The larger part of the emergency assistance burden is born today, as it was in the nineteenth century, by poor households themselves. By rough estimates, the scale of "doubled up" families in public housing alone in New York City outnumbers those who are officially homeless by 20 to 1.

V. THE ROLE OF LEGAL ADVOCACY

Arguably the most distinctive feature of the current public policy deliberations has been the role of legal advocacy.[47] At no time in the history of public shelter has the court played so central and persisting a role as in the original right to shelter case, filed in October 1979 on behalf of homeless men in New York City, *Callahan v. Carey*.[48] After a preliminary injunction in December 1979 which directed the city to provide shelter to all "needy, indigent men," the public system began to expand for the first time in fifteen years. Conditions, however, remained dismal and the treatment of the men harsh and degrading. Faced with a situation of de facto deterrence, the advocates insisted that the case go to trial.

Formal proceedings commenced in December 1980 and testimony on shelter conditions was solicited from both homeless men and local experts. Confronted with steadily amassing evidence of the gross insufficiency in capacity and intolerable situations within the shelter system, abetted by mounting pressure from Judge Richard Wallach, the city and state entered into prolonged negotiations with counsel for the defense in early spring 1981. The result, in August 1981, was a court-entered consent decree that not only reaffirmed a right to shelter but set minimal standards of decency for public shelters, and provided for ongoing monitoring of conditions in them. A major victory appeared won. No longer would a tradition that had made contempt for the homeless man its operating premise be acceptable.

In the nearly eight years that have elapsed since, the court has issued dozens of orders directing the city to comply with one or another of the terms of the decree. Shelter capacity has exploded: from a haphazard collection of Bowery flophouses and floor space at a central intake facility, with a maximum capacity of 1600 to a network of some twenty shelters throughout the city, with a total bed capacity of over 9,000. Quality, which had improved in the immediate aftermath of the decree, now fluctuates considerably, owing both to variations in the sheer size of facilities (up to 1200 on a single floor) and to the intensity of demand on a given night. There has been no noticeable decline in the street-dwelling population; just last fall (October 1988) a survey by the Transit Authority put the number of people sleeping in the subway system at over 1400. Overall costs for emergency shelter in New York City now top $0.3 billion annually.

A. Callahan Revisited

Judicial decrees may be blunt instruments for making policy, but the pressure they generate for immediate action, the continuing oversight by informed parties they offer, and the leverage they wield with notoriously unresponsive bureaucracies, make them all but matchless as catalysts for reform. At the same time, severe limitations are placed on the exercise of that power in practice. The implementation of reforms (especially costly reforms) is subject to myriad compromises and exceptions; the scope of application may be arbitrarily drawn; and obsessive concern with the details of the decree and subsequent orders may well eclipse the long-term goal. As such compromises have multiplied and the shelter system itself has mushroomed, advocates have found themselves hoist on their petard—seeking to maintain standards in an emergency enterprise that nearly everyone agrees is a shambles, and that threatens nonetheless to become the "crisis management" solution to homelessness.

I can put it simply: improvised as temporary measures under exigent circumstances, these institutional makeshifts soon developed inertial force of their own. Satellite apparatuses (health, mental health, drug rehab and job training programs) were spun off, adding to the service density of this new institutional niche. Whole systems evolved where jury-rigged stopgaps had been planted.

If there is one substantive advance, aside from the sheer gain in capacity, it is the provision for ongoing monitoring. Doggedly, the court has refused to cede oversight responsibility for the system, and has proven responsive to evidence of infractions of the terms of the decree. But if the recent history of the Willowbrook case is any guide, this will become an increasingly tenuous position as managerial responsibilities expand and external pressure mounts for less costly—or, more to the point, less privileged—forms of relief.

B. The Willowbrook Consent Decree

Six years into the implementation of a community placement plan for former residents of a state institution for the developmentally disabled, the state defendants appealed to the court to relax the size limit on transitional facilities (raising the ceiling from 15 to 50 beds per facility). The state cited improved conditions at the Willowbrook hospital, a tightening real estate market, and growing community opposition in support of its petition. The lower court ruled that the state failed to show that sufficient cause for a modification of the decree—"grievous wrong evoked by new and unforeseen conditions"—applied in this case. To the surprise of nearly all concerned, the appeals court reversed. It is the logic of its reasoning that concerns me.

The appeals court's ruling hinged on what it construed as the artificiality of the judicial laboratory that had spawned the consent decree in the first place. "In judicial reform litigation such as this," the court wrote,

> judicially imposed remedies must be open to...accommodation of a wider constellation of events than is represented in the adversarial setting of the courtroom.[49]

The court took particular note of the exigencies of budgetary constraints and neighborhood resistance to the transitional housing. The error in the lower court's ruling, in effect, was to have arrogated to the judiciary decisions about the implementation of public policy that are properly left to the legislature and the free play of the political arena. In a word, the lower court had mistaken for an *exception* a set of interests that warranted no special consideration.

Such a conservative construction of judicial redress was precisely what city and state defendants had been urging all along in *Callahan*. Had it prevailed, the course of public interest litigation in this case would have been rather different. Indeed, one may already glimpse what the end of an era that has only recently learned to treat the homeless as exceptions might look like.

VI. BY WAY OF CONCLUSION

If not the person, then at least the image of homelessness has undergone significant rehabilitation in recent years. Indeed, there is a steadily mounting store of evidence, largely ethnographic and increasingly longitudinal in nature, that most homeless people are homeless on an episodic basis; that many manage to retain old ties and may even cultivate new contacts with friends and kin who remain housed; that a good many still work, if only part-time, or at least scavenge in order to lay claim to some income; that, in short, the received image of the homeless poor as "abject" in their helplessness is dead wrong. Indeed, there are signs—fleeting and haphazard though they may be to date—that something of an inversion in our image of the homeless may be under sway. One can discern an almost celebratory tone in reports that purport to have found surprising evidence of resiliency and resourcefulness among some segments of the homeless poor.

At the same time, however, calls to "Bring Back Asylums"[50] resound with numbing frequency in the popular press, as though disorders of mind— perhaps compounded by pathologies of place—were the only issue.

My concern is less the accuracy of either of these versions than it is the implications to which they lend themselves in policy circles. Two proposals in particular I found troublesome. Both seem to me premised upon a principle of economy of social effort: resort to old institutions is less costly, in terms both of cultural reckoning and budgetary outlays, than would be serious and as yet untried attempts to grapple with the underlying issues of dispossession and resource scarcity that widespread homelessness raises.

The first is the recently initiated (October 1987) practice in New York City of forcibly removing street-dwellers found to be so "gravely disabled" that they are unable to care for themselves. In the first thirteen months of operation, over 300 persons were admitted to a special unit of a city hospital set up for this purpose. Over half were subsequently sent to a state hospital where most remain today. (The disposition of the others discharged is unclear, although it appears that for some number, families were located and agreed to receive them.) Recently, the advocates' worst fears about the absence of any long-term planning for permanent housing for these individuals were confirmed in a breathtaking announcement by the mayor, made over the objections of two of his commissioners, that manages to ignore both elementary axioms of community psychiatry and two decades of bitter experience. Discharge to the municipal shelter system will henceforth be considered an "appropriate" aftercare placement for psychiatric patients in municipal hospitals.[51]

Two objectives are thus accomplished. By fiat, a reclassification of the figure and meaning of homelessness is effected. From vagrants to patients: we now know what to do with such people, where to send them, what they need—at least up to the time of their discharge, when the warrant of their need again becomes ambiguous. We need not riddle the awful immediacy of their presence amidst us, nor invest it with any deeper resonances than those of mere pathology. We need not ponder what they had been offered, the grounds for their refusal of past assistance, or the strange logic that may be discerned in the art of their necessities.

The second achievement merely extends the first: we need not inquire—because the issue is never seriously broached—into the specifics of long-term provision for their subsistence. It is enough, apparently, that the semblance of competent care has been initiated and the rough theatre of their misery brought to an end. In the event our memories fail us, eighteen months later, when we are informed that it was not their homelessness (or, indeed, their hypothesized underlying disorder) that was the object of the intervention: shelter residents are, after all, still homeless. It was rather their visibility.

Thus, the shelter, now recast as a quasi-therapeutic institution, is made to reenact not only the legacy of the almshouse but that of the asylum as well. And, like that nineteenth century institution, it remains, "a convenient way of getting rid of inconvenient people."[52]

The second proposal, to my mind, is a bit trickier, building as it does on solid evidence of the support networks of the urban poor. It has been made most clearly (and, I hasten to add, constructively) by Peter Rossi.[53] The suggestion is to subsidize the spontaneous support of kin by establishing a categorical assistance program—Aid to Families with Dependent *Adults*. Leave aside for the moment the administrative nightmare such a program would present;[54] I want to concentrate on the principle of reform it embodies.

As a provisional measure, such an interim proposal has merit, recognizing as it does the sheer scale of housing development needed to close the gap between need and supply and the time that will take. The difficulty, of course, is that transitional demands have a way of settling into established precedents. It is that prospect of institutionalizing dependency for "redundant" adults that I found troubling.

The problem is that the proposal takes dependency as a given rather than as a contingent status. Arguable, the whole point of a public assistance program (or a social insurance program, as the European versions are known) is to introduce a buffer into the interface between worker household and labor market. Such programs are premised on a recognition, long in coming and contested in application, that unemployment is not primarily a function of individual character but of market forces operating according to their own logic. This logic is indifferent to the demands on or consequences for the laboring men and women subject to its sway. Confusions about the casual arrow in this dynamic have, of course, been the stuff of vigorous debate for centuries. To take but one instance, throughout the nineteenth and well into the twentieth century, "vagrancy" was thought to be the cause of unemployment, rather than the other way around.[55]

My point is the obvious one: once we accept that failure to procure a job—even in a labor market as hostile to the skills and capacities of many minority youth as ours is today—is equivalent to the surrender of the adult claim to independence, we will have ceded significant territory in the ground won by the welfare state in the last fifty years. We can, to my mind, ill-afford such a concession today, at a time when the mills of impoverishment grind ever more unerringly in the minority households of urban areas.

As a stopgap—an emergency, voluntary measure of limited duration—I can see the point to such a program. But as a long-term measure, it seems to me misguided and defeatist. Far more productive, I would argue, would be to open debate on the issue of "General Relief"—at present, a state funded and administered program of shamefully low benefit levels and minuscule coverage. That at least would build on the precarious achievements of past struggles to wrest the prospect of livelihood away from sheer market determination.

These are parlous times for the poor. Formally to assign responsibility for the provisioning of adult citizens to the uncertain scaffolding of custom and kinship is to redirect a demand that ought properly be made of government. That such a proposal seems, on the face of it, so prudent and well-grounded is, I would suggest, a measure of the ground we have lost in the last eight years.

NOTES

1. *New York Review of Books*, October 27, 1988, at 19.
2. "A *thes* [a propertyless laborer who worked for hire when he could find it and begged a living otherwise], not a slave, was the lowest creature on earth that Achilles could think of. The terrible thing about a *thes* was his lack of attachment, his not belonging." M.I. Finley, The World of Odysseus 57 (2d ed. 1978).
3. *The Odyssey* 251 (R. Fitizgerald, Trans.) (1961).
4. *See generally* P. Salter, Some Early Tracts on Poor Relief SV–XX (1926); N.Z. Davis, *Poor Relief, Humanism, and Heresy: The Case of Lyon*, 5 Studies Med. & Renaissance Hist. (1968); J. Garraty, Unemployment in History (1978); G. Himmelfarb, The Idea of Poverty (1983).
5. de Vives, *De Subventione Pauperum*, in P. Salter, *supra* note 4.
6. Tierney, *The Decretists and the Deserving Poor*, 1 Comp. Stud. Soc. & Hist. 341 (1959–60).
7. A.L. Beier, Masterless Men 4–5 (1985).
8. "[M]endicity is now their trade, which some practice well, others better; miracles of self-denial are demanded of them, and behold, on the contrary, prodigies of selfishness. It is no longer religion, it is their order which must be protected." J. Jusserand, English Wayfaring Life in the Middle Ages 298 (1897).
9. *Id.* at 350–351.
10. S. Wenzel, The Sin of Sloth 86–90, 174–75 (1967).
11. F. Braudel, The Wheels of Comemrce 506–12 (1982).
12. *Id.* at 508.
13. N.Z. Davis, *supra* note 4, at 258, 267.
14. *See generally* I. Wallerstein, The Modern World System, (1974).

15. P. Salter, *supra* note 4, at xvi.
16. J. Garraty, *supra* note 4, at 27.
17. S. Webb & B. Webb, English Poor Law History 350 (1927).
18. K. Marx, Capital (B. Fowkes Rev. ed. 1976) (1st ed. 1867); *cf.* C.J. Ribton-Turner, A History of Vagrants and Vagrancy and Beggars and Begging (1887).
19. For a fuller discussion of the "distributive dilemma," see generally D. Stone, The Disabled State (1984).
20. M. Mollat, The Poor in the Middle Ages: An Essay in Social History 231 (1986).
21. O. Hufton, The Poor of Eighteenth Century France 1750–1789 69–127 (1974).
22. P. Aries Centuries of Childhood 392 (1962); *cf.* F. Braudel, The Structures of Everyday Life 283–85 (1981).
23. *See* H. Waddell, The Wandering Scholars 161–84 (1927).
24. For a fascinating discussion of distinctive psychiatric disorders as cultural "commentary," see Karp, *Deconstructing Culture-Bound Syndromes*, 21 Soc. Sci. & Med. 221 (1985).
25. J. Jusserand, *supra* note 8.
26. A.L. Beier, *supra* note 7.
27. F. Braudel, *supra* note 11, at 510–511.
28. F. Braudel, *supra* note 22, at 285.
29. *See generally* K. Norberg, Rich and Poor in Grenoble, 1600–1814 295–296 (1985).
30. Jones, *The Strolling Poor: Transiency in Eighteenth-Century Massachusetts*, 8 J. Soc. Hist. 28 (1975).
31. *See generally* N. Anderson, The Hobo (1923) and E. Bradwin, The Bunkhouse Man (1928).
32. *Will ours be the Century of Homelessness,* 232 Saturday Evening Post 10 (September 12, 1958).
33. N. Anderson, The Homeless in New York City 2 (1934).
34. *See* A. Scull, Decarceration: Community Treatment and The Deviant—A Radical View 26–31 (1977).
35. Main, *The Homeless of New York,* 72 Pub. Interest 3 (1983).
36. The principle of less eligibility states that the situation of the assisted pauper was to be less attractive (or "eligible") than that of the most menial laborer, so as to keep sharp the spur of necessity and preserve the incentive to work.
37. In fact, for most of its history, the municipal lodging house in New York enforced monthly limits of stay.
38. Josephson, *The Other Nation,* 75 New Republic 16 (May 17, 1933).
39. Rice, *The Failure of the Municipal Lodging House,* 11 Nat'l. Mun. Rev. 358–59 (1922).
40. "In the care of [the local homeless] there had been neither application of the generally accepted standards of institutional care required of other city departments furnishing institutional care on a long time basis, nor the recognition of individual budgetary needs generally accepted in the care of resident families on relief. . . . A philosophy of temporariness characterized the program . . . " Governor's Comm'n on Unemployment, Public Relief for Transient and Non-Settled Persons in the State of New York 145 (1936).
41. A. Keyssar, Out of Work: The First Century of Unemployment in Massachusetts 156 (1986).
42. *See generally* U.S. Department of Housing and Urban Development, A Report on the 1988 National Survey of Shelters for the Homeless (1989).
43. They do *not* differ with respect to age, sex, ethnicity, residential history, substance abuse, or the role of economic factors or family crisis in causing their homelessness. *See* R.C. Tessler & D.L. Dennis, A Synthesis of NIMH-Funded

Research Concerning Persons Who Are Homeless and Mentally Ill 28, 36 (February 1989).

44. See Hopper, Susser, & Conover, *Economies of Makeshift: Deindustrialization and Homelessness in New York City*, 14 Urb. Anthropology 183 (1986).

45. Notably in the Steward B. McKinney Homeless Assistance Act of 1987, Pub. L. No. 100–77, 101 Stat. 482 (1987).

46. *See* Koegel & Burnam. *Traditional and Nontraditional Alcoholics*, 11 Alcohol Health and Research World 28 (1987); I. Piliavin, *Stayers and Leavers among the Homeless*, Paper Presented at the NIAAA and UCSD Conference on Homelessness, Alcohol and Other Drugs, San Diego (February 2–4, 1989); P. Rossi, Without Shelter: Homelessness in the 1980s 37–43 (1989); and Hopper, Susser & Conover, *supra* note 44.

47. *Cf.* K. Hopper and L. Cox, *Litigation in Advocacy for the Homeless,* in Housing the Homeless (J. Erickson and C. Whilhelm, Eds. 1986). *See also* Langdon & Kass, *Homelessness in America: Looking for the Right to Shelter*, 19 Colum. J.L. & Soc. Probs. 305 (1985).

48. 188 N.Y.L.J., Dec. 11, 1979, at 10, Col. 4 (N.Y. Sup. Ct., December 5, 1979).

49. As cited in D. Rothman & S. Rothman, The Willowbrook Wars 352 (1984).

50. Blake Fleetwood, New York Daily News, Apr. 9, 1989, at 1, Col. 1.

51. New York Times, Mar. 6, 1989, at 16, col. 1.

52. A. Scull, *supra* note 34, at 33.

53. P. Rossi, *supra* note 46, at 57–9.

54. Think only of the difficulties of establishing ongoing residence, of apportioning payment to family and supported member(s), of setting appropriate eligibility criteria.

55. *See generally* P.T. Ringenbach, Tramps and Reformers, 1873–1916 (1973).

Making Shelter Work: Placing Conditions on an Employable Person's Right to Shelter

Dennis D. Hirsch

Homelessness in America is a problem of significant dimensions. Current estimates of the number of homeless[1] vary from 250,000[2] to 3,000,000,[3] with a recent count giving a figure of 500,000-600,000.[4] This national tragedy has sparked many efforts to help. One of the major responses by members of the legal community has been to argue for a right to shelter that would obligate the government (generally state or local) to provide housing to all homeless persons who request it.[5] Legal scholars have attempted to define the grounds for such a right,[6] and litigators have brought lawsuits seeking to establish it.[7]

Generally, these advocates have argued for an unqualified guarantee of shelter to any person without a home.[8] For example, in an early article Frank Michelman described the right to shelter as

> an ironclad assurance that no one, no matter his profligacy or obstinacy, shall ever be deprived of decent shelter. Reference to a right to be housed suggests ...an assurance that acceptable housing will be available irrespective of the market returns commanded by one's endowments of talent, influence, or capital; and irrespective, even, of voluntary choices in one's remote past which results in present inability to pay the true costs of acceptable housing.[9]

Recently, however, judges and legal commentators have begun to question the unqualified nature of the right to shelter and to argue that, where the right is established, it be more narrowly defined. For example, Judge Neely of the Supreme Court of West Virginia, dissenting in a case that established a right to shelter in that state, took issue with the majority opinion because

> [it does] not establish with any particularity the class of people for whom the Commissioner is required to provide housing. Does it include people in certain income brackets only? Does it include those with sufficient income to pay rent who prefer to spend their income on alcohol? Does it include those who simply don't like the shelters currently run by charitable organizations?... [T]he

> new program...appears to contemplate permanent housing for anyone un-
> willing or unable to pay rent[.] Can anyone be turned down?[10]

A recent commentator offered a similar critique of right-to-shelter cases, stating that "[c]ourts that have recognized a legal right to shelter...have had difficulty defining the nature and the scope of the right.... [T]he lack of an adequate definition of a right to shelter is a major defect in decisions granting the right."[11]

Though voices such as these have begun to call for limits on the right to shelter, none as yet have suggested parameters for the right. This Note recommends a way for courts to proceed. While recognizing that the establishment of an unqualified right to shelter is, for some sectors of the shelter population, a positive development, it argues that, for the employable homeless, it is not. The Note will show that an unqualified right to shelter prevents the implementation of potentially useful policies targeted at this group. It will then argue that courts or settling parties establishing a right to shelter should define it more narrowly: the right should not extend to an employable homeless person who refuses, without good cause, to participate in an employment-related activity of which he or she is capable. Shelter administrators should be able to condition an employable person's right to shelter on such participation.

The Note will support this argument by examining New York City's experience with the right to shelter. In the 1979 case of *Callahan v. Carey,* advocates for the homeless brought suit against the City and State of New York claiming that state constitutional and statutory law guaranteed a right to shelter for all homeless men in New York City.[12] The litigation resulted in a consent decree effectively establishing an unqualified right to shelter.

This Note will show that in the years since the consent decree, increasing numbers of employable[13] single adults have moved into the New York City shelters.[14] By drawing on interviews with shelter administrators, and on current trends in social welfare policy, the Note will argue that the most effective way to help such people achieve self-sufficiency may well be to require them to participate in employment-related programs.

Under the current regime of an unqualified right to shelter, however, shelter administrators in New York City cannot implement such requirements because they cannot deny housing even to an employable person who refuses to participate in an employment-related program. Thus, an unqualified right to shelter constrains shelter administrators from testing new approaches that may be more effective in assisting shelter residents.

This Note suggests, therefore, that the parties to the *Callahan* litigation revise the consent decree so that it can permit administrators to implement employment-related requirements for employable shelter residents. Such a qualified right to shelter, the Note will show, is more consistent with the laws of New York State than is a broader right which would preclude requirements. The Note will also examine the constitutions of other states where lawsuits have established a right to shelter or where the basis for such a right might exist. This review will demonstrate that, as in New York, state law is consistent with placing employment-related conditions on the right to shelter of employable homeless persons. Courts finding a right to shelter should therefore define a narrower right which allows for such conditions.

I. *CALLAHAN V. CAREY:* THE CASE OF NEW YORK CITY

The disadvantages of an unqualified right to shelter become evident when one examines how such a right operates in practice. This Note begins with a look at New York City's experience with a broad-reaching right to shelter.

A. The Right-to-Shelter Litigation

In *Callahan v. Carey,*[15] a class of homeless men in New York City, represented by the Coalition for the Homeless (CFTH), sued the City and State of New York claiming that state constitutional and statutory law obligated defendants to provide them with food and shelter. The court granted plaintiffs' motion for a preliminary injunction requiring defendants to provide meals and lodging to those homeless men requesting it.[16] In issuing the preliminary injunction, the court cited the legal sources on which plaintiffs had grounded their arguments,[17] an indication that it was prepared to find a right to shelter based on New York State statutory and constitutional law.[18] Possibly because they anticipated this, defendants agreed to a liberally worded consent decree settling the litigation.[19] While the decree expressly left all issues of fact and law unresolved,[20] it established, de facto, an unqualified right to shelter.[21]

B. Changes in the Shelter Population Lead to Changing Concerns

To understand the policy implications of this unqualified right to shelter it is important, first, to become familiar with the make-up of the shelter population. In 1979, when the *Callahan* litigation began, the homeless plaintiffs were a relatively small group of highly incapacitated men, many of whom suffered from alcoholism, drug abuse, or mental illness.[22] People in this condition are generally not able to participate in employment and training programs, which may explain why the parties to the initial litigation do not appear to have raised the issue of employment-related requirements.

In the years since the decree, however, the shelter population has changed in two ways that make employment-related activities much more relevant. First, the number of people using the shelters has increased dramatically. Fewer than 2,000 single adults utilized the shelter system each night in 1978.[23] By the first half of fiscal year 1989, that number had expanded to 12,500.[24] Cost has grown commensurate with size. Operating costs for New York City's homeless programs for adults have grown from $6.8 million in 1978, to projected budgets (as of January 1988) of $156 million in fiscal year 1988 and $285 million in 1992.[25] This growth in size and expense makes it important to focus not just on providing beds for the homeless, but also on how to help them become self-sufficient.

The second change which increases the importance of this issue is that in the years following the decree the homeless population has come to include an increasing number of employable persons who are able to participate in employment-related programs. One of the first studies to point to this population shift was a 1932 City of New York Human Resources Administration (HRA) report.[26] HRA researchers interviewing homeless men who had lived in the shelters for two months or more found that nineteen percent of those interviewed "had in the past been able to function at quite high levels, both occupationally and socially," and many did not suffer from any evident disabilities.[27] As such, this group did not fit the 1979 mold of dysfunctional homeless.

Later studies have confirmed the finding that people with significant work histories and levels of functioning now make up a sizeable proportion of the shelter population. One study by the New York State Psychiatric Institute found that a considerable proportion of the shelter residents had recent work experience.[28] In addition, the report found that twenty-one percent of the shelter residents were capable of independent living, and an additional forty-six percent could handle living in their own apartment with "modest" supportive services.[29]

A 1988 City of New York Human Resources Administration report also confirms this trend. According to this report, fully thirty-three percent of those utilizing the shelters in 1988 were "employable," meaning that they suffered from no "major barriers to employment, such as psychiatric, serious medical, or substance abuse problems, criminal histories, limited education, or lack of work experience."[30] These figures contradict the general perception of the homeless as an incapacitated group. They demonstrate that a sizeable percentage of the current homeless population could participate in, and potentially benefit from, employment-related programs.

C. Extended Stays and Shelterization

Studies which examine the course of an employable person's stay in the shelter system give added weight to the importance of helping these residents to find jobs and become independent. These studies show that many do not use the shelters simply as temporary stopping places but move in on a long-term basis. According to a recent Human Resources Administration report, fifty-four percent of the employable single adults who entered the shelters stayed for at least four months, and thirty-one percent remained for more than seven months.[31]

Moreover, recent evidence suggests that extended stays in the shelter system have just the type of deleterious effects on persons staying there that one would least like to see with regard to the employable homeless. An in-depth study of shelter residents carried out by the New York State Psychiatric Institute in 1988 documents that many of those who remain in the shelters for significant periods adapt to their surroundings, give up on getting back out on their own, and begin to see the shelters as their permanent home.[32] Many "eventually gave up the battle and adjusted to permanent living in the shelter system."[33] This phenomenon appears to affect all residents, including those without mental or physical disabilities.[34] As the report concluded, "[a]pparently when choices were limited, perceptions were altered and adaptation took place."[35]

A pair of researchers, including a psychiatrist from Columbia University, reached remarkably similar conclusions in a 1990 study of New York City shelter residents. The report identifies a process known as "shelterization" whereby residents adapt to the shelter as a permanent home and lose their drive to return to life on the outside.[36] As one of the authors of the report stated, "[i]n short, people give in. They lose will and hope and all interest in improving themselves."[37]

These research findings indicate the development of a disturbing problem. Not only are substantial numbers of able-bodied people moving into the New York City shelter system, but many are staying for long periods and may be remaining on a permanent basis. To alleviate this problem it is important that shelter administrators develop effective means of aiding such people to achieve self-sufficiency.

D. How Most Effectively to Serve Employable Shelter Residents.

1. Controversy in New York. Those directly involved in working with employable homeless single adults express differing opinions about how best to help this group towards self-support and independent living. On the one hand, shelter administrators in New York stress the importance of requiring participation in some form of structured program—job placement, education or job training—as a way of combatting the apathy engendered by shelter life. For example, one New York City report cited the "need to develop employment referrals, supported work, and other means of fostering economic self-sufficiency"[38] and stressed that "[i]t will be important to carefully assess client needs and resources, *to impose appropriate structure and make appropriate demands on clients' own efforts.*"[39]

Karen Davis, former Director of Operations for the New York City Adult Shelters, supports this view, stating in an interview that "[a]ny way of introducing more structure would be helpful. We need to start creating some requirements since right now we ask nothing of our clients."[40] Davis believes that it would make sense to condition employable shelter residents' right to shelter on participation in work experience programs coupled with job placement or skills training activities.[41]

Leading advocates for the homeless in New York, however, disagree with the notion of imposing requirements on shelter residents. Keith Summa of CFTH, for example, believes the homeless are strongly motivated to leave the shelters and will voluntarily take advantage of employment activities that increase their opportunity to become self-sufficient.[42] Requiring participation, Summa contends, sets the wrong tone for the relationship between shelter provider and recipient and as a consequence is more destructive than helpful.[43]

2. The Philadelphia Approach.   In New York, advocates and shelter administrators differ on the issue of employment-related requirements. This is, perhaps, predictable given the logic of their roles. If one were to find a case where advocates and administrators concurred, however, their shared opinion would be entitled to additional weight since agreement would indicate that their respective roles had not unduly shaped their viewpoints. Philadelphia provides such an example.

Philadelphia faced a homelessness situation in many respects similar to New York's: litigation established a broad, unqualified right to shelter,[44] and this was followed by rapid increase in the size of the shelter population and in the cost of housing them.[45] In Philadelphia, however, after three years experience with an unqualified right to shelter, the advocates who had brought the litigation and the shelter administrators whom they had sued, jointly agreed on employment-related requirements.[46] They negotiated a new settlement which authorized the implementation of a client "protocol" whereby shelter applicants deemed employable were required to sign up for job-readiness, job-referral, and work-experience programs. The protocol gave shelter administrators the right to deny housing to employable shelter residents who refuse to comply with the conditions.[47]

It is especially interesting to examine the Philadelphia advocates views on the need for employment-related requirements, since their perspective differs so sharply from that of their New York counterparts. Steven Gold, General Counsel for the Committee on Dignity and Fairness, the group which brought the original right-to-shelter litigation in Philadelphia, and Phyllis Ryan, Executive Director of the Philadelphia Committee on the Homeless, both initially resisted the idea of requirements but eventually concluded that they were necessary and desirable.[48] According to Gold, a guaranteed right to shelter creates passivity both in the political sphere, where the homeless will be less likely to lobby for the building of more low-income housing, and in the personal sphere, where people become more dependant.[49] Employment-related requirements are one way to combat the debilitating effects of shelter life. In Gold's words, it is "absolutely critical to implement requirements, for people who are feeling psychologically down and disconnected may not take these steps voluntarily."[50] He recommends a model that his organization has implemented, run by the homeless themselves and mandating participation in employment, education, and community activities. Similarly, Ryan states that "we realized that in order to be most helpful we had to encourage the clients to take responsibility. They suffer from a great lack of self-esteem, and to get it back we need to encourage them to take on the task of shaping their own lives."[51] These are not words one would expect to hear from advocates for the homeless. Their source, and the experience on which they are based, make them especially worthy of consideration.

3. Insights From the AFDC Program. Lessons from the Aid to Families with Dependent Children (AFDC) program provide additional support for employment-related requirements. Research has shown that mandatory employment and training programs for welfare recipients can help raise the employment and earnings levels of participants and can be cost-effective.[52] This research provided support for the Family Support Act of 1988, which refocused the AFDC system to emphasize mandatory education, job search, and skills training programs.[53] The Act differs from prior approaches in that it seeks to increase the level of responsibility expected of clients at the same time as it augments the amount of services provided to them. Since both the AFDC program and the shelters serve highly dependent populations, the strong evidence and conclusions informing the Family Support Act provide support, by analogy, for those who advocate employment-related requirements for the employable homeless.

The AFDC experience also suggests an answer to the question of how to generate funding to pay for employment-related programs for the homeless. Because the Family Support Act combined increased client obligation with increased services, it broke new ground by receiving support both from conservatives, who agreed with the emphasis on client responsibility, and liberals, who liked the increase in supportive programs.[54] If employment-related requirements created a similar consensus with regard to programs for the homeless, they might increase the probability that proposals to fund increased services would be approved.

E. The Disadvantages of an Unqualified Right to Shelter

Social scientists have not yet directly proven the viability of mandatory employment-related programs for the homeless. The prior section has tried to show, however, that the issue is, at the very least, an open one. The interviews discussed above, and the evidence from the AFDC area, suggest that required skills training, job search, job placement, work experience, or education programs may well be the most effective way of aiding the employable homeless.[55] Shelter administrators should, therefore, have the opportunity to try out mandatory programs.

The unqualified right to shelter is problematic because it prevents such testing. By not allowing administrators to withhold shelter except in the most severe circumstances (e.g. violent behavior), it denies them the only effective means of sanctioning those who refuse to participate in mandated employment and training activities. Administrators cannot, therefore, set up meaningful requirements.

Shelter administrators in New York have run up against this problem. Attorneys for the Human Resources Administration state that while the Department has considered requirements of various types, it has not implemented them for fear of violating the guarantees of the consent decree and provoking further litigation.[56] Advocates for the homeless affirm that if employment-related requirements were adopted they would sue New York City to prevent their implementation.[57] Perhaps for this reason, New York City has put into place only voluntary employment-related activities.[58]

For New York City policy makers contending with the size and long-term dependency of the shelter population, this is not a satisfactory solution. They would prefer to have the option of implementing requirements.[59] Thus while a broad right to shelter may have been appropriate for the relatively small, incapacitated homeless population on whose behalf CFTH brought the initial *Callahan* litigation in 1979, it is not the correct solution for a population that includes significant numbers of employable homeless persons.[60]

F. *A More Narrowly Defined Right to Shelter*

This Note suggests that the parties to the *Callahan* litigation revise their consent decree to allow for employment-related conditions on the right to shelter.[61] For example, the eligibility section of the *Callahan* consent decree[62] could be modified to read:

> The City defendants shall provide shelter and board to each homeless person who applies for such, provided that (a) the person by reason of physical or mental dysfunction is in need of temporary shelter; or (b) the person meets the need standard to qualify for the Home Relief program established in New York State, except that the City defendants may, in their discretion, deny shelter to an employable homeless person who refuses, without good cause, to participate in employment- or training-related activities of which he or she is capable and which are intended to enable him or her to achieve self-support.

Language such as this would permit administrators to implement mandatory employment and training programs. As discussed above, no one has yet conclusively established that such programs will prove effective. Interviews with shelter administrators and advocates in Philadelphia, and the studies showing the positive effects of employment-related requirements in the welfare area, however, indicate that these programs may well have beneficial results.[63] Redefining New York's right to shelter in the manner suggested by this Note will allow shelter administrators to test the effectiveness of these potentially useful programs.

II. CONDITIONS ON AN EMPLOYABLE PERSON'S RIGHT TO SHELTER ARE CONSISTENT WITH THE LAWS OF NEW YORK STATE

The recommendation just stated may be beside the point. New York City is, after all, subject to a *right* to shelter established through litigation. If New York statutory and constitutional law compel an unqualified right to shelter, then the *Callahan* parties are constrained by this (at least until the legislature amends a controlling statute). The *Callahan* court's acceptance of plaintiffs' legal arguments in issuing the preliminary injunction makes it appear that the parties are constrained in this manner.[64] Importantly, however, the *Callahan* consent decree left all issues of law and fact unadjudicated.[65] No New York court opinion has settled this question on the merits.

This section will argue that shelter administrators would not offend New York law by placing employment-related conditions on the right to shelter of employable single adults. It will show that the plaintiffs' legal arguments in *Callahan,* and the court's opinion in issuing the preliminary injunction, depend on a perception of the homeless as a group of incapacitated persons. This concept of the homeless population is seriously out of date. Approximately one-third of those now living in New York's shelters are employable.[66] This section will reexamine plaintiffs' legal arguments in light of this change. It will argue that, with regard to the *employable* homeless, New York law does not preclude placing employment-related conditions on the right to shelter.

A. Premises of the Right-to-Shelter Litigation

Both the parties and the court in *Callahan* clearly viewed the homeless as a group of incapacitated individuals. For example, the plaintiffs' memo in *Callahan* supporting their motion for a preliminary injunction described the homeless population as "homeless men living in New York City, the overwhelming majority of whom are incapacitated due to physical and mental disabilities, often exacerbated by alcohol and drug additions."[67] Similarly the court, in issuing its preliminary injunction, described the group as "destitute and homeless alcoholics, addicts, mentally impaired derelicts, flotsam and jetsam"[68] and cited the Commissioner of the State Department of Social Service's description of the homeless as "'largely composed of individuals with histories of alcohol abuse, drug abuse, mental disorder or combination thereof. These conditions are chronic and seriously preclude or prevent independent functioning.' "[69] This perception of the homeless as people suffering from some form of disability served as a key premise of the *Callahan* plaintiffs' constitutional and statutory arguments.

1. The State Constitution.   Plaintiffs relied on section 1 of Article XVII of the New York State Constitution, which reads: "The aid, care and support of the needy are public concerns and shall be provided by the state and by such of its subdivisions, and in such manner and by such means, as the legislature may from time to time determine."[70] To construe this as a basis for a right to shelter, CFTH relied on a New York Court of Appeals decision, *Tucker v. Toia.*[71] The *Tucker* court interpreted the provision to mean that while the state retains "discretion in determining the means by which this objective is to be effectuated...and in classifying recipients and defining the term 'needy,' [the state constitution] unequivocally prevents the Legislature from simply refusing to aid those whom it has classified as needy."[72] The state, then, defines the term "needy," but once they have defined the term so that it covers a certain group they become obligated to provide aid to that group.

In *Callahan,* because the court and parties viewed the homeless as highly incapacitated, they accepted the "neediness" of this group without dispute. Plaintiffs, in their memo in support of the preliminary injunction, stated that "[o]bviously, indigent, homeless men seeking shelter are needy."[73] Defendants did not challenge this, probably because it seemed "obvious" to them as well.[74] The court, in granting the preliminary injunction, accepted that the homeless were "needy" and enforced the state obligation that follows from this. The perceived incapacitation of the homeless in 1979 was, therefore, an essential element of plaintiffs' state constitutional argument.

2. State Statutory Law.   As a second argument, the *Callahan* plaintiffs claimed that sections 131 and 62 of the New York State Social Services Law supported a right to shelter. They premised this assertion, too, on the incapacities of the 1979 homeless. Section 131 makes it the duty of state officials to "provide adequately for those unable to maintain themselves...."[75] Section 62 makes this obligation binding on local service providers such as New York City.[76] As with the term "needy" in Article XVII of the state constitution, the determination that a group is "unable to maintain themselves" affirmatively obligates the state to provide aid to them.[77] The incapacities of the homeless population as it existed in 1979 allowed the plaintiffs in *Callahan* to define their class as "homeless men...who are unable to provide for themselves."[78] Under such a definition, the homeless easily fit within the standards of sections 131 and 62. The defendants did not oppose this characterization in their memorandum.[79] Thus the incapacities of the homeless were integral to the *Callahan* plaintiffs' statutory argument as well.

B. The Arguments Reexamined

The premises of plaintiffs' arguments no longer hold for a significant proportion of shelter residents. As demonstrated above, up to thirty-three percent of the homeless single adults inhabiting the New York City shelters are functional and employable, not incapacitated.[80] Reexamined in this light, the state constitutional and statutory grounds advanced by the *Callahan* plaintiffs can be shown to be consistent with a right to shelter that permits requiring an employable person to participate in employment-related activities.

1. Conditions are Consistent With the State Constitution. As mentioned above,[81] plaintiffs based their state constitutional argument on the assertion that the homeless were "needy." New York courts have interpreted the term "needy," however, to exclude those employable persons who refuse to participate in employment-related programs and so contribute to the creation of their own need.

In *Barie v. Lavine,* the New York State Court of Appeals considered a case in which the state had sanctioned the Home Relief benefits of a poor but employable woman who had failed, without good cause, to attend a mandatory job interview.[82] The court held that the regulation under which the state sanctioned her grant did not violate the state's constitutional duty to aid the needy because

> [s]ection 1 of article XVII of the New York State Constitution mandates only that the "needy" and those unable to care for themselves be afforded aid and support.... The Legislature may in its discretion deny aid to employable persons who may properly be deemed not to be needy when they have wrongfully refused an opportunity for employment.[83]

The Appellate Division in *Barie* offered the clearest rationale for this decision, stating that:

> While the objective facts of hunger and a lack of sufficient assets to provide for one's own food, shelter and clothing establish prima facie a "needy" person, nevertheless, the word "needy" does not in its ordinary meaning encompass a person who is creating the need by consistently avoiding or refusing to provide for his needs.[84]

Under *Barie,* a person who is capable of participating in required employment-related activities but refuses, without good cause, to do so can be declared not "needy." The state, then, has no duty to provide aid to him or her. This holding has been reaffirmed consistently by New York courts.[85] While it might be argued that a shelter resident is distinguishable from a Home Relief recipient in that the very roof over his or her head is at stake, the *Barie* court's holding can be applied to the homeless. The Appellate Division in *Barie* explicitly recognized that Ms. Barie might be deprived of shelter as a result of the sanction, but upheld the regulation nonetheless.[86] Thus a shelter administrator could condition an employable shelter resident's benefits on the fulfillment of certain employment-related requirements without running afoul of the state constitution.

2. Conditions are Consistent with State Statutory Law.   Reexamining New York State statutory law in light of the changed nature of the homeless population shows that state statutes, like the state constitution, do not guarantee an unqualified right to shelter to the employable homeless. In 1979, the plaintiffs in *Callahan* could argue that the incapacitated homeless were *a priori* "unable to provide for themselves" and so were covered by sections 131 and 62.[87] An employable person who refuses to participate in employment-related activities, however, is *able* to take steps towards self-support. By definition, such a person is capable of participating in services which might allow him or her to become self-sufficient. The state, therefore, has no obligation to provide for such a person. In this respect, sections 131 and 62 are consistent with section 1, Article XVII of the state constitution.[88]

Moreover, section 131 explicitly provides that the state may condition an employable person's right to benefits on compliance with employment-related requirements. The statute states that "[n]o assistance or care shall be given to an employable person who has not registered with the nearest local employment agency. . . or has refused to accept employment in which he is able to engage."[89] The statute defines refusal to accept employment to include not only turning down a job, but also failing, without good cause, to report for a job interview,[90] failing to attend scheduled counseling, training or other appropriate job services,[91] or failing to participate in any other employment program deemed appropriate by local social service officials.[92] Rather than foreclosing employment-related conditions on the right to shelter, section 131 provides a basis on which to ground these conditions.[93]

In sum, neither the state constitution nor the statutory sources on which the litigants in *Callahan* based the right to shelter would preclude the parties from revising the consent decree to allow for employment-related conditions on an employable person's right to shelter.

III.   CONDITIONS ON AN EMPLOYABLE PERSON'S RIGHT TO SHELTER ARE CONSISTENT WITH THE LAWS OF OTHER JURISDICTIONS

Thus far, this Note has focused on New York State, arguing that the interested parties there can and should revise their consent decree to allow for employment-related conditions on the right to shelter of employable persons. New York, however, is not the only jurisdiction in which representatives of the homeless have brought right-to-shelter litigation. Such cases have also been brought in: Atlantic City, New Jersey; St. Louis, Missouri;

Hartford, Connecticut; and the State of West Virginia.[94] The amount of attention directed at the homelessness issue suggests that more cases are likely to follow. Moreover, studies have documented that, as in New York, the homeless population throughout the country is comprised of a sizeable number of employable persons.[95] Thus, the question of placing conditions on the right to shelter of employable homeless persons has national relevance.

This Note maintains that courts throughout the country who find a right to shelter should narrowly construe that right so that it does not preclude employment-related requirements. This Section will demonstrate that, as in New York, the laws of other states are consistent with such a qualified right.[96] This review focuses on state constitutional law because advocates for the homeless, responding to the lack of federal or common law grounds for a right to shelter,[97] have based their arguments primarily on state law.[98]

Many state constitutions do not offer direct support for a right to shelter. Even those that do, however, do not bar employment-related conditions on an employable person's right. To bar such conditions the state constitution would have to impose such a strong duty on the state that it would be unconstitutional to deny a bed even to a shelter resident who, although capable of participating in an employment program to which he or she was assigned, failed, without good cause, to do so. None would appear to create such an absolute duty.

The constitutions of thirty-three states do not contain any provisions dealing directly with aid to the poor.[99] They do not, therefore, offer explicit support for any form of a right to shelter, let alone an unqualified right.

There are seventeen state constitutions that do contain provisions concerning aid to the poor. Yet these too are unlikely to provide for an unqualified right to shelter. Two employ language wholly unrelated to the right-to-shelter issue.[100] Four empower the state or local governments to aid the poor but create no affirmative obligation to do so[101] and would, therefore, be highly unlikely to create any duty to provide shelter to the homeless.[102]

Five of the seventeen state constitutions do require the state to provide for the poor but contain only broadly worded language requiring the government to create public or charitable institutions.[103] The Wyoming Constitution, for example, provides that "[s]uch charitable, reformatory and penal institutions as the claims of humanity and the public good may require, shall be established and supported by the state in such manner as the legislature may prescribe."[104] These general words would not appear to create an affirmative obligation on the part of the state to house the homeless.[105] Even if this language were read to mandate homeless shelters as institutions required by "claims of humanity," the provision only prescribes the creation of an institution. The nature of the institution, its eligibility requirements, and its procedures are explicitly delegated to "the legislature," which would be free to place conditions upon entry into the shelter system.

The six remaining state constitutions provide more specifically for aid to the poor and present the closest cases. This Note has already considered one of these, the New York Constitution.[106] Two others, the North Carolina and Texas Constitutions, contain provisions which are of such narrow scope that they would not impede placing conditions on a right to shelter.[107]

The Oklahoma and Kansas Constitutions contain a broader duty to aid the poor, yet this obligation only reaches those who are needy due to "age, infirmity, or misfortune."[108] While this language may support a right to shelter, it does not preclude placing conditions on an employable person's right. Such a person is not, by definition, unable to function due to "age or infirmity." Nor does a person who has refused to participate in an employment-related activity need aid due to "misfortune" since this word implies "an instance of bad luck,"[109] not the failure to do something one is capable of doing.[110]

Finally, the Alabama Constitution contains the broadest language concerning aid to the poor: "It shall be the duty of the legislature to require the several counties of this state to make adequate provision for the maintenance of the poor."[111] If "maintenance" were held to include shelter, this provision might be construed to provide a right to shelter for all poor persons, employable or not, and so might preclude conditioning their right. On the other hand, it could be argued that providing shelter for employable persons only on the condition that they participate in employment-related programs is "adequate provision," especially where such requirements are intended to prevent dependency and shelter-induced apathy.

In sum, a review of state constitutions illustrates that the great majority, if not all, would permit placing employment-related conditions on an employable person's right to shelter. For the reasons discussed above, [112] courts finding a right to shelter should narrowly construe it to allow for such conditions.

IV. CONCLUSION

Considerable numbers of employable persons currently live in our nation's shelters. What can the legal community do that will best help such people to achieve self-sufficiency? This Note has argued that an unqualified right to shelter is not the optimal approach. Such a right precludes employment-related requirements that may well be the most effective means of assisting the employable homeless to fight the debilitating effects of shelter life and to take steps towards independence.[113] This Note recommends, therefore, that where courts or settling parties define a right to shelter they adopt a narrower formulation permitting employment-related conditions on an employable person's right.

NOTES

1. The homeless are generally defined as those lacking a permanent residence or living in public shelters, though a broader definition includes those living in unsafe or unsanitary housing. *See, e.g.,* Chackes, *Sheltering the Homeless: Judicial Enforcement of Governmental Duties to the Poor,* 31 J. Urb. & Contemp. Law 155, 155 (1987). Because this Note concerns the homeless who are living in the shelter system, it adopts the former definition.
2. Department of Housing & Urban Development, A Report to the Secretary on the Homeless and Emergency Shelters (1984).
3. M. Hombs & M. Snyder, Homelessness in America: A Forced March to Nowhere xvi (1983).
4. M. Burt & B. Cohen, America's Homeless: Numbers, Characteristics, and Programs That Serve Them 32 (Urban Institute Report 89-3, 1989).
5. *See, e.g.,* Werner, *Homelessness: A Litigation Roundup,* 18 Clearinghouse Rev. 1255 (1985).
6. *See, e.g.,* Langdon & Kass, *Homelessness in America: Looking for the Right to Shelter,* 19 Colum. J. L. & Soc. Probs. 305 (1985); Seibert, *Homeless People: Establishing Rights to Shelter,* 4 Law & Inequality 393 (1986); Note, *A Right to Shelter for the Homeless in New York State,* 61 N.Y.U. L. Rev. 272 (1986).
7. *See* Callahan v. Carey, No. 42582/79 (N.Y. Sup. Ct. Aug. 26, 1981) (final judgment by consent); McCain v. Koch, 502 N.Y.S.2d 720 (N.Y. App. Div. 1986); Eldredge v. Koch, 118 Misc. 2d 163, 459 N.Y. S.2d 960 (N.Y. Sup. Ct. 1983); Lubetkin v. City Manager of Hartford (Conn. Super. Ct. filed Feb. 4, 1983); Graham v. Schoemehl, No. 854-00035 (Mo. Cir. Ct. Nov. 15, 1985); Maticka v. Atlantic City, No. L-8306-84E (N.J. Super. Ct. Jan. 29, 1985); Hodge v. Ginsberg, 303 S.E.2d 245 (W. Va. 1983). *See also* Stille, *Seeking Shelter in the Law,* Nat'l. L.J. Feb. 10, 1986; Werner, *supra* note 5.
8. An unqualified right to shelter for the homeless is defined as an obligation on the part of the state or local government to provide shelter to all homeless persons who request it, excepting only those whose behavior, such as setting fire to the shelter or assaulting other residents, impinges too strongly on another's enjoyment of his or her right to shelter.
9. Michelman, *The Advent of a Right to Housing: A Current Appraisal,* 5 Harv. C.R.-C.L. L. Rev. 207, 207 (1970).
10. Hodge v. Ginsberg, 303 S.E.2d 245, 252 (W. Va. 1983) (Neely, J., dissenting).
11. Comment, *The Judiciary and the Ad Hoc Development of a Legal Right to Shelter,* 12 Harv. J.L. & Pub. Pol'y 193, 215-16 (1989) (footnote omitted).
12. Callahan v. Carey, No. 42582/79 (N.Y. Sup. Ct. Aug. 26, 1981) (final judgment by consent).
13. An employable person is defined as one who is not unable to participate in employment- or training-related activities due to significant incapacitation, either mental or physical. *See, e.g.,* N.Y. Soc. Serv.Law § 131(5) (Consol. Supp. 1989).
14. *See infra* notes 23-30 and accompanying text for a discussion of this change. While there have been other significant changes, such as the increasing numbers of homeless families utilizing New York City's shelters, these present quite different issues (e.g., the question of whether women with small children can or should be required to take on employment) which are beyond the scope of this Note. This Note will concern itself only with homeless single adults, not with homeless families.
15. Callahan v. Carey, No. 42582/79 (N.Y. Sup. Ct. Aug. 26, 1981) (final judgment by consent).

16. Callahan v. Carey, N.Y.L.J., Dec. 11, 1979, at 10, col. 5 (N.Y. Sup. Ct. Dec. 10, 1979) (order granting preliminary injunction).

17. *Id.*

18. McKittrick, *The Homeless: Judicial Intervention on Behalf of a Politically Powerless Group,* 16 Fordham Urb. L.J. 389, 406 n.111 (1988).

19. *Id.*

20. Callahan v. Carey, No. 42582/79, at 2 (N.Y. Sup. Ct. Aug. 26, 1981) (final judgment by consent).

21. The decree obligates New York City to provide shelter and board to a class of homeless men defined as: "each homeless man who applies for it provided that (a) the man meets the need standard to qualify for the home relief program established in New York State; or (b) the man by reason of physical, mental or social dysfunction is in need of temporary shelter." Callahan v. Carey, No. 42582/79, at 2–3 (N.Y. Sup. Ct. Aug. 26, 1981) (final judgment by consent). At first glance this provision may seem to establish a qualified right to shelter (i.e., conditioned on meeting eligibility requirements (a) or (b)), but in practice these "conditions" have proven impossible to implement, and New York's current policy is to provide a bed to any person who requests one. Interview with Karen Davis, Director of Operations for the New York City Adult Shelters, New York City Human Resources Administration in New Haven, Connecticut (Apr. 18, 1989). In large part, this situation stems from the phrase "social dysfunction," a term so broad that it has created a de facto entitlement for virtually everyone who applies. As one attorney for the New York City Human Resources Administration stated: "What is a 'social dysfunction'? How could we ask someone admitting applicants to assess whether an applicant suffers from a 'social dysfunction'? The City has got to give the term a broad reading and admit all who apply. We've got to err on that side of the issue, or risk a lawsuit." Interview with Dennis Young, Associate Attorney for the City of New York Human Resources Administration, in New York City (Apr. 25, 1989).

　　Later litigation extended the right to shelter established by the *Callahan* consent decree to homeless women, Eldredge v. Koch, 118 Misc. 2d 163, 459 N.Y.S.2d 960 (N.Y. Sup. Ct. 1983) (applying consent decree to women under equal protection analysis), and to homeless families, McCain v. Koch 117 A.D.2d 198, 212–14, 502 N.Y.S.2d 720, 729–30 (1986) (applying consent decree to homeless families under equal protection analysis).

22. *See infra* notes 67–69 and accompanying text.

23. City of New York Human Resources Administration, Revision of the Five-Year Plan for Housing and Assisting Homeless Single Adults 3 (1989).

24. *Id.*

25. City of New York Human Resources Administration, Five-Year Plan for Housing and Assisting Homeless Single Adults 49 (1988) (hereinafter Five-Year Plan).

26. Main, *The Homeless of New York,* 72 Pub. Interest 3 (1983), *reprinted in* Housing the Homeless 82 (J. Erickson & C. Wilhelm eds. 1986) (discussing and describing at length 1982 HRA report entitled "Chronic and Situational Dependency: Long-term Residents in a Shelter for Men").

27. *Id.* at 92–93.

28. N.Y. State Psychiatric Institute, A Study of Residents of the New York City Shelter System 14–16 (1986) [hereinafter A Study of Residents]. The researchers based their information on interviews with a representative sample of 832 male and female shelter residents. Twenty-nine percent of these, the report found, had worked for pay at least 20 hours per week for a month or more during the

past five months. During the prior three years, 42% had worked at a paying job at least 20 hours per week for 13 months or more, and 19% had worked at such a job for 25 to 36 months during this period.

29. *Id.* at 75–76.
30. Five-Year Plan, *supra* note 25, at 10.
31. *Id.* at 57.
32. A Study of Residents, *supra* note 28, at 88–89.
33. *Id.* at 87.
34. *Id.* at 86–87.
35. *Id.* at 89.
36. N.Y. Times, May 24, 1990, at B14, col. 4.
37. *Id.*
38. City of New York Human Resources Administration, New Arrivals: First Time Shelter Clients 2 (1982).
39. *Id.* (emphasis added).
40. Interview with Karen Davis, *supra* note 21.
41. Id.
42. Telephone interview with Keith Summa, CFTH (Nov. 14, 1989).
43. *Id.*
44. Philadelphia's right to shelter was initially put into place by a 1982 city ordinance passed by referendum. N.Y. Times, May 5, 1985, at 60, col. 3. In 1984, the Committee for Dignity and Fairness brought suit alleging inadequate provision of shelter and requesting an injunction to enforce the ordinance. *Id.* The parties settled by consent decree. *See* McKittrick, *supra* note 18, at 407 n.111.
45. In the three years following the consent decree the number of homeless using the Philadelphia shelters grew by 245%. Whitman, *Who's Who Among the Homeless: A Guide to Life on the Streets,* The New Republic, June 6, 1988, at 18, 20. Expenditures on shelter rose from approximately $4 million dollars in 1982 to over $23 million in 1989. Telephone interview with Steven Gold, General Counsel for the Committee for Dignity and Fairness (Nov. 20, 1989).
46. Telephone interview with Donald Felder, Outreach Administrator for the Philadelphia Office of Services to the Homeless and Adults (Nov. 7, 1989).
47. *Id.* The client protocol also requires substance abusers to sign up for treatment programs and requires those with an income from earnings or benefits to save a portion of it in anticipation of paying rent for an apartment.

    To date, no one has challenged the Philadelphia consent decree or the client protocols promulgated under it. This may be because the conditions agreed upon by the parties are consistent with the state laws. Alternatively, it may reflect the fact that advocacy groups, who helped develop the decree and protocols, do not wish to challenge them.
48. Telephone interview with Steven Gold, *supra* note 45. Telephone interview with Phyllis Ryan, Executive Director of the Philadelphia Committee for the Homeless (Nov. 7, 1989).
49. Telephone interview with Steven Gold, *supra* note 45.
50. *Id.*
51. Telephone interview with Phyllis Ryan, *supra* note 48.
52. S. Rep. No. 377, 100th Cong., 2nd Sess. 9, *reprinted in* 1988 U.S. Code Cong. & Admin News 2776, 2786.
53. *Id.* at 3–4 *reprinted in* 1988 U.S. Code Cong. & Admin. News, at 2780.
54. "[The bill] builds on a strong consensus, joined by liberals and conservatives alike, that the Nation's welfare system must stress family responsibility and community obligation...." *Id.* at 8, *reprinted in* 1988 U.S. Code Cong. & Ad-

min. News, at 2785. *See also* Gueron, *Work and Welfare: Lessons on Employment Programs,* 4 J. Econ. Persp. 79, 84 (forthcoming article) (Family Support Act represents compromise between liberal and conservative views of welfare reform).

55. Other commentators have suggested that requirements would be a useful means of getting the employable homeless to move towards employment and self-sufficiency. Thomas Main has proposed a work requirement for employable shelter residents which would deter them from using the shelter system and would send the message that society expects them to become self-supporting. Main, *supra* note 26, at 103–04. Robert Ellickson has also stated that employable shelter residents "must be encouraged to enter the job market," though he does not go so far as to suggest employment and training programs. Ellickson, *The Homelessness Muddle,* 99 Pub. Interest 45, 59 (1990). These proposals, however, do not include enough in the way of services. The mandatory employment and training programs envisioned by this Note would include such components as skills training, job placement, job search, work experience, or education programs.

   Such employment-related activities might be questioned on the grounds that high levels of unemployment, commonly assumed to be one of the causes of homelessness, make employment and training programs unlikely to succeed. Where there are few jobs to be found, some might argue, it makes less sense to require shelter residents to prepare for and seek work.

   It is true that employment and training programs will be less effective in economically depressed areas of the country, and more likely to show positive results in those regions where there are jobs. However, programs which train shelter residents in new work-related skills, or even in job search techniques with which they were not previously familiar, will better equip them to find work even in regions of significant unemployment. In addition, required program participation will keep shelter residents involved in work-related activities, helping them to combat the apathy and discouragement associated with life in the shelters and with unemployment. When the economy improves, they will then be better able to reenter the workforce.

56. Interview with Dennis Young, *supra* note 21.

57. Telephone interview with Keith Summa, *supra* note 42.

58. Five-Year Plan, *supra* note 25, at 24.

59. *See supra* notes 38–41 and accompanying text.

60. As one attorney for the HRA stated: "[The consent decree] prevents us from implementing the appropriate policies. For seventy percent of the shelter population, you can deal with them without violating the decree. For that other thirty percent [i.e, the functional and employable residents] though, the decree makes it extraordinarily difficult to deal with them." Interview with Dennis Young, *supra* note 21.

61. New York case law supports the idea that, in institutional reform litigation, consent decrees can be modified "with a free hand." New York State Ass'n for Retarded Children v. Carey, 706 F.2d 956, 970 (2d Cir. 1983) (modification of consent decree governing community for mentally retarded allowed so long as not in derogation of primary objective of decree). Moreover, in the *Callahan v. Carey* consent decree the court specifically retained jurisdiction to enable the parties to apply for any modifications which might be "necessary or appropriate." Callahan v. Carey, No 42582/79 at 15.

62. *See supra* note 21.

63. *See supra* notes 44–55 and accompanying text.

64. *See supra* notes 16–18 and accompanying text.
65. *See supra* note 20 and accompanying text.
66. *See supra* notes 26–30 and accompanying text.
67. Memorandum of Plaintiffs in Support of Their Motion for a Preliminary Injunction at 2, Callahan v. Carey, N.Y.L.J., Dec. 11, 1979, at 10, col. 5 (N.Y. Sup. Ct. Dec. 10, 1979) (No. 42582/79) [hereinafter Plaintiffs' Memorandum].
68. Callahan v. Carey, N.Y.L.J., Dec. 11, 1979, at 10, col. 5 (N.Y. Sup. Ct. Dec. 10, 1979).
69. *Id.*
70. N.Y. Const. art. XVII, § 1.
71. Tucker v. Toia, 43 N.Y.2d 1, 371 N.E.2d 449, 400 N.Y.S.2d 728 (1977).
72. *Id.* at 8, 371 N.E.2d at 452, 400 N.Y.S.2d at 731.
73. Plaintiffs' Memorandum, *supra* note 67, at 11.
74. *See* City Defendants' Memorandum of Law, Callahan v. Carey, N.Y.L.J., Dec. 11, 1979, at 10, col. 5 (N.Y. Sup. Ct. Dec. 10, 1979) (No. 42582/79) [hereinafter Defendants' Memorandum].
75. N.Y. Soc. Serv. Law § 131(1) (Consol. 1984).
76. N.Y. Soc. Serv. Law § 62 (Consol. 1984).
77. Barie v. Lavine, 40 N.Y.2d 565, 567–68, 357 N.E.2d 349, 350–51, 388 N.Y.S.2d 878, 879–80 (1976).
78. Plaintiffs' Memorandum, *supra* note 67, at 2.
79. Defendants' Memorandum, *supra* note 74.
80. *See supra* notes 26–30 and accompanying text.
81. *See supra* notes 70–74 and accompanying text.
82. Barie v. Lavine, 40 N.Y.2d 565, 566, 357 N.E.2d 349, 350, 388 N.Y.S.2d 878, 879 (1976).
83. *Id.* at 570, 357 N.E.2d at 352, 388 N.Y.S.2d at 881.
84. Barie v. Lavine, 48 A.D.2d 36, 38, 367 N.Y.S.2d 587, 590 (N.Y. App. Div. 1975).
85. *See e.g.* Kircher v. Perales, 112 A.D.2d 431, 433, 492 N.Y.S.2d 91, 94 (N.Y. App. Div. 1985) ("The Legislature has great discretion in setting criteria for defining the needy.... Moreover, the Legislature is free to exclude those who have purposely created their own 'need' in order to qualify for assistance." (citations omitted)); Flynn V. Bates, 67 A.D.2d 975, 977, 413 N.Y.S.2d 446, 448 (N.Y. App. Div. 1979) (noting that the word "needy" does not encompass a person who may create that need by failing or refusing to provide for her own needs.").
86. Barie v. Lavine, 48 A.D.2d 36, 38, 367 N.Y.S.2d 587, 589–90 (N.Y. App. Div. 1975).
87. *See supra* notes 75–79 and accompanying text.
88. *See* Barie v. Lavine, 48 A.D.2d 36, 38–39, 367 N.Y.S.2d 587, 590 (N.Y. App. Div. 1975); Hudson v. Sipprell, 76 Misc. 2d 684, 687, 351 N.Y.S.2d 915, 920 (N.Y. Sup. Ct. 1974).
89. N.Y. Soc. Serv. Law § 131(5) (Consol. Supp. 1989).
90. N.Y. Soc. Serv. Law § 131(5)(c) (Consol. Supp. 1989).
91. N.Y. Soc. Serv. Law § 131(5)(g) (Consol. Supp. 1989).
92. N.Y. Soc. Serv. Law § 131(7–a)(a)(g) (Consol. Supp. 1989).
93. *See* Barie v. Levine, 40 N.Y.2d 565, 567–68, 357 N.E.2d 349, 350–51, 388 N.Y.S.2d 878, 879–80 (1976).
94. See *supra* note 7.
95. Hagen, *The Heterogeneity of the Homeless,* 66 Soc. Casework 451, 456–57 (1987). The nature of homelessness, of course, varies in different parts of the country, and New York's homeless population is in some respects exceptional.

See P. Rossi, Down and Out in America (1989) (surveying homelessness in various parts of the United States).

96. This section draws on a thorough and useful survey of sate law provided by Langdon & Kass, *supra* note 6, at 324–34.

97. The Supreme Court has indicated that the federal Constitution contains no right to shelter. *See* Lindsey v. Normet, 405 U.S. 56, 74 (1972). No federal statutory right currently exists, and there does not appear to be a common law duty to provide assistance to the poor. *See, e.g.,* State v. City of Bristol, 139 Conn. 469, 95 A.2d 78 (1953); People *ex rel.* Heydenreich v. Lyons, 374 Ill. 557, 30 N.E.2d 46 (1940).

98. In addition to state constitutions, parties seeking a right to shelter might also rely on two other state law sources: general assistance statutes, *see, e.g.,* Callahan v. Carey, N.Y.L.J., Dec. 11, 1979, at 10, col. 5 (N.Y. Sup. Ct. Dec. 10, 1979), and state adult protective statutes, *see, e.g.,* Hodge v. Ginsberg, 303 S.E.2d 245, 252 (W. Va. 1983).

    General assistance statutes, such as section 131 relied upon in the *Callahan* litigation, establish programs that provide a minimal amount of aid to poor people not eligible for categorical federal programs. Even where these statutes could be construed to create a right to shelter, however, they would not create an unqualified right since most contain eligibility requirements that would permit placing employment-related conditions on an employable person's right. For example, the Virginia general assistance statute provides that "[n]o person shall be deemed to be in need of general relief, however, if he fails to accept available employment which is appropriate to his physical and mental abilities and training...." Va. Code Ann. § 63.1–106 (1987).

    Adult protective statutes require local or state officials to provide protective services to incapacitated adults who they determine to be abused, neglected, exploited or endangered. *See, e.g.,* Mich. Comp. Laws Ann. §§ 400.11–400.11f (West 1988). In *Hodge v. Ginsberg* advocates for the homeless in West Virginia successfully grounded a right to shelter on such a statute by arguing that lack of shelter and food creates a risk of death or injury which "endangers" homeless adults. Hodge v. Ginsberg, 303 S.E.2d 245, 252 (W. Va. 1983). Like general assistance statutes, however, most adult protective statutes would not provide grounds for an unqualified right to shelter. Most cover only "incapacitated" adults, disabled by mental or physical dysfunction or by age. Michigan's adult protective statute is representative. The statute applies only to those who are "[v]ulnerable," defined as "a condition in which an adult is unable to protect himself or herself... because of a mental or physical impairment or because of the frailties or dependencies brought about by advanced age." Mich. Comp. Laws Ann. § 400.11.(g). Employable shelter recipients would not, by definition, fit into such a category and so could not look to these statutes as grounds for an unconditional right to shelter.

99. *See* Langdon & Kass, *supra* note 6, at 332–34. They include in this category: Alaska, Arizona, Arkansas, California, Connecticut, Delaware, Florida, Georgia, Illinois, Iowa, Kentucky, Louisiana, Maine, Maryland, Massachusetts, Michigan, Minnesota, Nebraska, New Hampshire, New Jersey, New Mexico, North Dakota, Ohio, Oregon, Pennsylvania, Rhode Island, South Dakota, Tennessee, Utah, Vermont, Virginia, Washington, and Wisconsin.

100. The Colorado Constitution provides only that those residents who have reached age 60 receive a pension, Colo. Const. art. XXIV, § 3, and the West Virginia Constitution states simply that the county courts should appoint "overseers of the poor," W. Va. Const. art. IX, § 2.

101. *See* Haw. Const. art. IX, § 3; Ind. Const. art., IX, § 3; Miss. Const. art. IV, § 86; Mont. Const. art. 12 § 3(3).
102. *See* Langdon & Kass, *supra* note 6, at 333.
103. *See* Idaho Const. art X, § 1; Mo. Const. art IV, § 37; Nev. Const. art. XIII, § 1;S.C. const. art XII, § 1; Wyo. Const. art. 7, § 18.
104. Wyo. Const. art. VII, § 18.
105. *See* Langdon & Kass, *supra* note 6, at 332.
106. *See supra* notes 81–86 and accompanying text.
107. The North Carolina Constitution requires only that the legislature "provide for and define the duties of a board of welfare." N.C. Const. art. XI, § 4. The Texas Constitution mandates "the establishment of county poor houses and farms," but appears to leave to the legislature discretion to determine the practical details such as conditions for entry. Tex. Const. art. XI, § 2.
108. Okla. Const. art. XVII, § 3. ("The several counties of the State shall provide, as may be prescribed by law, for those inhabitants who, by reason of age, infirmity, or misfortune, may have claims upon the sympathy and aid of the country.") *See also* Kan. Const. art. VII, § 4.
109. Webster's Third New International Dictionary 1443 (1986).
110. The Fifth Circuit construed "misfortune," as used in this context, to exclude the "[a]blebodied. . . [who] are deemed indigent by choice and, as a matter of public policy, not entitled to maintenance." Brennan v. Harrison County, 505 F.2d 901, 903 (5th Cir. 1975).
111. Ala. Const. art. IV, § 88.
112. *See supra* notes 38–55 and accompanying text.
113. *See supra* notes 38–55 and accompanying text.

Decentralizing the Social Service System: A Reassessment

Michael R. Sosin

In recent years, Title XX of the Social Security Act and the Social Services Block Grant decentralized the social service system. This is claimed to be an improvement because decentralization strengthens the match between needs and services, added to the flexibility of workers and agencies, and increases efficiency. However, it is argued in this article that decentralization also contributes to some problematic service delivery patterns, such as specialization and selectivity, a lack of responsiveness to major shifts in patterns of needs, and a loss of effective advocacy to sustain appropriations. This argument is used to explain dilemmas in serving the homeless in Chicago and to question general assumptions about decentralization.

Title XX of the Social Security Act (1974) and the Social Services Block Grant (1981) decentralized the federal social service program that serves the poor.[1] The two sets of mandates granted states added discretion to determine which services to provide and which income groups to cover and eliminated most regulations concerning worker-client interactions.[2] As a result, not only did states become more active in determining priorities and procedures,[3] but counties also garnered some additional authority in the many states that gave them control over a portion of the revenues. Service delivery responsibilities also were delegated from the government to the private sector; a majority of the funds were transferred to private social services agencies through purchase-of-service contracts.[4]

The current system thus contrasts dramatically with the system of the early 1970s, when federal regulations promoted at least a limited degree of uniformity in the services and population groups covered, central mandates

Social Service Review (December 1990).
0037-7961/90/6404-0004$01.00
University of Chicago

ensured that public workers periodically visited a defined group of clients, and (perhaps because states needed to ensure that clients were visited and served in a specific manner) purchase-of-service contracts and delegation to local areas were less widely used. According to many academic observers, the service system has therefore been improved. The decentralization of policy decisions allegedly enables local areas to plan and deliver services without the encumbrance of detailed and stifling centralized regulations. When combined with the increased emphasis on delivery of services by counties and private agencies, it also is said to encourage accountability to the local community.[5] Accordingly, although some problems and substantial interstate variation are acknowledged,[6] observers generally conclude that local governments are increasingly likely to tailor their services and eligibility requirements to local needs; local public agencies modify the newly established priorities and procedures as the presented problems change, while public and private agency workers recognize and more fully respond to individual clients; and systems are relatively efficient in that states and counties limit the time spent proving compliance to federal regulations and are otherwise free to make sensible use of revenues.[7]

While these claims are partly valid, there are reasons to suspect that many state systems also have developed some troubling service delivery patterns. As both organizational theory and the public welfare literature warn, the local groups and individuals who gain control over programs, and the local advocates and interest groups who affect them, have many motives and vulnerabilities that can compromise the effectiveness of a service delivery system. For example, local governments may be unable to resist local constituencies that are not sympathetic to public welfare clients. Private social service agencies that governments fund have commitments to very specific service missions that may lead them to limit the scope of provided services. Local advocacy groups and agencies that receive funds may find it necessary to devote their energies to competing for government revenues rather than pursuing comprehensive long-term social aims. Certain local public agencies may lack the necessary resources to develop their own long-term plans.[8] Accordingly, while some states and counties may develop exemplary and creative systems, others are likely to settle for the selective, risk-avoiding, and routine service delivery pattern that is often found in government programs that encourage local control.[9]

More generally, it is argued in this article that theory and research suggest that decentralization of the type encouraged by Title XX and the Block Grant strongly influences the behavior of local governments, public agencies, private agencies, and advocacy groups. They often must limit the attention paid to meeting client needs or achieving other benefits commonly attributed to decentralization.

THREE ALLEGED BENEFITS OF DECENTRALIZATION

These themes become apparent when considering the three basic claims about the decentralized system: (1) that needs are better covered, (2) that there is enhanced responsiveness, and (3) that there is improved economic efficiency.

Coverage of Needs

Supporters of the first of the three claims, that decentralization helps develop an appropriate match between services and client needs, generally posit that local control and privatization increase the attention paid to local social conditions.[10] However, this proposition is usually stated without any analysis of the complex motives and actions of representatives of communities, public agencies, or advocacy groups involved in setting local priorities. Further, the evidence brought to bear often consists of examples of single, seemingly useful state service activities or descriptions of a few instances in which private agencies or local governments provide an innovative, needed service. Overviews and studies rarely consider patterns of service at the level at which the argument is phrased—that of the nature of the entire service delivery system.[11]

Specialization.—A wider theoretical perspective suggests one overlooked pattern that can compromise the development of the appropriate match between services and needs: the specialization of local delivery systems. This is particularly likely in communities that rely on private agencies to deliver services. As other literature on service organizations implies,[12] local governments that search for providers usually find that the relevant private agencies are highly specialized. These governments may favor this specialization when they dispense contracts in part because it allows private agencies to continue to provide services that they have proved they can deliver and in part because it gains the political support from a constituency that has become more critical in light of local accountability.

Given the bewildering number of contractual agreements that are made in many states, it also follows that many governments will favor specialized agreements because they offer ways of retaining some semblance of control over the complex system. That is, according to a well-documented theoretical proposition, organizational behavior often must involve a search for certainty in a threatening environment.[13] Literature suggests that, because specialization enables responses to be targeted to the strongest demands, the strategy of organizing around specific activities increases certainty when organizations face contradictory pressures from the community.[14] And as noted in the introduction, strong demands are common in locally accountable social service systems.

A similar blend of logic and theory suggests that specialization can threaten local government agencies that continue to directly deliver services in the Title XX or Block Grant program. For example, specialization limits the commitment of resources while allowing public workers to respond to the strongest of the many local demands for service. Similarly, governments can attain certainty by organizing contract officers into specialized units. Research on complex organizations in fact suggests that specialization of an agency's departments typically occurs when organization leaders perceive that strong pressures come from diverse sources.[15]

The problem with specialization.—Specialization is not necessarily problematic; indeed, it has some well-known advantages.[16] However, it can lead to difficulties when taken to extremes. For example, it is widely recognized that at least some generalist workers are needed to ensure that clients are informed about available services, that individuals who are theoretically eligible for programs are served, and that those who have multiple problems receive help in coping with a series of specialized agencies. The need or generalists is particularly great when a system contains many rigidities and gaps in coverage.[17]

Unfortunately, the literature suggests that such gaps often occur in service systems that have considerable local discretion. Locally powerful groups or individuals can demand coverage for one type of service or population group and can veto coverage for another. Local governments cannot easily resist public demands for such differentials. They quite often must highlight a few priorities—sometimes reasonable and sometimes not—while limiting aid to less favored groups of clients.[18]

Evidence—Although state and county systems vary considerably,[19] there is a good deal of evidence that the problems of specialization occur in many locales. The lack of generalist workers is particularly well documented. Studies suggest that public service workers were common in earlier years because caseworkers were mandated by federal laws to periodically visit clients and help with difficulties but that they are no longer typical in many local areas. Currently, few public workers inform welfare clients about the availability of services, diagnose problems during the regular visits, refer those with particular needs to more specialized service workers or to emergency financial units, act as case managers, or advocate for clients.[20] Studies also argue that recent changes in the service system (which are not tied to decentralization in these essays) are partly responsible for reduced participation in the Aid to Families with Dependent Children (AFDC) program of eligible individuals who are not informed of ways of obtaining benefits by financial assistance workers.[21]

Two studies also suggest that private agencies rarely provide generalist service,[22] while descriptions of private agencies that receive government funds indicate that specialization is common.[23] One national study finds that the private agencies funded by the government are more specialized than is typical—that is, public funds are generally distributed to organizations that focus on an age group, social problem, professional method, or even an ethnic group.[24]

Available information also suggests that local systems are not usually comprehensive.[25] One study of 1983 expenditures by 18 states in eight service areas shows that three apparently narrow services account for the majority of spending: adoption and foster care (24.9% of reported state expenditures on average), protective services for children (16.6%), and day care for children (20.8%). While it is not possible to extract an exact summary of expenditures for generalist services, it is notable that only half of the surveyed states report any expenditures for information and referral and that those expenditures account for less than 3 percent of reported budgets.[26]

Responsiveness

The second common claim is that decentralization encourages flexibility. One aspect of the suggestion, that workers respond to needs of individual clients, is clearly suspect. Scholars do not consider the possibility that, even if private agency workers tend to treat clients with respect and compassion, they often work in specialized agencies and thus can only cover a few types of needs.

There also are reasons to question the assertion that, because state or county officials face few regulations, they have the flexibility to adjust the program as the needs of the community change. Local political pressures that can create barriers to responsiveness are not considered within the common theoretical frameworks. Further, the evidence that is cited includes single examples of awarding contracts to private agencies, along with descriptions of small changes in state priorities. Authors rarely consider the extent to which basic priorities change over time or compare these shifts to the nature of the developing social problems.

Setting priorities in service delivery.—Literature and theory suggest the lack of flexibility of the decentralized system at the policy level in particular. For example, local governments can be pressured by private agencies that wish to obtain funds. Further, literature suggests that these agencies often are important political actors.[27] It follows that localities that rely on private agencies tend to face pressures to focus on problems and technologies that are normally stressed by the private sector, thus limiting change and responsiveness.

To be sure, responsiveness is not fully compromised when decentralization first increases; community activism is at a high point, a relatively small proportion of revenues are dispensed to private agencies, and the private agencies are unusually likely to lobby for broad service strategies at this time. However, literature suggests that responsiveness is likely to decrease. Community groups that do not have a direct financial interest in the service program become less active. More important, once purchase-of-service contracts become common, the private agencies that receive revenues are virtually forced to advocate for the continuation of the support from the government on which they come to depend.[28] They also become committed to the services for which they receive contracts.[29] Further, their yearly reports document that the services they deliver are in demand, while documentation of the need for services that are not delivered is not as complete. Although this is not intentional, such patterns bias the flow of information to the government in favor of currently delivered items.[30] One likely result is that the agencies garner a stable or even growing proportion of the financial support so that it becomes more difficult to find revenue to reallocate to new purposes.

Some authors suggest and find evidence that decentralization allows state and local administrators to withdraw funds from a particularly problematic private agency.[31] But this is distinct from drastically reallocating funds given to well-conceived private agency programs that are no longer in keeping with prime community needs. When contracts are used, a massive change requires a redistribution of many agreements; organizational change of this type is so taxing that it is rarely accomplished. For example, public agencies will find it difficult to undertake massive change, even if desired, because it threatens a variety of existing relationships with referral agencies and providers of services.[32]

Quite similar arguments suggest that the services directly delivered by state and local governments will change only slowly. As was noted, the public sector is pressured to establish specialized units under decentralization. These units become committed to the continuation of their programs. In addition, once such units are in operation, clients who have problems that are covered will be counted, while those who have other problems will be less likely to come to the agency, will be turned away, or will be relabeled. Thus, the process of gathering information reinforces the provision of the covered services. Further, as suggested by traditional literature on the problem of delegation, decentralization generally creates problems for community advocates or interest groups. Responsibility for any given need is divided among so many levels of government and units that advocates cannot easily argue that any one administrative unit should cover a new problem. States that delegate responsibility have little power to fund a new type of service and thus suggest that this is a local responsibility. Local governments rely on limited state appropriations and thus suggest that change must be a state responsibility. At each level, departments cover only specific services and cannot be faulted for failing to deal with a new need.[33]

Evidence.—The above argument is supported by numerous studies of specific agencies in social service systems that rely on decentralization—although only a few of these focus on Title XX and the Social Services Block Grant. Research indicates notable stability in that contracts are often distributed to private agencies that previously existed and prospered,[34] while

powerful agencies continue to receive large appropriations and similar contracts each year once they are supported. Only small agencies on the
"fringes" experience considerable turnover in funding.[35] Research also suggests that states and counties often dispense contracts in response to proposals from agencies and that powerful agencies that already receive
contracts tend to successfully apply for new awards.[36] Many studies conclude
that those private agencies that receive funds from decentralized programs
are not forced to change technologies[37] and that governments provide few
controls that might change their behavior.[38]

Support is also found in one interstate study that focuses on expenditures in eight service areas under the Social Services Block Grant in 1981,
1982, and 1984 (although the authors of this report come to different conclusions). One way of determining the stability of the services is to compare the
extent to which there are changes in the relative expenditures devoted to various service areas. Calculations based on the report reveal that in five of 18
surveyed states there were no changes in rank across the 3 years; in another
five, there was just one change; and four others evinced just two changes.
The report states that small reallocations in the percentages given to such activities by certain states, which occurred as federal revenues were reduced between 1981 and 1983, began to be reversed in 1984.[39]

Admittedly, there is no clear standard for determining whether the year-
by-year adjustments indicate a "reasonable" degree of responsiveness (and,
as noted, interest groups vie to obtain support for their specialty, which
leads to some such adjustment). But the above study provides details on the
nature of the changes in emphases that document a disturbing lack of responsiveness in a broader sense. Most shifts involve the relative priority
given to such traditional services as work-related day care (a prime recipient
of greater funding in eight states) or foster care and children's protective services (the recipient in four states). Shifts do not indicate a trend toward the
provision of new, innovative categories of services. Reported alterations in
eligibility also generally involve only the obvious reforms, promoting either
more emphasis on AFDC clients or a general relaxation of income standards. The lack of more profound change is particularly notable because such
problems as homelessness and teenage parenthood were becoming major
public issues, yet no state reported an increase in emphasis on either population group. While one state reported increasing the priority given to emergency home services, which could help those on the verge of homelessness,
no other listed change in service priorities seems to indirectly respond to
these developing social problems. Another study finds a pattern of stability
in earlier years of decentralization, discounting the activism in the first year
of implementation, and intimates that this stability is related to growing
pressures from providers.[40]

Efficiency and Revenue Patterns

One further claim of supporters of decentralization is that the reforms promote economic efficiency. Typical arguments are that private agencies are relatively efficient and that state and county governments also experience administrative savings because they are freed from burdensome federal requirements. However, these claims are not particularly convincing. For example, the local constraints that have been mentioned can also promote inefficiencies, while direct evidence on efficiency is weak.[41] Further, such efficiencies represent only a portion of issues related to revenue patterns. Studies rarely address a perhaps more fundamental issue, whether decentralization affects the funding level. That is, they do not consider ways in which structural reform can affect the politics of revenue allocation.

Day-care advocates suggest that the decentralized social service program strongly affects political processes. As they noted in response to a legislative proposal that would have folded additional revenue for this service into the general social service program, decentralization makes it difficult to achieve revenue increases, or even inflation adjustments, over time. Because the decentralized program is not controlled by federal authorities, it is difficult to use federal influence to assure that the service continues to be funded at local levels. Further, if there later is a need for increased provision of revenues, federal officials can deny responsibility and claim that the problem demands reallocation of the current resources granted to lower levels. But the lower levels can only accomplish this by cutting spending in another service area, which is troublesome. More generally, it is difficult to convince the federal legislature that growth in any one need in a given locality is sufficient to justify a revenue increase for the entire program.

Advocacy and coalitions.—Under decentralization, private service agencies (as well as other advocacy groups) that lobby the government in the contract-based systems may become more politically active. However, they may still be unlikely to undertake the high risk of working to raise the entire appropriation. As has been noted, they tend to be quite interested in obtaining revenues within a program and must thus spend time on the task of obtaining a portion of the funds that are dispensed through contracts at the local level. Indeed, if they do not, they lose out to other, more active advocates. This is likely to limit activism in the federal or state legislative arenas if for no other reason than each agency can only undertake a certain amount of advocacy within a given budget. Some scholars even posit that a system that encourages competition for part of a general appropriation promotes competitive relations among interested groups. This, in turn, disrupts the stability of the coalitions that are needed to achieve revenue increases or fight cutbacks.[42] In addition, when state and county governments gain authority to divide up revenues in the decentralized system, they come under pressure to be more involved in settling resulting local disputes rather than lobbying at higher levels to increase the total size of the appropriation.[43]

Evidence.—While it is difficult to discern a pattern in state spending during the earlier years of decentralization,[44] evidence clearly suggests that revenue growth at the federal level has been limited.[45] As is widely known, from 1974 up until 1981, federal appropriations for Title XX stayed roughly constant (moving from about 2.5 to 2.8 billion dollars), thus suffering a significant loss of value in a period of high inflation. Since then, federal revenues decreased (by 13.5% in real dollars by 1984). At least since 1977, state funding generally has not been sufficient to overcome the federal decrease; in fact, recent state funding patterns generally mirror the federal trends.[46]

To be sure, the gradual reduction in revenues in strongly affected by broad trends in the economy and in tax policies. It also is affected by structural changes whose relation to decentralization is debatable, such as those of the early 1970s, which placed a financial ceiling on federal appropriations, and the 1981 provision, which allowed states to withdraw their financial contribution. Nevertheless, Title XX and the Social Services Block Grant lost more revenues than other federal service programs that had ceilings on expenditures and that limited state funding requirements—notably, the child welfare programs. This suggests that decentralization contributes to the greater decline in revenues compared to inflation.

Further, there is evidence to support the contention that, beginning in 1975, the number of advocacy groups expanded, while coalitions were less active at the national, and perhaps state, level. Currently, advocates appear to be most active at levels at which priorities are set rather than at the levels at which overall appropriations are determined.[47]

Some speculation on substitution.—In addition to the problems of maintaining revenue, it is also likely that the increased governmental financial support of private agencies is not fully used to expand the total number of individuals served. Rather, it may encourage substitution, that is, the replacement of private resources by government revenue. This is a common pattern in governmental programs, as suggested by an often-cited study of the urban economic development program in Oakland, California, which found that those businesses that applied for available funds were already considering the types of projects for which they obtained revenues from government. One firm provided only eight new jobs on obtaining $423,000 in federal aid, apparently because revenue was viewed as a way of reducing the cost of a previously planned expansion.[48]

The social service system might experience unusually large amounts of substitution. This is made possible by the similarity (noted above) between activities of private agencies and the activities that government funds, as well as by the limited public control of the agencies. In addition, private agencies can feel pressured to substitute. For example, raising funds through donations is an onerous task for many service-oriented executives; it also involves enormous mouth-to-mouth uncertainty, which can be minimized by replacing the revenues with public contracts. Further, by substituting funds, private agencies increase their security because they know they can return to their original funding arrangements if their support is reduced as the government program suffers financial setbacks.[49]

There is evidence that agencies that obtain or lose public contracts maintain their revenues because government revenues and funds received from private resources are substituted. One study of total state service program revenues finds no relation between the level of governmental support and the per capita budgets of private agencies; when public support is higher, private donations are correspondingly reduced.[50] Similarly, recent Urban Institute publications suggest that many private agencies suffered only small net losses from the reductions in funding in the early 1980s because they substituted fees for service and other private revenue. Substitution was particularly easy for the types of services that are frequently funded under the Social Services Block Grant program, such as day care or child welfare services.[51] More directly, one study finds that, since contracting became common, there has been little expansion of the network of private agencies in one major city.[52]

HOMELESSNESS IN ILLINOIS AND CHICAGO

These arguments about the problematic consequences of decentralization are particularly relevant to the response of social services to growing social problems. One example is the response to homelessness in Chicago, which was analyzed to determine the pattern of services in a city that is concerned about the social problem but operates within a fully decentralized system.[53] The discussion is divided into separate examinations of the case-level system from the mid-1970s to the early 1980s, the response to homelessness during this period, the policy-level response in later years, and patterns of spending in these years.

Specialization and Related Difficulties: 1975–1982

Before the mid-1970s, poor individuals in Chicago were served by workers who were supervised by the state and who were attached to each AFDC office. While some of the workers were organized into units that specialized in such tasks as child welfare, a large number were given geographically determined caseloads. These workers were directed to periodically visit AFDC clients and determine if new needs were developing. Each client was given the name of a service worker to contact for help with such problems as evictions.

In 1975, following the implementation of Title XX (the first of the two federal programs aimed at decentralizing the service system), Illinois all but eliminated the caseload-based model in response to the added responsibility and corresponding need for control. While the state continued to provide one public liaison worker in AFDC offices in Chicago, nearly all other service activities were coordinated by specialized units, some of which were newly created for this purpose. Each unit was in charge of covering such problems as the need for battered women's shelters or developmental disabilities. Units generally dispensed their funds through purchase-of-service contracts and, in some instances (particularly in the child welfare unit), relied on state public workers who covered aspects of the specialized problem. As the first part of this article suggests, the services provided through contracts or directly delivered by state workers were selective because the units focused on high priorities. For example, there was (and is) little coverage of advocacy services or of population groups such as single men.[54]

As is common under decentralization, other service activities were expected to be provided by Chicago workers who were supported by a loosely structured state contract to the city (although counties are the more typical recipient in other jurisdictions in Illinois). But by the early 1980s, Chicago developed specialized units that focused on services that involved potentially controversial urban social problems:[55] workers lectured high school students on the problems of dropping out and using drugs, responded to complaints about family violence or disruptive individuals, or dispensed food baskets and managed the emergency energy program (using funds from another Block Grant). This specialization was made necessary by the pressures of decentralization. One city social service executive suggested that, in the late 1970s and early 1980s, pressures to meet these types of high-priority needs (accompanied by revenue shortages, which I argue may be increased by decentralization), were so intense that generalist workers could not be maintained.

Homelessness in Chicago: Case-Level Responses in the Early 1980s

While it is difficult to completely eliminate homelessness or even help certain individuals reverse or prevent the fall into this state, there is evidence that at least some homeless individuals in Chicago experience concrete events that can be managed through services. Almost half of the homeless individuals in a Chicago survey report that a combination of an argument with others and the lack or loss of welfare benefits caused their homelessness. A similar proportion note that they were formally or informally evicted for nonpayment of rent (multiple responses were possible). Clearly, some of the crises that immediately cause homelessness could be ameliorated if generalist workers could intervene in family arguments, advocate with income maintenance workers, forestall eviction, or locate or provide cash for a security deposit.[56]

As noted above, however, state or city workers could not routinely provide the needed services in Chicago in the late 1970s and early 1980s, even though these were typical tasks of the workers of the early 1970s. Indeed, the dilemmas that homelessness created for Chicago public system workers are well documented.[57] In response to direct questions, city officials acknowledge that an underlying barrier is organizational; it is difficult to develop a structure that places workers in the position to deliver many of the needed services (although one Chicago unit did help individuals obtain entry into homeless shelters and responded to certain other crises among the homeless). It is particularly likely that the decentralized service system is partly responsible for limiting the response to homelessness because many homeless individuals desire and would be able to make use of such tangible services if they were still available.[58]

Policy Response: 1983–1989

The relevant case advocacy and case management services also were rarely developed during the mid- or late 1980s. City officials had little discretion to develop these services, although they at one point tried to add a dozen workers to deal with general problems of families. Similarly, the needed services did not clearly fit into the existing specialized state structure. At the state level, modest improvements in services primarily occurred in mental health, where new appropriations were made available through federal programs. City and state officials who were asked about the extent to which workers might more generally deal with such problems as access to the income maintenance system suggest that is difficult to implement such services through the usual types of government contracts and public system units.[59]

While aware of some shortages of needed services, Chicago advocates suggest that service reform is difficult to achieve because no agency or specialized wing of the service system clearly has the responsibility (or ability) to provide case management or advocacy services for homeless individuals who are not chronically mentally ill or otherwise disabled and because it is very difficult to document the resulting lack of services when there are so many purchase-of-service contracts. Such problems clearly reflect common features of the decentralized system. Some advocates lend support to the suggestion that there are barriers to developing coalitions, confirming that it is difficult to argue for the provision of funds for the needed services without threatening the existing contracts dispensed to other respected private agencies.[60]

Revenue Responses: 1983–1989

In Chicago, as nationally, the increase in homelessness has nevertheless received considerable public attention. As a result, the number of shelter beds nearly tripled between 1983 and the end of 1989. City and state officials were clearly sympathetic and could provide financial support for shelter beds by readjusting contractual arrangements (the new shelter funds are allocated to private agencies in most cases). This response reflects an advantage of the purchase-of-service contracts used in the decentralized system, in that it is possible to readjust services, albeit in ways that favor shelters over services that cannot as easily be provided through limited purchase-of-service contracts.

Even in the case of shelter, however, decentralization creates dilemmas for officials. For example, one of the few sources of public funds that officials could use covers general housing programs; thus, shelters, and longer-term housing needs were forced to compete with each other.[61] (While the funds do not necessarily emanate from the Social Services Block Grant, the fact that they stem from other Block grants provides general evidence about the development of competition in a decentralized system.) The lack of expansion of the state funding base under the decentralized system is also evident because, with the exception of federal funds made available under the McKinney Act and the Federal Emergency Management Act, neither the state nor city found much new revenue. Neither level could successfully lobby for an increase in block grant appropriations on the basis of the needs of the homeless.

CONCLUSION

It must be concluded that many scholars need to revise their evaluation of the decentralized social service system. There is evidence that decentralization at times results in a high degree of specialization, limited responses to changing types of demands, and restricted ability to obtain new revenues.[62] To be sure, some of these problems only crop up in selected localities, are balanced by the commonly mentioned benefits, or represent continuations of problems of the centralized system. They also may not be fully applicable in all types of service systems. However, the problems are sufficient to at least warrant some consideration in discussions of decentralized systems.

It may be argued that the more problematic patterns are results of coincidental revenue shortages not related to decentralization. However, this seems unlikely for at least three reasons. First, there is evidence that the trends toward specialization, selectivity, and other problems are linked to the implementation of structural changes as well as to the imposition of revenue limits. It thus is notable that, under the centralized system, states did not fully resort to specialization when placed under a financial ceiling.[63] Second, this article provides evidence that decentralization affects advocacy and relations between levels of governments in ways that account for part of the limitation in total revenues; thus, it is likely to be implicated in whatever problems are caused by shortages of funds. Finally, because of substitution effects, it is likely that decentralization limits the scope of service provision beyond the degree dictated by revenue shortages.

It may also be argued that the potentially negative features reflect peculiar aspects of federal or state legislation surrounding Title XX and the Social Services Block Grant rather than the basic nature of the decentralization of decision making and service delivery. This, too, is doubtful because the existence of these features is supported not only by specific examples and by reference to specific provisions of federal legislation but also by an analysis of general reactions to increased state authority, delegation to counties, and use of private agencies in a broadly aimed service program. Most trends were, in fact, explicated with the help of theoretical literature about the demands and cross pressures encountered by local governments, the well-documented tendency of public agency executives to minimize uncertainty, and the incentives facing advocacy groups.[64]

In light of the sources of evidence, it is reasonable to suggest that similar problems might occur in instances other than Title XX and the Social Services Block Grant. This speculation seems warranted because many authorities point to this service delivery system and, in particular, its reliance on private agencies, to claim that a new, dominant "model" of delivery has developed. Evidence from this system is even used to suggest that the new model ameliorates some of the problems of inflexibility, waste, and indifference to the needs of individual clients that are allegedly inherent in federal "bureaucracy."[65] However, as noted, such literature fails to analyze the system as a whole. While private agencies may be exemplary when they operate without local government financing or the responsibility to take on the major burden of delivering services, they are pressured to interact with governments within the decentralized approach in ways that create problems.

The findings do not mean that decentralization is a complete failure. Nevertheless, the problems are quite significant. In contrast, evidence for the benefits of decentralization is generally limited.[66] The type of local control described in this article spawns difficulties that are at least as great as the benefits that have so far been demonstrated.

NOTES

The research on which this article is based was partly supported by the Chicago Community Trust. However, the conclusions are mine. I also wish to acknowledge the helpful comments of professors Evelyn Brodkin, Irving Piliavin, Steven Smith, research assistant Susan Grossman, and anonymous reviewers.

1. Neil Gilbert, *Capitalism and the Welfare State* (New Haven, Conn.: Yale University Press, 1983); Lester M. Salamon, "Partners in Public Service: The Scope and Theory of Government—Non-profit Relations," in *The Nonprofit Sector: A Research Handbook,* ed. Walter W. Powell (New Haven, Conn.: Yale University Press, 1986), pp. 115–16; Paul Terrell, "Private Alternatives to Public Human Services Administration," *Social Service Review 53 (March 1979):* 56–74.
2. John Yancey, "Public Social Services," in *Encyclopedia of Social Work,* 18th ed. (Silver Spring, Md.: National Association of Social Workers, 1987), 2:417–25;

Bill Benton, Tracey Field, and Rhona Millar, *Social Services: Federal Legislation vs. State Implementation* (Washington, D.C.: Urban Institute, 1978); Frances E. Zorn, Leilani S. Rose, and Beryl A. Radin, "Title XX and Public Participation: An Overview," *Public Welfare* 34 (Fall 1976): 20–25. The previous requirements for client-worker interactions included mandates that service needs are assessed periodically, that workers and clients develop specific contracts, and that AFDC clients receive a service worker.

3. Restrictions on the income levels of clients were primarily relaxed by the Social Services Block Grant and not by Title XX.

4. Benton, Feild, and Millar (n. 2 above). The use of purchase-of-service contracts doubled between the early and late 1970s. Further reasons for decentralization to lower levels or private agencies can be derived from literature about the tendency of public welfare systems to delegate authority when they are not under extreme pressure to control decisions. For example, see Joel F. Handler and E. J. Hollingsworth, *The Deserving Poor: A Study of Welfare Administration* (Chicago: Markham Publishing Co., 1971); Joel F. Handler and Michael R. Sosin, *Last Resorts: Emergency Assistance and Special Needs Programs in Public Welfare* (Orlando, Fla.: Academic Press, 1983). Also note that I use "counties" to refer to the lowest level of government even though cities may also be the primary unit.

5. When establishing priorities, states must consult with the community in a formal way.

6. For example, mandated state-level advisory boards failed to remain active in the Title XX state-level planning process. See Leilani S. Rose, Frances E. Zorn, and Beryl A. Radin, "Title XX and Public Participation: An Initial Assessment," *Public Welfare* 35 (Winter 1977): 24–31; Peter M. Kettner and Lawrence L. Martin, "Making Decisions about Purchase of Service Contracting," *Public Welfare* 44 (Fall 1986): 30–37.

7. Gilbert (n. 1 above); Gordon Manser and Rosemary Higgens Cass, *Voluntarism at the Crossroads* (New York: Family Service Association of America, 1976). Some authorities suggest that union contracts and civil service regulations cause some inefficiencies.

8. The specification of services that can be covered matches interest groups with the program, e.g., day care is defined as a potential service in this program but not in certain other federal efforts.

9. Michael Lipsky, *Street-Level Bureaucracy: Dilemmas of the Individual in Public Services* (New York: Russell Sage, 1980); Handler and Hollingsworth (n. 4 above); J. M. Prottas, *People Processing* (Lexington, Mass.: D. C. Heath, 1979).

10. I do not examine all aspects of the relevant patterns of delivery. Rather, I suggest some patterns in the current system that differ from those implemented under previous, more centralized legislation. This method focuses on the consequences of change and may uncover some overlooked contemporary patterns. I also do not attempt to summarize what might be "constant" features of delivery systems, such as the extent to which characteristics of the delivery system, no matter what the structure, continue to reflect a commitment to quality.

11. George E. Peterson, Randall R. Bovbjerg, Barbara A. Davis, Walter G. Davis, Eugene C. Durman, and Theresa A. Gullo, *The Reagan Block Grants: What Have We Learned?* (Washington, D.C.; Urban Institute, 1986).

12. Benton, Field, and Millar (n. 2 above).

13. Two of the early sources of this conventionally accepted view are James D. Thompson, *Organizations in Action* (New York: McGraw-Hill, 1967); and Michel Crozier, *The Bureaucratic Phenomenon* (Chicago: University of Chicago Press, 1964).

14. This literature is complex and suggests that the lack of specialization may be retained under some situations of external pressure. However, these situations involve more intensive pressures than those affecting most counties and states. The most politically pressured states may specialize less. Two relevant theoretical studies are Michael T. Hannan and John Freeman. "The Population Ecology of Organizations," *American Journal of Sociology* 82 (March 1977): 929–66; and Glenn R. Caroll, "Organizational Ecology," *Annual Review of Sociology* 10 (1985): 71–93.

15. It might be argued that governments still may find a way to avoid complete specialization. This was the case in the allegedly decentralized system of Community Action Agencies under the War on Poverty programs. The War on Poverty, however, contained some centralization and virtually mandated generalist services. In contrast, the legislation of the 1970s and 1980s relaxed such notable pressures toward generalist services as the federal mandate that workers regularly visit clients to conduct general needs assessments. (It also allows states and counties to cover only the areas of services they desire.) Paul Lawrence and Jay Lorsch, *Organization and Environments* (Boston: Harvard Business School, 1967); Howard Aldrich, *Organizations and Environments* (Englewood Cliffs, N.J.: Prentice-Hall, 1979).

16. Michael R. Sosin, *Private Benefits: Material Assistance in the Private Sector* (Orlando, Fla.: Academic Press, 1986).

17. Mark R. Yessian and Anthony Broskowski, "Generalists in Human-Service Systems: Their Problems and Prospects," *Social Service Review* 51 (June 1977), 265–88.

18. Handler and Hollingsworth (n. 4 above). Most local public emergency assistance programs focus on only some population groups—sometimes the elderly, sometimes poor single mothers, but almost never single adults. The programs also often systematically exclude items that are in theory covered by normal welfare grants, such as security deposits. This selectivity continues to reflect controversies over such issues as whether certain groups should not be helped, or whether coverage rewards those who voluntarily refuse to live within budgets. See Handler and Sosin (n. 4 above).

19. Handler and Hollingsworth (n. 4 above). New York and California are examples, at least according to data found in Peterson et al. (n. 11 above). This seems to follow from general organization theory, which implies that specialization can occur in response to potential conflict and the resulting uncertainty as well as to actual conflict.

20. Handler and Sosin (n. 4 above); Alfred J. Kahn, *Social Policy and Social Services* (New York: Random House, 1973). This is despite some general similarities in the social problems covered in the two systems. One study finds that the separation of services from eligibility might cause the reduction in referrals for services. But the separated model tested appears to be one in which regular visits were no longer mandated; thus, the lack of generalist work is also implicated. Irving Piliavin and Alan E. Gross, "The Effects of Separation of Services and Income Maintenance on AFDC Recipients," *Social Service Review* 51 (September 1977): 389–406.

21. Jan L. Hagen, "Income Maintenance Workers: Technicians or Service Providers?" *Social Service Review* 61 (June 1987): 261–71; Evelyn Brodkin and Michael Lipsky, "Quality control in AFDC as an Administrative Strategy," *Social Service Review* 57 (March 1983): 1–34; Michael Sosin, "Legal Rights and Welfare Change: 1960–1980," in *Fighting Poverty: What Works and What Doesn't,*

ed. Sheldon Danziger and Daniel H. Weinberg (Cambridge, Mass.: Harvard University Press, 1986), pp. 260–82.

22. Sosin, *Private Benefits* (n. 16 above); Richard Cloward and Irwin Epstein, "Private Social Welfare's Disengagement from the Poor: The Case of Family Adjustment Agencies," in *Social Welfare Institutions,* ed. Meyer Zald (New York: Wiley, 1965).

23. Arnold Gurin and Barry Friedman, *Contracting for the Delivery of Human Services: A Study of Contracting Practices in Three Human Service Agencies in Massachusetts,* report to the Office of Human Development Services (Washington, D.C.: Department of Health and Human Services, 1980); Madeline Kimmich, *American's Children, Who Cares: Growing Needs and Declining Assistance in the Reagan Era* (Washington, D.C.: Urban Institute, 1985); Martha Gibleman, "Are Clients Better Off When Services Are Purchased?" *Public Welfare* 39 (Fall 1981): 26–33.

24. Sosin, *Private Benefits* (n. 16 above).

25. Because it is likely that the priorities established before 1975 continue to dominate, it is not clear that decentralization resulted in greater selectivity in every local area. However, it is fairly clear that the expected expansion of services and of eligibility criteria did not generally materialize.

26. The eight items account for 65 percent of total program expenditures; it is unclear whether the remaining expenditures are contracts to cities that are not tallied, other expenses, or miscellaneous items. Peterson et al. (n. 11 above).

27. Bruce Fireman and William A. Gamson, "Utilitarian Logic in the Resource Mobilization Perspective," in *The Dynamics of Social Movements: Resource Mobilization, Tactics, and Control,* ed. M. N. Zald and J. D. McCarthy (New York: Sage, 1978); Terry Moe, *The Organization of Interests: Incentives and the Internal Dynamics of Political Interest Groups* (Chicago: University of Chicago Press, 1980); Richard Scott, "The Factory as a Social Service Organization: Goal Displacement in Workshops for the Blind," *Social Problems* 15 (March 1967): 160–75. This and the line of reasoning to follow also imply that private agencies obtain the type of discretion at the case level that can encourage flexibility by may also result in arbitrary worker behavior.

28. Although these boards may not be particularly powerful (see Benton, Feild, and Millar (n. 2 above)), the fact that the federal government mandates that priorities be set with the help of advisory boards might, if anything, contribute to this situation. These boards in fact exemplify a type of formal accountability that organizational theorists suggest might favor increased interest of the more powerful. Such boards are often composed of representatives of traditional service agencies and other powerful groups because it is the purpose of the boards to reflect current interests. See Philip Selznick, *TVA and the Grassroots* (Berkeley: University of California Press, 1949); Meyer Zald, "The Power and Function of Boards of Directors: A Theoretical Synthesis," *American Journal of Sociology* 75 (July 1969); 97–111; Stephen B. Heintz, "Dividing Scarce Dollars," *Public Welfare* 43 (Summer 1985): 19–24.

29. Sosin, *Private Benefits* (n. 16 above).

30. Irwin Epstein, "Advocates and Advocacy: An Exploratory Study," *Social Work Research and Abstracts* 17, no. 1 (1981): 5–12; Sosin, *Private Benefits* (n. 16 above). They could not easily do otherwise because individuals rarely apply to providers who do not already cover the desired service (and the few potential clients who do apply often turned away quickly and may not be formally counted). J. R. Greenley and Stuart S. Kirk, "Organizational Characteristics of Agencies

and the Distribution of Services to Applicants," *Journal of Health and Social Behavior* 14 (March 1973): 70–79.

31. Some degree of flexibility is apparent in changes in the early years of Title XX, in which the number of agencies and funded services expanded. however, the possible trade-off between adding new private services and reducing traditional public sector services has not been well documented. At least one authority claims that responsiveness is also demonstrated by the fact that, when revenues were reduced in the early 1980s, states, to some degree, changed the focus of programs to more fully cover the poor and emphasize such "crisis" specialties as protective services. Benton, Feild, and Millar (n. 2 above); Peterson et al. (n. 11 above).

32. The argument about change is supported by literature summarized in Gerald Zaldman and Robert Duncan, *Strategies for Planned Change* (New York: Wiley, 1977). More specific support for the suggestion about reluctance to alter agreements follows from the "resource dependency" perspective on organizations, as summarized in Jeffrey Pfeffer and Gerald R. Salancik, *The External Control of Organizations* (New York: Harper & Row, 1978).

33. Daniel Katz and Robert L. Kahn, *The Social Psychology of Organizations* (New York: Wiley, 1966); Handler and Hollingsworth (n. 4 above).

34. In this city, as well as nationally, governments generally supply only about one-third of the funds of a typical agency and, thus, usually support units that are difficult to control because they have other sources of support. Nelly Hartogs and Joseph Weber, *Impact of Government Funding on the Management of Voluntary Agencies* (New York: Greater New York Fund/United Way, 1978); Filer Commission, *Giving in America: Towards a Stronger Voluntary Sector* (Washington, D.C.: Commission on Private Philanthropy and Public Need, 1977).

35. Malcolm Bush, *Public, Private, and Civic: The Organized Response to Troubled Families* (Berkeley and Los Angeles: University of California Press, 1987).

36. Jeffrey Pfeffer and Gerald R. Salancik (n. 32 above).

37. Ralph Kramer, "Voluntary Agencies and Personal Social Services," in *The Nonprofit Sector: A Research Handbook,* ed. Walter W. Powell (New Haven, Conn.: Yale University Press, 1986), pp. 240–57; Camile Lambert and Leah R. Lambert, "Impact of Poverty Funds on Voluntary Agencies," *Social Work* 15 (April 1979): 53–61; Felice Davidson Perlmutter, "Public Funds and Private Agencies," *Child Welfare* 50 (May 1971): 264–70. There is some evidence of a broader public role in funding new agencies or in promulgating new types of services. However, these (and other) instances are structurally distinct from the general service programs in that funds are specifically dispensed for social problems not normally handled by the private sector; thus, powerful private agencies are not so fully involved. One example is Daniel J. Finnegan, "Federal Categorical Grants and Social Policies: An Empirical Study," *Social Service Review* 62 (December 1988): 614–31.

38. Ralph Kramer and Paul Terrell, *Social Service Contracting in the Bay Area* (Berkeley: University of California, Center for Governmental Studies, 1984).

39. Benton, Feild, and Millar (n. 2 above); Peterson et al. (n. 11 above). If one item increases in rank, all others become relatively lower priorities. In the text, this is included as one change. Note, however, that most shifts in priorities involve switches among items.

40. The advisory boards are particularly unimportant. Welfare executives thus claim that the boards played a major role only in the first year of the program. Perhaps continuing relations with funded agencies are more important. See Benton, Feild, and Millar (n. 2 above).

41. Decreases in state staff occurred under the Block Grant, but these may not suggest efficiency of decentralization compared to centralization because they lower costs that grew with decentralization under Title XX. Peterson et al. (n. 11 above); Benton, Feild, and Millar (n. 2 above).

42. It has been argued that private agencies are the intermediaries between citizens and society. See Barbara J. Nelson, *Making an Issue of Child Abuse: Political Agenda Setting for Social Problems* (Chicago: University of Chicago Press, 1984); Jay Pressman and Aaron Wildavsky, *Implementation* (Berkeley: University of California Press, 1973). Recent literature on coalitions also suggests that advocacy often takes a limited scope in situations in which small reforms can be easily achieved while larger scale reforms are less probable. See Mancur Olson, *The Logic of Collective Action* (Cambridge, Mass.: Harvard University Press, 1965); James Q. Wilson, *Political Organizations* (New York: Basic, 1973); Terry Moe (n. 27 above); Anthony Oberschall, "Loosely Structured Collective Conflict: A Theory and an Application," in *Research in Social Movements, Conflicts and Change,* ed. Louis Krisberg (Greenwich, Conn.: JAI, 1980), 3:45–68; Joel F. Handler, *Social Movements and the Legal System* (New York: Academic Press, 1978).

43. J. H. Calper, *The Politics of Social Services* (Englewood Cliffs, N.J.: Prentice-Hall, 1975); Benton, Feild, and Millar (n. 2 above). This alteration in the level of greatest controversy would not take place if interest groups had unusually powerful interests and backing—under such a situation the 1975 legislation might not even have been adopted. However, due to the nature of social services, it is rather easy to disrupt a general coalition promoting federal responsibility. See Gilbert Steiner, with Pauline Milius, *The Children's Cause* (Washington, D.C.: Brookings Institution, 1986).

44. Though Title XX allowed states only a limited appropriation, it is unclear whether all states made use of all of their allocation until the late 1970s.

45. Martha Burt and Karen J. Pittman, *Testing the Social Safety Net* (Washington, D.C.: Urban Institute, 1985); Peterson et al. (n. 11 above).

46. Burt and Pittman (n. 45 above).

47. Gilbert Y. Steiner, *The Futility of Family Policy* (Washington, D.C.: Brookings Institution, 1981); Steiner and Milius (n. 43 above). Steiner attributes this reduction in activism to factors other than structure, such as the lack of a clear consensus about social service goals and the lack of evidence about what strategies would help clients the most. But these problems seem endemic to the social services in any era, while the level of advocacy has apparently decreased since decentralization became policy. Nevertheless, the controversies over services and the lack of a consensus are important ingredients in the change to a decentralized system. Such a change did not occur in the income maintenance programs, e.g., even though the Reagan administration recommended decentralization of AFDC.

48. Pressman and Wildavsky (n. 42 above).

49. As has been noted, the quest for such certainty is generally considered a typical organizational strategy. See Pfeffer and Salancik (n. 32 above).

50. Burt Weisbrod and J. Schifl, "Collective Provision of Social Services: The Role of the Nonprofit Sector," discussion paper (University of Wisconsin—Madison, Institute for Research on Poverty, 1982).

51. Kirsten Gronbjerg, James C. Musselwhite, and Lester Salamon, *Government Spending and the Nonprofit Sector* (Washington, D.C.: Urban Institute, 1984); Kimmich (n. 23 above); Burt and Pittman (n. 45 above).

52. Hartogs and Weber (n. 34 above). Another way of summarizing the data and focusing on the same problem is to suggest that private agencies have little choice but to substitute to some degree because private sources are less likely to be generous when the public sector provides higher levels of financial support. See Michael Sosin, "Do Private Agencies Fill Gaps in the Public System?" *Administration in Social Work* 8 (Summer 1984): 13–24.

53. For details on the methods, which involved 70 interviews in which 90 individuals took part, see Michael Sosin, Paul Colson, and Susan Grossman, *Homelessness in Chicago: Poverty and Pathology, Social Institutions and Social Change* (Chicago: University of Chicago, School of Social Service Administration, 1988).

54. I avoid the strong argument that any particular unfavored group is always denied aid. Rather, I argue that discretion allows the priorities of local areas to vary so that, in each area, some groups of poor that are not favored (or are not served by the private agencies that receive contracts) are minimally served.

55. Recall that the theory suggests that potential as opposed to actual controversy promotes specialization. In addition, theory suggests that those services for which there is very high demand, strong equity claims, or an unusually high degree of controversy will be administered by the state.

56. See Sosin, Colson, and Grossman (n. 53 above).

57. Dan Salerno, Kim Hopper, and Ellen Baxter, *Hardship in the Heartland: Homelessness in Fight U.S. Cities* (New York: Community Service Association of New York, 1984).

58. Sosin, Colson and Grossman (n. 53 above).

59. They also suggest that these activities are at most dealt with by nonfunded agencies within the private sector, but few such services existed. Beyond shelters and legal aid agencies, the study of Chicago uncovered only three agencies active in case advocacy for the homeless—even until 1989. None used public funds for this purpose. Very few agencies served single, poor individuals who compose the majority of the homeless population. See Sosin, Colson, and Grossman (n. 53 above).

60. For suggestions that the problems may be general, see Kim Hopper and Ellen Baxter, *Public Lives/Private Spares* (New York: Community Service Society of New York, 1981); Kim Hopper and Jill Hamburg, *The Making of America's Homeless: From Skid Row to New Poor* (New York: Community Service Society of New York, 1984).

61. The federal government provided new funds for days spent in shelters and, later, for building new housing units. This seems to be a typical response under a generally centralized service system. Each new problem that manages to overcome the many barriers to achieving federal attention receives a specific, closed-ended, decentralized, and perhaps easy to eventually eradicate, response. The federal legislation also promoted some provision of case management services to the chronically mentally ill.

62. These tendencies may be controlled, but this does not negate the point that they are common in the decentralized system.

63. A temporary limit was adopted in the previous, centralized program in 1973.

64. Not all centralized programs have generalist workers, and some are selective; but I argue that decentralized systems may more often face such pressures.

65. Peter L. Berger and Richard John Neuheus, *To Empower People: The Role of Mediating Structures in Public Policy* (Washington, D.C.: American Enterprise Institute for Public Policy Research, 1977); Charles Murray, *Losing Ground: American Social Policy, 1950–1980* (New York: Basic, 1984), p. 232.

66. For example, some literature suggests that the reliance on the private sector leads to only marginal improvement because there are only moderate degrees of private agency innovation and advocacy for public innovation. As has been mentioned, literature on efficiency and effectiveness is mixed. A review of much of the evidence is contained in Kramer, "Voluntary Agencies and Personal Social Services" (n. 37 above). See also Ralph Kramer, *Voluntary Agencies in the Welfare State* (Berkeley and Los Angeles: University of California Press, 1981).

The Diversity of Case Management Needs for the Care of Homeless Persons

Dorothy Stephens, MHS
Elaine Dennis, MSP
Monica Toomer
Joan Holloway

Synopsis

Health care providers have been attempting to meet the special needs of homeless people on a national level since 1984. The need to implement strategies specific to serving the diversity of services required by homeless people has been apparent. To devise appropriate strategies, clinical information was drawn from the Health Resources and Services Administration-Health Care for the Homeless (HRSA-HCH) projects, which were created in 1987 primarily to fill such a need. In addition, data gathered by the HCH projects (1984-87) funded by the Robert Wood Johnson and Pew Memorial Trust were used. It is suggested that the past mode of providing health care for the homeless has been found to be inadequate when confronting the complex problems of the homeless person of today.

In general, health care providers need to focus more on case management activities, which may include activities not necessarily associated with the provision of health care services (for example, finding and providing food, clothing, shelter, and assessing entitlement eligibility) to achieve the ultimate goal—stabilization—and when possible, reintegration of the homeless person back into society.

The homeless are a heterogeneous group of people. Although in the past they may have been associated exclusively with the alcohol and substance

Ms. Stephens, Ms. Toomer, and Ms. Holloway are with the Division of Special Populations Program Development, Health Resources and Services Administration (HRSA). Ms. Stephens and Ms. Toomer are Staff, and Ms. Holloway is the Director, Ms. Dennis was formerly with HRSA.

Tearsheet requests to Dorothy Stephens, MHS, HRSA, Rm. 7A-22, Parklawn Bldg., 5600 Fishers Lane, Rockville, MD 20857.

abuse subculture, today a new type of homeless person is emerging. Thus, although the previous methods of treating the health care, psychosocial, and economic needs of these persons may have been effective, independent of one another, today a new comprehensive strategy must be implemented. This strategy must be flexible and tailored to the homeless person's needs.

The Stewart B. McKinney Homeless Assistance Act of 1987 provided $75 million during calendar years 1988–89 to provide health care to homeless people. As a result of the influx of funds, in 1987 the Health Care for the Homeless (HCH) Program of the Health Resources Services Administration (HRSA) was created.

The HRSA-HCH Program was modeled after the HCH Program funded by the Robert Wood Johnson and Pew Memorial Trust (RWJ), which funded health care for the homeless projects in 19 major metropolitan areas from August 1984 through November 1987. Under this earlier program, outpatient health services, including primary care, substance abuse treatment, and mental health, and case management services were provided.

This paper presents a discussion of the diversity of the homeless population, using HRSA-HCH calendar years (CY) 1988 and 1989 data in relation to the type of case management activities the homeless might require to restore them eventually to the mainstream of society.

DEMOGRAPHICS

As defined, the homeless population is a group of people whose common thread includes, but may not be limited to, people for whom permanent housing is unavailable, including persons whose primary residence during the night is a supervised public or private facility that provides temporary living accommodations. As such, the homeless population includes families with children, mentally ill persons, substance abusers, runaway youth, and people with acquired immunodeficiency syndrome (AIDS). Given the diversity of this population, it is natural to assume that their needs would be different and, thus, the intensity of care would be different.

As a group, the homeless are at high risk for many minor health care problems, which if not treated, could potentially develop into life-threatening illnesses (1–4). In addition, many resources were available for the homeless people, that is, food, clothing, and shelter. However, there was a paucity of organizations that acted on the behalf of homeless people, either to provide health care services or to channel them to the appropriate sources for nonmedical care.

In response, on July 22, 1987, President Reagan signed the Stewart B. McKinney Homeless Assistance Act of 1987. The act is designed to provide a wide array of Federal help to communities through organizing and providing a comprehensive package of services to homeless people. During December of 1987, HRSA awarded 109 HCH grants to 43 states, Puerto Rico, and the District of Columbia for the provision of comprehensive health care services to homeless people. Awards ranged from $62,000 to $2 million, and most projects began serving patients in March 1988. In 1989, projects received approximately $45 million and an additional $31.5 million in 1990 to serve people from January through September.

Although not all projects' staff responded to all questions, the following represents service data derived from the first 2 years of operation of the HRSA projects:

Category	*CY 1988*	*CY 1989*
Total persons served....................	231,000	352,000
Total visits	783,000	1,356,000

The demographic profile of the homeless, derived from CY 1989 data, is

- 36 percent were black,

- 47 percent were white,

- 11 percent were Hispanic,

- 16 percent were in some other category,

- 20 percent or 72,000 were women ages 15–44; of these 5,998 were pregnant, and 27 percent of those were teenagers,

- 21 percent were children and their parent(s) living as a family unit or were homeless runaway youths.

Following the RWJ model, HRSA-HCH projects were designed to meet the health care needs of homeless people where they congregate. Thus, HCH providers sought out homeless people in settings where they gathered. The following CY 1988 data show their housing status:

- 38 percent were residents of emergency shelters,

- 13 percent were living on the street,

- 6 percent were living in transitional housing, and

- 8 percent were doubled up, that is, persons or families living with friends or relatives in other than a permanent arrangement.

Health Problems of the Homeless

Based on CY 1988–89 data, the following is a breakdown of the services received:

Service	Person Seen in 1988	1988 visits	1989 visits[1]
Primary care	315,000	101,000	592,000
Mental health	8,000	55,000	103,000
Substance abuse	15,000	60,000	210,000
Case management..............	38,000	202,000	343,000

[1]Data for persons seen in 1989 have yet to be compiled.

The data from the RWJ projects have been used to estimate the leading health problems of the homeless.

- 38 percent suffer from alcohol abuse (47 percent of the men, 16 percent of the women),

- 33 percent suffer from mental illness (MI); however, women have twice the rate of MI disorder than men,

- less than 10 percent are chronically mentally ill (2).

The most common physical health problems encountered in the RWJ-HCH projects were acute episodic disorders, including upper respiratory infections, traumas (injuries), and skin ailments, in that order. The principal chronic or major disorders, also in order of frequency, have been hypertension, gastrointestinal ailments, peripheral vascular disease, problems with dentition, neurological disorders, eye disorders, cardiac disease, genitourinary problems, musculoskeletal ailments, ear disorders, and chronic obstructive pulmonary disease (2, 3). Overall, it is estimated that 41 percent of the RWJ-HCH clients are afflicted with some chronic physical disorder, compared with 25 percent of the U.S. ambulatory patient population in general (2).

In addition, approximately one client in six is afflicted with some infectious or communicable disorder that represents a potential risk to the public's health. Most of these are minor conditions—skin ailments, lice infestations. Still, serious respiratory infections (that is, pneumonia and pleurisy) are observed among more than 3 percent; sexually transmitted venereal infections, about 2 percent; and active tuberculosis, approximately 0.5 percent (2).

According to CY 1988 HRSA-HCH data, the leading diagnoses among patients ages 15 or older were alcohol and other substance abuse, skin disorders, mental illness, hypertension, pulmonary disease, and trauma (5).

Similar findings were reported by Nyamathi and Shuler in a 1989 study of urban homeless adults in Los Angeles (6). According to this study, the top five medical problems reported by the homeless included upper respiratory infections, rashes, sores, or swelling of the extremities, hypertension, and injuries.

HOMELESS FAMILIES AND CHILDREN

The image of homeless people as ravaged by chronic mental illness, alcoholism, and drugs has been a popular characterization of this population. However true this may have been in the past, the demographics indicate that a different image of a homeless person is emerging. A 1985 survey of 26 major cities conducted by the U.S. Conference of Mayors showed a 33 percent increase in the number of families with children seeking shelter services (7), and the 1988 National Survey of Shelters for the Homeless found that families make up two of every five homeless persons that use the shelters (8).

CY 1988 HRSA-HCH providers reported the six most common diagnosis for homeless children ages 0–14 as follows: anemia, undernutrition, incomplete immunizations, skin disorders, pulmonary disease, and developmental delay (5).

Many of these families have entered the ranks of the homeless because of economic problems ranging from loss of employment to the lack of availability of affordable, low-cost housing (1, 9). Most are made up of single women and children as opposed to single males accompanied by children. As a group, their health problems differ from those of single males. For example, mothers are afflicted by psychological distress resulting from the unstable housing situation, from the situation from which they have come, and increased incidence of low birth weight and mortality of their infants. The children suffer from malnutrition, lack of immunizations, and increased prevalence of chronic physical disorders (2, 10). The incidence of acute disease and prevalence of chronic disease among this group may depend on the duration of their homelessness.

HOMELESS MENTALLY ILL AND SUBSTANCE ABUSERS

The chronically mentally ill (CMI) person and the substance abuser (alcohol and drug) become homeless, in some instances, as a result of some of the same reasons as do families (2, 9). However, the CMI and substance abuser require more than an economic intervention to resolve the condition for which they are afflicted. And, should they be dually diagnosed, their need for services intensifies to an even greater degree (11).

The CMI and substance abuser most often require an array of services ranging in some cases from supervised living environments to education and job training, as well as psychosocial rehabilitation (12). The application of treatment regimens for CMI and substance abusers should be contained in a treatment plan that outlines the incremental steps in assisting the homeless in obtaining the highest level of functioning possible. The overall monitoring of the patient's progress should be the responsibility of a case manager who provides health care as well as coordination of auxiliary services (that is, training, education, job) for the patient (13).

AIDS AND HOMELESSNESS

The past 2 years have been substantial improvements in the diagnosis and treatment of opportunistic infections and certain other manifestations of human immunodeficiency virus (HIV) infected patients, according to reports given at a recent conference AIDS (14). This has meant that the quality and duration of life for infected persons has improved. However, homeless people who are HIV positive may not have as optimistic a prognosis due to environmental and physical deprivation resulting from their homeless status. This problem may become more prevalent as the number of intravenous (IV) drug abusers with HIV infection increases.

There is a high probability that the number of HIV positive homeless people will increase as the infection spreads in the population of IV drug abusers. The unstable living arrangements of this group will be further threatened by the onset of HIV infection.

RUNAWAY YOUTH

For thousands of adolescents, home is any place that they can sleep for the night. In many metropolitan areas, these young people are the fastest growing segment of the homeless populations. Their stories are as unique as they are, yet a common bond holds them together—some have been sexually abused and have chosen to end it by leaving home. Others are discipline problems, and still others are substance abusers who select the street over parental control. They all seek to escape victimization by fleeing from their environment; the irony is that they are again victims on the streets. If not victims, they must victimize others.

The rate of pregnancy among homeless females can be looked to as a prime example of their victimization. The highest rate is approximately 25 percent and occurs for the cohort 16–19-year-olds; in the next oldest cohort, 20–24-year-olds, the rate exceeds 20 percent. This demonstrates a rate of pregnancies of about two times that of the national rate (15). Late or no prenatal care and little social support contribute to the high rate of low birth weight and infant mortality seen in this population (16).

The Juvenile Justice and Delinquency Prevention Act, Public Law 93–415, provides funding for 311 runaway shelters. These shelters are managed by the Family and Youth Services Bureau in the Department of Health and Human Services. The shelters have an advocate in the National Network of Runaway Youth Services, a nonprofit foundation, based in Washington, DC, and seek to provide food, lodging, and other social services to homeless youth.

The HRSA-HCH and the Family and Youth Services Bureau work together to provide primary care to this population through the 109 medical projects funded under the McKinney Act. According to CY 1989 data, approximately 21 percent of persons seen in HCH facilities were homeless families, including runaway youth.

In cities where there are common project sites, efforts are being made to coordinate the provision of services. The range of services will span the range of needs. Optimally, shelters for runaways should provide access to primary care services and material on communicable diseases, substance abuse information for runaway youth, and related training for shelter staff. Formal linkages have been formed between agencies, but more importantly, homeless youths will benefit—for example, increased access to primary and preventive health services, including prenatal care.

CASE MANAGEMENT, COORDINATION OF CARE

The implementation of a case management system in programs providing health care services to homeless people is essential, given the environmental and psychosocial deficits often found in this population (1, 17). A case management system should be operational to assure both internal as well as external coordination of services and to provide followup and monitoring of the patient's progress (1, 18, 19).

As such an important facet of care, case management activities were funded under the HRSA-HCH Program. CY 1988 case management activities provided a ratio of 5 visits per person at approximately 202,000 visits per 38,000 persons. Preliminary CY 1989 data reveals a 59 percent increase in visits over 1988. (The 1989 data for persons has yet to be compiled.)

There are certain basic elements that compose a case management system: (a) definition of the role and responsibilities of the case manager, such as patient advocate, should be defined in terms of functions; (b) the case manager should have access to all of the providers involved in the treatment of the patient; and (c) the case manager should function as the "overseer" of the entire case from a system point of view, and as such needs to have more than a passing familiarity with the treatment plan developed for the patient. Because of the complexity of the health and psychosocial problems faced by homeless people, it is important for the case manager to have a multidisciplinary approach and to "broker" the system on behalf of the patient (17, 18, 20, 21).

CONCLUSION

Given the diversity of this population, it is highly desirable that each local program be tailored to the needs of the population found within that project's service area. An integrated approach to addressing not only the health but the psychosocial and economic needs of the homeless population is critical; they cannot be separated.

REFERENCES

1. Winkleby, M. A.: Comparison of risk factors for ill health in a sample of homeless and nonhomeless poor. Public Health Rep 105: 404–410, July–August 1990.
2. Wright, J. D., and Weber, E.: Homelessness and health. McGraw-Hill, Inc., Washington, DC, 1987
3. Ropers, R. H., and Boyer, R.: Homelessness as a health risk. Alcohol Health Res World 11: 38–41, 89–90 (1987).
4. Smith, L. G.: Teaching treatment of mild acute diarrhea and secondary dehydration to "homeless" parents. Public Health Rep 102: 539–542, September–October 1987.
5. Health Resources and Services Administration: The Health needs of the homeless: a report on persons served by the McKinney Act's health care for the homeless program. National Association of Community Health Centers, Inc., Washington, DC, September 1989.
6. Nyamathi, A., and Shuler, P.: Factors affecting prescribed medication compliance of the urban homeless adult. Nurse Pract 14: 47–54 (1989).
7. U.S. Conference of Mayors: Health care for the homeless: a forty-city review. Washington, DC, 1985.
8. U.S. Department of Housing and Urban Development: The report on the 1988 national survey of shelters for the homeless. U.S. Government Printing Office, Washington, DC, (1989).
9. Rossi, P. H., and Wright, J. D.: The determinants of homelessness. Health Affairs 6: 19–32 (1987).
10. Gelberg, L., and Lawrence, L.: Psychological distress among homeless adults. J Nerv Ment Dis 177: 291–295 (1989).
11. Wolfe, H. L., and Sorensen, J. L.: dual diagnosis patients in the urban psychiatric emergency room. J Psychoactive Drugs 21: 169–175 (1989).
12. Riesdorph-Ostrow, W.: Deinstitutionalization: a public policy perspective. J Psychosoc Nurs 27: 4–8 (1989).
13. Levine, I., and Fleming, M.: Human resource development: issues in case management. University of Maryland, College Park, MD. 1985.
14. Gayle, H., Porter, V., Greene, Y., and Hunter, G.: An analysis of national trends. Delivered at "From Cries and Whispers to Action: Black Women and AIDS," sponsored by the National Black Women's Health Project. Washington, DC, Oct. 17–18, 1988.
15. Westoff, C.: Fertility in the United States. Science 234: 554–559, Oct. 31, 1986.
16. Bachrach, L. L.: Homeless women: a context for health planning. Milbank Q 65: 371–396 (1987).
17. Committee on Health Care for Homeless People: Homelessness health and human needs. Institute of Medicine, Washington DC, 1988.
18. Breakey, W. R.: Treating the homeless. Alcohol Health Res World 11: 42–46, 90 (1987).
19. Welch, W. M., and Toff, G.: Service needs of minority persons who are homeless and homeless mentally ill. In Proceedings of the third of four knowledge development meetings on issues affecting homeless mentally ill people. George Washington University, Washington, DC, December 14–15, 1987, pp. 1–77.
20. Bargmann, E.: Washington, D.C.: the Zacchaeus Clinic—a model of health care for homeless people. In Health care of homeless people, P. W. Brickner, L. K.

Scharer, B. Conanan, A. Elvy, and M. Savarese, editors. Springer-Verlag, New York, 1985, pp. 323–332.
21. Brickner, P. W., et al., editors: Health care of homeless people. Springer-Verlag, New York, 1985.

Status of Programs Under the Stewart B. McKinney Homeless Assistance Act and Related Legislation

OVERVIEW OF MCKINNEY ACT

The Stewart B. McKinney Homeless Assistance Act (P.L. 100-77) became law in July 1987. The McKinney Act includes nearly twenty different provisions to address the needs of homeless people by providing for emergency shelter, food, health care, mental health care, housing, educational programs, job training, and other community services. The initial authorization for the McKinney Act was for two years and expired on September 30, 1988.

On November 7, 1988, President Reagan signed the Omnibus McKinney Homeless Assistance Act of 1988 (P.L. 100–628), which reauthorized the McKinney Act for another two years. The reauthorization bill authorized $634 million in fiscal 1989 and $676 million in fiscal 1990 for McKinney programs. President Bush's 1990 budget proposes full funding the McKinney programs at $676 million for fiscal 1990. Congress appropriated only $388 million for the McKinney programs for fiscal 1989. The reauthorization bill contains provisions to make certain housing programs under the Act more flexible for states to administer. It also establishes a mechanism to facilitate the coordination and dissemination of McKinney program information.

For a list of authorization and appropriation levels for the McKinney Act, refer to Appendix A.

INTERAGENCY COUNCIL ON THE HOMELESS

Agency. Independent Agency within the Executive Branch.

Composition. The Secretary of HUD is chairperson of the council. The council is composed of the heads of ten Cabinet departments (Agriculture, Commerce, Defense, Education, Energy, Health and Human Services,

Housing and Urban Development, Interior, Labor, and Transportation) and five independent agencies (ACTION, Federal Emergency Management Agency [FEMA], General Services Administration [GSA], Veterans' Administration [VA], and the Postmaster General). HUD appointed an executive director of the council in December 1987. The council must report annually to the President and Congress on its assessment of the nature and extent of the problems of the homeless and the activities of federal agencies in addressing these needs.

Functions. The Council was established by the McKinney Act to review, monitor, evaluate, and recommend improvements in federal programs to assist the homeless; to collect and disseminate information relating to the homeless; to reduce duplication of effort among federal agencies and to provide technical assistance to states, local government, and private or nonprofit organizations serving the homeless. The council collects and disseminates information relating to the homeless and is required to distribute a bimonthly bulletin on federal resources available under the McKinney Act including application deadlines and federal agency contact persons.

Technical Assistance. The council is required to employ a minimum of two regional coordinators and a maximum of five to help interpret federal regulations, assist in the application process for federal assistance, coordinate McKinney programs with other federal programs, and develop recommendations for regional solutions to homeless issues. The regional coordinators are required to schedule biennial regional workshops in each of the ten federal regions and to hold at least five of these workshops by September 30, 1989.

Program Timetables. Each federal agency that is responsible for administering a program under the McKinney act is required to provide a timetable to the council regarding program funding availability and application deadlines. This must occur within 90 days after the date of the reauthorized law's enactment. The council is then required to provide this information to each state (including the state contact person).

Encouragement of State Involvement. States are required to designate a state contact person to receive and disseminate information received from the council, including the bimonthly bulletin. States are encouraged to establish state interagency councils to coordinate with the council and state and local agencies to effectively disseminate and utilize information on McKinney homeless assistance programs. For more details on the possible functions of the state contact person and the interagency councils, refer to Appendix B.

Funding.   For fiscal 1989, $1.1 million was appropriated as a separate budget item. In fiscal 1988, the council received $750,000 which came from the $65 million for the Supportive Housing Demonstration program. In fiscal 1987 the council received $200,000, which came from the Federal Task Force on Hunger and Homeless that had been functioning in HHS.

Comments.   The council submitted its first report to Congress in the fall of 1987 and completed its first annual report in January, 1989.

The Council publishes a newsletter, *Council Communique.* To receive a copy of the newsletter, contact the Interagency Council at 451 7th Street, S.W., Room 10158, Washington, D.C. 20410, (202)755–1480.

Contact.   Tricia Rodgers, (202) 755-1480

COMPREHENSIVE HOMELESS ASSISTANCE PLAN

Agency.   U.S. Department of Housing and Urban Development (HUD)

Overview.   States, eligible cities, and urban counties must have developed, and have approved, Comprehensive Homeless Assistance Plans (CHAPs) to participate in McKinney Act programs administered by HUD. The CHAP is also required in connection with programs administered by the U.S. Department of Labor.

Timeline.   CHAPs must be submitted annually. The deadline for submission of Comprehensive Homeless Assistance Plans (CHAPS) was February 13, 1989.

Comments.   CHAPs contain a statement of need, a brief inventory of facilities and services to assist the homeless, a strategy to meet the needs of the homeless and recognize special needs, and an explanation of how federal funds will complement and enhance available services. A CHAP must also describe how facilities and services will be used to meet the needs of the homeless.

The CHAP must include assurances that each grantee and project sponsor will administer, in good faith, a policy designed to ensure that the homeless facility is drug and alcohol-free.

Each CHAP must identify the appropriate person or agency to contact regarding the contents of the plan. In addition, CHAPs are required to be exchanged between participating states, cities, and counties to help improve state and local coordination and planning.

In 1988, plans were submitted and approved for all fifty states and Puerto Rico, and for 322 of 327 eligible cities and urban counties. Progress reports in carrying out the CHAPs were due January 31, 1989, covering the period ending December 31, 1988. HUD will issue information regarding the content of the review later this year.

Contact. (Cities and Counties) James R. Broughman (202) 755-5977. (States) James N. Forsberg (202) 755-6322.

EMERGENCY SHELTER GRANT PROGRAM (ESG)

Agency. Community Planning and Development, U.S. Department of Housing and Urban Development (HUD)

Eligible Applicants. States, cities, urban counties, and local governments.

Timeline. Notice of funding availability was published January 9, 1989. Applications were due February 13, 1989.

Use of Funds. This program provides grants on a formula basis to states, eligible cities, urban counties, and local governments for renovation, major rehabilitation, or conversion of buildings for use as emergency shelters for homeless persons. Funds also can be used for certain operating costs, social services, and homeless prevention activities, including financial assistance to families who have received eviction notices or notices of termination of utility service. States can distribute ESG assistance directly to private nonprofit organizations, if local governments certify their approval of the project.

ESG funds can be used for 20 percent of essential services. The 20 percent setaside of the ESG grant is taken from the aggregate amount of assistance that is given to the state or local government.

About half of the funds are distributed through the Community Development Block Grant-Small Cities formula to local governments. The balance is allocated to formula jurisdictions, with a minimum allocation of $25,000.

Match Requirement. Each program recipient must match federal funds on a dollar-for-dollar basis. The match may include the value of any donated material or building, leases, staff salaries, or the value of volunteer services.

Range of Awards. In fiscal 1987, applications were received and approved for all fifty states, as well as Puerto Rico. All of the 318 applications received from eligible cities and urban counties were also approved. Fiscal 1988 funds were distributed to all 50 states and Puerto Rico and to over 300 metropolitan areas and urban counties. The average grant was $66,200 for states and $14,700 for cities and urban counties.

Comments. When grantees receive funds for shelter operations and essential services, the building must be used as a shelter as long as federal assistance is received. The shelter site can be changed only if the assistance is for operating funds or essential services and the new site would continue to serve essentially the same population. If funds are used for rehabilitation, other than major rehabilitation or conversion, the building must be used as a shelter for at least 3 years. If funds are used for major rehabilitation or conversion, the building must be used as a shelter for a minimum of 10 years.

Contacts. Jim Forsberg (states), (202) 755-6322 and Jim Broughman (metro cities and urban counties), (202) 755-5977

IDENTIFICATION OF UNDERUTILIZED FEDERAL BUILDINGS FOR FACILITIES TO ASSIST THE HOMELESS

Agency. U.S. Department of Housing and Urban Development (HUD), U.S. Department of Health and Human Services (HHS) and General Services Administration (GSA).

Overview. The McKinney Act requires that federal agencies identify all underutilized buildings and properties for possible use by states, local governments, and non-profit organizations as facilities to assist the homeless. HUD, in consultation with the U.S. Department of Health and Human Services (HHS) and the General Services Administration (GSA), must then determine which of these properties are suitable for use. New suitable properties are to be listed in the Federal Register each week.

Eligible Applicants. States, local governments and private non-profit organizations.

Timeline. Applications for use of a property must be submitted to HHS within 30 days (this may be changed to 90 days) after the property is listed in the *Federal Register*. HHS must make a decision on the application within 15 days of receipt. If you are interested in applying for use of a property, write immediately to HHS (address listed below) to alert them of your interest. This may give you more time to complete the application. Applicants interested in a property that have missed the 30-day deadline should still contact HHS to discuss the option of applying (if the property has not already been leased).

For the list of properties recently published in the *Federal Register* refer to Appendix C.

Comments. In applying, applicants should request a ten year lease. Ownership of buildings and property cannot be transferred from the federal government. To be deemed suitable, buildings must have functioning utilities and meet minimum structural standards. Vacant land sites must be accessible by roads.

Due to a federal court order issued December 12, 1988, HUD must release listings of sites that are deemed eligible for use by the homeless. Please note that while some properties may have been deemed suitable, they may not be available. Prior to the court order, few steps had been taken by appropriate agencies to make surplus properties available for the homeless.

Contacts. For further information or an application, contact:

Judy Brietman, Department of Health and Human Services, Division of Public Health Services, Room 17A-10, Parklawn Building, 5600 Fisher Lane, Rockville, Maryland 20857, (301)443-2265. (send a letter of intent if interested in a property). Tim Leshan, National Coalition for the Homeless, (202) 659-3310. Wendy Adler, National Governor's Association, (202) 624-7819.

SECTION 8 ASSISTANCE FOR
SINGLE ROOM OCCUPANCY (SRO) DWELLINGS

Agency. U.S. Department of Housing and Urban Development (HUD)

Eligible Applicants. Grants are awarded based on a national competition to state,city, urban county, or tribal public housing agencies that currently administer Section 8 Moderate Rehabilitation Assistance Programs.

Timeline. Notice of funding availability was published January 9, 1989. Applications for fiscal 1989 funds are due April 10, 1989.

Use of Funds. The SRO program increases funding for HUD Section 8 Moderate Rehabilitation Assistance Program to be used to rehabilitate SRO units for occupancy by the homeless. SRO assistance can also be used to rehabilitate efficiency units that contain kitchen or bathroom facilities if the project owner agrees to pay the additional costs of rehabilitation and operation of the units. The per unit cost limit on SRO dwellings of $14,300 will be increased annually based on increases in construction costs.

Range of Awards. For fiscal 1988, one hundred public housing agencies applied for a total of $350 million in funding, ten times the available amount of funds. Thirty-five million dollars was awarded to twenty-one public housing agencies to support 1,048 single room occupancy units in their communities.

Comments. No city or urban county can receive more than 10 percent of the funds. Applications should describe the non-profit organizations that are to receive funds for SRO rehabilitation under the program. Contracts are for fifteen years, and rehabilitation must be completed within twelve months of execution of an agreement between HUD and the public housing agency.

Contacts. Larry Goldberger, (202) 755-5720. Mary Maher, (202) 755-6650

SUPPLEMENTAL ASSISTANCE FOR FACILITIES TO ASSIST THE HOMELESS (SAFAH)

Agency. U.S. Department of Housing and Urban Development (HUD)

Eligible Applicants. States, metropolitan cities, urban counties, tribes, or private nonprofit organizations.

Timeline. No funds were appropriated for SAFAH in either fiscal 1988 or 1989. President Bush's 1990 budget proposes funding the program at $11.0 million.

Use of Funds. The SAFAH program provides discretionary grants to cover costs beyond those covered by the emergency shelter grant or supportive housing programs. The additional funds are to address the special needs of homeless families with children, elderly homeless, or handicapped homeless persons, and to facilitate the transfer and utilization of public buildings to assist the homeless. The SAFAH program also provides funds for innovative programs designed to meet the needs of the homeless by assisting in the purchase, lease, renovation, or conversion of facilities to assist the homeless or provide support services. Funds can be used for the costs of supportive services to the homeless beyond those costs covered in the ESG and supportive housing programs and to cover the operation costs of facilities to assist the homeless.

Range of Awards. In fiscal 1987, HUD received 231 applications for close to $100 million. In December 1987, HUD awarded the $15 million appropriated to thirty-nine applicants for their supplemental assistance projects. Two states (Pennsylvania and Vermont), local governments, and nonprofit organizations were funded.

Contact. Edward Stromberg, (202) 426-1520

SUPPORTIVE HOUSING DEMONSTRATION PROGRAM

Agency.   U.S. Department of Housing and Urban Development (HUD)

Overview.   This program is designed to develop innovative approaches for providing housing and support services to homeless persons.

This program contains two components: the Transitional Housing Demonstration Program and the Permanent Housing for the Handicapped Program.

1. Transitional Housing Demonstration Program

Eligible Applicants.   States, metropolitan cities, urban counties, tribes, and nonprofit organizations.

Timeline.   Notice of funding availability was published January 9, 1989. Applications are due March 30, 1989.

Use of Funds.   This program provides discretionary grants to states, metropolitan cities, urban counties, tribes, and nonprofit organizations for projects that facilitate the movement of homeless persons to independent living by providing temporary housing and support services.

Funds can also be used to establish and operate employment assistance programs for the residents of transitional housing. Grants are to be used to employ residents in operating and maintaining the housing and to pay residents' transportation costs to their jobs. Transitional housing projects that contain an employment assistance program will be a priority in funding decisions.

The program is targeted to serve deinstitutionalized homeless persons, other homeless persons with mental disabilities, and homeless families with children.

Match Requirement.   Program recipients are required to provide a 50 percent match from non-federal sources which may include state or local funds, salaries paid to staff, salaries paid to transitional housing residents who participate in an employment assistance program, the value of services and time donated by volunteers and the value of any donated material or building or any lease on a building. Recipients are required to provide housing and supportive services for a minimum of ten years.

Limit on Residence for Transitional Housing.   A homeless person can remain in transitional housing up to 24 months, or a longer period if the secretary of HUD determines it is necessary.

Range of Awards.   In 1987, 118 projects were funded with the $54.3 million for transitional housing services for the homeless. In 1988, two hundred seventy-nine applications were received and 108 were funded. The average total grant in 1988 equaled $509,600.

Comments.   HUD will provide, upon request, an application package describing the information and documents that transitional housing applicants must submit.

Contact.   Morris Bourne, (202) 755-9075

2. Permanent Housing for the Handicapped

Eligible Applicants.   States can apply for funds to distribute to nonprofit organizations or public housing authorities that provide community-based long-term housing and supportive services in projects that have no more than eight handicapped homeless persons.

Timeline.   Notice of funding availability was published January 9, 1989. Applications are due by April 27, 1989.

Use of Funds.   Supportive housing program funds can be used for annual operating costs of permanent housing for the handicapped projects. If used for operating costs, the funds cannot exceed 50 percent of these costs in the first year and no more than 25 percent of the operating cost for the second year. Projects can have no more than eight persons. The secretary of HUD can waive the eight-person limit if the applicant demonstrates that local market conditions dictate the development of a larger project, and that the development will still achieve the neighborhood integration objectives of the program.
   Projects must either be group homes designed solely for housing handicapped homeless persons or dwelling units in a multifamily housing project, condominium project, or a cooperative project. Project sponsors are required to provide housing and support services for a minimum of ten years.

Match Requirements.   States must certify that they will match program funds with 50 percent of non-federal sources that are to be used solely for acquisition or rehabilitation. Non-federal sources include state or local funds, salaries paid to staff, salaries paid to transitional housing residents who participate in an employment assistance program, the value of time donated by volunteers, and the value of any donated material or building or any lease on a building.

Range of Awards. Due to the lateness of the fiscal 1987 appropriation, fiscal 1987 and 1988 funds were combined. A total of $30 million was available for permanent housing for the handicapped for fiscal 1987 and 1988. In the first round of funding in 1988, applications were received from 24 states, the District of Columbia, Puerto Rico, and the Virgin Islands for a total of 57 projects. HUD awarded $3.2 million to 37 projects in 20 states. For the second round of funding, HUD received applications for 62 projects. Forty-one projects were approved and received $3.6 million. Approximately $23 million remaining from the permanent housing appropriation for fiscal years 1987 and 1988 was transferred to the 1989 appropriation for the transitional housing program.

Comments. Applicants should be sure to specify the amounts and sources of their matching funds. If requested, HUD will provide states with an application package describing the information and documents required for assistance for permanent housing projects. Applications are also available from the state contact person.

Contact. Morris Bourne, (202) 755-9075

SECTION 202/HOUSING AND COMMUNITY DEVELOPMENT ACT OF 1987

Agency. U.S. Department of Housing and Urban Development (HUD)
Section 202 of the Housing and Community Development Act of 1987 (P.L. 100–242) was amended to ensure that the Section 202 program would meet the special housing needs of non-elderly handicapped families and individuals. The amendments provide for the adoption of standards and procedures for improved shelter and supportive services for mentally ill people that would otherwise be homeless.

Eligible Applicants. Non-profit organizations.

Timeline. Notification of funding availability for fiscal 1989 will be issued in mid-April, 1989. Applications will be due in mid-June, 1989.

Use of Funds. Section 202 contains two forms of housing assistance targeted for lower-income elderly and handicapped persons and families. This includes construction and permanent financing loans for the development of rental units, with funds borrowed by HUD from the Treasury to the extent permitted in legislation. HUD couples this loan assistance with a subsidy from Section 8 funds for all units. The amount available for this use is designated in the appropriation for all Section 8 funding. Thus, the number of units actually produced must be a combination of available loan and Section 8 funding.

The program targets 25 percent of its funds to provide loans for projects for the handicapped, with the mentally ill homeless handicapped receiving priority.

Range of Awards. For fiscal 1988, $566 million was appropriated and for the first time the handicapped were targeted under Section 202. Congress appropriated $480 million for fiscal 1989.

Comments. HUD field offices will provide examples of approved applications upon request.

Contacts. Bob Wilden, (202) 426-8730. Sharon Mizell, (202) 755-5866

COMMUNITY DEMONSTRATION PROJECTS FOR ALCOHOL AND DRUG ABUSE TREATMENT

Agency. National Institute on Alcohol Abuse and Alcoholism (NIAAA), in consultation with the National Institute on Drug Abuse (NIDA).

Eligible Applicants. State agencies and community-based public and private nonprofit organizations. Fiscal 1989 funds will be available, on a competitive basis, to the 9 projects already funded. No new applications will be accepted.

Timeline. Notification of funding availability was published in February, 1989. The 9 eligible programs must submit renewal applications by mid-April, 1989.

Use of Funds. The program provides discretionary grants for demonstration projects that develop and expand alcohol and drug abuse treatment services for homeless individuals, many of whom are mentally ill.

Range of Awards. Nine grants totaling $8.1 million were awarded in 1988. Grants were targeted to communities of 200,000 and above, but open to cities of all sizes. The average grant award was $914,000.

Comments. The program is intended to fund research and evaluation projects, rather than service projects. Each grant recipient is required to set aside 25% of its budget for project evaluation.

Contacts. Barbara Lubran, (301) 443-0786. Robert Huebner, (301) 443-0786.

COMMUNITY MENTAL HEALTH SERVICES
DEMONSTRATION PROJECT

Agency. Alcohol, Drug Abuse and Mental Health Administration (ADAMHA), U.S. Department of Health and Human Services (HHS) in collaboration with the National Institute of Mental Health (NIMH).

Eligible Applicants. State mental health authorities. Fiscal 1989 funds will be available, on a competitive basis, to the 12 projects already funded. No new applications will be accepted.

Timeline. The 12 eligible projects must submit renewal applications by early May, 1989.

Use of Funds. This demonstration project provides discretionary grants for community-based mental health services to the homeless or those at risk of becoming homeless. The program is intended to fund up to twelve comprehensive, two-year community-based demonstration projects for homeless adults with severe, long-term mental illness and up to four grants for two-year innovative demonstration projects serving severely emotionally disturbed homeless children and adolescents. Services can include outreach, case management, treatment and rehabilitation, transitional housing, and staff training.

Range of Awards. Thirty-three applications were submitted by state mental health authorities for fiscal 1987–1988. Of the applications, twenty-four were targeted for adult programs; nine for children. Nineteen applications were approved, but due to insufficient funds only 12 of these projects were funded and one of those for only one year. Three of the projects funded were for children; nine for adults.

Comments. Comprehensive local demonstration projects should supply services such as outreach, case management, treatment and rehabilitation, transitional housing, and staff training. State applicants must designate the local entity(ies) or organization(s) that will carry out the grant activities in the local demonstration area. Each state may submit only one application and must specify whether the application is for a project serving adults or children. Only one local area may be served within a state.

Contacts. Dr. Irene Shifren Levine, (301) 443-3706. Dr. Deborah Rog, (301) 443-3706.

EMERGENCY ASSISTANCE DEMONSTRATION PROGRAM (AFDC)

Agency.   No decision has been made as to which agency will administer the demonstration program once it is funded. Questions about the program are being handled by the Office of Community Services, U.S. Department of Health and Human Services (HHS).

Eligible Applicants.   States that participate in the emergency assistance program are eligible to participate and must use public or private non-profit agencies to carry out the projects.

Timeline.   The Demonstration Program received no appropriation for fiscal 1989. For fiscal 1990, President Bush's budget proposes funding the program at $20.0 million.

Use of Funds.   The reauthorized McKinney Act included at least two but no more than three demonstration projects designed to reduce the number of homeless families on AFDC living in hotels by encouraging the rehabilitation or construction of transitional facilities.

States that participate are to use project funds to rehabilitate or construct transitional housing facilities, which can be converted to permanent housing, and provide on-site social services at the facilities. Demonstration projects shall meet the conditions and requirements that the secretary prescribes.

To be approved as a demonstration project, a state AFDC agency must demonstrate that the project will provide transitional facilities only for homeless families who are AFDC recipients; reduce the number of rooms that are used to house homeless families on AFDC in transient facilities by the number of units made available in transitional facilities; and indicate that the total cost of federal financial assistance provided under the project to families residing in transitional facilities plus the total cost of grants made to the state cannot exceed the federal share in currently housing these families in transient facilities (including payments made to cover basic needs and services).

Comments.   The McKinney reauthorization bill extends the current moratorium on implementing regulations proposed by the Department of Health and Human Services (HHS) to restrict states' use of AFDC emergency assistance and special needs allowances to help meet the needs of homeless families. The moratorium is extended until September 30, 1989. The proposed regulatory changes are described below:

Standard of Need.   The proposed regulations would affect those states that operate an emergency assistance program and those states that provide special need allowances based on type of housing. They would allow federal authority to limit or define the amount the state determines is necessary to meet special needs or emergencies (AFDC standard of need and payment levels).

Currently, states have the flexibility to establish a statewide standard of need including the cost of "basic needs" (food, clothing, shelter, etc.) and may include "special needs" of AFDC recipients. Some states are providing several kinds of allowances for shelters as a basic or special need. The state plan must specify the circumstances under which payments will be made for special needs.

The proposed regulations would prohibit states from varying their special need allowances or providing multiple shelter allowances for shelter due to the type of housing occupied by AFDC recipients.

Emergency Assistance. Under current law, states receive federal matching funds (50 percent) for emergency assistance authorized by the state for one period of thirty consecutive days in twelve consecutive months. Emergency assistance may include payments for services to meet needs that arose before or extend beyond this period. Some states use emergency assistance and/or special needs funds to provide assistance to homeless families. including shelter in welfare hotels.

The proposed regulations would limit emergency assistance so states could provide only one period of assistance of thirty consecutive days in twelve consecutive months. Needs beyond thirty days would not be subject to matching funds, though states could provide for these needs through their own funds. The regulations also would require states to include in the state plan maximum benefits to be provided for each type of emergency need specified in the plan.

Study of Program. The McKinney Act directs HHS to study current policy and recommend changes, both statutory and regulatory, designed to improve the ability of the AFDC program to respond to the emergency needs of homeless families and eliminate the use of AFDC funds for shelter costs in "welfare hotels." The report is due to Congress by July 1, 1989.

Contact. Jan Fox, (202) 252-5254

EMERGENCY COMMUNITY SERVICES
HOMELESS GRANT PROGRAM

Agency. Office of Community Services, U.S. Department of Health and Human Services (HHS).

Eligible Applicants. State agencies designated by the governor of their state to administer the Emergency Community Services Homeless Grant Program.

Timeline. States were sent notices of funding availability in February, 1989. Applications are due March 31, 1989.

Use of Funds. This program provides grants to states through the Community Services Block Grant (CSBG) formula. State agencies distribute the funds to eligible entities such as community action agencies to provide emergency assistance to the homeless. States must release funds to the eligible entities within 60 days of receipt of funds. Indian tribes apply directly to the U.S. Department of HHS and funds are allocated using the CSBG formula.

Funds may be used to expand services to the homeless and to promote private sector assistance. Funds for this program may be used to assist those at risk of becoming homeless. Assistance may be used to help with mortgage, rental, or utility payments. Not more than 25 percent of the program funds received can be used for these purposes.

Range of Awards. In fiscal 1988, 126 applications, which included all states and territories plus 69 Indian tribes, were received. Grants were awarded to all 126 applicants.

Contacts. Jane Checkan, (202) 252-5260. Jan Fox, (202) 252-5254.

HEALTH CARE SERVICES FOR THE HOMELESS

Agency. U.S. Health Resources and Services Administration (HRSA), U.S. Department of Health and Human Services (HHS)

Eligible Applicants. Public and private non-profit organizations, including community mental health centers such as those supported under the Robert Wood Johnson Foundation initiative. Fiscal 1989 funding is restricted to the 109 projects already funded. No new applications were accepted for fiscal 1990.

Timeline. The notification of funding availability for fiscal year 1989 funds was published November 30, 1988. Applications were due December 30, 1988. Notification of funding availability for fiscal year 1990 is expected to be published in late summer or early fall of 1989.

Use of Funds. The Secretary of HHS under the Public Health Service Act (section 340) awards discretionary grants to support the delivery of health care services to the homeless, including primary care services, drug and alcohol abuse treatment, and optional mental health services.

Residents of transitional housing are eligible for health care services under this program. Also, grantees may continue providing health care services to an individual for up to a year after the individual has become a resident in permanent housing and is no longer homeless. Grantees may, at their option use funds to provide dental, vision, or podiatry services to the homeless where medically necessary.

Match Requirement. Grants may not exceed 75 percent of service costs and each grantee is required to provide a 25 percent match, (the first year) which may be in cash or in kind (plant, equipment, or services). In the second or subsequent year of funding, the grantee must provide a 33 1/3 percent match. The Secretary can waive the match requirement in exceptional circumstances for all nonprofit entities.

Range of Awards. In fiscal 1987 and 1988, 153 applications were received for a total of $83 million. Of these, 109 grantees were funded ranging in grants from $63,000 to $2 million. The average grant was $285,000.

Comments. Grants are awarded through a competitive application process with preference given to applicants with experience in direct client delivery of primary health services and substance abuse treatment for the homeless or underserved populations.

Contacts. Harold Dame, (301) 443-8134. Joan Holloway, (301) 443-8134.

MENTAL HEALTH BLOCK GRANT

Agency. Alcohol, Drug Abuse and Mental Health Administration (ADAMHA), U.S. Department of Health and Human Services (HHS).

Eligible Applicants. State agencies designated to administer the Mental Health Block Grant Program.

Timeline. Notice of funding availability was sent to the states on December 5, 1988. State agencies have until September 30, 1989 to apply for fiscal 1989 funds. Funds are distributed as applications are received and approved.

Use of Funds. State agencies receive formula-based block grants to distribute, at their discretion, to community mental health centers and local programs providing services to chronically mentally ill homeless persons. Funds may be used for community mental health services, outreach services, case management, referrals to health services, substance abuse treatment, supportive and supervisory residential services, and staff training, including training of individuals who work in shelters, mental health clinics, and other sites where the homeless receive services.

Funding Mechanism.   If the amount appropriated for the program in any year is not sufficient to fund a minimum allotment of $150,000 to each state, then the secretary of HHS is required to convert the program to a competitive application process (instead of by formula). The current formula is based on the proportion of a state's population in urbanized areas relative to that of the nation's population in urbanized areas.

State Match.   States are required to provide a 25 percent match, which may be in cash or kind.

State Compliance.   If a state fails to submit an application, to prepare an application in compliance with the application procedures, or the state does not spend the full amount of its allotment, the Secretary must use the unalloted funds to make grants to public and nonprofit entities in that state to provide mental health services to the homeless.

Range of Awards.   For fiscal 1989 the appropriation is $14.1 million, resulting in an allotment of approximately $267,000 to each state. To date, ten states have submitted applications for fiscal 1989 funds.

Comments.   Applicants should closely follow the instructions in the application packet to avoid delays in funding approval.

Contacts.   Gary Palsgrove, (301) 443-3820. Dr. Irene Shifren Levine, (301) 443-3706.

RUNAWAY AND HOMELESS YOUTH PROGRAM

Agency.   Administration for Children, Youth and Families (ACYF), Office of Human Development Services (OHDS) and U.S. Department of Health and Human Services (HHS).
   This program is not authorized under the McKinney Act; it is part of the Runaway and Homeless Youth Act, Section 331.

Overview.   The program addresses the needs of runaway and homeless youth and their families by providing grants to state and local governments and private agencies. It contains two components: the Basic Center Grants and Coordinated Network Grants.

Each year a portion of the total appropriation of both programs is used to fund a toll-free runaway and youth hotline (1-800-621-4000). Approximately 260,000 youth and families are served by the hotline.

1. Basic Center Grants

Eligible Applicants. States, localities, private and nonprofit agencies, and Indian tribes. Applicants submit applications directly to the Administration for Children, Youth and Families, and applications received are subject to a competitive review process. Initial grant years differ for states due to a staggered three-year approval process.

Timeline. The notification of funding availability will be published in the first week of March, 1989. Applications will be due 60 days after publication (first week of May, 1989).

Use of Funds. Basic Center Grants are used to develop or strengthen community-based centers that are not in the law enforcement structure and juvenile justice system. Funds for this program are allocated to state jurisdictions by formula. The formula is based on the state youth population under eighteen years of age in proportion to the national total.

Range of Awards. The Administration for Children, Youth and Families awarded $21.9 million in Runaway and Homeless Youth Basic Center Grants for fiscal 1988. One hundred eighty-three applications were received for the competitive grants and approximately one-third of the total funds ($7.6 million) were awarded to 127 of these applicants. Another $13.8 million was awarded to current basic center grantees who had one or two years remaining in their project periods. Approximately 200 non-competing grants were also awarded as part of the three-year grant cycle. Of the 1987 grantees who had a year remaining in their project periods only 4 were not refunded.

Comments. Applications should describe how the center fits into the overall system of services for runaway and homeless youths in the area. The application should indicate how other support services are coordinated with services offered by the center.

Contact. Pamela Johnson, (202) 755-7800.

2. Coordinated Network Grants

Eligible Applicants. Eligible applicants include coordinated networks of agencies, if they are not part of the law enforcement structure or juvenile justice system. A coordinated network of agencies is defined as an association of two or more private organizations whose purpose is to develop or strengthen services to runaway or homeless youth and their families.

Timeline. No new grants will be awarded until the next 3-year funding cycle begins in fiscal 1991.

Use of Funds. Coordinated Network Grants, a discretionary grant program, funds projects that support and strengthen the work of centers. These include training and technical assistance activities; research and demonstration projects; and methods to improve program administration, outreach, prevention, and family reunification.

Range of Awards. Approximately $750,000 was available for Coordinated Network Grants for fiscal 1988, and a one time supplemental of $383,000 was divided among the 10 networks according to the number of states and grantees in their area. Grant awards ranged from $50,000 to $85,000. For fiscal 1989, $750,000 is the base amount available for the Coordinated Network Grants.

Comments. The project period for Coordinated Networking Grants is for three years. The next funding cycle will begin in 1991. Grantees are initially funded for one year; continued funding is based on satisfactory performance.

Contact. Pamela Johnson, (202) 755-7800.

Emergency Food and Shelter Program

Agency. Federal Emergency Management Agency (FEMA)

Eligible Applicants. The Emergency Food and Shelter Program National Board allocates program funds to Local Emergency Food and Shelter Program Boards. Funds are distributed to local boards based on a formula that includes the unemployment rate, total number of unemployed persons, total number of persons below the poverty line, and the total population. A portion of the funds are distributed to state set-aside committees for distribution to local boards. The local boards then allocate these funds to local nonprofit and government organizations using their own criteria. Communities that do not receive a direct allocation may apply to a state board if state setaside funds are available.

Timeline. All funds have been distributed for fiscal 1989. Local boards will be notified of funding availability for fiscal 1990 in October, 1989. The local boards will then have 30 days to reply, indicating which local agencies are to receive funds.

Use of Funds. Funds are used to supplement the purchase of food for shelters and mass feeding facilities, small equipment, limited leasing of capital equipment, utility and central assistance, emergency lodging, and minor rehabilitation of shelter facilities. Emergency food and shelter appropriations are distributed within 105 days after funds are made available.

Comments. The national board, chaired by the director of FEMA, consists of six members selected by the director. One member is selected from each of the following agencies: United Way of America, Salvation Army, National Council of Churches of Christ in the U.S.A., Catholic Charities U.S.A., Council of Jewish Federations, Inc., and the American Red Cross. The local boards are composed of members of the same agencies, excluding the director, who is replaced by a representative of local government. The state set-aside committee has the same representation as the local and national boards, with state government occupying the government position.

Contacts. Wiley Cooper, (703) 683-1166. Fran McCarthy, (202) 646-3652.

ADULT EDUCATION HOMELESS PROGRAM

Agency. U.S. Department of Education (DOE)

Eligible Applicants. State education agencies.

Timeline. The program is operating on a delayed cycle for fiscal year 1989. Notification of funding availability will be published in Spring or Summer, 1989. Applications for fiscal 1989 funds will be due in the fall. Specific deadlines will be determined by April, 1989.

Use of Funds. The program provides discretionary grants to state education agencies to design and implement literacy training and basic skills remediation programs for adult homeless individuals. Fiscal 1989 funds may be used both for previously funded programs and programs that were not funded in 1987 or 1988. State education agencies can implement programs either directly or through contracts and grants.

Range of Awards. In fiscal 1987 and 1988, funds were distributed to state education agencies based on a formula whereby each state received a minimum allocation of $75,000. The range of awards was $75,000 to $499,000 for fiscal 1987; and $75,000 to $526,000 for fiscal 1988.

Comments. Applications for fiscal 1989 funding should describe the educational programs the state education agency plans to implement itself and/or programs that will be implemented by subgrantees. Applications should describe how ancillary support programs such as housing, health care and food assistance will complement the educational program.

Contacts. Sarah Newcomb, (202) 732-2390. Ronald Pugsly, (202) 732-2272.

EDUCATION FOR HOMELESS CHILDREN AND YOUTH PROGRAM

Agency. U.S. Department of Education (DOE)

Eligible Applicants. State education agencies.

Timeline. Notification of funding availability for fiscal 1988 was sent to state contacts on November 10, 1988. The program operates on a delayed cycle with both state plans and applications for funding due April 30, 1989. Funds are distributed as applications and state plans are received and approved through April, 1989. The notification of funding availability for fiscal 1989 funds will be issued in December, 1989.

Use of Funds. The program provides formula grants to state education agencies to develop and implement programs for the education of homeless children. Funds are distributed on the basis of the Chapter 1 Basic Grant formula, which includes both the number of low-income children and the average state expenditure per pupil from the previous year. State education agencies receive a minimum allocation of $50,000.

State Plan. For 1987 funding, state education agencies had to assess strategies to assure homeless children access to education. For fiscal 1988, the agencies must submit state plans that provide a strategy for the education of homeless children and procedures to resolve disputes regarding the educational placement of homeless children. The plans do not need to address specific details of programs the staate intends to use to impelement the strategy. However, each plan must ensure, to the extent practicable under local education law, that:

- Local education authorities continue the education of the child in the original school district for the rest of the school year or place the child in the district he or she is actually living in, whichever is in the child's best interest;

- Each homeless child is provided the same services as other children;

- The records of each homeless child who is transferred to a new school district are available i a timely manner in the new district.

State Coordinator. Each state is required to establish a coordinator to implement this program. The coordinator of the education for the homeless children and youth program is required to gather and evaluate data on the number and location of homeless children in the state and the problems in meeting their educational needs. This data must be collected annually. In addition, the coordinator must file a report based on the data collected with the Secretary of Education by December 31 of each year.

Range of Awards. The fiscal 1988 appropriation is $4.7 million. Grants range from $50,000-$400,000. All 50 states, the District of Columbia, and Puerto Rico applied for 1987 federal funds, and all applicants received funds.

Comments. States were required to file final reports on the number and location of homeless children in the state and the difficulties experienced in meeting their educational needs by December 31, 1988.

Contacts. Edward E. Smith, (202) 732-4726 Tom Fagan, (202) 732-4682

HOMELESS VETERANS' REINTEGRATION PROJECT

Agency. U.S. Department of Labor (DOL) under the Assistant Secretary of Labor for Veterans' Employment and Training.

Eligible Applicants. State, county, or local governments. Fiscal year 1989 funding is restricted to the 15 projects already funded. No new applications will be accepted.

Timeline. The notification of funding availability for fiscal 1989 will be issued March 14, 1989. Renewal applications (for the 15 eligible projects) must be submitted no later than 60 days prior to the project's current expiration date. These deadlines fall between May 1, 1989 and July 30, 1989 for all 15 eligible projects.

Use of Funds. This reintegration project is a competitive grant program established under the McKinney Act to provide job training, remedial education, basic literacy instruction, job counseling, and outreach referrals to homeless veterans.

Range of Awards. For fiscal 1988, fifteen of 33 agencies that submitted applications were permitted to submit full applications by June 30, 1988 and all fifteen applications were accepted. Grants ranged from $50,000 to $200,000.

Comments.   Projects must hire homeless or fomerly homeless veterans as outreach workers. Projects must also demonstrate coordination with other local McKinney Act programs and homeless service providers.

A similar program has been run by this agency since November 1986 called the Jobs for Homeless Veterans which funded fourteen cities to run job training programs for veterans.

Contact.   Christine Chudd, (202) 523-9110

JOB TRAINING FOR THE HOMELESS
DEMONSTRATION PROGRAM

Agency.   U.S. Department of Labor(DOL)

Eligible Applicants.   State and local public agencies, nonprofit organizations and privately owned businesses.

Timeline.   The notice of funding availability will be issued in March, 1989. Applications are due 45 days later (early May, 1989).

Use of Funds.   This program involves a competitive grant application process under which the Secretary of Labor makes grants for job training demonstration projects for the homeless. Grants may be used for basic skills instruction, remedial education activities, basic literacy instruction, job search activities, job counseling, and job preparatory training, including resume writing and interviewing skills.

State Match.   Each state is required to provide a 10 percent to 50 percent match as determined for each project by the secretary. The match may be in cash or in kind. Grants per state are limited to 15 percent of the total appropriation.

Range of Awards.   Thirty-three of 175 applicants were approved and received grants in fiscal 1988.

Comments.   Proposals for funding must be consistent with the state's Comprehensive Homeless Assistance Plan, in which the state describes how it will coordinate projects with other services for homeless persons under the McKinney Act.

Contacts.   John Heinberg, (202) 535-0682. Jack Mitchka, (202) 535-0682.

JOB TRAINING PARTNERSHIP ACT (JTPA)

When first enacted, the McKinney Act amended JTPA in two ways to assist homeless individuals in obtaining employment and training services.

- It added the homeless to the definition of who are eligible for JTPA programs, in Section 4(8) of the act.

- It changed the requirements for proof of residency under Section 141(E) of JTPA to permit services to individuals who cannot prove residency within the service delivery area if its job training plan permits services to homeless individuals.

Contact. John Heinberg, (202) 535-0682.

HOMELESS CHRONICALLY MENTALLY ILL VETERANS

Agency. Veterans Administration (VA)

This program is part of the Veterans' Benefits and Services Act of 1988 (P.L. 100-322; section 115) and the reauthorized McKinney Act (P.L. 100-628; section 401).

Eligible Applicants. VA Medical Centers. At this time, the Veteran's Administration plans to limit fiscal year 1990 funding to the program sites previously funded.

Timeline. Fiscal year 1989 funds have already been distributed.

Use of Funds. This program provides discretionary grants to VA Medical Centers to provide treatment and rehabilitative services to homeless veterans who have a chronic mental illness. Not more than $500,000 of the funding appropriated for this program shall be used to monitor services nor maintain more than 10 full-time employees in the VA. This program should not result in the reduction of the conversion of hospital-care beds to nursing-home-care beds by the VA.

Range of Awards. In 1988, the program received ninety-two applications and funded forty-three sites.

Comments. Community-based residential treatment facilities that currently serve VA Medical Center clients, or intend to serve these clients in the future, may apply to the local VA Medical Center for funding.

Contact. Gay Koerber, (202) 233-5194

VETERAN'S DOMICILIARY CARE PROGRAM

Agency. Veterans' Administration (VA)
The program is not authorized under the McKinney Act; it is part of the Supplemental Appropriations Act of 1987 (P.L. 100-71).

Eligible Applicants. VA Medical Centers in urban areas. For fiscal 1989, funds were distributed only to the existing 20 program sites.

Timetable. Fiscal year 1989 funds have already been distributed. The Bush budget proposes an appropriation of $15.0 million for fiscal year 1990.

Use of Funds. This program provides funding for conversion of surplus space in VA Medical Centers to domiciliary beds for homeless veterans.

Range of Awards. Ten sites were selected in October 1987, and funds were distributed to them in December 1987. In addition, funds were provided to ten existing domiciliaries to start specialized homeless veterans treatment programs.

Contacts. Richard Olsen, James Kelly, (202) 233-3692.

U.S. DEPARTMENT OF DEFENSE—THREE PROGRAMS

Agency. U.S. Department of Defense (DOD)
The Department of Defense provides assistance to the homeless under three separate programs. Two of the programs, the *Homeless Support Initiative Program* and *Shelter for the Homeless Program*, are funded directly by federal appropriations. These two programs are authorized under Section 2456 of Title 10, United States Code. The third program, *Commissary Food Bank Program*, is authorized under the Defense Authorization Act (P.L. 99-145). The Interagency Council on the Homeless is required to report to Congress on the status of these programs, among other homeless programs.

1. Homeless Support Initiative Program

Eligible Applicants. State and local governments and shelter operators.

Timeline. Applications are accepted at any time on a continuing basis.

Use of Funds. The Department of Defense provides blankets to state and local governments and shelter operators throughout the country.

Range of Awards. A total of $3.2 million worth of blankets was supplied to shelters in fiscal 1987 and 1988. To date, $1.5 million worth of blankets have been supplied for fiscal 1989.

Comments. State and local governments and shelter providers should call or write to the Defense Logistics Agency for information on participating in this program.

Contact. Bill Gola, Defense Logistics Agency, BLA-DRSO-M, Cameron Station, Alexandria, VA 22304–6100, (202) 274-6383.

2. Shelter for the Homeless Program

Eligible Applicants. State and local governments.

Timeline. Applications are accepted at any time on a continuing basis.

Use of Funds. The Department of Defense makes funds available to renovate and repair underutilized facilities on military installations for use by state and local governments in conjunction with charitable organizations for the homeless.

Range of Awards. The program received appropriations of $700,000 in fiscal 1987, and $800,000 in fiscal 1988. Nine hundred thousand dollars was appropriated for fiscal 1989. Since 1983, 15 facilities have been renovated for emergency and transitional housing for the homeless.

Comments. State and local government agencies should contact the commander of their local military installation for information on available facilities.

Contact. Steven Kleiman, (202) 697-8241

3. Commissary/Food Bank Program

Eligible Applicants. The Department of Defense has an agreement with the Department of Health and Human Services (HHS) to designate the local food bank recipients in different geographical areas.

Timeline. Applications are accepted at any time on a continuing basis.

Use of Funds. The Department of Defense makes unmarketable items from military commissaries available to the homeless.

Range of Awards.   The program involves 600,000 pounds of food a year and no direct federal appropriation. Four hundred and eighty-six commissaries and food banks are currently participating in the program.

Comments.   Food banks should contact the Regional Director of HHS for information on participating in this program.

Contact.   Lt. Col. Jay Gordon, (202) 697-9283

FOOD STAMP OUTREACH PROGRAM

Agency.   U.S. Department of Agriculture (USDA)
In its initial authorization, the McKinney Act amended the Food Stamp Act as described below. Changes to the Food Stamp program are no longer included in the McKinney Act, but in the Hunger Prevention Act of 1988 (P.L. 100–435).

Eligible Applicants.   State agencies designated to administer food stamp programs.

Timeline.   There is no deadline for applications. Agencies must notify the USDA of their intention to establish an outreach program for the homeless.

Use of Funds.   States may, at their option, receive federal matching funds (50 percent) to conduct food stamp outreach to homeless persons. This outreach may include public service announcements, brochures and informational materials, and employment of outreach workers or ombudsmen.

Range of Awards.   President Bush's proposed 1990 budget authorizes $70.0 million for food stamp provisions aimed at helping the homeless.

Comments.   The McKinney Act and Hunger Prevention Act of 1988 also mandated changes in food stamp eligibility requirements to allow increased access by the homeless in obtaining food stamps. These changes include the following: permit families who are living with other relatives to receive their own food stamp allotments; provide expedited service to the homeless so that they may receive benefits not later than the fifth calendar day after filing an application; and preclude homeless persons from monthly reporting of changes in income. Rent paid by the government to house the homeless in hotels may not be counted as part of homeless persons' income for purposes of determining food stamp allotments. To help prevent homelessness, the cap on shelter expenses used to determine food stamp allotments was increased from $147 to $170 for persons whose shelter expense exceeds 50% of their income after other deductions.

Contact. Food Stamp Outreach: Cecilia Fitzgerald, (703) 756-3384. Food Stamp Eligibility: Certification Policy Branch, (703) 756-3520, (803) 756-3024.

TEMPORARY EMERGENCY FOOD ASSISTANCE PROGRAM (TEFAP)

Agency. U.S. Department of Agriculture (USDA)

When originally enacted, the McKinney Act extended TEFAP's authorization through 1988. In 1988, TEFAP was reauthorized under the Hunger Prevention Act of 1988 (P.L. 100–435).

Eligible Applicants. State agencies which have been designated by the governor of their state to administer the program.

Timeline. The next distribution cycle will begin in fiscal year 1991 for food banks, and fiscal year 1992 for emergency shelters and soup kitchens.

Use of Funds. TEFAP funds are used to purchase and distribute certain commodities to states for use by emergency shelters, soup kitchens, and food banks. TEFAP also reimburses states for administrative costs of distributing surplus government commodities. Commodities are distributed based on a formula that includes data on state unemployment and poverty levels.

Range of Awards. All 50 states receive commodities for emergency shelters and soup kitchens for the homeless, and all states except Alaska receive commodities for food banks.

Comments. TEFAP was originally designed only to reimburse the states for administrative costs of distributing surplus government commodities. The supply of most surplus commodities was exhausted in early 1988 and the program was revised to permit purchase of commodities as well.

Contact. Alberta Frost, (703) 756-3680

Homesteading: A Solution for the Homeless?

Jerome I. Weinstein

Homesteading stands unique among federal housing programs. Unlike many federal programs, its roots date back to the 19th century. In the 1970s, it was recognized as a tool for fighting urban decay. Since then, its success and the lessons learned through its use show that, if properly applied, it can be a vibrant resource enabling the use of our marginal housing inventory.

Although it is not a program that can house everyone or solve every problem everywhere, it should be keyed for use in our core cities. Here, the variations of housing abandonment provide a variety of lands within public responsibility or ownership that can be made available to those with the greatest need. Where property vacancy and homelessness coexist, homesteading can play a vital role if given the proper consideration by those concerned with housing.

The current federally funded program uses foreclosed government-owned property. New methods await development. One new method can capitalize on municipally owned single-family properties using the experience from the HUD-funded demonstrations and the ongoing Section 810 program. Another method can use occupied but abandoned multi-family housing—under the format of homesteading cooperatives.

SECTION 810

Homesteading, specifically urban homesteading, can be a valuable tool. Currently, it is simply another way to dispose of federally owned foreclosed property that had met minimum property standards—quality vacant

Jerome I. Weinstein is a Housing Specialist in the Department of Housing and Urban Development's Regional Office in Philadelphia, Pennsylvania. The comments set forth in this article reflect the author's opinions and not necessarily those of his employer.

stock. Critically, it could be considered an adjunct of HUD's single family property disposition system.

Presently, Section 810 funds pay for properties that, in fact, would be sold into the private market through the normal federal property disposition system.

The Local Urban Homesteading Agency (LUHA) buys, with federal funds, houses from the federal government. In all but a few cities suffering from upset market conditions, these houses would be bought by individuals. During fiscal year 1988, HUD sold 7,946 houses. With homesteading funds, LUHAs purchased 818 houses. The odds are 99 to 1 that HUD through ordinary property disposition, could have sold these 818 houses. Their ordinary sale could permit a higher use of federal funds than current reimbursement to the agency for the value of its property.

Under the Section 810 Program, property acquisition averages $18,000 per unit. If these funds were used to write down the cost of only health and safety repairs, they would have a three-to-one leveraging effect. Three times as many units could be repaired and more homeless persons housed.

Repairs average $27,000. If only 50 percent of the repairs are necessary to meet health and safety requirements, federal funds could then be used to subsidize the interest rate, making entrance into the program possible for the working homeless. And, if a community wanted to establish a program goal with high neighborhood improvement standards, they could do so using state or local funds. Therefore, it is proposed that to support the homesteading of municipally owned properties HUD funds should be used toward the cost of essential repairs instead of paying the federal government for a property than can be sold in another manner.

Because of the risks to lenders, and the high cost of improvements, financing is generally unavailable for the homesteading of municipally owned property. If 810 funds were used to assist with the cost of only essential repairs limited to health and safety, these properties could provide relief to the employed and homeless. Other repairs deemed necessary could be resolved through sweat equity or with local level assistance. Even the self-help energy inherent in the concept is ignored and lost.

The program appears to be a lottery for low/moderate-income families, limited to only those who can meet market mortgage criteria, enabling financing for repairs. The current program is structured to avoid failure. But some failure, the result of taking the risk necessary to house poor families, is a healthy indication the program is actually serving the families Congress has directed to be helped.

Congress sets the level of improvements necessary and the occupancy conditions which must be met before the homesteader obtains complete ownership or title. At the local level, the municipality again imposes a grid of requirements raising costs, thereby limiting the use of the program for many needy who could be successful homesteaders. Average repair costs in 1987 were $23,000 per property.

By its legislation, Congress establishes two levels of property repair. The first enables the homesteader to take possession of the property: "Repair all defects in the property that pose substantial danger to the health and safety within one year of the date of such initial conveyance."

The second repair requirement is "Make sure such repairs and improvement to the property as may be necessary to meet applicable local standards for decent, safe and sanitary housing within three years after date of initial conveyance."

The legislation establishes bi-level standards for repair, primarily health and safety and secondarily, those decent, safe, and sanitary concerns which are determined by local codes. This two-level pattern of repair requirements can be used to relieve the high rehabilitation costs impeding the wider use of homesteading.

NEW METHODS

The Federal Homesteading Program for the 1990s should bring together the problems of abandoned properties and homeless, impacted (overcrowded), working, or otherwise income-stable families, and reach more of a spectrum of the needy than any current programs can. The current program, despite its limitations, provides a network of 130 cities with experienced, capable local urban homesteading agencies. When provided with the authority, the mechanisms, and appropriate state and local resources, they can be the force to house people. To do so, it is necessary for these agencies to focus on the vacant property within their jurisdictions.

Municipally owned vacant property has been obscured by the common use of the term "abandoned." Unfortunately, the simple definition also underlies the common belief that foreclosed properties under one of the federal mortgage guaranteed programs are in fact abandoned. That is not the case; they are being held for resale by the government.

Expediting the foreclosure process which returns properties to the municipality, organizing data about their availability, and facilitating their reuse for mechanisms like homesteading, will help core cites. Because of the unavailability of these properties and/or their condition, municipalities quickly turned to using federal properties when Congress authorized the Section 810 program in 1974.

Within core cities there are vacant or abandoned houses municipally owned, or about to be. Others about to be, are identifiable as tax delinquent or have moved to the tax foreclosure procedure.

Federal Section 810 homesteading funds should be redirected to resolve ownership of these properties or to finance essential repairs, rather than for purchasing from the federal government houses which could be sold through regular methods.

The same federal expenditures could provide a means that would shelter many more families.

DEMONSTRATIONS

Fortunately, HUD completed two congressionally authorized demonstrations: one for single-family properties, and one for multi-family properties. The demonstrations provide an understanding of the mistakes that prevent homesteading from reaching broader needs. Each provides the basis for growth.

In both demonstrations, the desire for program success (or fear of failure) set aside the basic concept or the principles of homesteading:

• the use of government-owned property, and

• self-help or sweat equity.

The single-family local property urban homesteading demonstration conducted from 1985 to 1987 provided local communities with cash to acquire local properties for homesteading. Most cities were unable to acquire as many properties as they had anticipated and the original grants were underutilized.

So-called abandoned properties cost up to $15,000 to acquire. After two years, of 129 properties acquired for the demonstration, less than 17 percent had been fully rehabilitated.

The problems encountered included lack of information about the local inventory, tax foreclosure, abandonment, ownership, and liens. Also, there were large rehabilitation costs due to ultra-high rehabilitation standards and the absence of subsidized mortgages and administrative costs which ranged from $1,265 to $10,709 per property.

All show the need for rethinking the methods needed for a basic program. Using two principles, an analysis of the demonstrations and the operating experience of the past 15 years, a responsible format for new methods of homesteading can be proposed.

In the demonstrations, the identification of candidate properties was difficult. Because municipal lists contained no information on vacancy, status, condition of the structure, or appraised value, they did not generally prove to be helpful.

Most municipalities lack a central property database. There are separate tax records, legal department lists of properties in foreclosure, assessment records, ownership data, inspection records, etc. Current information as maintained is usually unindexed, fragmented, and unreliable.

A standardized, uniform property information system should be developed. It would provide comprehensive, specific information on the status and availability of property within the city. This would be a valuable tool for homesteading and all community development programs.

SELF HELP

No issue in the operation of homesteading is more vital and yet more misunderstood than self-help. With homesteading it is one-half of the basic concept. As a practical issue, it represents the primary method to obtain cost savings in the rehabilitation process.

Self-help or sweat equity is essentially limited or factored out of homesteading by the local agencies as administrators perceive the needs of program operation. The bureaucracy places effectiveness and the program goals above the concept.

The cutting edge, the self-help concept is prostituted for production. Aren't people being charged to fish, instead of taught to fish, when self-help and sweat equity is reduced to activities such as "...participation in planning design, decision making, and management?"

REHABILITATION

Most of the municipalities in the Local Property Demonstration reported that they maintained a high degree of control over the rehabilitation process. Extensive work write-ups based on local housing codes were completed.

Average rehabilitation costs were reported at $31,098 per property, compared with $21,545 under the regular program for fiscal year 1987. This is a large sum for houses which cost $15,000 to acquire. How much of this is necessary?

This issue must be carefully examined. Nowhere is the overkill through standards more obvious than the activity in Milwaukee where, within certain limitations, all repairs and improvements must be of a quality which will last for 20 years. This is 20 times the period for an ordinary property insured by HUD under any regular FHA program for resale to ordinary people.

Standards, as identified within the national statute, establish two rehabilitation levels. Those items which are critical—plumbing, heating, electrical and roofing to provide safe and sanitary housing—are essentials. The second category consists of local code requirements for all housing and includes decorating, energy efficiency, and items which families may choose to do at their own pace, and at levels of workmanship and expenditure acceptable to them.

Had the LUHAs in the Local Property Demonstration dealt with city-owned houses—truly abandoned properties—the demonstration could have been the basis for a valid test. If municipally owned properties were to be homesteaded, it would not cost $15,000 to obtain a house.

The purpose of the homesteading program is to assist, preserve, and revitalize neighborhoods. The cost of repair cannot be the primary criterion for property selection nor should those costs be charged to the homesteader.

SUBSIDIES

Many assume that, under the homesteading program, the subsidized loan for repairs is made to provide for the needs of the family. But a subsidized loan can be used to offset the risks and costs that homesteaders undertake during the redevelopment of vacant houses.

Their actions benefit the larger community. When a family moves into a vacant property, the neighborhood benefits. The family provides housing for itself. It also provides energy for neighborhood improvements.

The direct costs to the public are obvious. To support the homesteading of municipal properties, public funds should be provided to finance essential repairs, rather than paying the federal government for properties. It is ironic that most, if not all, programs that purport to house people require the eligible program participants to be "credit worthy." After all, the costs of repair and rehabilitation must be met through borrowing.

Of course, most homeless people are not credit worthy because they happen to be poor. We put forth a real paradox when we require someone to be "needy" and at the same time "credit worthy" in order to participate in housing programs.

As a major criterion, credit worthiness, in the traditional sense, is invalid for meeting the needs of the underhoused. If we want a family to take the risk of ownership in a declining neighborhood, it logically follows that we should be willing to risk money to make their efforts successful. That money should be recognized as a subsidy and should be available from the public because it serves the general public good.

LEGAL ISSUES

The success of federal housing policy, programs, and assistance depends upon the legal environment provided by each state. For homesteading, one consistent problem results from the restrictions on the disposal of government-owned property. In many states, a city cannot give away a house for a nominal sum. There has to be a public sale.

Other states prohibit conveyance at less than market value, and even then the buyer cannot be restricted to a homesteader or a preselected community group. Some jurisdictions even lack the authority to forgive municipal taxes and allow a property to be donated for homesteading.

State action is necessary in these matters. The foremost problem is the lack of expeditious legal mechanisms to deal with the so-called abandoned property. Tax foreclosure and condemnation (eminent domain) powers are inadequate to stimulate reuse of abandoned property.

Historically, homesteading made available vacant farmland and it was believed this idea could be applied to vacant urban property. Through appropriate criteria, this was to be to the benefit of low-income families who, through their efforts, would benefit the neighborhood. The value of the demonstration is that it identified the obstacles to a new federal homesteading effort. With the appropriate federal direction, homesteading can be an effective local program.

RESOURCES

The multi-family occupied building that is abandoned or neglected by owners provides a rich resource for homesteading. Such buildings are still usable and can still provide shelter.

At the same time, the occupants, those who would be forced to move or would be added to the homeless rolls if a building is closed, are prime homesteader candidates.

To facilitate the continued use of such buildings, special legislation should be enacted. The appropriate judicial process is "receivership."

Federal homesteading funds are currently used at the rate of $18,000 per house. These funds should be made available to communities to move a property through the receivership process. This would provide 25 times the number of units provided under the current program.

The foreclosure process for tax delinquent properties has been rightfully restrictive to provide the maximum reasonable protection from loss of property ownership due to temporary financial hardship. This protection of the owner's right, however, fails to consider the disruption that occurs when property is neglected or abandoned.

The owner's neglect of legal responsibilities to the tenants and tax obligations to the city are the obvious results of property abandonment. Yet in most states, an expeditious method of dealing with the problem does not exist.

Receivership places the property's control into the hands of a bipartisan advocate who represents the general community and whose goal is the property's orderly use. It is expeditious, selective, and presents an ideal method for the intercession of the community in the abandonment process.

Receivership is established by the court with jurisdiction to provide justice for all parties concerned: the tenants, the landlord, lenders, the city, and others with possible financial interests in the property. The use of receivership on problem buildings provides a technique to preserve a deteriorating asset while protecting the welfare of the occupants, neighboring owners, and the general community.

Receivership activities in tandem with multi-family homesteading provide a viable tool to combat the abandonment of multi-unit buildings and the deterioration taking place within the inner city.

Upon court action, the receivership may borrow money to maintain, service, and repair the property. These monies, loans, become a first lien like a mortgage. As a first lien on an occupied property, a cooperative homesteading entity can be a secure investment opportunity for a lender. Receivership established by state legislation, tested both in courts and in practice, provides a unique opportunity for the Federal National Mortgage Association (Fannie Mae) to participate actively in lending. It is a vehicle to meet the requirements of the Community Reinvestment Act for local lenders which can be effective nationwide.

Using municipally owned houses could result in a tripling of units available to the income-stable poor. Or the same dollars, if used in those states and cities with receivership capacity and the proper housing inventory, could recover as many as 25 times the units provided now.

Homesteading is a tool both for housing people and for reversing neighborhood decay within ailing core cities. It is not the single solution to all urban housing problems, but it does not meet some current needs and can be used to meet the needs of many of the homeless.

Creating More Dynamic Public Housing: A Modest Proposal

Frederick Brown

Originally, the federal housing department recognized that its mission was to help a community or neighborhood remain dynamic. Those responsible for federal housing programs intended that people of many income strata would live in the same area. The "working poor," as the more highly motivated people in public housing, were to provide examples of heightened attitudes, a sense of self-dependence, and a knowledge of the value of one's own work. They were to interact with those less fortunate and share experiences. The families with higher skills and better social behavior were to serve as models for the others to follow.

In the beginning stages of public housing (from 1937 to 1950) sites were self-sufficient, relatively well-run operations. Government dollars were used to build the units and to stimulate the housing industry. Below market rate rents were set and charged to eligible families. These rates, however, were high enough to cover the cost of PHA operations.

Families were selected according to very strict criteria. Each family had to be headed by two parents, who had to show they had total control of their household. For example, school age children had to demonstrate good attendance at school. The family could not have a history of problems in the neighborhood or the community. To be eligible, the parents had to work and be able to pay the rent. (See Chart 1, next page.)

Mr. Brown is the Executive Director of the Housing Authority of the County of Chester, Pennsylvania. The ideas expressed in this article originally were presented by Mr. Brown and representatives of the Pennsylvania Association of Housing and Redevelopment Officials to Senator Arlen Specter (R-PA) in March, 1990. During this meeting, Mr. Brown presented ideas to transform national public housing policy and improve public housing nationwide. Senator Specter requested that these ideas be submitted in writing. The following article is based on Mr. Brown's proposal.

In the past, the public supported assisted housing because it helped people attain the "American Dream," which promised those who were willing to work that they could one day own a home. After World War II, the federal government began to provide subsidies for training, education, and alternative housing.

Of the new subsidies, one of the most far reaching was the GI Bill, which gave people who would have otherwise relied on public housing the opportunity to get a college education and receive home buying benefits.

Chart I

Family of 2

| Very low-income | $14,600* | Low-Income | $25,350 |

Family of 4

| Very low-income | $18,250* | Low-income | $29,200 |

Family of 6

| Very low-income | $21,150* | Low-income | $32,850 |

**"Very Low-income" = 50% of Area Mean Income. "Low-income" = 80% of Area Mean Income. The figures used are for Chester County, Pennsylvania. The Area Mean for Chester County is $38,000. Only Those With very low-incomes are eligible for public housing units.

By changing the income eligibility rate to allow more "low- income" people to become tenants, the housing authorities would receive more rent revenue and this requires less HUD subsidies. With this increase in money available for other purposes, HUD could add to the "new housing fund" and provide more needed housing for both "low and very low-income" families.

In the 1970s, the "Brooke Amendment" (sponsored by Senator Edward Brooke of Massachusetts) dramatically changed public housing by tapping rents that PHAs charged tenants. All a tenant family had to pay for rent was 25 percent of its joint income.

Once this amendment was instituted, the amount of money that tenants provided to the housing authorities dropped drastically. HUD then had to rescue housing authorities by paying an approximation of the operating subsidies PHAs required.

Another result of this amendment was to change the selection process for families. Since there was no longer an established rent which required families to have a certain income to be eligible for public housing, families could become PHA tenants no matter how little income they earned.

THE PROBLEM

According to the selection process prior to the Brooke Amendment, when the housing authorities had two equally qualified people for a unit, criteria other than income were significant. Now, the lack of adequate income is the chief tenant selection criterion.

The result was that, during the 1970s, thousands of "very low-income" people with limited work and social skills flooded into public housing. The more capable and responsible tenants then began to leave.

The housing authorities were left with less revenues to serve a more needy population. Housing authorities also became more and more dependent on HUD subsidies. These subsidies were much less than, and not related to, actual PHA operating expenses.

As a person or family stabilizes in public housing and moves toward self-sufficiency, the household income often rises. In addition, as the children grow older, the parent or parents are free to pursue education and/or employment.

When the sons and daughters of public housing residents become old enough, they usually join the work force and contribute to the total household income. This income growth, which should be a benefit, often has a negative impact on the family.

Because the rent policy requires that tenants must pay 30 percent of their adjusted incomes for rent, working tenant families are often required to pay an amount that exceeds what they would pay if they rented in the private market.

On March 19, 1990, HUD Secretary Jack Kemp, addressing the NAHRO Legislative Conference at the Ramada Renaissance Hotel in Washington, D.C., noted the problems that the present rent policy creates.

"Wealth is not measured in GNP," Kemp stated, "it's not in gross national product, it's not in brick and mortar. The wealth of our cities is our people. They are a resource in and of themselves and we have to tap that resource...I think of Ohio, where a public housing resident took a $19 an hour construction job and found out that his income based rent would go well over $650 a month. He was put in a position of trying to figure out how he could make do with that job. He left it...The rewards for working should be dramatically changed. I think we've got to look at the rent structures that are discouraging families."

THE SOLUTION

There is a solution to this problem. HUD and Congress must establish a ceiling rent policy so that aspiring, ambitious tenants are not penalized for getting a good job—but are rewarded and encouraged to continue working so that they may one day acquire the American Dream, their own home.

Our current policies all too often work against two parent families. We need a realistic ceiling rent program. We should be rewarding the families that stay together, not forcing them apart.

We should explore phasing in rent increases over longer periods of time. During the job training phase, we ought to disregard income altogether. We need to give people a greater incentive to get into the work force and get a job.

Consider the plight of a family in a Chester County, Pennsylvania, public housing site that exemplifies Secretary Kemp's point. This family, headed by a working mother and father, succeeded in earning a combined yearly income of $37,000. Because their rent would be $950 a month, however, the husband and wife decided to break up so that the wife's yearly income—about $16,000—would be the basis for their rent.

HUD and the Congress should change the law to establish a fair rent for tenants in public housing based on, but lower than, the private market rate in an area. This ceiling rent would not increase if the tenant family made more money. The established rate would take into consideration the total cost of maintaining the units in top condition, thus providing safe, decent, and sanitary housing.

This change also would allow the tenants to save income earned that is above the fair market rent. This extra income could be placed, either in mandatory escrow held by the housing authority, or some other form of documented savings that would be available to tenants when they move into housing in the private sector.

An additional benefit of this change would be the reduction of subsidies from HUD to the housing authorities as rent revenues increased. Families with increasing incomes would remain intact and within public housing.

In his March speech, Kemp stated, "I did not take the position of HUD Secretary to destroy public housing. I have become HUD Secretary to be a builder and a rehabilitator..." HUD could use the "new-found money" from decreased subsidies to develop sorely needed new low-income housing, thus helping Secretary Jack Kemp to accomplish his mission.

Chart II

Family of 2

Very low-income - $14,600*   Low-income - $23,350

Family of 4

Very low-income - $18,250*   Low-income - $29,200

Family of 6

Very low-income - $21,150*   Low-income - $32,850

Very Low-income = 50% of Area Mean Income. Low-income = 80% of Area Mean Income. The area mean for Chester County, PA, is $38,000. Only Those With Very Low-income are eligible for public housing units"

ELIGIBILITY

Increasing income eligibility so that the working poor may acquire public housing units is another part of the solution. We can and should enrich residents of public housing communities with the qualities of those who work and dream of bettering themselves. Their example will inspire other tenants.

We can develop opportunities for the working poor to enter public housing by increasing the amount of money that those applying for public housing may earn and remain eligible. These working poor are "low-income" people who earn 80 percent of an area's mean income. At present, "low-income families," that is, the "working poor," are excluded from public housing.

Consider the following example: A family of four consists of two working adults, both making a minimum wage of $5 a hour, eight hours a day, for five days a week. If that family applies for public housing, it cannot be accepted. Their gross family income would be $20,800—which exceeds the income eligibility limit ($18,250 in Chester County, Pennsylvania) for a family of four with a "very low-income." Only those "very low-income" people who make no more than 50 percent of the area mean income are now eligible for public housing. (See Chart II, above.)

By changing the income eligibility rate to allow more "low-income people" to become tenants, housing authorities would receive more rent revenues and thus require less HUD subsidies. With this increase in money available for other purposes, HUD could again add to the "new housing fund," and provide more needed housing for both "low-" and "very low-income" families.

DYNAMIC HOUSING

Motivated working people would thus help create a more dynamic environment in public housing communities. HUD and the housing authorities should reward those on the route to self-sufficiency. Those already on this route, the most active tenants, would save their money and eventually move into their own homes and apartments. Their vacated public housing units would become available for other low-income people.

Very low-income families would learn through the example of their more hard working neighbors to become responsible for their own lives and responsible for public property. The American dream of success, of owning property, would be rekindled in these people.

If this approach were followed, public housing would become what it was intended to be—a temporary dwelling place that families could rely on when difficulties struck, not a stopping place.

Housing authority officials who serve very low-income people—and these, as stated, are the only people now served in public housing—know that, too often, public housing becomes a community of hopelessness and apathy. Just helping these tenants survive requires increasing amounts of public funds for social service programs.

If public housing is to be the housing of last resort, PHAs will need major increases in public subsidies. In the past, before housing authorities were expected to house the very poor, the average cost of labor and material for rehabilitating a vacated unit was $1,000. Today, the average cost for rehabilitating a similar unit is $3,000.

HUD and housing authorities need to change their programs to meet the present reality. We should begin to reward those who strive toward economic independence, self-reliance, and the dream of owning their own home.

Enterprise Zones:
Do They Work?

Robert Guskind

Ten years after enterprise zones entered the America political debate,the jury is still out. There are hundreds of state-run enterprise zones, but critics say many of them are simply sales-pitch items for local economic development hustlers scouring the country for footloose companies. Few look anything like the entrepreneurial paradise that animate Jack Kemp, Secretary of the Department of Housing and Urban Development.

Embraced by President Reagan, supported by Bush, backed by congressional Democrats and Republicans alike, and enacted by conservative and liberal governors, enterprise zones have fueled controversy for the better part of the 1980s. Kemp and his conservative allies, along with Democrats willing to try another approach in areas where programs of the 1960s and 1970s fell short, have lined up on one side to espouse a deceptively simple concept.

Take parcels of land, even entire neighborhoods, in depressed areas and single them out for special treatment. Businesses that set up shop within the zones will get hefty tax breaks, including an exemption from the capital gains tax, some investment tax credits, and some credits for hiring unemployed workers.

Regulations will be relaxed to lighten the "burden" of government. States and cities will pitch in with their own tax incentives and, possibly, public money.

If all this works, according to theory, thriving businesses will spring up in place of shuttered storefronts and gutted buildings. The marketplace, not government programs, will be the engine of revival. And it will be done with far less money than it cost for old-fashioned government grants.

Robert Guskind writes for the *National Journal*. This article, originally authored for that publication, appears here in an edited version with that magazine's permission.

Versions of this theory are being tested in more than 500 "active" state enterprise zones (more than 1,500 have been designated). The state enterprise zones come in all size and regions. Louisiana has designated 750 of them. Illinois has 68. A small slice of inner-city Hartford, Connecticut, is a zone. Nearly the entire Ohio cities of Toledo and Cleveland are zones, plus all of the prosperous Jersey City waterfront across from Manhattan. A 46-square mile parcel in and around Louisville, Kentucky, is a zone, so is an 111-square-mile area around the rural Missouri town of Cuba.

Most of the zones offer a combination of local property tax abatements, tax credits for hiring new employees, sales tax breaks, deductions for capital improvements, low-interest loans, and outright grants to businesses. Often, there are job training funds and, in many cases, fresh public spending for infrastructure and government-subsidized marketing for the zone.

Additionally, the majority of the enterprise zones have to meet state criteria for distress that include above-average unemployment and poverty rates, and some measure of physical decline.

The states boast of spectacular results for their programs. Based on state estimates, HUD, in 1987, reported that enterprise zones had saved or created about 180,000 jobs and attracted $8.8 billion in private capital.

A more recent survey by *Business Facilities* magazine estimated that enterprise zones had created 184,600 new jobs, retained 169,100 jobs and attracted $18.1 billion in investment through 1988. HUD is currently updating its figures.

The way Kemp has always seen it, enterprise zones are a way to uncork the entrepreneurial spirit that lies dormant in every downtrodden urban neighborhood. Yet, as the zones have worked in practice—whatever their purported results in jobs and investment—most states have eschewed Kemp's "small is beautiful" approach.

They have opted instead to use enterprise zones as another offering in their industrial recruitment packages of tax breaks, loans, and grants to snare companies from other jurisdictions.

"In many instances cities and states have created things they call enterprise zones," said Stuart Butler, the Heritage Foundation's Director of Domestic Policy Studies who popularized the British version of enterprise zones in the United States. "But they're not fundamentally different from traditional economic development policies of special tax breaks and assistance and the earmarking of money."

The questions of who would show up to take advantage of enterprise zone tax breaks and whether one area's gain is another area's loss have always been at the heart of the debate.

"If you only think about taking someone else's business, you are going to miss the point about enterprise zones," Kemp said, "because the incentives are driven by the attraction to the entrepreneur, [and are] not [aimed at] the Fortune 500."

Many state and local economic development officials, however, disagree with Kemp and take a keen interest in wooing big firms.

Around the country, enterprise zones have been custom-made for big companies or routinely extended to fit their plants and offices within zone boundaries. In 1985, when Chrysler Corporation threatened to shut down an Illinois plant employing 4,200 workers, Republican Governor James R. Thompson, Jr., declared the plant an enterprise zone, entitling the automaker to industrial revenue bonds, tax abatements and job training funds, for a total subsidy of $15 million. Chrysler kept the assembly line rolling.

A short time later, Illinois set up an enterprise zone to benefit a Chrysler-Mitsubishi Motors Corporation joint venture plant in Bloomington. That package totaled more than $100 million.

Jersey City has routinely used enterprise zone benefits in the area it set up along its waterfront as part of the financial packages it offers firms that are thinking about defecting from New York City. Retailers in New Jersey enterprise zones are entitled to charge customers a sales tax that's only half the state's usual 6 percent. Among the beneficiaries: a glitzy, upscale shopping mall on the Jersey City waterfront.

All through the 1980s, reviews of the state programs have been rolling in. Any many of them are lukewarm. Most have concluded that state and local tax breaks are of only minimal importance in persuading businesses to set up shop in enterprise zones, and that the incentives can't be credited with creating jobs. Several studies have raised the specter of rewarding businesses for decisions they would have made in any case. Others have concluded that state and local estimates of investments or "new" and "saved" jobs are wildly unreliable.

"Across the board, whether you are talking about employment or community and neighborhood revitalization, the enterprise zones set up by the states are not producing the desired effects," said Earl Jones, a University of Illinois professor of urban planning who has studied enterprise zones in Bridgeport, Connecticut, and Decatur, Illinois. In both cases, Jones concluded, the programs were not contributing to economic activity.

MODEL PROGRAMS

In the world of enterprise zones, Evansville, Indiana, has a "model" program in a state considered to have one of the country's more successful zone programs. Evansville has one of 12 enterprise zones scattered across Indiana and another two are slated to open in the state next year. Businesses in the zones can take advantage of a total exemption on inventory taxes, which accounts for more than 90 percent of the tax credits that have been handed out under the program. The state, meanwhile requires businesses that get tax credits to plow about 15 percent of the money back into the local organizations that run the enterprise zones.

Evansville set up its two-and-half-square-mile enterprise zones in 1984 in a neighborhood that, back in the 1950s, hosted 15,000 workers, mostly in factory jobs. By the time the zone opened, employment had plummeted to 4,400. Evansville first snared a big retailer, T.J. Maxx Corporation, which opened a $55 million distribution and warehouse center in the zone. That brought in 1,500 jobs. Meanwhile, Evansville and the state invested about $4 million in public money in the zone to upgrade water mains, build a firehouse, set up a day-care center for employees and provide other amenities.

The investment appears to have paid off. There were 260 businesses in the zone when it opened. Today, there are 340. Total employment has jumped more than 50 percent. "The enterprise zone is a targeted, focused program," said Alan Eric Jones, executive director of the Evansville Urban Enterprise Association. "It doesn't just throw money around. And it creates high paying jobs, not hotel jobs."

Cornell University professor Margaret G. Wilder and Indiana University professor Barry M. Rubin have studied the Evansville zone. Their findings confirmed the economic growth. But the reasons, they concluded, were the characteristics of the land, the local enterprise zone association, the local director, and factors beyond tax incentives. "Financial incentives are useful but not critical," Wilder and Rubin determined. "Financial and regulatory incentives, by themselves, are very unlikely to lead to the success of enterprise zone programs."

Wilder and Rubin figured that from 1985 to 1987, the zone's tax incentives had cost Evansville $5.9 million. They found that 36 percent of the tax breaks went to firms with almost no employees, firms that were using the zone as a tax shelter for warehouses where trucks simply unloaded and picked up materials.

Indiana University professor Bruce Nissen has calculated that, statewide, Indiana's enterprise zones cost $43.2 million in lost property taxes from 1984 to 1987 and that the losses have been escalating at 30 percent a year. Nissen also estimated that property tax bills in cities with enterprise zones had increased by $10 to $100 a year to offset the lost revenue from the zones. "There's no evidence that the program has made any difference," Nissen said. "And it's not fair to home owners, businesses and other property owners not located within the zone. Enterprise zones shift the tax burden in an inequitable manner.

Another state that has amassed evidence on enterprise zones is Maryland, which set up its program in anticipation of the federal tax breaks that Reagan promised but never delivered.

Now, Maryland's program is at the center of a little war over whether its enterprise zones are working as intended—or flopping expensively.

The Park Circle Enterprise Zone, in the middle of Baltimore's bedraggled Park Heights neighborhood, hosts a Londontown Corporation raincoat factory. On the surface, Park Circle, a site that Kemp visited in last April, is a thriving enterprise zone.

Maryland and Baltimore have poured $10 million in public money into the industrial park, which opened in 1982. Jobs and investment have followed.

Businesses in the enterprise zone currently have more than 1,000 employees, and the zone has attracted $26 million in private investment. A Control Data Corporation-owned small business incubator, which has gathered more than $500,000 in tax credits since 1984, has spawned more than 150 small firms, keeping in tune with the small business bent favored by Jack Kemp.

The new Londontown raincoat plant was to employ 500 workers. To persuade the manufacturer to open a plant in the city, Baltimore offered enterprise zone benefits, which included an 80 percent property tax abatement for five years and $3.5 million in state and city loans.

The enterprise zone program, said J. Randall Evans, Maryland Secretary of Economic and Employment Development, offered certain financial advantages to the company which enabled them to continue cost effective production in the state.

Maryland officials offer Londontown as an example of their enterprise zone program in action. But only a short distance from the new factory ground recently was broken for a new $13 million Parks Sausage Company plant that might represent a darker side of enterprise zones.

In the Parks Sausage case, the enterprise zone's tax breaks had become part of a multi-state bidding war. Baltimore won the factory after beating out Michigan, Philadelphia, and Washington, D.C., for the facility.

The city piled on incentives that included a $23 million urban development action grant on top of the standard enterprise zone offerings. After the dust settled, the sausage maker's president admitted that a move out of Baltimore had been unlikely. Some Baltimore officials muttered that they'd been had.

Maryland officials said that, all told, the 13-zone state program has created 1,600 jobs and attracted $40 million in investment at a cost of at least $13 million in lost revenue and state spending, not counting local incentives.

But last December, when the General Accounting Office (GAO) issued a report requested by Kemp and Representative Robert Garcia (D-NY), it had few kind words for the program. Maryland's enterprise zones, the GAO auditors concluded, "did not stimulate local economic growth as measured by employment or strongly influence most employers' decisions about business location."

Employers, the report said, "may have legally won financial windfalls from program credits for decisions that they had already made or would have potentially made in the absence of the program. A federal program should be designed to avoid this potentially expensive and wasteful trap."

The report suggested that the federal government experiment with enterprise zones on a small scale before launching a full-fledged program.

Stung by the GAO criticism, Maryland Governor William Donald Schaefer, who had proposed the Maryland program when he was Baltimore's mayor, ordered his economic development staff to respond to the GAO audit. The governor's report concluded that the GAO report was "fundamentally flawed" and that, among other things, the three zones that the GAO studied weren't representative of the state's zone and that the GAO had ignored the benefits of the zones other than job creation, among them, hiring of disadvantaged workers.

DOUBTS

And so, doubts linger on the topic of tax-incentive based urban revitalization. Opponents have long argued that tax incentives fly in the face of countless studies that show taxes at the bottom of the list of the factors businesses consider in selecting sites for offices and plants.

And even if they attract some businesses, the argument goes, enterprise zones that depend on tax-incentives won't offer enough to help truly distressed areas.

"The future boils down to investing more in human capital to be competitive," said author David Osborne, who recently wrote a *New Republic* article highly critical of enterprise zones. (Kemp angrily denounced the article at a congressional hearing.).

Osborne argued that to expect revitalization through cuts in taxes and regulations is "simplistic" and that Kemp should focus instead on using the forgone revenue to finance community development organizations or a series of local development banks that would finance neighborhood projects.

"Tax breaks invest in new plants and buildings," Osborne said. "They drain away the money that we need to invest in human capital."

Kemp readily acknowledges that it will take more than tax breaks to make enterprise zones work. But he and other zone supporters say that passing judgement on the state zones isn't fair because those zones were never intended to work without federal incentives.

"If there's no place in the United States where we've abolished the capital gains tax, enterprise zones will never have a chance to be totally judged," Kemp has said.

At most, state taxes generally amount to 5 percent of a company's income, said Richard Cowden, Executive Director of the American Association of Enterprise Zones, the Washington representative for enterprise zone directors. He calls the state programs "a modest experiment in reducing some state taxes."

In fact, a number of studies of state enterprise zones have found large numbers of businesses that don't even apply for state tax breaks, ostensibly because the tax breaks are too small.

Butler of The Heritage Foundation concurs. "What we have in effect, is a system of enterprise zones, limited by the lack of potent federal tax incentives," he said.

If Kemp gets his way and manages to refocus enterprise zones on small businesses in rundown neighborhoods, a number of states and cities will soon discover that their versions of enterprise zones aren't what Kemp and the program's other spiritual godfathers have in mind.

In 1987, Congress passed an enterprise zone measure that authorized HUD to designate 100 federal enterprise zones that would get priority treatment in receiving federal aid. Two-thirds of the zones were to be in cities and the remaining third in rural areas. By January, 1989, HUD had received about 250 applications for the 100 slots.

But Kemp effectively put the applications on ice when he announced last March that he wouldn't select any zones for federal designation until Congress enacted a package of tax incentives to go along with zone designation.

"We've got to put some incentives, some teeth, some carrots out there," Kemp told the House Banking, Finance and Urban Affairs Subcommittee on Economic Stabilization.

The most prominent of the bills to come before Congress in 1989 has been introduced by Garcia, Kemp's longtime co-sponsor on enterprise zone legislation, and Representative Charles B. Rangel (D-NY), a former opponent of the concept.

Their bill would include a 50 percent tax credit for wages paid to disadvantaged employees, a 10 percent credit for annual increases in payroll expenditures, a 10 percent tax credit for new construction, a waiver on capital gains taxes, a 37.5 percent credit for research and development and deductions of up to $100,000 per individual for investment in enterprise zone businesses.

The measure Kemp will propose is expected to take a similar tack, but Kemp will probably also ask for safeguards to limit the size of the zones and cap credits and deductions so that they'll appeal primarily to small businesses.

"The design of the bill, the design of the criteria, the design of the tax incentives and the competitive process, I think, are the fail-safe mechanisms by which you make sure that the South Bronx doesn't try to steal business from Michigan or Alabama," Kemp said. He also believes that with some latitude to pick and choose zones based on the sophistication of their approach, he can make sure the zones benefit inner-city entrepreneurs.

"There will be winners and losers here," said Thomas M. Humbert, HUD's Deputy Assistant Secretary for Policy. "Only 70 enterprise zones are going to be chosen. That leaves more than 400 to fend for themselves without federal tax incentives."

Meanwhile, in state capitals from Trenton to Honolulu, state officials are keeping a wary eye on the debate in Washington.

In Hawaii, Thomas J. Smyth, who heads the business services division of the state's Business and Economic Development Department, said that a federal program would be welcome. But Smyth worries that "the compromises can end up being an incentive for no one."

The enterprise zone debate has now come full circle. Washington has bobbled the ball for 10 years. In the interim, more than two-thirds of the states have picked up the ball and run with it.

Some have come up winners and some losers. And now the ball is back in Kemp's hands.

"Kemp's a political entrepreneur with a good track record," said Butler, who barely a year ago was quoted in *California Journal* as saying that enterprise zones were an idea "whose time had gone." Now Butler says, "If anyone can pull it off, Kemp can. He has a clear vision of what he'd like the zones to accomplish. His challenge is leading economic development in the cities in a new direction."

And deep down, Kemp knows that he doesn't have much time to spare. "If it isn't done [in 1989] or early in the next year, it won't get done," Kemp said. "I'm not a pessimist. But if we let this moment go by it would certainly make it tougher. If we fail in this environment, the consequences are disastrous for the country."

A Bush/Kemp Report Card

Michael A. Stegman

Despite promises to get HUD back into a leadership position in the housing debate, the only major initiative sponsored by the Bush Administration during its first 14 months in office was a reform bill (enacted by Congress in December of last year) designed to breathe new life and impose a new management system on the scandal-plagued housing agency.

The decision to push management reform at HUD without a simultaneous move to advance the nation's housing agenda was the outcome of a significant policy debate within the Administration. Two of Jack Kemp's senior advisors urged the Secretary to seize the opportunity to make reform an integral part of a bold, audacious, visionary policy that included changing the department's name from HUD to HOME—a policy intended to get the nation's mind off scandal and mismanagement.

According to C. Austin Fitts, Assistant Secretary of Housing (and the FHA Commissioner), and Ken Blackwell, then-Assistant Secretary for Intergovernmental Affairs, Jack Kemp's program should have revolved around the empowering effects of homeownership, and should have been targeted toward "the 37 percent of all Americans who are renters."

In a private, though widely leaked, memo sent to Kemp last September, Fitts and Blackwell laid out their concept of what the Secretary's vision should be:

"Your vision is HOME. The American Dream is to own a home. The strength of the country is that we are not a nation of landless peasants, but a nation of homeowners. The man on the street needs a simple concept to

Michael A. Stegman is a Professor and Chairman of the Department of City and Regional Planning, University of North Carolina at Chapel Hill. This article is an edited version of remarks Mr. Stegman made during the 1990 Annual Meeting of the Urban Affairs Association in Charlotte, North Carolina, last April.

grasp onto, and it should not be 'reform.' It should be 'home.' Every initiative will be designed to enhance the possibility of home ownership, even the rental assistance programs."

The centerpiece of the proposed Fitts/Blackwell housing policy was not a new low-income construction program—probably no Bush housing policy will ever center on building new housing for the poor. Rather, the quantum increase in homeownership was supposed to come from a veritable "fire sale" of the thousands of FHA foreclosed single family homes across the country. The cost the federal government incurred by holding those properties had risen to intolerable levels. Fitts and Blackwell suggested:

"The HUD Secretary will lead FHA in selling essentially all of its inventory of single family homes in one nation-wide sale. The price of the homes would start at the appraised value, and go down 1 percent for every day not sold. The key is a major, nationwide advertising campaign. There is a powerful frontier of homes, a 'Go West, Young Man' attitude."

While nothing as dramatic as the Fitts/Blackwell program was unveiled by the Administration during its early months in office, Jack Kemp has aggressively embraced the policy of empowerment through homeownership as his own. And in a November, 1989 speech in Dallas before the National Association of Homebuilders, President Bush sketched out the broad parameters of what such a policy might look like—his so-called HOPE initiative.

Though the concept of promoting self-sufficiency through homeownership was very much in evidence in the President's Dallas speech, the Fitts/Blackwell rhetoric of near-universal homeownership had been stripped away. There was no commitment to raise the homeownership rate just a little, or even to keep it from falling further than it has fallen in recent years.

Rather, somewhere between September and November of last year, between Washington and Dallas, an audacious homeownership-oriented, national housing policy had been watered down to a resident conversion measure that would give occupants of HUD-assisted housing, especially those in public housing, the opportunity to buy their units.

Roughly three months after President Bush's HOPE speech in Dallas—in February of this year—the Administration released its Fiscal Year 1991 low-income budget, and, on March 13th, unveiled the Homeownership and Opportunity for People Everywhere (HOPE) Act, which, if enacted, would, according to some critics, make it a crime to be a renter.

BUDGET

Despite the Administration's high-sounding rhetoric about major increases for low-income housing, when stripped of budgetary gimmickry, the President's FY 1991 HUD budget proposes outlays that are only a meager $28 million more than those provided a year ago.

According to an LIHIS, Special Memorandum, *The Fiscal Year 1991 Budget and Low Income Housing,* issued in February, the 1991 HUD budget, would extend housing assistance to "a total of only 82,049 new households, the same number, on average, that were committed during the Reagan years."

The woeful inadequacy of the low-income housing budget is, perhaps, most strikingly reflected in the fact that HUD is consistently forced to address some of the most urgent housing priorities by "anecdote," or through small-scale demonstration programs that can meet only a tiny fraction of demonstrated need.

No more clear-cut example of this scandalous situation exists than in HUD's proposed $44 million demonstration program that would provide a combination of housing vouchers and supportive services to approximately 1,500 very poor, frail elderly individuals during the next five years.

In point of fact, there is relatively little in this program that can be "demonstrated." During the past 40 years, the size of the older population has increased dramatically. In 1950, only 12 million Americans were 65 or older. Today, the number is close to 30 million, and is projected to increase to 65 million by the year 2030.

Furthermore, the oldest of the old, those age 85 or older, make up the fastest growing segment of the population. By 2030, their numbers will triple, accounting for more than 8.6 million persons.

This group of elderly—the need for services and places considerable demands on service delivery systems. Studies show, for example, that persons aged 85 and older are four times more likely than those aged 65 to 74 to require long-term care services.

Projected growth of the older population, especially among the extremely aged, could place an enormous strain on services and programs that serve the elderly.

It is outrageous that the best we can do here is to extend assistance to 1,500 very needy persons. It is even more shameful that in order to mount this inadequate effort, HUD will cancel funding for its ongoing Congregate Housing Services Program that currently serves 2,000 elderly people.

Moreover, neither of these small initiatives provides the much-needed support to older people who already live in federally assisted housing. According to some estimates, approximately 25 percent of the aging population in assisted housing require some kind of support service for meals, health maintenance, or other needs. The HUD-proposed frail elderly program, however, doesn't touch upon this group.

The President's budget does contain nearly $8 billion in new budget authority to renew nearly 285,000 expiring Section 8 Certificates and Vouchers for another five years—an obligation that the Reagan Administration was never willing to acknowledge.

GRANTS AND AID

In a stunning reversal of form, the current politics of low-income hous-ing find a conservative Administration rejecting a Democratic call for a Republican-style block grant type of housing assistance.

Block grant assistance would deliver flexible federal resources to states and localities in favor of a series of rigid, democratic-style categorical pro-grams that would be micro-managed from Washington.

There are, perhaps two practical reasons that explain this phenomenon. Since states and localities are probably not as excited about privatizing pub-lic housing and converting HUD-held multifamily inventory to tenant own-ership as the Administration seems to be, limiting funds solely to these uses appears to be the best way of assuring the funding of these programs.

Presumably due to the scandals it inherited at HUD, the Bush Adminis-tration has a morbid fear that, left to their own devices, jurisdictions would use their unfettered funds to develop new housing.

The Administration appears to be convinced that all low-income pro-duction programs are systemically flawed and that the term "cost-effective new construction" is a contradiction in terms. Thus, the Administration is doing all in its power to minimize local discretion.

In rejecting the block grant-oriented Housing Opportunity Partnership Program, the centerpiece of the Cranston-D'Amato National Affordable Housing Act, Jack Kemp recently urged the Senate Banking Committee to "take a long and critical look at any proposed policy initiatives which would effectively decentralize failures and institutionalize them at the local level."

COST-SHARING

No major housing bill stands a serious chance of enactment unless it contains some provision for state and local cost-sharing. While most legisla-tive proposals call for a 25 percent state or local match, HOPE contains a higher, one-third matching requirement.

The real danger, however, comes not from the higher match, but from the fact that HOPE would allow localities to use their federal community development block grant funds to meet their cost-sharing responsibilities.

This approach continues the Reagan Administration's practice of view-ing the CDBG program as a universal solvent, a cheap elixir to cure all ur-ban ills. It is a thinly veiled power play by the federal government to coerce communities into using their scarce community development dollars to build new low-income housing.

At the same time that it expands the array of CD-eligible activities to include new construction, the HOPE legislation proposes to reduce CDBG funding next year by $161 million.

While states and localities should bear some program costs, the Congress should reject the HOPE plan to force localities to use CDBG funds to further the Administration's privatization policies.

SECTION 8

Consistent with the Fitts/Blackwell sentiment that appears to say "if you are not a homeowner, there must be something wrong with you," HOPE would authorize HUD to use Section 8 certificates and vouchers in certain homeownership situations. The Administration proposes to limit these flexible forms of homeownership assistance to its public housing privatization and other resident conversion initiatives.

Rather than giving all localities greater flexibility in their use of Section 8 funds, HOPE merely replaces public housing operating subsidies with Section 8 funds to support tenant conversions—which deprives very low-income families who are not now receiving any type of housing assistance from gaining any aid at all. This is just one more example of how hard budget realities can run roughshod over a welcome policy innovation.

TAX CREDITS

Except for moving federally owned stock into private ownership and privately owned, assisted inventory into non-profit and tenant ownership, the Administration's housing policies are decidedly voucher-oriented. Indeed, HUD even proposes substituting a leading option for new construction in its most popular production program—Section 202 housing for the elderly and handicapped. Under this initiative, nonprofit sponsors would receive commitments of five-year Section 8 project-based contracts, allowing them to lease new or existing homes and apartments for their elderly and handicapped clients.

Kemp's only concession to new construction is his support of a one-year extension of the low-income housing tax credit, the federal cost of which, of course, is not charged against the HUD budget.

Jack Kemp's enthusiastic support for low-income housing tax credits rings just a little hollow.

Three out of every four low-income housing projects that received tax credits in 1988 required at least one additional source of subsidy to reduce their rents to levels affordable by the poor. Sixty percent contained at least one federal subsidy in addition to tax credits. In 1988, nearly a third (31.2 percent) of all tax credit projects were in rural areas. Of these, nearly half (45.8 percent) combined the tax credit with Farmer's Home Administration Section 515 below market rate financing.

Despite the probable extension of the tax credit, the job of creating new low-income housing in rural areas next year will be much more difficult if Congress and the Administration stay their present budgetary course. This is because the Administration proposes to cut the Section 515 program by 31 percent to substitute a total of 8,000 rural housing vouchers to offset this and other rural housing program cuts.

Similarly, nearly 40 percent of all 1988 tax credit projects planned to combine the tax credit with other HUD subsidies, including Section 8 Moderate Rehabilitation funds, Housing Development Action Grants (HoDAG), and Community Development Block Grants (CDBG). In addition, one-fifth of all tax credit projects were planned for use with Section 8 certificates and vouchers.

As mentioned, the Administration plans cutbacks in CDBG funds. Congress has already banned the use of Moderate Rehabilitation with tax credits. The President's budget recommends the outright cancellation of HoDAG, and competition and vouchers will increase as this vital source of rental assistance is channeled to public housing buy-outs and other Administration-sponsored resident conversion ventures.

Advocates of community-sponsored housing who view the low-income tax credit as the centerpiece of a decentralized system of creative finance that is supported largely by states and localities through the growing network of public/private partnerships, are wrong on both counts. The fact is that about 90 percent of all projects and 97 percent of housing units supported by tax credits in 1988 were sponsored, not by non-profits, but by for-profit developers.

Moreover, despite the recent rapid growth in state and local housing finance, just 10 percent of all tax credit projects contained one or more state subsidies, while an even smaller 4 percent contained a local subsidy. And the financial condition of many large states and cities is rapidly deteriorating, as is their willingness and capacity to fund new low-income housing.

In this regard, it should be pointed out that California, Connecticut, Massachusetts, and New York are contending with revenue shortfalls ranging from $250 million to more than $1 billion in 1988, and state and local budget woes have spread more broadly during the last eighteen months.

Recently, for example, funding for Massachusetts' two most significant housing construction programs, which replaced federal housing subsidies cut by President Reagan, have been eliminated in the state budget submitted by Governor Dukakis.

To help close a large projected deficit in the current fiscal year, the Mayor of New York City, with the concurrence of the Governor, will redirect $150 million into the city's general fund from Battery Park City leases that had been previously earmarked for low-income housing.

In short, even if the tax credit is extended, unless the Congress enacts housing legislation other than HOPE, (which contains virtually no funds for new construction) the production of low-income housing will be cut to a fraction of what it has been during the last two or three years.

PRIVATIZATION

Those among us who believed that the sale of public housing would never gain enough policy momentum to be taken seriously had better take a hard look at Title I of the HOPE bill. While the fiscal 1991 authorization for public housing sales is just $96 million, it rises nearly threefold in fiscal 1992 to $260 million, and increases nearly half again in 1993, to $400 million.

Despite enormous budget pressures, the Administration plans to spend at least three-quarters of a billion dollars over the next three years to privatize public housing. Since HOPE authorizes 15 percent of program funds to be used for planning grants (which will amount to nearly $13 million next year, and to $60 million two years thereafter), HOPE can be expected to spawn a new generation of resident conversion consulting firms.

More important than the fact that HOPE expands upon the Reagan Administration's infatuation with public housing homeownership as a way of getting the federal government out of the operating subsidy business, is that HOPE is the first privatization bill to explicitly recognize many of the heretofore ignored complexities and largely hidden costs of mounting a major public housing sales program.

In addition to recognizing the need to provide resident management councils who want to buy their projects with extensive amounts of technical assistance, HOPE also authorizes HUD to use Section 8 certificates to help the new homeowners meet their ongoing obligations. The legislation limits post-sales assistance to no more than a total of five years worth of public housing operating subsidies, which may not last long enough for some buyers to keep up with their housing costs after that time period.

This is the first time that HUD has admitted that privatization cannot work without providing homebuyers post-sale operating assistance.

HOPE also removes other constraints to a volume privatization program. It vastly enlarges the potential pool of resident management councils that can qualify to buy their projects.

The current law requires resident management councils to have completed at least three years of effective project management before they can buy their project. HOPE proposes amending the law by including the new phrase "or by arranging for management by a qualified management entity."

Theoretically, tenant organizations that meet all requirements for purchase, with the exception of the self-management provision of the current law, could form a resident management council on Monday, execute a private contract with a competent management firm on Tuesday, and qualify to acquire their project from HUD on Wednesday.

While existing legislation limits the sale of public housing units to qualified residents, HOPE broadens the group of eligible buyers by converting the residency requirement to a preference, and then opening sales to Section

8 recipients who have participated in HUD's Operation Bootstrap, or other Secretary-approved economic self-sufficiency programs.

A possible consequence of this more liberal selection process is that HOPE would permit a housing authority or resident council to bypass low-income families on their waiting lists who cannot qualify for home-ownership in favor of higher income families further down on the list who can qualify to buy.

Finally, HOPE proposes to liberalize the strict one-for-one replacement housing requirements that Congress attached to the privatization measure it passed in the 1987 Housing and Community Development Act. HOPE would allow Section 8 certificates to qualify as replacement housing units, even though they will expire in five years.

HOPE would also permit housing authorities to count as replacement housing those units built with state or local housing assistance, as well as housing built with low-income housing tax credits.

Title IV of the HOPE bill proposes requirements for localities to apply to HUD for designation of Housing Opportunity Zones within their juris-dictions. These are specific geographic areas within communities that are willing to reduce regulatory barriers to the construction of new homes for low- and moderate-income families.

Title IV authorizes the Secretary of HUD to select 50 Housing Oppor-tunity Zones in as many communities for participation in this incentive-driven demonstration of regulatory reform. While the concept of Housing Opportunity Zones is a good one, the problem is that HUD is offering pre-cious few incentives to entice communities to compete for zone designation while requiring a great deal from those that do.

In addition to the promise that low-income people will have special ac-cess to certain mortgage insurance programs that would be liberalized just for Zone designees, the legislation would increase by 10 percent a locality's Rental Rehabilitation Grant entitlement if it contains an approved Housing Opportunity Zone.

While this incentive is better than nothing, the President's 1991 budget proposes to cut the Rental Rehab program by 45 percent, from $128 million to $69.9 million. Even with the bonus, localities can expect to receive sub-stantially lower rehabilitation entitlements than they received this year. In short, unless HUD sweetens the pie considerably more than it has done thus far, Housing Opportunity Zones may do no more to promote the construc-tion of new homes for low-income families than Enterprise Zones have done to promote job creation and economic development in inner cities and de-pressed rural areas.

CONCLUSIONS

While many take issue with the Administration's housing priorities, others find it gratifying that, unlike the previous administration, HUD is at least talking about the same set of issues as the housing community.

In his short time as the Administration's bleeding heart conservative, Jack Kemp has sought to marshall HUD resources in ways that will reduce dependency and increase self-sufficiency.

His unbridled support for homeownership and traditional values has made him, according to William Safire, "a kind of Secretary of Family."

No amount of enthusiasm, sensitivity, or family centeredness, however, can substitute for hard resources, and Jack Kemp's ambitious agenda for HUD cannot be advanced on the budget that the President has made available to him.

Rethinking Rental Housing:
A Progressive Strategy

John I. Gilderbloom, Richard P. Appelbaum

Housing the poor is one of the most serious domestic problems facing our country today. A recent national opinion poll found that, next to AIDS, inadequate housing was considered the important domestic problem facing America today. The proportion of income going into rent has reached record levels, with one-half of the nation's renters paying rents that are unaffordable by government standards.

Between 1970 and 1983, median rents tripled, while renters' income barely doubled. Waiting lists for public housing have grown dramatically, forcing over two-thirds of the nation's cities to close off their lists to new applicants. These unfortunate conditions have been instrumental in creating an estimated million or more homeless persons in America—perhaps the greatest shame of the richest nation in the world. We believe that as our nation moves into the next decade the crisis will only worsen.

Conservatives blame government regulation in the form of planning, zoning and rent control as the major cause of this housing crisis. Yet, the experience of Houston—the much ballyhooed Free Enterprise City—seriously questions this assumption. Houston would appear to be ideal from the viewpoint of housing affordability. The city has an astounding 20 percent rental vacancy rate, little planning, no rent control, and lacks even zoning ordinances.

Yet, Houston nonetheless suffers from a serious housing affordability problem. The reality is that Houston's problems mirror those of rest of the

This article is drawn from the themes of the authors' current book *Rethinking Rental Housing* (Philadelphia: Temple University, 1988). Mr. Gilderbloom is an Associate Professor of Urban Policy at the University of Louisville in Kentucky. Mr. Appelbaum is Professor and Chair of the Department of Sociology at the University of California, Santa Barbara.

nation: a large homeless population, enormous waiting lists for public housing, half a million low- and moderate-income persons paying more than they can afford for housing, one-fourth of the low income population forced to live in overcrowded housing, and a zero vacancy rate for housing accessible to the disabled.

A recently completed study by the University of Houston's Center for Public Policy found that only 6 percent of qualifying low- and moderate-income people receive any form of governmental housing assistance. Despite this enormous housing emergency, thousands of rental units are demolished every year.

Houston's wide-open approach to growth and development notwithstanding, Barton Smith, Senior Associate at the Center for Public Policy, has predicted that the problem of high housing costs will worsen in the coming decade, with rents doubling between 1988 and 1992. Clearly, the free enterprise approach Houston has taken has not worked. Nor will it work in other cities.

The truth is that the supposedly private rental housing market is far from free. Constraints exist not only in the form of local interventions (zoning, land-use planning, rent controls, regulations on development, and so forth), but as exogenous interferences as well—the most significant of which include federal interest and tax policies, which are among the worst influences on local housing markets. Yet, the Reagan Administration has modeled its housing policies on the fiction of the existence of free enterprise.

Reagan has made drastic cut-backs in all low-income housing programs, greatly reducing the federal role in providing affordable housing for lower-income families which supposedly shifted responsibility to the private market. In the face of continuously rising rents, housing assistance funds have been slashed by more than two-thirds during the Reagan Administration.

Such deep budget cuts are justified with the assertion that, in reality, no rental housing crisis exists: in the words of The President's Commission on Housing, "Americans today are the best-housed people in history, with affordability problems limited to the poor."

When President Reagan assumed office, the federal government was spending seven times as much on defense as low-income housing; by the time he leaves office, the ratio will have grown to forty-four to one.

Housing assistance has been slashed by 78 percent, while defense spending has increased by 31 percent. Money targeted for Section 8 housing allowance programs has been cut by 82 percent; and the Section 202 loan program for elderly and handicapped housing has been abolished, as has the Section 235 home ownership program.

Although adequate housing is presumably a top priority of the federal government—first enunciated in the 1949 Housing Act as the right to a "decent home and a suitable living environment"—there has never been a federal commitment to assuring such an objective. On the contrary, American housing policy is grounded in traditional economic theory, which has dominated and guided housing policy for both Democratic and Republican administrations for years.

Such theory—which holds that home prices and rents are the straightforward result of marketplace supply and demand factors—has never been convincingly challenged either from within economics itself or from other disciplines in the social sciences. As a result, public policy has sought primarily to buttress the private marketplace, rather than directly provide affordable housing to those in need.

LONG-TERM APPROACH

Our research indicates, for example, that rental housing markets are far from competitive as is assumed, but rather embed significant institutional barriers to simple supply-side responses to changes in demand.

Among these barriers we would include mortgage interest rates whose fluctuations bear no relationship to local supply conditions; tax laws that encourage speculation; significant concentration of ownership and management of apartments; and government housing programs that treat housing not as a community good but as a commodity.

As a consequence, we concluded, policies aimed only at increasing housing supply will not necessarily result in lowered rents or prices. We argue, in fact, that neither the conventional market-driven response (build additional housing) nor its opposite (control rents) are likely, by themselves, to do much towards solving the rental housing crisis. We argue that government cannot rely on the "unregulated marketplace" to supply decent and affordable housing, any more than tenants can rely exclusively on rent controls.

Instead, we believe, a comprehensive national housing policy along the lines pioneered by Sweden is needed to combat the housing crisis. Such a policy would greatly expand the currently miniscule *Third Stream* of existing non-market housing [the other two streams being private ownership and rentals], to serve the increasing numbers of persons whose needs are not being met by the present system.

We offer an Omnibus Housing Program, based on the Institute for Policy Study's "Progressive Housing Program for America" recently introduced in Congress as the Dellums Housing Bill (H.R. 4727). While the program does propose some regulation of existing rental housing to help secure affordability, it primarily focuses on non-market alternatives.

These include federal, state, and local programs designed to promote the construction, rehabilitation, and conversion of housing to non-market forms (e.g., community-owned housing, public housing, and tenant-owned equity-controlled cooperatives). Under the Program, virtually all federal housing funds would be directed towards the Third-Stream, non-market sector. Funding would be by means of direct federal grants, thereby ending reliance on volatile and costly private credit markets.

Reforms of national credit and tax policies are also proposed which would make the federal role both more effective and efficient, while discouraging the speculative practices that presently help fuel housing inflation.

SHORT-TERM INITIATIVES

As we move into the 1990s, affordable housing will become a critical national issue. At the local level there are a number of short-term programmatic responses that can be made, assuming that the comprehensive approach previously discussed is not likely to be enacted in the immediate future.

For example, a significant portion of existing community development block grants (or, alternatively, a newly funded program of housing block grants) should be designated for the exclusive funding of nonprofit housing. This approach is already seen in Congressman Joseph Kennedy's "Community Housing Partnership Act" (H.R. 3891), which calls for $500 million to subsidize low-income housing efforts on the part of community development corporations and other nonprofits.

Given the presently limited capacity of the nonprofit sector, a portion of funding should be directed towards providing them with training and other forms of technical support.

ELDERLY & DISABLED

Block grants should also be used to create and fund an Independent Housing Service, which would be charged with providing technical assistance to builders who wish to construct or convert housing for use by the elderly and disabled. The Service would provide assistance in the placement, design, and financing of housing for disadvantaged populations.

Such assistance would include, for example, free architectural consultation to landlords and developers interested in modifying units for the disabled. In addition, the Service would also provide grants or loans to cover the costs of constructing a barrier-free living environment. To make sure that these units remain affordable, rents and sales prices would be strictly controlled.

Finally, the Service could also serve as an advocate for the disabled community. Local planning should be directed at providing affordable and barrier-free housing environments, with all new multifamily housing units required to afford ground floor accessibility to wheel chair users.

The cost of designing such units is minimal—a few hundred dollars, compared to the thousands of dollars it takes to modify an existing unit. All new housing developments should provide sidewalks with curb cuts, timed lights and bus shelters.

Large housing developments should also be required to have a certain number of units that are accessible. All cooperative and urban homesteading programs should set aside at least 15 percent of the units for persons with disabling conditions.

LIMITED EQUITY COOPERATIVES

Cooperatives with resale restrictions offer a useful example of attractive multifamily community-based housing, since they provide many of the guarantees ordinarily associated with home ownership. Such cooperatives are customarily operated through a democratically run, non-profit corporation which holds a single mortgage on the property.

Under a typical arrangement, each new owner purchases a share for a minimal down payment (for example, 10 percent of the value of the unit). Monthly payments then include each owner's portion of the common mortgage, plus a fee for maintenance and operating expenses.

When an owner wishes to move, he or she sells the share back to the cooperative, which then is resold to a new owner. Since the whole process takes place within the cooperative corporation, no new financing or real estate fees are ever involved.

Such cooperatives are termed *limited equity* both because the member's equity is limited to his or her share rather than the value of the unit itself, and because the appreciation in the value of that share is limited by common agreement to a low level. Cooperative members cannot sell their shares for what the market will bear.

In this way the sales price of units falls below the market price for comparable housing. While a typical home or condominium is sold and refinanced at ever-inflating prices many times over its life span, a limited-equity cooperative is never sold.

The original mortgage is retained until it is fully paid off, at which time the monthly payments of the owners decrease to the amount necessary to operate and maintain the units. The principal difference between cooperative and private ownership is that within cooperatives, owners may change many times without the cooperative itself ever changing owners.

Owners share the full rights and privileges of private owners, including the tax benefits which are not available to tenants in rental housing. Ownership rests in the hands of residents, public agencies, or community organizations.

In all instances, management would be structured to promote resident involvement and encourage resident control over the use of space.

Numerous countries (Canada, Sweden, Finland, France, and Italy) have enacted programs to create cooperative housing. These actions have contributed to substantial decreases in the percentage of income paid into housing. The development of a sizeable cooperative housing sector could result in significant increases in affordable low- and moderate-income housing.

It would also result in greater control over the existing housing environment on the part of low-income residents, contributing to the "pride of place" often experienced by home owners. Ronald Lawson's survey of tenants in low-income housing cooperatives in New York City indicates that their level of satisfaction was quite high. ("Owners of Last Resort: An Assessment of the Track Record of New York City's Early Low Income Cooperative Conversions," New York City Department of Housing Preservation and Development.)

Tenants were almost unanimous in viewing their cooperative arrangements as preferable to—and less expensive than—rental housing. Many claimed that they were offered a sense of control that they had not previously known.

Many were saved from displacement by being afforded the opportunity to live in affordable cooperative units.

Tenants scored well, collectively, on basic indicators of effective management; experienced low vacancy rates and below-average turnover rates; and generally gave their cooperatives good marks on services provided. Moreover, the tenants stated overwhelmingly that they preferred cooperative living to private rental housing.

Writing in the **JOURNAL OF HOUSING** in 1981, (Volume 38, Number 7, *"Housing cooperatives: a viable means of home ownership for low-income families,"* page 392) Scott B. Franklin has summarized the benefits of cooperatives as follows:

- protection against rising costs;

- home ownership;

- tax advantages;

- community of interest: a sense of "we-ness" and less crime;

- lower maintenance costs;

- less turnover;

- protection against eviction;

- equity accrual; and,

- control and selection of incoming owners.

The drawbacks, on the other hand, says Franklin, include:

- owner default;

- difficulty in financing; and,

- restricted sovereignty.

The significant cost savings of cooperatives can be even greater when self-help rehabilitation is involved, with residents providing "sweat equity" in the rehabilitation of abandoned or foreclosed units. Sweat equity generally involves exerting physical labor to rehabilitate the housing unit, which can range from replacing or repairing major structural elements of the house to improving the plumbing, heating, electricity, and other necessities.

HOMESTEADING

When self-help rehabilitation is done the cost of bringing multi-family housing up to code can be 50 percent of the cost of conventional rehabilitation by private developers. Churches, poverty organizations, and nonprofits serving disadvantaged groups can sponsor non-profit housing development and rehabilitation. Abandoned and dilapidated units could be renovated by these organizations.

New York and Boston have been able to revitalize many declining neighborhoods by developing innovative homesteading programs. These programs result in greater housing opportunities for disadvantaged persons, an increase in tax revenue, more jobs, and the renewal of neighborhoods.

A state wide receivership program could be coupled with such programs, under which landlords who repeatedly refuse to fix code violations can be forced by the courts to cede rents for needed repairs (and, under certain circumstances, ownership of the unit as well).

Housing receivership programs have worked well in New Jersey. Poor neighborhoods could be dramatically turned around with the adoption of a large scale homesteading and receivership program.

CONCLUSION

The private market alone cannot provide affordable housing for all citizens—especially for the disabled, elderly and poor. The conservative approach, based on encouraging free enterprise, has proven a failure in reaching those most in need.

On the other hand, the traditional liberal strategy of providing massive tax breaks and subsidies for builders and landlords has proven to be costly, inefficient, and largely ineffective as well.

New and bold measures, we believe, must be used to combat the housing crisis. We call for a new urban populist housing program where residents are empowered to develop their own solutions for the housing crisis. We believe that our Third-Stream housing program would go a long way towards providing decent and affordable housing in a humane and efficient fashion.

Our program emphasizes local control, the benefits of ownership, and pride in community.

Paul Goodman wrote in *Growing Up Absurd* that "a man has only one life and if during it he has no great environment, no community, he has been irreparably robbed of a human right." Cities are judged great, not by the number of monumental buildings or people within their borders, but by their ability to provide justice and civility.

How well does the average American city address the needs of its citizens—whether they are rich or poor, black or white, old or young, abled or disabled? Great cities are measured by the kinds of employment, housing, educational, aesthetic, and spiritual opportunities they afford their residents. All urbanites should live with dignity and without fear.

Great cities provide for all and exclude no one. By these standards— how many American cities would today be judged as great?

Community Development: A National Perspective

Dr. Mark L. Matulef

For forty years local community development agencies (CDAs) have responded to the ever-changing needs of America's cities and towns. The nation's 3,000 CDAs have worked to eliminate slums and blight, build community service centers, rehabilitate housing and revitalize neighborhoods. CDAs have adopted their programs to face today's compelling urban problems: plant closings, aging physical infrastructures, and the growing homeless problem.

Yet, at the same time that the need for investment in the nation's economic residential, and public infrastructure is growing, the sources of funding for local community development programs have been cut back. Community Development Block Grants have been cut 30 percent since 1981. Local bond issues have fallen dramatically since the passage of the Tax Reform Act of 1986. (The Act placed different categories of public purpose bonds under a single, state-wide volume cap. Local redevelopment and housing bonds were forced to compete with bonds for hospitals and student loans. The Act also reduced the volume of bonds that state and local agencies could issue.) The gap left by cut-backs in federal spending and a smaller bond market have not been filled by state government. State general expenditures for housing and community development made up less than one percent of state budgets in 1987.

Local government contributions to community development increased between 1985 and 1986, although not enough to offset the cuts in contributions from federal programs and bond issues. Despite cut-backs in financial

Dr. Matulef is Research Director for the National Association of Housing and Redevelopment Officials in Washington, D.C. This article is excerpted from the larger study **This is Community Development** available from NAHRO at $10 per copy.

resources, however, local CDAs continue to work to revitalize housing, public facilities, and businesses—although at a slower pace.

In 1987, the National Association of Housing and Redevelopment Officials conducted a survey to get statistical information on the local community development industry. The survey addressed agency organization and powers, their use of federal funds, and their impact on housing, jobs, and business development.

The final sample included 139 local agencies. Of these sample agencies that participated in the NAHRO survey 52 were community development agencies or departments; 59 were other departments of local government; 12 were redevelopment authorities which maintain some independence from local government; seven were public housing authorities; and the remaining nine were city, town, or county governments that do not have a distinct community development department. (For the distribution of CD agencies in the NAHRO Survey on which this information is based, see page 242.)

The agencies in the survey sample made $1.88 billion in expenditures in 1985 and $1.91 billion in 1986. In 1985, 1986, and 1987, most local community development activities were funded by intergovernmental grants.

CDBG

There is one thing that 80 percent of the nation's community development agencies have in common: Community Development Block grants. CDBG is the largest federal government funding source for community neighborhood revitalization. CDBG is not so much a single program as a vehicle that allows local agencies to tailor their own programs to the particular needs of their respective cities, towns, and counties.

In 1987, Congress terminated the General Revenue Sharing program. The eligible uses of CDBG had been expanded every year since the program's creation in 1974. Congressional appropriations for CDBG have been reduced nearly 20 percent since 1981. While funding levels declined, however, the number of communities participating in CDBG increased.

CDBG has assumed an increasingly important role in community revitalization. It represents three-quarters of the funding under the Office of Community Planning and Development in the federal Department of Housing and Urban Development.

Local CD agencies have had to make the shrinking federal dollars go further by leveraging private investment, by forming partnerships with nonprofit community based groups, by devising new financial mechanisms, and by providing a strong leadership and planning role.

In 1986, the sample CD agencies supplemented their $834 million in CDBG funds with $176 million in leveraged private sector investment. During the same year, the sample agencies used CDBG funds to rehabilitate 11,890 units of housing occupied by low- and moderate income people.

There is evidence, however, that CD agencies are losing ground as funds have been reduced.

Surveys conducted by NAHRO in 1986 and 1987 revealed that fewer units of housing were being rehabilitated and fewer elderly persons were receiving social services in programs using CDBGs. Local community development programs have made good use of HUD programs never-the-less. These programs have benefitted communities of all sizes and all regions of the country.

HOUSING

Housing for low- and moderate-income people is one of the chief program areas of local community development agencies. Community development agency support for housing takes many forms. The chart on page 246 shows the extent of financial support for housing provided by the agencies in the sample in the mid-1980s.

SINGLE FAMILY HOUSING

Community development support for single family housing declined between 1985 and 1986. In 1986, Congress passed the wide sweeping Tax Reform Act. The act reduced the volume of tax-exempt mortgage revenue bonds housing finance agencies could issue, imposed new income and price limits, and restricted the HFA's ability to build reserves.

Bond proceeds are a substantial source of capital for CD agencies' single family programs. CD agencies' bond issuing capacity was reducing during the time CDBG appropriations were declining. Most CD agency assistance is made directly to home owners. The declining number of units assisted reflect rising costs and declining CD appropriations.

MULTI-FAMILY HOUSING

Most of the agencies in the NAHRO database support efforts to improve multifamily housing. Of the 139 agencies in the survey database, 60 percent provided rehabilitation finance for multifamily housing. The following figures illustrate community development agency involvement in multifamily housing development and rehabilitation.

Activity	*Percent of Sample Agencies*
Rehabilitation	60.4%
Finance	42.4%
Site Improvements	38.1%
Land Assembly	36.7%
Site Selection	33.8%
Construction Finance	33.8%
Long-term (Mortgage) Finance	31.7%

Seventy-six community development agencies in the NAHRO sample helped rehabilitate 66,869 units of multifamily housing between 1985 and 1987. Seven agencies in the sample helped build 9,000 units. Most of the multifamily housing assisted by the CD agencies was targeted to low-income families, senior citizens, or disabled persons.

The chart on page 245, Multifamily Housing Program Sample summarizes CD agency participation in several intergovernmental multifamily housing programs between 1985 and 1987. (The units-by-programs do not add to the totals because not all intergovernmental programs are listed. Also the totals reflect housing activity undertaken at the local agency's initiative.)

SOCIAL SERVICES

Most community development agencies are distinct from local social services units: human resource, public welfare, public health, recreation, employment departments and so forth. Yet many community development agencies play an important role in supporting social services, most often by providing financial support. It is also more common for local CD agencies to provide referrals to service agencies than to provide services directly.

The chart on page 242, Support Services Provided by CDAs, shows the number of agencies in the NAHRO sample that provided support for social services. "Direct services or support" refers to the actual provision of servcies by an agency or the provision of financial assistance. "Agencies providing service referrals" are those which do not provide direct services or financial assistance, but which refer individuals to service providers.

Multi-family Housing Program Sample

Program	Agencies	Units
CDBG (rehabilitation)	54	23,855
Federal Low-Rent Public housing:		
Modernization	8	8,931
New Construction	4	2,630
Federal Rental Rehabilitation Program	37	8,157
Local Rehabilitation Programs	6	3,402
State Rehabilitation Programs	14	2,991
UDAG	3	2,378
Section 312 Loans	16	1,052
Total Units Rehabilitated	76	66,899
Total Units Constructed	7	9,000

ECONOMIC REVITALIZATION

Community development agencies provide job training and placement services, participate in assisted housing management, and engage in economic revitalization activities. Sixty-five percent of the agencies participating in the NAHRO survey participated in area-wide physical improvements to support economic development. Financial assistance was the most common CD agency contribution.

Financial Assistance for Low- and Moderate-Income Housing

Programs	Community Development Agencies	All Surveyed Communities Providing Assistance
Loans to Private Entities	54.7%	79.9%
Grants to Private Entities	52.5%	76.3%
Creation of a Special Assessment District	7.9%	66.2%
Property Tax Abatement or Exemption	8.6%	643.7%
Tax Increment Financing	20.1%	59.0%
Loan Guarantees	36.0%	55.4%
Mortgage Purchase Program	23.0%	35.3%
Venture Capital	18.7%	23.1%
Mortgage or Loan Insurance	13.7%	23.7%
Sales Tax Abatement	1.4%	19.4%

Assistance for Single Family Housing

Program	Agencies	Units 1985	Units 1986
Direct rehabilitation services to bring homes up to code	58	6,680	6,505
Other Rehabilitation Loans	55	5,580	5,412
Mortgage Subsidies	17	2,425	1,116
Weatherization Loans	14	2,296	2,471
Purchase/Rehabilitation Loans	14	598	418
Homesteading	14	263	240
Downpayment Subsidy	10	532	387
Construction Finance	4	467	137
Other forms of Single Family Assistance	22	16,505	11,900
Total Assisted Units	93	35,088	28,121

Homeless Services

Shelter and other services for homeless persons and families have become increasingly important components of local community development programs.

In the months after NAHRO conducted its 1987 Community Development Survey, Congress enacted the Stuart B. McKinney Homeless Assistance Act of 1987. The McKinney Act provided grants to local agencies and community-based, nonprofit organizations for housing and service programs for the homeless.

Estimates of the homeless population range from 350,000 to three million persons. The concensus of the nation's mayors is that families with children are the fastest growing component of the homeless population.

Programs to assist homeless persons include the provision of meals and health care, the provision of sanitary facilities for washing, overnight and temporary shelter, and permanent housing opportunities. Local government agencies and community groups are the principle providers of services for homeless persons.

The accompanying chart summarizes the response of the agencies in the NAHRO survey sample to the problem of homelessness (before the Stuart B. McKinney Act was passed).

"Second stage housing" refers to transitional shelter—bridging the gap between homeless shelters and permanent housing.

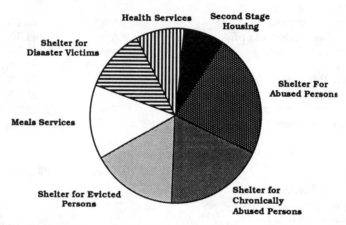

For additional information on the homeless, including a state by state survey of the efforts of housing and community development agencies, states, and local entities; legislation, policies, and programs, see *Assistance for the Homeless Persons: A NAHRO Resource Book* by Mary K. Nenno.

Efficient
Use of
CDBG Dollars

Community Development agencies have developed financial mechanisms to make efficient use of CDBG dollars. One of the most popular mechanisms is the Revolving Loan Fund. CDBG is used to capitalize a fund that is replenished by loan repayments. RLFs have been used for both economic development and residential rehabilitation. Among the NAHRO sample, 70 agencies used $335.6 million in 1986 CDBG dollars to capitalize RLFs.

Sixty-seven CD agencies used $22 million in 1986 CDBG dollars to acquire property. Thirty-eight agencies used $4.6 million in CDBG funds to reduce interest rates paid by developers, landlords, and home owners on a variety of loans. Sixteen agencies used $1.2 million for guarantees on loans. Guarantees are used to reduce risk and thereby reduce interest rates on rates.

Another device, the Community Development Interim Loan Fund program, enables cities, counties, and states to loan community development block grant funds. The funds are on deposit in a letter of credit with the U.S. Department of Housing and Urban Development and are loaned to businesses for short-time financing of a CDBG-eligible project.

The lending agency must require an assisted firm guarantee that loaned funds will be repaid whenever they are needed to pay expenses of the local CDBG program. The loans must be guaranteed by an unconditional and irrevocable private letter of credit payable to the lending agency on demand.

These interim loans generate interest earnings that increase the amount available for allocation to other eligible CDBG projects. All funded projects must meet HUD's benefit criteria.

Fifty-six percent of the agencies contributed to building facade improvements and fifty percent contributed to the improvement of building interiors.

Transportation and waterfront development activities were supported by 29 percent of the agencies surveyed. Fifty-one percent of the agencies reported that their communities were authorized to undertake tax-increment financing projects and about half of the agencies surveyed have participated in historic preservation activities.

CONCLUSION

As federal funds for community development have been cut, and as state and local government bond issuing ability has been restricted, so have the achievements of CDAs declined. Nevertheless, in the mid-1980s, CDAs have made substantial contributions to the cities and towns they serve.

Between 1985 and 1986, the 139 CDAs in the NAHRO Community Development Survey sample assisted more than 60,000 households purchase or rehabilitate their single-family homes.

Between 1985 and 1987, the 139 CDAs helped build or rehabilitate 75,000 low- and moderate-income multifamily housing units. These agencies used Community Development Block Grants to create or preserve more than 24,000 jobs in 1986—74 percent of which were held by low- and moderate-income persons.

And, between 1985 and 1987, these community development agencies used Urban Development Action Grants to generate $8.4 million in additional local taxes, create or retain more than 19,000 jobs (most for low- and moderate-income workers), and induce more than $750 million in private investment.

Local community development agencies are the catalysts for neighborhood preservation and improvement. They have been able to use federal, state, and local funds wisely and well.

New Directions in Welfare and Housing Assistance

The welfare assistance and the housing assistance systems of the federal government are undergoing significant change. As welfare assistance moves from an income maintenance program only to a system that also promotes self-sufficiency, the housing relationship is assuming a new and special importance.

Limited housing choices affect a family's ability to attain self-sufficiency by curtailing mobility and obstructing the pursuit of new jobs, education, and improved social conditions.

A suitable home, free from the anxieties and dangers of hazardous structural and unhealthful conditions, is basic to family well-being. Without it, attempts at self-support and independence are severely hampered.

Housing conditions affect the well-being of individuals. The physical health of families is directly affected by poor housing conditions, i.e., rodent infestation, lack of heat, lead-based paint poisoning, and unsound structural conditions.

Anxieties and stress resulting from poor housing conditions can seriously affect the mental health of an individual.

A child's ability to develop intellectually and socially is significantly affected by his or her environment.

Welfare reform enacted by the 100th Congress, and signed into law by President Reagan on October 13, 1988, represents a first step toward reducing poverty among American children and families. It emphasizes a program of self-sufficiency, in addition to providing income maintenance.

This article is an edited excerpt from the forthcoming publication, Findings, Initiatives and Recommendations on the Housing Component in Welfare Reform, scheduled for publication this fall by NAHRO and the American Public Welfare Association.

The Family Support Act of 1988 (P.L. 100–485) calls for comprehensive state education, training, and employment programs for welfare recipients with children aged three and over, provided agencies can secure adequate child care and other support services. It provides one year of transitional medical assistance and child care for families entering the work-force. It calls for stronger child support enforcement, including automatic wage withholding from absent parents' wages and federal support for paternity determination.

And it provides for a two- year study of benefit alternatives, including the Family Living Standard proposed by the American Public Welfare Association and the nation's governors.

In the report, *One Child In Four,* APWA proposed a series of national policies designed to reduce poverty among American families and children. The Family Living Standard (FLS) was proposed as a way to assure that poor families would have a stable economic environment from which to move to self-sufficiency.

The FLS would be a nationally mandated, state-specific benefit plan designed to meet family needs based upon actual living costs (including those for food, clothing, transportation, housing and furnishings, utilities, and other maintenance costs). Under the APWA recommendations, the FLS would be incorporated into federal law and regulation and would be adjusted for inflation.

Family Support Act Provisions	*Fiscal Year 1989–1993*
Job Opportunities and Basic Skills Training	$1.3 billion
Supportive and Transitional Assistance for Families Working to Leave Welfare	$1.2 billion
AFDC-UP Program Benefits for Two-Parent Families	$1.2 billion
	$3.7 billion
Less Revenues from Mandating of Child Support and Other Provisions	$0.4 billion
TOTAL	$3.3 billion

Each state's FLS could be calculated based on local living costs. A given state could have more than one standard to take into account living cost differentials, most notably the differences in housing costs between rural and urban areas.

The process for implementing the 1988 reform provisions will be a gradual one over a five-year period, with a total authorization of $3.3 billion.

To fully address the issue of poverty in America, other steps are clearly needed, including reform of the cash assistance program once the congressionally mandated study of welfare benefits has been completed. Another major step involves access to housing for poor families. A prerequisite for strong, self-sufficient families is the ability to live in safe, decent, affordable housing.

Today, steadily rising housing costs and steadily diminishing resources—both wages and the value of cash assistance—force many American families into housing that is neither safe nor decent. Where safe, decent housing is available, it is often not affordable. Cooperative efforts by human service officials, in concert with housing and other public officials, are needed to address the national housing need.

Because of cut-backs in assistance at the federal level, the declining availability of affordable housing, and the growth of homelessness in recent years, human service agencies have assumed an increasingly larger role in housing poor people. In many cases, the welfare system in the United States has assumed a housing function of last resort for poor people, particularly homeless persons.

Within the context of the 1988 Family Support Act, public human service agencies are now focusing their efforts on promoting family self-sufficiency. These agencies provide counseling, case management services, income support, and other services to poor families in need of assistance.

The percentage of welfare recipients required to work or enroll in education or job training programs (minimum participation rates) would begin for single parents at seven percent of the welfare caseload in 1990 and rise in four steps to 20 percent in 1995. There are exceptions for mothers of children under age three (or under one, at the option of the state) and for a few other categories of people, such as those too old or unable to work.

The new Family Support Act also continues support for state demonstrations. Title V contains seven different demonstration programs. It is clear that the 1988 legislation is only the first step in the evolving changes in welfare assistance.

Over the past decade, there have been significant changes also in federal housing assistance programs. Most significant has been the expansion, beginning with the 1974 Housing and Community Development Act, of Section 8 rent certificates to place low-income families in existing private housing. This was supplemented by the institution of five-year vouchers earlier in the 1980s.

Both rent certificates/vouchers and the traditional housing construction and rehabilitation programs have received devastating cuts in new authorizations since 1981, from a level of $30.9 billion in FY 1980 to $7.5 billion in 1989.

Because they do not cost as much as new construction/rehabilitation, certificates and vouchers have been increasingly favored. New construction has been virtually eliminated.

Looking ahead to the next five years, there are two matters that will determine further federal housing assistance. The first matter is that the 15-year Section 8 certificates, authorized under the 1974 Housing Act, will soon expire, and will require re-authorization of funds to be continued. Even if the term for these certificates is reduced from 15 to five years, the refunding cost will be significant.

Refunding requirements for expiring certificates/vouchers over the next four years make it extremely difficult to foresee any significant expansion in the level of housing assistance under the federal budget.

Refunding Costs by Fiscal Year//Section 8 Certificates and Vouchers

Fiscal Year	Expiring Certificates	Expiring Vouchers	Refunding Costs
1990	12,573	11,063	$680 million
1991	140,765	39,773	$5.6 billion
1992	134,263	73,262	$6.6 billion
1993	130,451	49,000	$6.1 billion

The second matter that will dominate future housing assistance is the growing importance of state and local housing initiatives since 1980. While the full scope and depth of this change is not yet clear, several significant observations can be made:

- State governments are increasingly active in housing development and rehabilitation. In addition, state-administered human services are increasingly recognizing their responsibility to provide fundamental linkages between housing and services for persons with special needs.

- Nonprofit, neighborhood-based community organizations are gaining new capabilities in housing development and rehabilitation, and particularly in serving homeless persons and other vulnerable populations.

- Local government and local public agencies are becoming increasingly innovative in financing housing development and rehabilitation, particularly in joint public/private ventures and partnerships.

An overriding significant constraint to this new activity is that almost all of it has centered on the financing of new housing construction, and neighborhood housing rehabilitation and improvement. Very few states or localities have committed long-term funding for the income support (rent supplements) required to bring the newly financed housing within the reach of persons on public assistance and lower income persons. Discussion about future federal housing legislation are now under way, and it is clear that there are issues demanding attention:

- How to provide federal assistance to further stimulate and expand new state and local initiatives in housing construction and rehabilitation.

- How to develop an expanded certificates/vouchers program to provide income support (rent supplements) for low-income households to occupy available existing housing, as well as the newly financed housing developed by state and local entities.

- How to tie human services to assisted housing for families with special needs, including the frail elderly, handicapped and disabled, homeless, and single parents.

These issues are reflected in the efforts of the Senate Subcommittee on Housing and Urban affairs. The Subcommittee undertook intensive study and consultations in 1988 in preparation for the introduction of new housing assistance legislation in 1989. The House of Representatives has also introduced 1989 legislation (HR 1180).

Implementing the Family Living Standard to provide adequate financial support for welfare families to compete in the housing market, following the congressionally mandated study, and increasing the available low-income housing stock for low-income families are basic to making long-term gains in self-sufficiency for poor families with children.

For the foreseeable future, federal funding for both welfare assistance and housing assistance will be restricted by the federal budget deficit. In the case of housing assistance, there is the further constraint of the need to refund Section 8 certificates and vouchers which are expiring (see table, page 185). Budget requirements for this refunding for fiscal years 1991, 1992, and 1993 will be almost at the level of the recent total new authorization for HUD housing assistance ($7.5 billion in FY 1989).

Under these budget circumstances, it is important that available resources be utilized in the most effective ways. There are opportunities to use federal housing assistance to expand and supplement state and local housing initiatives. There are also opportunities to link the resources of the housing assistance and welfare assistance programs to serve welfare families better.

Sheltering the Homeless: Creating Permanent Housing

Kerron R. Barnes

In recent years, Orange County, New York, has experienced a substantial growth in its homeless population. In 1987, the number of people without housing reached 650. In 1988, the county provided services to 989 adults and 513 children. In an effort to house these people, the county was forced to rely on hotels and motels. The cost for hotel/motel services was as high as $1,500 per month. Often, clients stayed in these hotels for nine to twelve-month periods.

Attempts to find more suitable and less expensive emergency housing have met with community resistance, and have been hampered by the limits on the allowances available to pay for rental housing.

To address the growing problem and rising costs, Orange County devised a unique program to provide adequate and permanent housing for the homeless, a program that reduced long-term costs and provided a supply of affordable rental housing.

The plan involved private, county, state, and federal funding; utilized the resources of banks, non-profit agencies, and several county departments; and is expected to produce 48 units during the first year. Ironically, the program accomplishes its objectives while adhering to the New York State Constitution's prohibition against counties having a direct role in providing housing.

CONCEPT

Under this program, non-profit sponsors purchase scattered-site rental buildings containing two to four units. These units are rented to clients of

Kerron R. Barnes is the Director of the Office of Community Development of the City of Goshen, Orange County, New York.

the Department of Social Services at the rate paid for emergency (motel) housing for a period of 18 months. The funds to purchase the structure are provided by bank loans at the usual commercial rate. The down payment and closing costs are provided through HUD community development funds or, in some cases, UDAG loan repayment funds derived from an Urban County Community Development Grant.

The shelter rent paid by the Orange County Department of Social Services is augmented by a state housing assistance payment grant that provides for a complete array of social services, including job counseling, training, life skills education, and other services needed to help the client become self-sufficient. The non-profit sponsor either provides these services or purchases them from other agencies.

The high rate of rental payments for the first 18 months enables the sponsors to reduce the mortgage principal significantly. At the end of the period during which the apartment is used as emergency housing, the apartment can be rented at the Section 8 Fair Market Rent and still finance all expenses. Thus, the program gradually will produce a permanent supply of affordable rental housing at a cost roughly equal to that which would have been paid for motel rooms.

Since many of the buildings purchased require rehabilitation, the program provides for HUD Rental Rehabilitation Loans from the Orange County Office of Community Development (OCD). OCD also provides inspection services and construction management. In some cases, community development or UDAG repayments are used to supplement the rental rehabilitation funds. All funds from OCD are provided as either 18-month or 10-year loans, thus saving funds to be recycled to other buildings.

The Orange County Department of Social Services manages the overall program through a contract with the sponsors. Clients considered for participation must be housed in a hotel or motel, and must show some promise of success. Final decisions on inclusion are made jointly by the Orange County Department of Social Services and the non-profit sponsor.

Clients are advised upon acceptance that they will be required to engage in all programs offered during the transitional period. Programs and services include, but are not limited to, apartment maintenance, child rearing and employment training and various referral services. Individual service packages are supervised by a project manager employed by the property owner. The property owner meets routinely with Department of Social Services staff members on matters concerning a client's acceptance and progress.

Clients who fail to meet program expectations despite case management intervention are terminated from the program, and returned to emergency shelter. Replacements are drawn from the Department of Social Services' pool of homeless families. Successful completion of the transitional program earns the client an offer of a permanent lease. To assure project viability, Section 8 Certificates for the 48 units in the initial phase have been secured.

The Department of Social Services and the owners agreed that tenants who break their leases, or who choose not to renew, will be replaced by other homeless clients. These clients will be eligible for Section 8 and will pay rent as the previous tenants did, however, they also will receive the benefits of the Transitional Service Program and will have the same responsibilities and opportunities as those earlier clients.

A fee, agreed upon between the Department of Social Services and the owners, will be paid to cover such services. The agreement limits the amount of income a tenant may earn and remain eligible for this housing. The agreement also assures that the housing will remain available for lower income or homeless persons. The agreement also guarantees that 50 percent of the clients entering the program will be employed at the end of the transitional phase.

OPERATIONS

The Department of Social Services operates the program through contracts, letters of approval, and operational plans in cooperation with OCD. The contract between the Department of Social Services and property owners specifically states the role of both parties, but is silent on the dollar amounts that are to be exchanged.

Each property requires the owner to submit a financial *pro forma* and service budget demonstrating the financial viability of the property. Budgets are reviewed by Department of Social Services and Division of Budget staff members.

If the financial materials pass inspection, a letter of approval—which becomes part of the contract—is sent. An inspection by OCD is conducted to assure physical and financial feasibility.

Owners are compensated monthly, after submission of vouchers. To assure prompt payment, the owners and the department have agreed to use agency couriers between offices, and special handling to assure check receipt by the 15th of each month.

The Department of Social Services may pay only for eligible clients receiving services, the use of a facility, and damages and associated compensation from the project budget. The ability to take up to 24 months to "spend down," the principal allows flexibility for repayment in the event of an unforeseen vacancy or emergency.

Services provided are a legitimate cost over current motel/hotel expenditures. Cost effectiveness is expected to be shown in the decline of recidivism for families successfully completing the program, and in the savings resulting from a client's employment. Over the long term, the county expects to realize some savings.

The lease offered after the transitional period requires continuation of apartment maintenance and other skills acquired.

Orange County's Transitional Housing Program is intended to produce the following results in its first year:

- The acquisition and operation of 48 units of rental housing specifically for families housed in hotels, motels, or shelters.

- Production of a permanent supply of affordable rental housing.

- Promotion of self-sufficiency among 50 percent of the participating families.

- Reduction of the incidence of homelessness and the rising cost of providing emergency housing.

- Involvement of the private sector, nonprofit sponsors, and government agencies in a new cooperative relationship.

- Improvement of the program's performance and operation so it can be expanded in the future.

After about one year of intertwining numerous programs, funds, agencies, and staffs, Orange County is about to make significant progress toward meeting the housing needs of its homeless population. The most significant element is the channeling of emergency shelter payments into more suitable forms of permanent housing.

The program is replicable in any area where a local agency pays rents for motel rooms, where housing sponsors can leverage that cash flow into permanent financing, and where properties can be purchased at reasonable costs. The specific path to the desired outcome may vary, as will the participants, but similar results can be anticipated.

Bibliography

Ades, Paul. The unconstitutionality of 'antihomeless' laws: ordinances prohibiting sleeping in outdoor public areas as a violation the right to travel. 77 *California Law Review* May 1989:595–628.

America's homeless mentally ill: falling through a dangerous crack. *New England Journal on Crime and Civil confinement* Summer 1989:277–299.

Arnold, Craig Anthony. Beyond self-interest: policy entrepreneurs and aid to the homeless. *Policy Studies Journal.* Fall 1989: 47–67.

Baker, James N. Needing a place to die; activist rally with new urgency for a troubling cause: the plight of homeless people with AIDS. *Newsweek.* April 4, 1988: 24–2.

Bates, Andrew. Mental health spas; how money intended for homeless psychotics went to suburban neurotics. 22 *Washington Monthly.* December 1990:26–30.

Belcher, John R. Rights versus needs of homeless mentally ill persons. 33 *Social Work.* September–October 1988:398–493.

Belcher, John R. and Frederick A. DiBlasio. The needs of depressed homeless persons: designing appropriate services. 26 *Community mental Health Journal.* June 1990: 255.

Bryson, D. B. Crime, drugs and subsidized housing. *Clearinghouse. review* 1990: 435–447.

Burt, Martha R. and Barbara E. Cohen. *America's homeless: numbers, characteristics, and programs that serve them.* Urban Institute Report 89–3: University Press of America, July 1989.

Callison, J. W. Low-income housing credit now even more complex. *Journal of Taxation.* March 1990: 148–155.

Caton, Carol L. M. *Homeless in America:* Oxford University Press, 1990.

Carrillo, Teresita E., Judit A. Gilbridge and Mabel M. Chan. Soup kitchen means: an observation and nutrient analysis. *Journal of the American Diatetic Association* July 1990: 989–922.

Coates, R. C. Legal rights of homeless Americans. 24 *University of San Francisco Law Review.* Winter 1990: 297–362.

Curtin, John J. Hope for the homeless. 76 *ABA Journal.* December 1990:8.

Dreier, Peter and John Atlas. Grassroots strategies for the housing crisis: a national agenda. *Social Policy.* Winter 1989:25–39.

Dreier, Peter and Richard Applebaum. Nobody home: the housing crisis meets the nineties. *Tikkun*. September–October 1990: 15–19.

Elickson, Robert C. The homeless muddle. *Public Interest*. Spring 1990:45–60.

Failing America's mentally ill. 108 *U.S. News & World Report*. September 24, 1990: 21.

Ferguson, Mary Ann. Psychiatric nursing in a shelter for the homeless. 89 *American Journal of Nursing*. August 1989:1060–1063.

Fox, Elaine R. and Lisa Roth. Homeless Children: Philadelphia as a case study. *506 Annals of the American Academy*. November 1989: 141–151.

Gelberg, Lillian and Lawrence S. Linn, Assessing the physical health of homeless adults. *The Journal of the American Medical Association*. October 13, 1989: 1973–1980.

Gibbs, Nancy R. Begging: to give or not to give; with panhandlers at every corner, people are running out of patience and change. *Time*. 5 September 1988: 68–75.

Gore, Albert Jr., Public policy and the homeless. *The American Psychologist*. August 1990:960–963.

Greenhouse, Linda. U.S. Supreme Court leaves intact a ban on subway begging. *The New York Times*. November 27, 1990:A1.

Hanrahan, Patricia M. and Katherine Rankin. Ignoring the homeless: an American pastime. *Human Rights*. Summer 1990:36–40.

Holden, Constance, Health problems of the homeless. 242 *Science*. October 14, 1988: 188–190.

Hombs, Mary Ellen. Federal policy for the homeless. 1 *Stanford Law and Policy Review*. Fall 1989:57–68.

Homeless: a dialogue on welfare and housing strategies. 23 *Clearinghouse Review*. June 1989: 104–115.

How attempts to help the homeless can backfire. *U.S. News & World Report*. February 29, 1988:32–34.

Housing and participation. *Community Development Journal*. January 1990:9–74.

Kelly, Elinor, J. Clyde Mitchell and Susan J. Smith. Factors in the length of stay of homeless families in temporary accommodation. *The Sociological Review*. November 1990:621–634.

Kircheimer, Donna Wilson. Sheltering the homeless in New York City; expansion in an era of government contraction. 104 *Political Science Quarterly*. Winter 1989/ 1990: 607–623.

Kirkpatrick, David. How we can win the war on poverty. *Fortune*. April 10, 1989:124–133.

Kozol, Jonathan. Distancing the homeless. *Yale Review*. Winter 1988:153–168.

Krauthammer, Charles. How to save the homeless mentally ill: Brown vs. Board of Re-education. *The New Republic*. February 8, 1988:22–26.

Lang, Michael H. *Homelessness Amid Affluence: Structure and Paradox in the American Political Economy*. Praeger: 1989.

Leo, John. Homeless rights, community wrongs. *U.S. News and World Report*. 24 July 1989: 56.

Levine, Irene S. and Debra J. Rog. Mental health services for homeless mentally ill persons: federal initiatives and current service trends. *The American Psychologist*, August 1990:963–9.

Marotto, Robert A. Are those street people part of the new poor, too? toward an applied sociology of social problems. 20 *American Sociologist*. Summer 1989:111–122.

Meyer, J.A. Establishing a right to shelter: lessons from Connecticut. *University of Bridgeport Law Review*. 1990:1–30.

Molotsky, Irvin. Upset by beggars, Washington is arresting them; an old law is res- urrected. But is it constitutional? *The New York Times.* November 7, 1990:A9.

National Academy of Sciences. The dynamics of homelessness. *Children Today.* May–June 1989: 2–4.

Novogradac, M. J. and E. J. Fortenbach. The low-income housing tax credit: im- pact of the changes wrought by the Revenue Reconciliation Act of 1989. 17 *Jour- nal of Real Estate Taxation.* Spring 1990:219–30.

Poor, not crazy. *The Economist.* September 10, 1988:33–35.

"Rays of hope" for the homeless. 160 *America.* January 7, 1989: 3.

Rossi, Peter H. The old homeless and the new homeless in historical perspective. *The American Psychologist.* August 1990:954–160.

Schiff, Laurence. Would they be better off in a home? Why do people become homeless? *National Review.* March 5, 1990:33–36.

Sherman, Rory. Legal help in a frigid N.Y.C. *The National Law Journal.* January 8, 1990.

Snow, David A., Susan G. Baker and Leon Anderson. On the precariousness of measuring insanity in insane contexts. *Social Problems.* April 1988:192–197.

Taub, T.C. The future of affordable housing. 22 *Urban Law.* Fall 1990:659–692.

The impact of federal antidiscrimination laws on housing for people with mental disabilities. 59 *George Washington Law Review.* January 1991: 413–50.

The unconstitutionality of 'antihomeless' laws: ordinances prohibiting sleeping in outdoor public areas as a violation of the right to travel. 77 *California Law Re- view.* May 1989:595–628.

Torrey, E. Fuller. Thirty years of shame: the scandalous neglect of the mentally ill homeless. *Policy Review.* Spring 1989:10–16.

United States. Congressional Joint Economic Committee. The Underclass: hearing, May 25, 1989.

United States. House. Committee on Ways and Means. Subcommittee on Human Resources. How to help the working poor; and problems of the working poor: hearings, February 28–April 27, 1989.

United States. House. Select Committee on Aging. Subcommittee on Human Serv- ices. Expansion of community-based services to special populations: hearing. July 19, 1989.

United States. House. Select Committee on Hunger. International Task Force. Im- proving the health of the poor: a development cornerstone: hearing, April 6, 1989.

United States. Senate. Committee on Banking, Housing, and Urban Affairs. Sub- committee on Housing and Urban Affairs. The role of state and local govern- ments developing housing strategies with emphasis on S. 566; hearing, June 6, 1989, to authorize a new corporation to support state and local strategies for achieving more affordable housing; to increase homeownership; and for other purposes: the National Affordable Housing Act.

United States. Senate. Committee on Banking, Housing, and Urban Affairs. Sub- committee on Housing and Urban Affairs. Roundtable hearing on the Housing Opportunity Partnership (HOP) and Home Corporation provisions hearing, June 7, 1989, on S. 566, to authorize a new corporation to support state and local strat- egies for achieving more affordable housing; to increase homeownership; and for other purposes; the National Affordable Housing Act. 1990.

United States. Senate. Committee on Banking, Housing, and Urban Affairs. Sub- committee on Housing and Urban Affairs. Supportive housing needs of elderly and disabled persons: hearing, June 2, 1989, on S. 566, to authorize a new corpo- ration to support state and local strategies for achieving more affordable housing;

to increase homeownership; and for other purposes; the National Affordable Housing Act. 1989.

United States Senate. The "Homeownership and Opportunity for People Everywhere" [HOPE], initiatives: joint hearings, March 20 and 29, 1990 before the Committee on Banking, Housing, and Urban Affairs and the Subcommittee on Housing and Urban Affairs, on the budget and legislative proposals of the Bush administration to preserve low-income housing and provide new affordable housing opportunities for low-income families; expand opportunities for homeownership; and create jobs and economic development in our distressed urban and rural communities. 1990

Welfeld, Irving. Our nonexistent housing crisis. *The Public Interest.* Fall 1990:55–62.

Westerfelt, Herb and Elsa Elliott. Estimating mental illness among the homeless: the effects of choice-based sampling. *Social Problems.* December 1989:525–532.

Whitman, David. Shattering myths about the homeless; new research finally reveals how many there are and what they need. *U.S. News & World Report.* March 20, 1989:26–8.

Wittman, Friedner D. Housing models for alcohol programs serving homeless persons. *Contemporary Drug Problems.* Fall 1989:483–504.

Wohl, A. Gimme shelter. Lawyering for the homeless. *A.B.A. Journal.* August 1990:58–60 + .

Winkleby, Marilyn A. Comparison of risk factors for ill health in a sample of homeless and nonhomeless poor. *Public Health Reports.* July–August 1990: 404–411.

Wright, James D. The mentally ill homeless: what is myth and what is fact? *Social Problems.* April 1988:182–192.

NTC DEBATE BOOKS

1991/92 Topic
HELPING THE HOMELESS, Goodnight et al.
THE PLIGHT OF THE HOMELESS, Rowland
HOMELESSNESS: A SOCIAL DILEMMA, Goodnight

Debate Theory and Practice
ADVANCED DEBATE, Thomas & Hart
BASIC DEBATE, Fryar, Thomas, & Goodnight
COACHING AND DIRECTING FORENSICS, Klopf
CROSS-EXAMINATION IN DEBATE, Copeland
DICTIONARY OF DEBATE, Hanson
FORENSIC TOURNAMENTS: PLANNING AND ADMINISTRATION, Goodnight & Zarefsky
GETTING STARTED IN DEBATE, Goodnight
JUDGING ACADEMIC DEBATE, Ulrich
MODERN DEBATE CASE TECHNIQUES, Terry et al.
MOVING FROM POLICY TO VALUE DEBATE, Richards
STRATEGIC DEBATE, Wood & Goodnight
STUDENT CONGRESS & LINCOLN-DOUGLAS DEBATE, Giertz & Mezzera

Debate Aids
DEBATE AWARD CERTIFICATES
DEBATE LECTERN
DEBATE PINS
DEBATE TIMER
CASE ARGUMENTS FLOW CHARTS
PLAN ARGUMENT FLOW CHARTS
LINCOLN-DOUGLAS DEBATE AUDIO TAPE

For a current catalog and information about our complete line
of language arts books, write:
National Textbook Company,
a division of NTC Publishing Group
4255 West Touhy Avenue
Lincolnwood (Chicago), Illinois 60646-1975 U.S.A.